Pearls of Wisdom

THE BOOK OF THE LAW

Marbi Burnette

Copyright © 2022 by Marbi Burnette

All rights reserved. No part of this publication may be reproduced, distributed or transmitted in any form or by any means, including photocopying, recording, or other electronic or mechanical methods, without the prior written permission of the publisher, except in the case of brief quotations embodied in critical reviews and certain other noncommercial uses permitted by copyright law. For permission requests, write to the publisher, addressed "Attention: Permissions Coordinator," at the address below.

Marbi Burnette/Rejoice Essential Publishing
PO BOX 512
Effingham, SC 29541
www.republishing.org

The Holy Bible, English Standard Version® (ESV®) Copyright © 2001 by Crossway, a publishing ministry of Good News Publishers. ll rights reserved. The ESV text may not be quoted in any publication made available to the public by a Creative Commons license. The ESV may not be translated into any other language. ESV Text Edition: 2016

ISBN: 978-1-956775-35-8

Contents

Genesis 1..1
Genesis 2..7
Genesis 3..12
Genesis 4..17
Genesis 5..22
Genesis 6..27
Genesis 7..32
Genesis 8..37
Genesis 9..42
Genesis 10..47
Genesis 11..52
Genesis 12..57
Genesis 13..62
Genesis 14..66
Genesis 15..71
Genesis 16..75
Genesis 17..79
Genesis 18..84
Genesis 19..90
Genesis 20..96
Genesis 21..101
Genesis 22..107

Genesis 23	112
Genesis 24	116
Genesis 25	125
Genesis 26	130
Genesis 27	136
Genesis 28	143
Genesis 29	148
Genesis 30	154
Genesis 31	160
Genesis 32	168
Genesis 33	174
Genesis 34	179
Genesis 35	184
Genesis 36	189
Genesis 37	195
Genesis 38	201
Genesis 39	206
Genesis 40	211
Genesis 41	216
Genesis 42	224
Genesis 43	230
Genesis 44	236
Genesis 45	242
Genesis 46	247
Genesis 47	252
Genesis 48	258
Genesis 49	263
Genesis 50	268

Exodus 1 273
Exodus 2 278
Exodus 3 283
Exodus 4 288
Exodus 5 294
Exodus 6 299
Exodus 7 304
Exodus 8 309
Exodus 9 315
Exodus 10 321
Exodus 11 327
Exodus 12 331
Exodus 13 339
Exodus 14 344
Exodus 15 350
Exodus 16 355
Exodus 17 361
Exodus 18 365
Exodus 19 370
Exodus 20 375
Exodus 21 380
Exodus 22 386
Exodus 23 391
Exodus 24 397
Exodus 25 401
Exodus 26 407
Exodus 27 413
Exodus 28 418

Exodus 29..425

Exodus 30..432

Exodus 31..438

Exodus 32..442

Exodus 33..448

Exodus 34..453

Exodus 35..465

Exodus 36..471

Exodus 37..476

Exodus 38..482

Exodus 39..482

Exodus 40..488

Leviticus 1...494

Leviticus 2...498

Leviticus 3...502

Leviticus 4...506

Leviticus 5...512

Leviticus 6...517

Leviticus 7...523

Leviticus 8...529

Leviticus 9...535

Leviticus 10...540

Leviticus 11...545

Leviticus 12...552

Leviticus 13...556

Leviticus 14...564

Leviticus 15...572

Leviticus 16...578

Leviticus 17	584
Leviticus 18	588
Leviticus 19	593
Leviticus 20	599
Leviticus 21	604
Leviticus 22	609
Leviticus 23	615
Leviticus 24	622
Leviticus 25	627
Leviticus 26	635
Leviticus 27	642
Numbers 1	648
Numbers 2	655
Numbers 3	660
Numbers 4	667
Numbers 5	674
Numbers 6	680
Numbers 7	685
Numbers 8	695
Numbers 9	700
Numbers 10	705
Numbers 11	711
Numbers 12	717
Numbers 13	721
Numbers 14	726
Numbers 15	733
Numbers 16	740
Numbers 17	747

Numbers 18...751

Numbers 19...757

Numbers 20...762

Numbers 21...768

Numbers 22...774

Numbers 23...781

Numbers 24...786

Numbers 25...791

Numbers 26...795

Numbers 27...803

Numbers 28...808

Numbers 29...814

Numbers 30...820

Numbers 31...824

Numbers 32...831

Numbers 33...837

Numbers 34...844

Numbers 35...849

Numbers 36...855

Deuteronomy 1..859

Deuteronomy 2..866

Deuteronomy 3..872

Deuteronomy 4..878

Deuteronomy 5..886

Deuteronomy 6..892

Deuteronomy 7..897

Deuteronomy 8..903

Deuteronomy 9..908

Deuteronomy 10 914
Deuteronomy 11 919
Deuteronomy 12 925
Deuteronomy 13 931
Deuteronomy 14 936
Deuteronomy 15 941
Deuteronomy 16 946
Deuteronomy 17 951
Deuteronomy 18 956
Deuteronomy 19 961
Deuteronomy 20 966
Deuteronomy 21 971
Deuteronomy 22 976
Deuteronomy 23 982
Deuteronomy 24 987
Deuteronomy 25 992
Deuteronomy 26 997
Deuteronomy 27 1002
Deuteronomy 28 1007
Deuteronomy 29 1016
Deuteronomy 30 1022
Deuteronomy 31 1027
Deuteronomy 32 1033
Deuteronomy 33 1040
Deuteronomy 34 1045

Genesis 1

English Standard Version

The Creation of the World

1 In the beginning, God created the heavens and the earth.

2 The earth was without form and void, and darkness was over the face of the deep. And the Spirit of God was hovering over the face of the waters.

3 And God said, "Let there be light," and there was light.

4 And God saw that the light was good. And God separated the light from the darkness.

5 God called the light Day, and the darkness he called Night. And there was evening and there was morning, the first day.

6 And God said, "Let there be an expanse in the midst of the waters, and let it separate the waters from the waters."

7 And God made the expanse and separated the waters that were under the expanse from the waters that were above the expanse. And it was so.

8 And God called the expanse Heaven. And there was evening and there was morning, the second day.

9 And God said, "Let the waters under the heavens be gathered together into one place, and let the dry land appear." And it was so.

10 God called the dry land Earth, and the waters that were gathered together he called Seas. And God saw that it was good.

11 And God said, "Let the earth sprout vegetation, plants yielding seed, and fruit trees bearing fruit in which is their seed, each according to its kind, on the earth." And it was so.

12 The earth brought forth vegetation, plants yielding seed according to their own kinds, and trees bearing fruit in which is their seed, each according to its kind. And God saw that it was good.

13 And there was evening and there was morning, the third day.

14 And God said, "Let there be lights in the expanse of the heavens to separate the day from the night. And let them be for signs and for seasons, and for days and years,

15 and let them be lights in the expanse of the heavens to give light upon the earth." And it was so.

16 And God made the two great lights—the greater light to rule the day and the lesser light to rule the night—and the stars.

17 And God set them in the expanse of the heavens to give light on the earth,

18 to rule over the day and over the night, and to separate the light from the darkness. And God saw that it was good.

19 And there was evening and there was morning, the fourth day.

20 And God said, "Let the waters swarm with swarms of living creatures, and let birds fly above the earth across the expanse of the heavens."

21 So God created the great sea creatures and every living creature that moves, with which the waters swarm, according to their kinds, and every winged bird according to its kind. And God saw that it was good.

22 And God blessed them, saying, "Be fruitful and multiply and fill the waters in the seas, and let birds multiply on the earth."

23 And there was evening and there was morning, the fifth day.

24 And God said, "Let the earth bring forth living creatures according to their kinds—livestock and creeping things and beasts of the earth according to their kinds." And it was so.

25 And God made the beasts of the earth according to their kinds and the livestock according to their kinds, and everything that creeps on the ground according to its kind. And God saw that it was good.

26 Then God said, "Let us make man in our image, after our likeness. And let them have dominion over the fish of the sea and over the birds of the heavens and over the livestock and over all the earth and over every creeping thing that creeps on the earth."

27 So God created man in his own image, in the image of God he created him; male and female he created them.

28 And God blessed them. And God said to them, "Be fruitful and multiply and fill the earth and subdue it, and have dominion over the fish of the sea and over the birds of the heavens and over every living thing that moves on the earth."

29 And God said, "Behold, I have given you every plant yielding seed that is on the face of all the earth, and every tree with seed in its fruit. You shall have them for food.

30 And to every beast of the earth and to every bird of the heavens and to everything that creeps on the earth, everything that has the breath of life, I have given every green plant for food." And it was so.

31 And God saw everything that he had made, and behold, it was very good. And there was evening and there was morning, the sixth day.

Genesis 2

English Standard Version

The Seventh Day, God Rests

1 Thus the heavens and the earth were finished, and all the host of them.

2 And on the seventh day God finished his work that he had done, and he rested on the seventh day from all his work that he had done.

3 So God blessed the seventh day and made it holy, because on it God rested from all his work that he had done in creation.

The Creation of Man and Woman

4 These are the generations of the heavens and the earth when they were created, in the day that the Lord God made the earth and the heavens.

5 When no bush of the field was yet in the land and no small plant of the field had yet sprung up—for the Lord God had not caused it to rain on the land, and there was no man to work the ground,

6 and a mist was going up from the land and was watering the whole face of the ground—

7 then the Lord God formed the man of dust from the ground and breathed into his nostrils the breath of life, and the man became a living creature.

8 And the Lord God planted a garden in Eden, in the east, and there he put the man whom he had formed.

9 And out of the ground the Lord God made to spring up every tree that is pleasant to the sight and good for food. The tree of life was in the midst of the garden, and the tree of the knowledge of good and evil.

10 A river flowed out of Eden to water the garden, and there it divided and became four rivers.

11 The name of the first is the Pishon. It is the one that flowed around the whole land of Havilah, where there is gold.

12 And the gold of that land is good; bdellium and onyx stone are there.

13 The name of the second river is the Gihon. It is the one that flowed around the whole land of Cush.

14 And the name of the third river is the Tigris, which flows east of Assyria. And the fourth river is the Euphrates.

15 The Lord God took the man and put him in the garden of Eden to work it and keep it.

16 And the Lord God commanded the man, saying, "You may surely eat of every tree of the garden,

17 but of the tree of the knowledge of good and evil you shall not eat, for in the day that you eat of it you shall surely die."

18 Then the Lord God said, "It is not good that the man should be alone; I will make him a helper fit for him."

19 Now out of the ground the Lord God had formed every beast of the field and every bird of the heavens and brought them to the man to see what he would call them. And whatever the man called every living creature, that was its name.

20 The man gave names to all livestock and to the birds of the heavens and to every beast of the field. But for Adam[g] there was not found a helper fit for him.

21 So the Lord God caused a deep sleep to fall upon the man, and while he slept took one of his ribs and closed up its place with flesh.

22 And the rib that the Lord God had taken from the man he made into a woman and brought her to the man.

23 Then the man said, "This at last is bone of my bones and flesh of my flesh; she shall be called Woman, because she was taken out of Man."

24 Therefore a man shall leave his father and his mother and hold fast to his wife, and they shall become one flesh.

25 And the man and his wife were both naked and were not ashamed.

Genesis 3

English Standard Version

The Fall

1 Now the serpent was more crafty than any other beast of the field that the Lord God had made. He said to the woman, "Did God actually say, 'You shall not eat of any tree in the garden'?"

2 And the woman said to the serpent, "We may eat of the fruit of the trees in the garden,

3 but God said, 'You shall not eat of the fruit of the tree that is in the midst of the garden, neither shall you touch it, lest you die.'"

4 But the serpent said to the woman, "You will not surely die.

5 For God knows that when you eat of it your eyes will be opened, and you will be like God, knowing good and evil."

6 So when the woman saw that the tree was good for food, and that it was a delight to the eyes, and that the tree was to be desired to make one wise, she took of its fruit and ate, and she also gave some to her husband who was with her, and he ate.

7 Then the eyes of both were opened, and they knew that they were naked. And they sewed fig leaves together and made themselves loincloths.

8 And they heard the sound of the Lord God walking in the garden in the cool of the day, and the man and his wife hid themselves from the presence of the Lord God among the trees of the garden.

9 But the Lord God called to the man and said to him, "Where are you?"

10 And he said, "I heard the sound of you in the garden, and I was afraid, because I was naked, and I hid myself."

11 He said, "Who told you that you were naked? Have you eaten of the tree of which I commanded you not to eat?"

12 The man said, "The woman whom you gave to be with me, she gave me fruit of the tree, and I ate."

13 Then the Lord God said to the woman, "What is this that you have done?" The woman said, "The serpent deceived me, and I ate."

14 The Lord God said to the serpent, "Because you have done this, cursed are you above all livestock and above all beasts of the field; on your belly you shall go, and dust you shall eat all the days of your life.

15 I will put enmity between you and the woman, and between your offspring and her offspring; he shall bruise your head, and you shall bruise his heel."

16 To the woman he said,"I will surely multiply your pain in childbearing; in pain you shall bring forth children. Your desire shall be contrary to your husband, but he shall rule over you."

17 And to Adam he said, "Because you have listened to the voice of your wife and have eaten of the tree of which I commanded you, 'You shall not eat of it,' cursed is the ground because of you; in pain you shall eat of it all the days of your life;

18 thorns and thistles it shall bring forth for you; and you shall eat the plants of the field.

19 By the sweat of your face you shall eat bread, till you return to the ground, for out of it you were taken; for you are dust, and to dust you shall return."

20 The man called his wife's name Eve, because she was the mother of all living.

21 And the Lord God made for Adam and for his wife garments of skins and clothed them.

22 Then the Lord God said, "Behold, the man has become like one of us in knowing good and evil. Now, lest he reach out his hand and take also of the tree of life and eat, and live forever—"

23 therefore the Lord God sent him out from the garden of Eden to work the ground from which he was taken.

24 He drove out the man, and at the east of the garden of Eden he placed the cherubim and a flaming sword that turned every way to guard the way to the tree of life.

Genesis 4

English Standard Version

Cain and Abel

1 Now Adam knew Eve his wife, and she conceived and bore Cain, saying, "I have gotten a man with the help of the Lord."

2 And again, she bore his brother Abel. Now Abel was a keeper of sheep, and Cain a worker of the ground.

3 In the course of time Cain brought to the Lord an offering of the fruit of the ground,

4 and Abel also brought of the firstborn of his flock and of their fat portions. And the Lord had regard for Abel and his offering,

5 but for Cain and his offering he had no regard. So Cain was very angry, and his face fell.

6 The Lord said to Cain, "Why are you angry, and why has your face fallen?

7 If you do well, will you not be accepted? And if you do not do well, sin is crouching at the door. Its desire is contrary to you, but you must rule over it."

8 Cain spoke to Abel his brother. And when they were in the field, Cain rose up against his brother Abel and killed him.

9 Then the Lord said to Cain, "Where is Abel your brother?" He said, "I do not know; am I my brother's keeper?"

10 And the Lord said, "What have you done? The voice of your brother's blood is crying to me from the ground.

11 And now you are cursed from the ground, which has opened its mouth to receive your brother's blood from your hand.

12 When you work the ground, it shall no longer yield to you its strength. You shall be a fugitive and a wanderer on the earth."

13 Cain said to the Lord, "My punishment is greater than I can bear.

14 Behold, you have driven me today away from the ground, and from your face I shall be hidden. I shall be a fugitive and a wanderer on the earth, and whoever finds me will kill me."

15 Then the Lord said to him, "Not so! If anyone kills Cain, vengeance shall be taken on him sevenfold." And the Lord put a mark on Cain, lest any who found him should attack him.

16 Then Cain went away from the presence of the Lord and settled in the land of Nod, east of Eden.

17 Cain knew his wife, and she conceived and bore Enoch. When he built a city, he called the name of the city after the name of his son, Enoch.

18 To Enoch was born Irad, and Irad fathered Mehujael, and Mehujael fathered Methushael, and Methushael fathered Lamech.

19 And Lamech took two wives. The name of the one was Adah, and the name of the other Zillah.

20 Adah bore Jabal; he was the father of those who dwell in tents and have livestock.

21 His brother's name was Jubal; he was the father of all those who play the lyre and pipe.

22 Zillah also bore Tubal-cain; he was the forger of all instruments of bronze and iron. The sister of Tubal-cain was Naamah.

23 Lamech said to his wives: "Adah and Zillah, hear my voice; you wives of Lamech, listen to what I say: I have killed a man for wounding me, a young man for striking me.

24 If Cain's revenge is sevenfold, then Lamech's is seventy-sevenfold."

25 And Adam knew his wife again, and she bore a son and called his name Seth, for she said, "God has appointed for me another offspring instead of Abel, for Cain killed him."

26 To Seth also a son was born, and he called his name Enosh. At that time people began to call upon the name of the Lord.

Genesis 5

English Standard Version

Adam's Descendants to Noah

1 This is the book of the generations of Adam. When God created man, he made him in the likeness of God.

2 Male and female he created them, and he blessed them and named them Manwhen they were created.

3 When Adam had lived 130 years, he fathered a son in his own likeness, after his image, and named him Seth.

4 The days of Adam after he fathered Seth were 800 years; and he had other sons and daughters.

5 Thus all the days that Adam lived were 930 years, and he died.

6 When Seth had lived 105 years, he fathered Enosh.

7 Seth lived after he fathered Enosh 807 years and had other sons and daughters.

8 Thus all the days of Seth were 912 years, and he died.

9 When Enosh had lived 90 years, he fathered Kenan.

10 Enosh lived after he fathered Kenan 815 years and had other sons and daughters.

11 Thus all the days of Enosh were 905 years, and he died.

12 When Kenan had lived 70 years, he fathered Mahalalel.

13 Kenan lived after he fathered Mahalalel 840 years and had other sons and daughters.

14 Thus all the days of Kenan were 910 years, and he died.

15 When Mahalalel had lived 65 years, he fathered Jared.

16 Mahalalel lived after he fathered Jared 830 years and had other sons and daughters.

17 Thus all the days of Mahalalel were 895 years, and he died.

18 When Jared had lived 162 years, he fathered Enoch.

19 Jared lived after he fathered Enoch 800 years and had other sons and daughters.

20 Thus all the days of Jared were 962 years, and he died.

21 When Enoch had lived 65 years, he fathered Methuselah.

22 Enoch walked with God after he fathered Methuselah 300 years and had other sons and daughters.

23 Thus all the days of Enoch were 365 years.

24 Enoch walked with God, and he was not, for God took him.

25 When Methuselah had lived 187 years, he fathered Lamech.

26 Methuselah lived after he fathered Lamech 782 years and had other sons and daughters.

27 Thus all the days of Methuselah were 969 years, and he died.

28 When Lamech had lived 182 years, he fathered a son

29 and called his name Noah, saying, "Out of the ground that the Lord has cursed, this one shall bring us relief from our work and from the painful toil of our hands."

30 Lamech lived after he fathered Noah 595 years and had other sons and daughters.

31 Thus all the days of Lamech were 777 years, and he died.

32 After Noah was 500 years old, Noah fathered Shem, Ham, and Japheth.

Genesis 6

English Standard Version

Increasing Corruption on Earth

1 When man began to multiply on the face of the land and daughters were born to them,

2 the sons of God saw that the daughters of man were attractive. And they took as their wives any they chose.

3 Then the Lord said, "My Spirit shall not abide in man forever, for he is flesh: his days shall be 120 years."

4 The Nephilim were on the earth in those days, and also afterward, when the sons of God came in to the daughters of man and they bore children to them. These were the mighty men who were of old, the men of renown.

5 The Lord saw that the wickedness of man was great in the earth, and that every intention of the thoughts of his heart was only evil continually.

6 And the Lord regretted that he had made man on the earth, and it grieved him to his heart.

7 So the Lord said, "I will blot out man whom I have created from the face of the land, man and animals and creeping things and birds of the heavens, for I am sorry that I have made them."

8 But Noah found favor in the eyes of the Lord.

Noah and the Flood

9 These are the generations of Noah. Noah was a righteous man, blameless in his generation. Noah walked with God.

10 And Noah had three sons, Shem, Ham, and Japheth.

11 Now the earth was corrupt in God's sight, and the earth was filled with violence.

12 And God saw the earth, and behold, it was corrupt, for all flesh had corrupted their way on the earth.

13 And God said to Noah, "I have determined to make an end of all flesh, for the earth is filled with violence through them. Behold, I will destroy them with the earth.

14 Make yourself an ark of gopher wood. Make rooms in the ark, and cover it inside and out with pitch.

15 This is how you are to make it: the length of the ark 300 cubits, its breadth 50 cubits, and its height 30 cubits.

16 Make a roof for the ark, and finish it to a cubit above, and set the door of the ark in its side. Make it with lower, second, and third decks.

17 For behold, I will bring a flood of waters upon the earth to destroy all flesh in which is the breath of life under heaven. Everything that is on the earth shall die.

18 But I will establish my covenant with you, and you shall come into the ark, you, your sons, your wife, and your sons' wives with you.

19 And of every living thing of all flesh, you shall bring two of every sort into the ark to keep them alive with you. They shall be male and female.

Genesis 6

20 Of the birds according to their kinds, and of the animals according to their kinds, of every creeping thing of the ground, according to its kind, two of every sort shall come in to you to keep them alive.

21 Also take with you every sort of food that is eaten, and store it up. It shall serve as food for you and for them."

22 Noah did this; he did all that God commanded him.

Genesis 7

English Standard Version

1 Then the Lord said to Noah, "Go into the ark, you and all your household, for I have seen that you are righteous before me in this generation.

2 Take with you seven pairs of all clean animals, the male and his mate, and a pair of the animals that are not clean, the male and his mate,

3 and seven pairs of the birds of the heavens also, male and female, to keep their offspring alive on the face of all the earth.

4 For in seven days I will send rain on the earth forty days and forty nights, and every living thing that I have made I will blot out from the face of the ground."

5 And Noah did all that the Lord had commanded him.

6 Noah was six hundred years old when the flood of waters came upon the earth.

7 And Noah and his sons and his wife and his sons' wives with him went into the ark to escape the waters of the flood.

8 Of clean animals, and of animals that are not clean, and of birds, and of everything that creeps on the ground,

9 two and two, male and female, went into the ark with Noah, as God had commanded Noah.

10 And after seven days the waters of the flood came upon the earth.

11 In the six hundredth year of Noah's life, in the second month, on the seventeenth day of the month, on that day all the fountains of the great deep burst forth, and the windows of the heavens were opened.

12 And rain fell upon the earth forty days and forty nights.

13 On the very same day Noah and his sons, Shem and Ham and Japheth, and Noah's wife and the three wives of his sons with them entered the ark,

14 they and every beast, according to its kind, and all the livestock according to their kinds, and every creeping thing that creeps on the earth, according to its kind, and every bird, according to its kind, every winged creature.

15 They went into the ark with Noah, two and two of all flesh in which there was the breath of life.

16 And those that entered, male and female of all flesh, went in as God had commanded him. And the Lord shut him in.

17 The flood continued forty days on the earth. The waters increased and bore up the ark, and it rose high above the earth.

18 The waters prevailed and increased greatly on the earth, and the ark floated on the face of the waters.

19 And the waters prevailed so mightily on the earth that all the high mountains under the whole heaven were covered.

20 The waters prevailed above the mountains, covering them fifteen cubits deep.

21 And all flesh died that moved on the earth, birds, livestock, beasts, all swarming creatures that swarm on the earth, and all mankind.

22 Everything on the dry land in whose nostrils was the breath of life died.

23 He blotted out every living thing that was on the face of the ground, man and animals and creeping things and birds of the heavens. They were blotted out from the earth. Only Noah was left, and those who were with him in the ark.

24 And the waters prevailed on the earth 150 days.

Genesis 8

English Standard Version

The Flood Subsides

1 But God remembered Noah and all the beasts and all the livestock that were with him in the ark. And God made a wind blow over the earth, and the waters subsided.

2 The fountains of the deep and the windows of the heavens were closed, the rain from the heavens was restrained,

3 and the waters receded from the earth continually. At the end of 150 days the waters had abated,

4 and in the seventh month, on the seventeenth day of the month, the ark came to rest on the mountains of Ararat.

5 And the waters continued to abate until the tenth month; in the tenth month, on the first day of the month, the tops of the mountains were seen.

6 At the end of forty days Noah opened the window of the ark that he had made

7 and sent forth a raven. It went to and fro until the waters were dried up from the earth.

8 Then he sent forth a dove from him, to see if the waters had subsided from the face of the ground.

9 But the dove found no place to set her foot, and she returned to him to the ark, for the waters were still on the face of the whole earth. So he put out his hand and took her and brought her into the ark with him.

10 He waited another seven days, and again he sent forth the dove out of the ark.

11 And the dove came back to him in the evening, and behold, in her mouth was a freshly plucked olive leaf. So Noah knew that the waters had subsided from the earth.

12 Then he waited another seven days and sent forth the dove, and she did not return to him anymore.

13 In the six hundred and first year, in the first month, the first day of the month, the waters were dried from off the earth. And Noah removed the covering of the ark and looked, and behold, the face of the ground was dry.

14 In the second month, on the twenty-seventh day of the month, the earth had dried out.

15 Then God said to Noah,

16 "Go out from the ark, you and your wife, and your sons and your sons' wives with you.

17 Bring out with you every living thing that is with you of all flesh—birds and animals and every creeping thing that creeps on the earth—that they may swarm on the earth, and be fruitful and multiply on the earth."

18 So Noah went out, and his sons and his wife and his sons' wives with him.

19 Every beast, every creeping thing, and every bird, everything that moves on the earth, went out by families from the ark.

God's Covenant with Noah

20 Then Noah built an altar to the Lord and took some of every clean animal and some of every clean bird and offered burnt offerings on the altar.

21 And when the Lord smelled the pleasing aroma, the Lord said in his heart, "I will never again curse the ground because of man, for the intention of man's heart is evil from his youth. Neither will I ever again strike down every living creature as I have done.

22 While the earth remains, seedtime and harvest, cold and heat, summer and winter, day and night, shall not cease."

Genesis 9

English Standard Version

1 And God blessed Noah and his sons and said to them, "Be fruitful and multiply and fill the earth.

2 The fear of you and the dread of you shall be upon every beast of the earth and upon every bird of the heavens, upon everything that creeps on the ground and all the fish of the sea. Into your hand they are delivered.

3 Every moving thing that lives shall be food for you. And as I gave you the green plants, I give you everything.

4 But you shall not eat flesh with its life, that is, its blood.

5 And for your lifeblood I will require a reckoning: from every beast I will require it and from man. From his fellow man I will require a reckoning for the life of man.

6 "Whoever sheds the blood of man, by man shall his blood be shed, for God made man in his own image.

7 And you, be fruitful and multiply, increase greatly on the earth and multiply in it."

8 Then God said to Noah and to his sons with him,

9 "Behold, I establish my covenant with you and your offspring after you,

10 and with every living creature that is with you, the birds, the livestock, and every beast of the earth with you, as many as came out of the ark; it is for every beast of the earth.

11 I establish my covenant with you, that never again shall all flesh be cut off by the waters of the flood, and never again shall there be a flood to destroy the earth."

12 And God said, "This is the sign of the covenant that I make between me and you and every living creature that is with you, for all future generations:

13 I have set my bow in the cloud, and it shall be a sign of the covenant between me and the earth.

14 When I bring clouds over the earth and the bow is seen in the clouds,

15 I will remember my covenant that is between me and you and every living creature of all flesh. And the waters shall never again become a flood to destroy all flesh.

16 When the bow is in the clouds, I will see it and remember the everlasting covenant between God and every living creature of all flesh that is on the earth."

17 God said to Noah, "This is the sign of the covenant that I have established between me and all flesh that is on the earth."

Noah's Descendants

18 The sons of Noah who went forth from the ark were Shem, Ham, and Japheth. (Ham was the father of Canaan.)

19 These three were the sons of Noah, and from these the people of the whole earth were dispersed.

20 Noah began to be a man of the soil, and he planted a vineyard.

21 He drank of the wine and became drunk and lay uncovered in his tent.

22 And Ham, the father of Canaan, saw the nakedness of his father and told his two brothers outside.

23 Then Shem and Japheth took a garment, laid it on both their shoulders, and walked backward and covered the nakedness of their father. Their faces were turned backward, and they did not see their father's nakedness.

24 When Noah awoke from his wine and knew what his youngest son had done to him,

25 he said, "Cursed be Canaan; a servant of servants shall he be to his brothers."

26 He also said, "Blessed be the Lord, the God of Shem; and let Canaan be his servant.

27 May God enlarge Japheth, and let him dwell in the tents of Shem, and let Canaan be his servant."

28 After the flood Noah lived 350 years.

29 All the days of Noah were 950 years, and he died.

Genesis 10

English Standard Version

Nations Descended from Noah

1 These are the generations of the sons of Noah, Shem, Ham, and Japheth. Sons were born to them after the flood.

2 The sons of Japheth: Gomer, Magog, Madai, Javan, Tubal, Meshech, and Tiras.

3 The sons of Gomer: Ashkenaz, Riphath, and Togarmah.

4 The sons of Javan: Elishah, Tarshish, Kittim, and Dodanim.

5 From these the coastland peoples spread in their lands, each with his own language, by their clans, in their nations.

6 The sons of Ham: Cush, Egypt, Put, and Canaan.

7 The sons of Cush: Seba, Havilah, Sabtah, Raamah, and Sabteca. The sons of Raamah: Sheba and Dedan.

8 Cush fathered Nimrod; he was the first on earth to be a mighty man.

9 He was a mighty hunter before the Lord. Therefore it is said, "Like Nimrod a mighty hunter before the Lord."

The beginning of his kingdom was Babel, Erech, Accad, and Calneh, in the land of Shinar.

11 From that land he went into Assyria and built Nineveh, Rehoboth-Ir, Calah, and

12 Resen between Nineveh and Calah; that is the great city.

13 Egypt fathered Ludim, Anamim, Lehabim, Naphtuhim,

14 Pathrusim, Casluhim (from whom the Philistines came), and Caphtorim.

15 Canaan fathered Sidon his firstborn and Heth,

16 and the Jebusites, the Amorites, the Girgashites,

17 the Hivites, the Arkites, the Sinites,

18 the Arvadites, the Zemarites, and the Hamathites. Afterward the clans of the Canaanites dispersed.

19 And the territory of the Canaanites extended from Sidon in the direction of Gerar as far as Gaza, and in the direction of Sodom, Gomorrah, Admah, and Zeboiim, as far as Lasha.

20 These are the sons of Ham, by their clans, their languages, their lands, and their nations.

21 To Shem also, the father of all the children of Eber, the elder brother of Japheth, children were born.

22 The sons of Shem: Elam, Asshur, Arpachshad, Lud, and Aram.

23 The sons of Aram: Uz, Hul, Gether, and Mash.

24 Arpachshad fathered Shelah; and Shelah fathered Eber.

25 To Eber were born two sons: the name of the one was Peleg, for in his days the earth was divided, and his brother's name was Joktan.

26 Joktan fathered Almodad, Sheleph, Hazarmaveth, Jerah,

27 Hadoram, Uzal, Diklah,

28 Obal, Abimael, Sheba,

29 Ophir, Havilah, and Jobab; all these were the sons of Joktan.

30 The territory in which they lived extended from Mesha in the direction of Sephar to the hill country of the east.

31 These are the sons of Shem, by their clans, their languages, their lands, and their nations.

32 These are the clans of the sons of Noah, according to their genealogies, in their nations, and from these the nations spread abroad on the earth after the flood.

Genesis 11

English Standard Version

The Tower of Babel

11 Now the whole earth had one language and the same words.

2 And as people migrated from the east, they found a plain in the land of Shinar and settled there.

3 And they said to one another, "Come, let us make bricks, and burn them thoroughly." And they had brick for stone, and bitumen for mortar.

4 Then they said, "Come, let us build ourselves a city and a tower with its top in the heavens, and let us make a name for ourselves, lest we be dispersed over the face of the whole earth."

5 And the Lord came down to see the city and the tower, which the children of man had built.

6 And the Lord said, "Behold, they are one people, and they have all one language, and this is only the beginning of what they will do. And nothing that they propose to do will now be impossible for them.

7 Come, let us go down and there confuse their language, so that they may not understand one another's speech."

8 So the Lord dispersed them from there over the face of all the earth, and they left off building the city.

9 Therefore its name was called Babel, because there the Lord confused the language of all the earth. And from there the Lord dispersed them over the face of all the earth.

Shem's Descendants

10 These are the generations of Shem. When Shem was 100 years old, he fathered Arpachshad two years after the flood.

11 And Shem lived after he fathered Arpachshad 500 years and had other sons and daughters.

12 When Arpachshad had lived 35 years, he fathered Shelah.

13 And Arpachshad lived after he fathered Shelah 403 years and had other sons and daughters.

14 When Shelah had lived 30 years, he fathered Eber.

15 And Shelah lived after he fathered Eber 403 years and had other sons and daughters.

16 When Eber had lived 34 years, he fathered Peleg.

17 And Eber lived after he fathered Peleg 430 years and had other sons and daughters.

18 When Peleg had lived 30 years, he fathered Reu.

19 And Peleg lived after he fathered Reu 209 years and had other sons and daughters.

20 When Reu had lived 32 years, he fathered Serug.

21 And Reu lived after he fathered Serug 207 years and had other sons and daughters.

22 When Serug had lived 30 years, he fathered Nahor.

23 And Serug lived after he fathered Nahor 200 years and had other sons and daughters.

24 When Nahor had lived 29 years, he fathered Terah.

25 And Nahor lived after he fathered Terah 119 years and had other sons and daughters.

26 When Terah had lived 70 years, he fathered Abram, Nahor, and Haran.

Terah's Descendants

27 Now these are the generations of Terah. Terah fathered Abram, Nahor, and Haran; and Haran fathered Lot.

28 Haran died in the presence of his father Terah in the land of his kindred, in Ur of the Chaldeans.

29 And Abram and Nahor took wives. The name of Abram's wife was Sarai, and the name of Nahor's wife, Milcah, the daughter of Haran the father of Milcah and Iscah.

30 Now Sarai was barren; she had no child.

31 Terah took Abram his son and Lot the son of Haran, his grandson, and Sarai his daughter-in-law, his son Abram's wife, and they went forth together from Ur of the Chaldeans to go into the land of Canaan, but when they came to Haran, they settled there.

32 The days of Terah were 205 years, and Terah died in Haran.

Genesis 12

English Standard Version

The Call of Abram

1 Now the Lord said to Abram, "Go from your country and your kindred and your father's house to the land that I will show you.

2 And I will make of you a great nation, and I will bless you and make your name great, so that you will be a blessing.

3 I will bless those who bless you, and him who dishonors you I will curse, and in you all the families of the earth shall be blessed."

4 So Abram went, as the Lord had told him, and Lot went with him. Abram was seventy-five years old when he departed from Haran.

5 And Abram took Sarai his wife, and Lot his brother's son, and all their possessions that they had gathered, and the people that they had acquired in Haran, and they set out to go to the land of Canaan. When they came to the land of Canaan,

6 Abram passed through the land to the place at Shechem, to the oak of Moreh. At that time the Canaanites were in the land.

7 Then the Lord appeared to Abram and said, "To your offspring I will give this land." So he built there an altar to the Lord, who had appeared to him.

8 From there he moved to the hill country on the east of Bethel and pitched his tent, with Bethel on the west and Ai on the east. And there he built an altar to the Lord and called upon the name of the Lord.

9 And Abram journeyed on, still going toward the Negeb.

Abram and Sarai in Egypt

10 Now there was a famine in the land. So Abram went down to Egypt to sojourn there, for the famine was severe in the land.

11 When he was about to enter Egypt, he said to Sarai his wife, "I know that you are a woman beautiful in appearance,

12 and when the Egyptians see you, they will say, 'This is his wife.' Then they will kill me, but they will let you live.

13 Say you are my sister, that it may go well with me because of you, and that my life may be spared for your sake."

14 When Abram entered Egypt, the Egyptians saw that the woman was very beautiful.

15 And when the princes of Pharaoh saw her, they praised her to Pharaoh. And the woman was taken into Pharaoh's house.

16 And for her sake he dealt well with Abram; and he had sheep, oxen, male donkeys, male servants, female servants, female donkeys, and camels.

17 But the Lord afflicted Pharaoh and his house with great plagues because of Sarai, Abram's wife. 1

8 So Pharaoh called Abram and said, "What is this you have done to me? Why did you not tell me that she was your wife?

19 Why did you say, 'She is my sister,' so that I took her for my wife? Now then, here is your wife; take her, and go."

20 And Pharaoh gave men orders concerning him, and they sent him away with his wife and all that he had.

Genesis 13

English Standard Version

Abram and Lot Separate

1 So Abram went up from Egypt, he and his wife and all that he had, and Lot with him, into the Negeb.

2 Now Abram was very rich in livestock, in silver, and in gold.

3 And he journeyed on from the Negeb as far as Bethel to the place where his tent had been at the beginning, between Bethel and Ai,

4 to the place where he had made an altar at the first. And there Abram called upon the name of the Lord.

5 And Lot, who went with Abram, also had flocks and herds and tents,

6 so that the land could not support both of them dwelling together; for their possessions were so great that they could not dwell together,

7 and there was strife between the herdsmen of Abram's livestock and the herdsmen of Lot's livestock. At that time the Canaanites and the Perizzites were dwelling in the land.

8 Then Abram said to Lot, "Let there be no strife between you and me, and between your herdsmen and my herdsmen, for we are kinsmen.

9 Is not the whole land before you? Separate yourself from me. If you take the left hand, then I will go to the right, or if you take the right hand, then I will go to the left."

10 And Lot lifted up his eyes and saw that the Jordan Valley was well watered everywhere like the garden of the Lord, like the land of Egypt, in the direction of Zoar. (This was before the Lord destroyed Sodom and Gomorrah.)

11 So Lot chose for himself all the Jordan Valley, and Lot journeyed east. Thus they separated from each other.

12 Abram settled in the land of Canaan, while Lot settled among the cities of the valley and moved his tent as far as Sodom.

13 Now the men of Sodom were wicked, great sinners against the Lord.

14 The Lord said to Abram, after Lot had separated from him, "Lift up your eyes and look from the place where you are, northward and southward and eastward and westward,

15 for all the land that you see I will give to you and to your offspring forever.

16 I will make your offspring as the dust of the earth, so that if one can count the dust of the earth, your offspring also can be counted.

17 Arise, walk through the length and the breadth of the land, for I will give it to you."

18 So Abram moved his tent and came and settled by the oaks of Mamre, which are at Hebron, and there he built an altar to the Lord.

Genesis 14

English Standard Version

Abram Rescues Lot

1 In the days of Amraphel king of Shinar, Arioch king of Ellasar, Chedorlaomer king of Elam, and Tidal king of Goiim,

2 these kings made war with Bera king of Sodom, Birsha king of Gomorrah, Shinab king of Admah, Shemeber king of Zeboiim, and the king of Bela (that is, Zoar).

3 And all these joined forces in the Valley of Siddim (that is, the Salt Sea).

4 Twelve years they had served Chedorlaomer, but in the thirteenth year they rebelled.

5 In the fourteenth year Chedorlaomer and the kings who were with him came and defeated the Rephaim in Ashteroth-karnaim, the Zuzim in Ham, the Emim in Shaveh-kiriathaim,

6 and the Horites in their hill country of Seir as far as El-paran on the border of the wilderness.

7 Then they turned back and came to En-mishpat (that is, Kadesh) and defeated all the country of the Amalekites, and also the Amorites who were dwelling in Hazazon-tamar.

8 Then the king of Sodom, the king of Gomorrah, the king of Admah, the king of Zeboiim, and the king of Bela (that is, Zoar) went out, and they joined battle in the Valley of Siddim

9 with Chedorlaomer king of Elam, Tidal king of Goiim, Amraphel king of Shinar, and Arioch king of Ellasar, four kings against five.

10 Now the Valley of Siddim was full of bitumen pits, and as the kings of Sodom and Gomorrah fled, some fell into them, and the rest fled to the hill country.

11 So the enemy took all the possessions of Sodom and Gomorrah, and all their provisions, and went their way.

12 They also took Lot, the son of Abram's brother, who was dwelling in Sodom, and his possessions, and went their way.

13 Then one who had escaped came and told Abram the Hebrew, who was living by the oaks of Mamre the Amorite, brother of Eshcol and of Aner. These were allies of Abram.

14 When Abram heard that his kinsman had been taken captive, he led forth his trained men, born in his house, 318 of them, and went in pursuit as far as Dan.

15 And he divided his forces against them by night, he and his servants, and defeated them and pursued them to Hobah, north of Damascus.

16 Then he brought back all the possessions, and also brought back his kinsman Lot with his possessions, and the women and the people.

Abram Blessed by Melchizedek

17 After his return from the defeat of Chedorlaomer and the kings who were with him, the king of Sodom went out to meet him at the Valley of Shaveh (that is, the King's Valley).

18 And Melchizedek king of Salem brought out bread and wine. (He was priest of God Most High.)

19 And he blessed him and said, "Blessed be Abram by God Most High, Possessor of heaven and earth;

20 and blessed be God Most High, who has delivered your enemies into your hand!" And Abram gave him a tenth of everything.

21 And the king of Sodom said to Abram, "Give me the persons, but take the goods for yourself."

22 But Abram said to the king of Sodom, "I have lifted my hand to the Lord, God Most High, Possessor of heaven and earth,

23 that I would not take a thread or a sandal strap or anything that is yours, lest you should say, 'I have made Abram rich.'

24 I will take nothing but what the young men have eaten, and the share of the men who went with me. Let Aner, Eshcol, and Mamre take their share."

Genesis 15

English Standard Version

God's Covenant with Abram

1 After these things the word of the Lord came to Abram in a vision: "Fear not, Abram, I am your shield; your reward shall be very great."

2 But Abram said, "O Lord God, what will you give me, for I continue childless, and the heir of my house is Eliezer of Damascus?"

3 And Abram said, "Behold, you have given me no offspring, and a member of my household will be my heir."

4 And behold, the word of the Lord came to him: "This man shall not be your heir; your very own son shall be your heir."

5 And he brought him outside and said, "Look toward heaven, and number the stars, if you are able to number them." Then he said to him, "So shall your offspring be."

6 And he believed the Lord, and he counted it to him as righteousness.

7 And he said to him, "I am the Lord who brought you out from Ur of the Chaldeans to give you this land to possess."

8 But he said, "O Lord God, how am I to know that I shall possess it?"

9 He said to him, "Bring me a heifer three years old, a female goat three years old, a ram three years old, a turtledove, and a young pigeon."

10 And he brought him all these, cut them in half, and laid each half over against the other. But he did not cut the birds in half.

11 And when birds of prey came down on the carcasses, Abram drove them away.

12 As the sun was going down, a deep sleep fell on Abram. And behold, dreadful and great darkness fell upon him.

13 Then the Lord said to Abram, "Know for certain that your offspring will be sojourners in a land that is not theirs and will be servants there, and they will be afflicted for four hundred years.

14 But I will bring judgment on the nation that they serve, and afterward they shall come out with great possessions.

15 As for you, you shall go to your fathers in peace; you shall be buried in a good old age.

16 And they shall come back here in the fourth generation, for the iniquity of the Amorites is not yet complete."

17 When the sun had gone down and it was dark, behold, a smoking fire pot and a flaming torch passed between these pieces.

18 On that day the Lord made a covenant with Abram, saying, "To your offspring I give this land, from the river of Egypt to the great river, the river Euphrates,

19 the land of the Kenites, the Kenizzites, the Kadmonites,

20 the Hittites, the Perizzites, the Rephaim,

21 the Amorites, the Canaanites, the Girgashites and the Jebusites."

Genesis 16

English Standard Version

Sarai and Hagar

1 Now Sarai, Abram's wife, had borne him no children. She had a female Egyptian servant whose name was Hagar.

2 And Sarai said to Abram, "Behold now, the Lord has prevented me from bearing children. Go in to my servant; it may be that I shall obtain children by her." And Abram listened to the voice of Sarai.

3 So, after Abram had lived ten years in the land of Canaan, Sarai, Abram's wife, took Hagar the Egyptian, her servant, and gave her to Abram her husband as a wife.

4 And he went in to Hagar, and she conceived. And when she saw that she had conceived, she looked with contempt on her mistress.

5 And Sarai said to Abram, "May the wrong done to me be on you! I gave my servant to your embrace, and when she saw that she had conceived, she looked on me with contempt. May the Lord judge between you and me!"

6 But Abram said to Sarai, "Behold, your servant is in your power; do to her as you please." Then Sarai dealt harshly with her, and she fled from her.

7 The angel of the Lord found her by a spring of water in the wilderness, the spring on the way to Shur.

8 And he said, "Hagar, servant of Sarai, where have you come from and where are you going?" She said, "I am fleeing from my mistress Sarai."

9 The angel of the Lord said to her, "Return to your mistress and submit to her."

10 The angel of the Lord also said to her, "I will surely multiply your offspring so that they cannot be numbered for multitude."

11 And the angel of the Lord said to her, "Behold, you are pregnant and shall bear a son. You shall call his name Ishmael, because the Lord has listened to your affliction.

12 He shall be a wild donkey of a man, his hand against everyone and everyone's hand against him, and he shall dwell over against all his kinsmen."

13 So she called the name of the Lord who spoke to her, "You are a God of seeing," for she said, "Truly here I have seen him who looks after me."

14 Therefore the well was called Beer-lahai-roi; it lies between Kadesh and Bered.

15 And Hagar bore Abram a son, and Abram called the name of his son, whom Hagar bore, Ishmael.

16 Abram was eighty-six years old when Hagar bore Ishmael to Abram.

Genesis 17

English Standard Version

Abraham and the Covenant of Circumcision

1 When Abram was ninety-nine years old the Lord appeared to Abram and said to him, "I am God Almighty; walk before me, and be blameless,

2 that I may make my covenant between me and you, and may multiply you greatly."

3 Then Abram fell on his face. And God said to him,

4 "Behold, my covenant is with you, and you shall be the father of a multitude of nations.

5 No longer shall your name be called Abram, but your name shall be Abraham, for I have made you the father of a multitude of nations.

6 I will make you exceedingly fruitful, and I will make you into nations, and kings shall come from you.

7 And I will establish my covenant between me and you and your offspring after you throughout their generations for an everlasting covenant, to be God to you and to your offspring after you.

8 And I will give to you and to your offspring after you the land of your sojournings, all the land of Canaan, for an everlasting possession, and I will be their God."

9 And God said to Abraham, "As for you, you shall keep my covenant, you and your offspring after you throughout their generations.

10 This is my covenant, which you shall keep, between me and you and your offspring after you: Every male among you shall be circumcised.

11 You shall be circumcised in the flesh of your foreskins, and it shall be a sign of the covenant between me and you.

12 He who is eight days old among you shall be circumcised. Every male throughout your generations, whether born in your house or bought with your money from any foreigner who is not of your offspring,

13 both he who is born in your house and he who is bought with your money, shall surely be circumcised. So shall my covenant be in your flesh an everlasting covenant.

14 Any uncircumcised male who is not circumcised in the flesh of his foreskin shall be cut off from his people; he has broken my covenant."

Isaac's Birth Promised

15 And God said to Abraham, "As for Sarai your wife, you shall not call her name Sarai, but Sarah shall be her name.

16 I will bless her, and moreover, I will give you a son by her. I will bless her, and she shall become nations; kings of peoples shall come from her."

17 Then Abraham fell on his face and laughed and said to himself, "Shall a child be born to a man who is a hundred years old? Shall Sarah, who is ninety years old, bear a child?"

18 And Abraham said to God, "Oh that Ishmael might live before you!"

19 God said, "No, but Sarah your wife shall bear you a son, and you shall call his name Isaac. I will establish my covenant with him as an everlasting covenant for his offspring after him.

20 As for Ishmael, I have heard you; behold, I have blessed him and will make him fruitful and multiply him greatly. He shall father twelve princes, and I will make him into a great nation.

21 But I will establish my covenant with Isaac, whom Sarah shall bear to you at this time next year."

22 When he had finished talking with him, God went up from Abraham.

23 Then Abraham took Ishmael his son and all those born in his house or bought with his money, every male among the men of Abraham's house, and he circumcised the flesh of their foreskins that very day, as God had said to him.

24 Abraham was ninety-nine years old when he was circumcised in the flesh of his foreskin.

25 And Ishmael his son was thirteen years old when he was circumcised in the flesh of his foreskin.

26 That very day Abraham and his son Ishmael were circumcised.

27 And all the men of his house, those born in the house and those bought with money from a foreigner, were circumcised with him.

Genesis 18

English Standard Version

1 And the Lord appeared to him by the oaks of Mamre, as he sat at the door of his tent in the heat of the day.

2 He lifted up his eyes and looked, and behold, three men were standing in front of him. When he saw them, he ran from the tent door to meet them and bowed himself to the earth

3 and said, "O Lord, if I have found favor in your sight, do not pass by your servant.

4 Let a little water be brought, and wash your feet, and rest yourselves under the tree,

5 while I bring a morsel of bread, that you may refresh yourselves, and after that you may pass on—since you have come to your servant." So they said, "Do as you have said."

6 And Abraham went quickly into the tent to Sarah and said, "Quick! Three seahs of fine flour! Knead it, and make cakes."

7 And Abraham ran to the herd and took a calf, tender and good, and gave it to a young man, who prepared it quickly.

8 Then he took curds and milk and the calf that he had prepared, and set it before them. And he stood by them under the tree while they ate.

9 They said to him, "Where is Sarah your wife?" And he said, "She is in the tent."

10 The Lord said, "I will surely return to you about this time next year, and Sarah your wife shall have a son." And Sarah was listening at the tent door behind him.

11 Now Abraham and Sarah were old, advanced in years. The way of women had ceased to be with Sarah.

12 So Sarah laughed to herself, saying, "After I am worn out, and my lord is old, shall I have pleasure?"

13 The Lord said to Abraham, "Why did Sarah laugh and say, 'Shall I indeed bear a child, now that I am old?'

14 Is anything too hard for the Lord? At the appointed time I will return to you, about this time next year, and Sarah shall have a son."

15 But Sarah denied it, saying, "I did not laugh," for she was afraid. He said, "No, but you did laugh."

16 Then the men set out from there, and they looked down toward Sodom. And Abraham went with them to set them on their way.

17 The Lord said, "Shall I hide from Abraham what I am about to do,

18 seeing that Abraham shall surely become a great and mighty nation, and all the nations of the earth shall be blessed in him?

19 For I have chosen him, that he may command his children and his household after him to keep the way of the Lord by doing righteousness and justice, so that the Lord may bring to Abraham what he has promised him."

20 Then the Lord said, "Because the outcry against Sodom and Gomorrah is great and their sin is very grave,

21 I will go down to see whether they have done altogether according to the outcry that has come to me. And if not, I will know."

Abraham Intercedes for Sodom

22 So the men turned from there and went toward Sodom, but Abraham still stood before the Lord.

23 Then Abraham drew near and said, "Will you indeed sweep away the righteous with the wicked?

24 Suppose there are fifty righteous within the city. Will you then sweep away the place and not spare it for the fifty righteous who are in it?

25 Far be it from you to do such a thing, to put the righteous to death with the wicked, so that the righteous fare as the wicked! Far be that from you! Shall not the Judge of all the earth do what is just?"

26 And the Lord said, "If I find at Sodom fifty righteous in the city, I will spare the whole place for their sake."

27 Abraham answered and said, "Behold, I have undertaken to speak to the Lord, I who am but dust and ashes.

28 Suppose five of the fifty righteous are lacking. Will you destroy the whole city for lack of five?" And he said, "I will not destroy it if I find forty-five there."

29 Again he spoke to him and said, "Suppose forty are found there." He answered, "For the sake of forty I will not do it."

30 Then he said, "Oh let not the Lord be angry, and I will speak. Suppose thirty are found there." He answered, "I will not do it, if I find thirty there."

31 He said, "Behold, I have undertaken to speak to the Lord. Suppose twenty are found there." He answered, "For the sake of twenty I will not destroy it."

Genesis 18

32 Then he said, "Oh let not the Lord be angry, and I will speak again but this once. Suppose ten are found there." He answered, "For the sake of ten I will not destroy it."

33 And the Lord went his way, when he had finished speaking to Abraham, and Abraham returned to his place.

Genesis 19

English Standard Version

God Rescues Lot

1 The two angels came to Sodom in the evening, and Lot was sitting in the gate of Sodom. When Lot saw them, he rose to meet them and bowed himself with his face to the earth

2 and said, "My lords, please turn aside to your servant's house and spend the night and wash your feet. Then you may rise up early and go on your way." They said, "No; we will spend the night in the town square."

3 But he pressed them strongly; so they turned aside to him and entered his house. And he made them a feast and baked unleavened bread, and they ate.

4 But before they lay down, the men of the city, the men of Sodom, both young and old, all the people to the last man, surrounded the house.

5 And they called to Lot, "Where are the men who came to you tonight? Bring them out to us, that we may know them."

6 Lot went out to the men at the entrance, shut the door after him,

7 and said, "I beg you, my brothers, do not act so wickedly.

8 Behold, I have two daughters who have not known any man. Let me bring them out to you, and do to them as you please. Only do nothing to these men, for they have come under the shelter of my roof."

9 But they said, "Stand back!" And they said, "This fellow came to sojourn, and he has become the judge! Now we will deal worse with you than with them." Then they pressed hard against the man Lot, and drew near to break the door down.

10 But the men reached out their hands and brought Lot into the house with them and shut the door.

11 And they struck with blindness the men who were at the entrance of the house, both small and great, so that they wore themselves out groping for the door.

12 Then the men said to Lot, "Have you anyone else here? Sons-in-law, sons, daughters, or anyone you have in the city, bring them out of the place.

13 For we are about to destroy this place, because the outcry against its people has become great before the Lord, and the Lord has sent us to destroy it."

14 So Lot went out and said to his sons-in-law, who were to marry his daughters, "Up! Get out of this place, for the Lord is about to destroy the city." But he seemed to his sons-in-law to be jesting.

15 As morning dawned, the angels urged Lot, saying, "Up! Take your wife and your two daughters who are here, lest you be swept away in the punishment of the city."

16 But he lingered. So the men seized him and his wife and his two daughters by the hand, the Lord being merciful to him, and they brought him out and set him outside the city.

17 And as they brought them out, one said, "Escape for your life. Do not look back or stop anywhere in the valley. Escape to the hills, lest you be swept away."

18 And Lot said to them, "Oh, no, my lords.

19 Behold, your servant has found favor in your sight, and you have shown me great kindness in saving my life. But I cannot escape to the hills, lest the disaster overtake me and I die.

20 Behold, this city is near enough to flee to, and it is a little one. Let me escape there—is it not a little one?—and my life will be saved!"

21 He said to him, "Behold, I grant you this favor also, that I will not overthrow the city of which you have spoken.

22 Escape there quickly, for I can do nothing till you arrive there." Therefore the name of the city was called Zoar.

God Destroys Sodom

23 The sun had risen on the earth when Lot came to Zoar.

24 Then the Lord rained on Sodom and Gomorrah sulfur and fire from the Lord out of heaven.

25 And he overthrew those cities, and all the valley, and all the inhabitants of the cities, and what grew on the ground.

26 But Lot's wife, behind him, looked back, and she became a pillar of salt.

27 And Abraham went early in the morning to the place where he had stood before the Lord.

28 And he looked down toward Sodom and Gomorrah and toward all the land of the valley, and he looked and, behold, the smoke of the land went up like the smoke of a furnace.

29 So it was that, when God destroyed the cities of the valley, God remembered Abraham and sent Lot out of the midst of the overthrow when he overthrew the cities in which Lot had lived.

Lot and His Daughters

30 Now Lot went up out of Zoar and lived in the hills with his two daughters, for he was afraid to live in Zoar. So he lived in a cave with his two daughters.

31 And the firstborn said to the younger, "Our father is old, and there is not a man on earth to come in to us after the manner of all the earth.

32 Come, let us make our father drink wine, and we will lie with him, that we may preserve offspring from our father."

33 So they made their father drink wine that night. And the firstborn went in and lay with her father. He did not know when she lay down or when she arose.

34 The next day, the firstborn said to the younger, "Behold, I lay last night with my father. Let us make him drink wine tonight also. Then you go in and lie with him, that we may preserve offspring from our father."

35 So they made their father drink wine that night also. And the younger arose and lay with him, and he did not know when she lay down or when she arose.

36 Thus both the daughters of Lot became pregnant by their father.

37 The firstborn bore a son and called his name Moab. He is the father of the Moabites to this day.

38 The younger also bore a son and called his name Ben-ammi. He is the father of the Ammonites to this day.

Genesis 20

English Standard Version

Abraham and Abimelech

1 From there Abraham journeyed toward the territory of the Negeb and lived between Kadesh and Shur; and he sojourned in Gerar.

2 And Abraham said of Sarah his wife, "She is my sister." And Abimelech king of Gerar sent and took Sarah.

3 But God came to Abimelech in a dream by night and said to him, "Behold, you are a dead man because of the woman whom you have taken, for she is a man's wife."

4 Now Abimelech had not approached her. So he said, "Lord, will you kill an innocent people?

5 Did he not himself say to me, 'She is my sister'? And she herself said, 'He is my brother.' In the integrity of my heart and the innocence of my hands I have done this."

6 Then God said to him in the dream, "Yes, I know that you have done this in the integrity of your heart, and it was I who kept you from sinning against me. Therefore I did not let you touch her.

7 Now then, return the man's wife, for he is a prophet, so that he will pray for you, and you shall live. But if you do not return her, know that you shall surely die, you and all who are yours."

8 So Abimelech rose early in the morning and called all his servants and told them all these things. And the men were very much afraid.

9 Then Abimelech called Abraham and said to him, "What have you done to us? And how have I sinned against you, that you have brought on me and my kingdom a great sin? You have done to me things that ought not to be done."

10 And Abimelech said to Abraham, "What did you see, that you did this thing?"

11 Abraham said, "I did it because I thought, 'There is no fear of God at all in this place, and they will kill me because of my wife.'

12 Besides, she is indeed my sister, the daughter of my father though not the daughter of my mother, and she became my wife.

13 And when God caused me to wander from my father's house, I said to her, 'This is the kindness you must do me: at every place to which we come, say of me, "He is my brother."'"

14 Then Abimelech took sheep and oxen, and male servants and female servants, and gave them to Abraham, and returned Sarah his wife to him.

15 And Abimelech said, "Behold, my land is before you; dwell where it pleases you."

16 To Sarah he said, "Behold, I have given your brother a thousand pieces of silver. It is a sign of your innocence in the eyes of all who are with you, and before everyone you are vindicated."

17 Then Abraham prayed to God, and God healed Abimelech, and also healed his wife and female slaves so that they bore children.

18 For the Lord had closed all the wombs of the house of Abimelech because of Sarah, Abraham's wife.

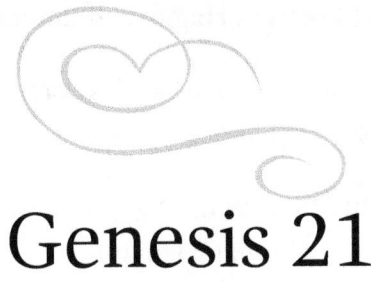

Genesis 21

English Standard Version

The Birth of Isaac

1 The Lord visited Sarah as he had said, and the Lord did to Sarah as he had promised.

2 And Sarah conceived and bore Abraham a son in his old age at the time of which God had spoken to him.

3 Abraham called the name of his son who was born to him, whom Sarah bore him, Isaac.

4 And Abraham circumcised his son Isaac when he was eight days old, as God had commanded him.

5 Abraham was a hundred years old when his son Isaac was born to him.

6 And Sarah said, "God has made laughter for me; everyone who hears will laugh over me."

7 And she said, "Who would have said to Abraham that Sarah would nurse children? Yet I have borne him a son in his old age."

God Protects Hagar and Ishmael

8 And the child grew and was weaned. And Abraham made a great feast on the day that Isaac was weaned.

9 But Sarah saw the son of Hagar the Egyptian, whom she had borne to Abraham, laughing.

10 So she said to Abraham, "Cast out this slave woman with her son, for the son of this slave woman shall not be heir with my son Isaac."

11 And the thing was very displeasing to Abraham on account of his son.

12 But God said to Abraham, "Be not displeased because of the boy and because of your slave woman. Whatever Sarah says to you, do as she tells you, for through Isaac shall your offspring be named.

13 And I will make a nation of the son of the slave woman also, because he is your offspring."

14 So Abraham rose early in the morning and took bread and a skin of water and gave it to Hagar, putting it on her shoulder, along with the child, and sent her away. And she departed and wandered in the wilderness of Beersheba.

15 When the water in the skin was gone, she put the child under one of the bushes.

16 Then she went and sat down opposite him a good way off, about the distance of a bowshot, for she said, "Let me not look on the death of the child." And as she sat opposite him, she lifted up her voice and wept.

17 And God heard the voice of the boy, and the angel of God called to Hagar from heaven and said to her, "What troubles you, Hagar? Fear not, for God has heard the voice of the boy where he is.

18 Up! Lift up the boy, and hold him fast with your hand, for I will make him into a great nation."

19 Then God opened her eyes, and she saw a well of water. And she went and filled the skin with water and gave the boy a drink.

20 And God was with the boy, and he grew up. He lived in the wilderness and became an expert with the bow.

21 He lived in the wilderness of Paran, and his mother took a wife for him from the land of Egypt.

A Treaty with Abimelech

22 At that time Abimelech and Phicol the commander of his army said to Abraham, "God is with you in all that you do.

23 Now therefore swear to me here by God that you will not deal falsely with me or with my descendants or with my posterity, but as I have dealt kindly with you, so you will deal with me and with the land where you have sojourned."

24 And Abraham said, "I will swear."

25 When Abraham reproved Abimelech about a well of water that Abimelech's servants had seized,

26 Abimelech said, "I do not know who has done this thing; you did not tell me, and I have not heard of it until today."

27 So Abraham took sheep and oxen and gave them to Abimelech, and the two men made a covenant.

28 Abraham set seven ewe lambs of the flock apart.

29 And Abimelech said to Abraham, "What is the meaning of these seven ewe lambs that you have set apart?"

30 He said, "These seven ewe lambs you will take from my hand, that this may be a witness for me that I dug this well."

31 Therefore that place was called Beersheba, because there both of them swore an oath.

32 So they made a covenant at Beersheba. Then Abimelech and Phicol the commander of his army rose up and returned to the land of the Philistines.

33 Abraham planted a tamarisk tree in Beersheba and called there on the name of the Lord, the Everlasting God.

34 And Abraham sojourned many days in the land of the Philistines.

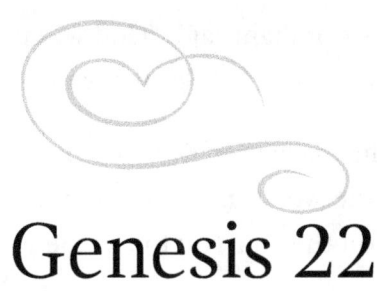

Genesis 22

English Standard Version

The Sacrifice of Isaac

22 After these things God tested Abraham and said to him, "Abraham!" And he said, "Here I am."

2 He said, "Take your son, your only son Isaac, whom you love, and go to the land of Moriah, and offer him there as a burnt offering on one of the mountains of which I shall tell you."

3 So Abraham rose early in the morning, saddled his donkey, and took two of his young men with him, and his son Isaac. And he cut the wood for the burnt offering and arose and went to the place of which God had told him.

4 On the third day Abraham lifted up his eyes and saw the place from afar.

5 Then Abraham said to his young men, "Stay here with the donkey; I and the boy will go over there and worship and come again to you."

6 And Abraham took the wood of the burnt offering and laid it on Isaac his son. And he took in his hand the fire and the knife. So they went both of them together.

7 And Isaac said to his father Abraham, "My father!" And he said, "Here I am, my son." He said, "Behold, the fire and the wood, but where is the lamb

for a burnt offering?" 8 Abraham said, "God will provide for himself the lamb for a burnt offering, my son." So they went both of them together.

9 When they came to the place of which God had told him, Abraham built the altar there and laid the wood in order and bound Isaac his son and laid him on the altar, on top of the wood.

10 Then Abraham reached out his hand and took the knife to slaughter his son.

11 But the angel of the Lord called to him from heaven and said, "Abraham, Abraham!" And he said, "Here I am."

12 He said, "Do not lay your hand on the boy or do anything to him, for now I know that you fear God, seeing you have not withheld your son, your only son, from me."

13 And Abraham lifted up his eyes and looked, and behold, behind him was a ram, caught in a thicket by his horns. And Abraham went and took the ram and offered it up as a burnt offering instead of his son.

14 So Abraham called the name of that place, "The Lord will provide"; as it is said to this day, "On the mount of the Lord it shall be provided."

15 And the angel of the Lord called to Abraham a second time from heaven

16 and said, "By myself I have sworn, declares the Lord, because you have done this and have not withheld your son, your only son,

17 I will surely bless you, and I will surely multiply your offspring as the stars of heaven and as the sand that is on the seashore. And your offspring shall possess the gate of his enemies,

18 and in your offspring shall all the nations of the earth be blessed, because you have obeyed my voice."

19 So Abraham returned to his young men, and they arose and went together to Beersheba. And Abraham lived at Beersheba.

20 Now after these things it was told to Abraham, "Behold, Milcah also has borne children to your brother Nahor:

21 Uz his firstborn, Buz his brother, Kemuel the father of Aram,

22 Chesed, Hazo, Pildash, Jidlaph, and Bethuel."

23 (Bethuel fathered Rebekah.) These eight Milcah bore to Nahor, Abraham's brother.

24 Moreover, his concubine, whose name was Reumah, bore Tebah, Gaham, Tahash, and Maacah.

Genesis 23

English Standard Version

Sarah's Death and Burial

1 Sarah lived 127 years; these were the years of the life of Sarah.

2 And Sarah died at Kiriath-arba (that is, Hebron) in the land of Canaan, and Abraham went in to mourn for Sarah and to weep for her.

3 And Abraham rose up from before his dead and said to the Hittites,

4 "I am a sojourner and foreigner among you; give me property among you for a burying place, that I may bury my dead out of my sight."

5 The Hittites answered Abraham,

6 "Hear us, my lord; you are a prince of God among us. Bury your dead in the choicest of our tombs. None of us will withhold from you his tomb to hinder you from burying your dead."

7 Abraham rose and bowed to the Hittites, the people of the land.

8 And he said to them, "If you are willing that I should bury my dead out of my sight, hear me and entreat for me Ephron the son of Zohar,

9 that he may give me the cave of Machpelah, which he owns; it is at the end of his field. For the full price let him give it to me in your presence as property for a burying place."

10 Now Ephron was sitting among the Hittites, and Ephron the Hittite answered Abraham in the hearing of the Hittites, of all who went in at the gate of his city,

11 "No, my lord, hear me: I give you the field, and I give you the cave that is in it. In the sight of the sons of my people I give it to you. Bury your dead."

12 Then Abraham bowed down before the people of the land.

13 And he said to Ephron in the hearing of the people of the land, "But if you will, hear me: I give the price of the field. Accept it from me, that I may bury my dead there."

14 Ephron answered Abraham,

15 "My lord, listen to me: a piece of land worth four hundred shekels of silver, what is that between you and me? Bury your dead."

16 Abraham listened to Ephron, and Abraham weighed out for Ephron the silver that he had named in the hearing of the Hittites, four hundred shekels of silver, according to the weights current among the merchants.

17 So the field of Ephron in Machpelah, which was to the east of Mamre, the field with the cave that was in it and all the trees that were in the field, throughout its whole area, was made over

18 to Abraham as a possession in the presence of the Hittites, before all who went in at the gate of his city.

19 After this, Abraham buried Sarah his wife in the cave of the field of Machpelah east of Mamre (that is, Hebron) in the land of Canaan.

20 The field and the cave that is in it were made over to Abraham as property for a burying place by the Hittites.

Genesis 24

English Standard Version

Isaac and Rebekah

1 Now Abraham was old, well advanced in years. And the Lord had blessed Abraham in all things.

2 And Abraham said to his servant, the oldest of his household, who had charge of all that he had, "Put your hand under my thigh,

3 that I may make you swear by the Lord, the God of heaven and God of the earth, that you will not take a wife for my son from the daughters of the Canaanites, among whom I dwell,

4 but will go to my country and to my kindred, and take a wife for my son Isaac."

5 The servant said to him, "Perhaps the woman may not be willing to follow me to this land. Must I then take your son back to the land from which you came?"

6 Abraham said to him, "See to it that you do not take my son back there.

7 The Lord, the God of heaven, who took me from my father's house and from the land of my kindred, and who spoke to me and swore to me, 'To

your offspring I will give this land,' he will send his angel before you, and you shall take a wife for my son from there.

8 But if the woman is not willing to follow you, then you will be free from this oath of mine; only you must not take my son back there."

9 So the servant put his hand under the thigh of Abraham his master and swore to him concerning this matter.

10 Then the servant took ten of his master's camels and departed, taking all sorts of choice gifts from his master; and he arose and went to Mesopotamia to the city of Nahor.

11 And he made the camels kneel down outside the city by the well of water at the time of evening, the time when women go out to draw water.

12 And he said, "O Lord, God of my master Abraham, please grant me success today and show steadfast love to my master Abraham.

13 Behold, I am standing by the spring of water, and the daughters of the men of the city are coming out to draw water.

14 Let the young woman to whom I shall say, 'Please let down your jar that I may drink,' and who shall say, 'Drink, and I will water your camels'—let her be the one whom you have appointed for your servant Isaac. By this I shall know that you have shown steadfast love to my master."

15 Before he had finished speaking, behold, Rebekah, who was born to Bethuel the son of Milcah, the wife of Nahor, Abraham's brother, came out with her water jar on her shoulder.

16 The young woman was very attractive in appearance, a maiden whom no man had known. She went down to the spring and filled her jar and came up.

17 Then the servant ran to meet her and said, "Please give me a little water to drink from your jar."

18 She said, "Drink, my lord." And she quickly let down her jar upon her hand and gave him a drink.

19 When she had finished giving him a drink, she said, "I will draw water for your camels also, until they have finished drinking."

20 So she quickly emptied her jar into the trough and ran again to the well to draw water, and she drew for all his camels.

21 The man gazed at her in silence to learn whether the Lord had prospered his journey or not.

22 When the camels had finished drinking, the man took a gold ring weighing a half shekel, and two bracelets for her arms weighing ten gold shekels,

23 and said, "Please tell me whose daughter you are. Is there room in your father's house for us to spend the night?"

24 She said to him, "I am the daughter of Bethuel the son of Milcah, whom she bore to Nahor."

25 She added, "We have plenty of both straw and fodder, and room to spend the night."

26 The man bowed his head and worshiped the Lord

27 and said, "Blessed be the Lord, the God of my master Abraham, who has not forsaken his steadfast love and his faithfulness toward my master. As for me, the Lord has led me in the way to the house of my master's kinsmen."

28 Then the young woman ran and told her mother's household about these things.

29 Rebekah had a brother whose name was Laban. Laban ran out toward the man, to the spring.

30 As soon as he saw the ring and the bracelets on his sister's arms, and heard the words of Rebekah his sister, "Thus the man spoke to me," he went to the man. And behold, he was standing by the camels at the spring.

31 He said, "Come in, O blessed of the Lord. Why do you stand outside? For I have prepared the house and a place for the camels."

32 So the man came to the house and unharnessed the camels, and gave straw and fodder to the camels, and there was water to wash his feet and the feet of the men who were with him.

33 Then food was set before him to eat. But he said, "I will not eat until I have said what I have to say." He said, "Speak on."

34 So he said, "I am Abraham's servant.

35 The Lord has greatly blessed my master, and he has become great. He has given him flocks and herds, silver and gold, male servants and female servants, camels and donkeys.

36 And Sarah my master's wife bore a son to my master when she was old, and to him he has given all that he has.

37 My master made me swear, saying, 'You shall not take a wife for my son from the daughters of the Canaanites, in whose land I dwell,

38 but you shall go to my father's house and to my clan and take a wife for my son.'

39 I said to my master, 'Perhaps the woman will not follow me.'

40 But he said to me, 'The Lord, before whom I have walked, will send his angel with you and prosper your way. You shall take a wife for my son from my clan and from my father's house.

41 Then you will be free from my oath, when you come to my clan. And if they will not give her to you, you will be free from my oath.'

42 "I came today to the spring and said, 'O Lord, the God of my master Abraham, if now you are prospering the way that I go,

43 behold, I am standing by the spring of water. Let the virgin who comes out to draw water, to whom I shall say, "Please give me a little water from your jar to drink,"

44 and who will say to me, "Drink, and I will draw for your camels also," let her be the woman whom the Lord has appointed for my master's son.'

45 "Before I had finished speaking in my heart, behold, Rebekah came out with her water jar on her shoulder, and she went down to the spring and drew water. I said to her, 'Please let me drink.'

46 She quickly let down her jar from her shoulder and said, 'Drink, and I will give your camels drink also.' So I drank, and she gave the camels drink also.

47 Then I asked her, 'Whose daughter are you?' She said, 'The daughter of Bethuel, Nahor's son, whom Milcah bore to him.' So I put the ring on her nose and the bracelets on her arms.

48 Then I bowed my head and worshiped the Lord and blessed the Lord, the God of my master Abraham, who had led me by the right way to take the daughter of my master's kinsman for his son.

49 Now then, if you are going to show steadfast love and faithfulness to my master, tell me; and if not, tell me, that I may turn to the right hand or to the left."

50 Then Laban and Bethuel answered and said, "The thing has come from the Lord; we cannot speak to you bad or good.

51 Behold, Rebekah is before you; take her and go, and let her be the wife of your master's son, as the Lord has spoken."

52 When Abraham's servant heard their words, he bowed himself to the earth before the Lord.

Genesis 24

53 And the servant brought out jewelry of silver and of gold, and garments, and gave them to Rebekah. He also gave to her brother and to her mother costly ornaments.

54 And he and the men who were with him ate and drank, and they spent the night there. When they arose in the morning, he said, "Send me away to my master."

55 Her brother and her mother said, "Let the young woman remain with us a while, at least ten days; after that she may go."

56 But he said to them, "Do not delay me, since the Lord has prospered my way. Send me away that I may go to my master."

57 They said, "Let us call the young woman and ask her."

58 And they called Rebekah and said to her, "Will you go with this man?" She said, "I will go."

59 So they sent away Rebekah their sister and her nurse, and Abraham's servant and his men.

60 And they blessed Rebekah and said to her, "Our sister, may you become thousands of ten thousands, and may your offspring possess the gate of those who hate him!"

61 Then Rebekah and her young women arose and rode on the camels and followed the man. Thus the servant took Rebekah and went his way.

62 Now Isaac had returned from Beer-lahai-roi and was dwelling in the Negeb.

63 And Isaac went out to meditate in the field toward evening. And he lifted up his eyes and saw, and behold, there were camels coming.

64 And Rebekah lifted up her eyes, and when she saw Isaac, she dismounted from the camel

65 and said to the servant, "Who is that man, walking in the field to meet us?" The servant said, "It is my master." So she took her veil and covered herself.

66 And the servant told Isaac all the things that he had done.

67 Then Isaac brought her into the tent of Sarah his mother and took Rebekah, and she became his wife, and he loved her. So Isaac was comforted after his mother's death.

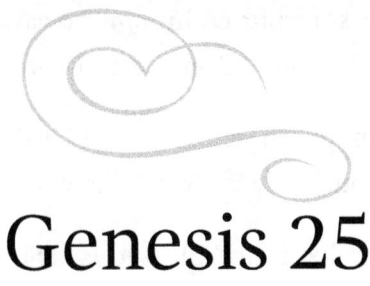

Genesis 25

English Standard Version

Abraham's Death and His Descendants

1 Abraham took another wife, whose name was Keturah.

2 She bore him Zimran, Jokshan, Medan, Midian, Ishbak, and Shuah.

3 Jokshan fathered Sheba and Dedan. The sons of Dedan were Asshurim, Letushim, and Leummim.

4 The sons of Midian were Ephah, Epher, Hanoch, Abida, and Eldaah. All these were the children of Keturah.

5 Abraham gave all he had to Isaac.

6 But to the sons of his concubines Abraham gave gifts, and while he was still living he sent them away from his son Isaac, eastward to the east country.

7 These are the days of the years of Abraham's life, 175 years.

8 Abraham breathed his last and died in a good old age, an old man and full of years, and was gathered to his people.

9 Isaac and Ishmael his sons buried him in the cave of Machpelah, in the field of Ephron the son of Zohar the Hittite, east of Mamre,

10 the field that Abraham purchased from the Hittites. There Abraham was buried, with Sarah his wife.

11 After the death of Abraham, God blessed Isaac his son. And Isaac settled at Beer-lahai-roi.

12 These are the generations of Ishmael, Abraham's son, whom Hagar the Egyptian, Sarah's servant, bore to Abraham.

13 These are the names of the sons of Ishmael, named in the order of their birth: Nebaioth, the firstborn of Ishmael; and Kedar, Adbeel, Mibsam,

14 Mishma, Dumah, Massa,

15 Hadad, Tema, Jetur, Naphish, and Kedemah.

16 These are the sons of Ishmael and these are their names, by their villages and by their encampments, twelve princes according to their tribes.

17 (These are the years of the life of Ishmael: 137 years. He breathed his last and died, and was gathered to his people.)

18 They settled from Havilah to Shur, which is opposite Egypt in the direction of Assyria. He settled over against all his kinsmen.

The Birth of Esau and Jacob

19 These are the generations of Isaac, Abraham's son: Abraham fathered Isaac,

20 and Isaac was forty years old when he took Rebekah, the daughter of Bethuel the Aramean of Paddan-aram, the sister of Laban the Aramean, to be his wife.

21 And Isaac prayed to the Lord for his wife, because she was barren. And the Lord granted his prayer, and Rebekah his wife conceived.

22 The children struggled together within her, and she said, "If it is thus, why is this happening to me?" So she went to inquire of the Lord.

23 And the Lord said to her, "Two nations are in your womb, and two peoples from within you[c] shall be divided; the one shall be stronger than the other, the older shall serve the younger."

24 When her days to give birth were completed, behold, there were twins in her womb.

25 The first came out red, all his body like a hairy cloak, so they called his name Esau.

26 Afterward his brother came out with his hand holding Esau's heel, so his name was called Jacob. Isaac was sixty years old when she bore them.

27 When the boys grew up, Esau was a skillful hunter, a man of the field, while Jacob was a quiet man, dwelling in tents.

28 Isaac loved Esau because he ate of his game, but Rebekah loved Jacob.

Esau Sells His Birthright

29 Once when Jacob was cooking stew, Esau came in from the field, and he was exhausted.

30 And Esau said to Jacob, "Let me eat some of that red stew, for I am exhausted!" (Therefore his name was called Edom.

31 Jacob said, "Sell me your birthright now."

32 Esau said, "I am about to die; of what use is a birthright to me?"

33 Jacob said, "Swear to me now." So he swore to him and sold his birthright to Jacob.

34 Then Jacob gave Esau bread and lentil stew, and he ate and drank and rose and went his way. Thus Esau despised his birthright.

Genesis 26

English Standard Version

God's Promise to Isaac

1 Now there was a famine in the land, besides the former famine that was in the days of Abraham. And Isaac went to Gerar to Abimelech king of the Philistines.

2 And the Lord appeared to him and said, "Do not go down to Egypt; dwell in the land of which I shall tell you.

3 Sojourn in this land, and I will be with you and will bless you, for to you and to your offspring I will give all these lands, and I will establish the oath that I swore to Abraham your father.

4 I will multiply your offspring as the stars of heaven and will give to your offspring all these lands. And in your offspring all the nations of the earth shall be blessed,

5 because Abraham obeyed my voice and kept my charge, my commandments, my statutes, and my laws."

Isaac and Abimelech

6 So Isaac settled in Gerar.

7 When the men of the place asked him about his wife, he said, "She is my sister," for he feared to say, "My wife," thinking, "lest the men of the place should kill me because of Rebekah," because she was attractive in appearance.

8 When he had been there a long time, Abimelech king of the Philistines looked out of a window and saw Isaac laughing with Rebekah his wife.

9 So Abimelech called Isaac and said, "Behold, she is your wife. How then could you say, 'She is my sister'?" Isaac said to him, "Because I thought, 'Lest I die because of her.'"

10 Abimelech said, "What is this you have done to us? One of the people might easily have lain with your wife, and you would have brought guilt upon us."

11 So Abimelech warned all the people, saying, "Whoever touches this man or his wife shall surely be put to death."

12 And Isaac sowed in that land and reaped in the same year a hundredfold. The Lord blessed him,

13 and the man became rich, and gained more and more until he became very wealthy.

14 He had possessions of flocks and herds and many servants, so that the Philistines envied him.

15 (Now the Philistines had stopped and filled with earth all the wells that his father's servants had dug in the days of Abraham his father.)

16 And Abimelech said to Isaac, "Go away from us, for you are much mightier than we."

17 So Isaac departed from there and encamped in the Valley of Gerar and settled there.

18 And Isaac dug again the wells of water that had been dug in the days of Abraham his father, which the Philistines had stopped after the death of Abraham. And he gave them the names that his father had given them.

19 But when Isaac's servants dug in the valley and found there a well of spring water,

20 the herdsmen of Gerar quarreled with Isaac's herdsmen, saying, "The water is ours." So he called the name of the well Esek, because they contended with him.

21 Then they dug another well, and they quarreled over that also, so he called its name Sitnah.

22 And he moved from there and dug another well, and they did not quarrel over it. So he called its name Rehoboth, saying, "For now the Lord has made room for us, and we shall be fruitful in the land."

23 From there he went up to Beersheba.

24 And the Lord appeared to him the same night and said, "I am the God of Abraham your father. Fear not, for I am with you and will bless you and multiply your offspring for my servant Abraham's sake."

25 So he built an altar there and called upon the name of the Lord and pitched his tent there. And there Isaac's servants dug a well.

26 When Abimelech went to him from Gerar with Ahuzzath his adviser and Phicol the commander of his army,

27 Isaac said to them, "Why have you come to me, seeing that you hate me and have sent me away from you?"

28 They said, "We see plainly that the Lord has been with you. So we said, let there be a sworn pact between us, between you and us, and let us make a covenant with you,

29 that you will do us no harm, just as we have not touched you and have done to you nothing but good and have sent you away in peace. You are now the blessed of the Lord."

30 So he made them a feast, and they ate and drank.

31 In the morning they rose early and exchanged oaths. And Isaac sent them on their way, and they departed from him in peace.

32 That same day Isaac's servants came and told him about the well that they had dug and said to him, "We have found water."

33 He called it Shibah; therefore the name of the city is Beersheba to this day.

34 When Esau was forty years old, he took Judith the daughter of Beeri the Hittite to be his wife, and Basemath the daughter of Elon the Hittite,

35 and they made life bitter for Isaac and Rebekah.

Genesis 27

English Standard Version

Isaac Blesses Jacob

1 When Isaac was old and his eyes were dim so that he could not see, he called Esau his older son and said to him, "My son"; and he answered, "Here I am."

2 He said, "Behold, I am old; I do not know the day of my death.

3 Now then, take your weapons, your quiver and your bow, and go out to the field and hunt game for me,

4 and prepare for me delicious food, such as I love, and bring it to me so that I may eat, that my soul may bless you before I die."

5 Now Rebekah was listening when Isaac spoke to his son Esau. So when Esau went to the field to hunt for game and bring it,

6 Rebekah said to her son Jacob, "I heard your father speak to your brother Esau,

7 'Bring me game and prepare for me delicious food, that I may eat it and bless you before the Lord before I die.'

8 Now therefore, my son, obey my voice as I command you.

Genesis 27

9 Go to the flock and bring me two good young goats, so that I may prepare from them delicious food for your father, such as he loves.

10 And you shall bring it to your father to eat, so that he may bless you before he dies."

11 But Jacob said to Rebekah his mother, "Behold, my brother Esau is a hairy man, and I am a smooth man.

12 Perhaps my father will feel me, and I shall seem to be mocking him and bring a curse upon myself and not a blessing."

13 His mother said to him, "Let your curse be on me, my son; only obey my voice, and go, bring them to me."

14 So he went and took them and brought them to his mother, and his mother prepared delicious food, such as his father loved.

15 Then Rebekah took the best garments of Esau her older son, which were with her in the house, and put them on Jacob her younger son.

16 And the skins of the young goats she put on his hands and on the smooth part of his neck.

17 And she put the delicious food and the bread, which she had prepared, into the hand of her son Jacob.

18 So he went in to his father and said, "My father." And he said, "Here I am. Who are you, my son?"

19 Jacob said to his father, "I am Esau your firstborn. I have done as you told me; now sit up and eat of my game, that your soul may bless me."

20 But Isaac said to his son, "How is it that you have found it so quickly, my son?" He answered, "Because the Lord your God granted me success."

21 Then Isaac said to Jacob, "Please come near, that I may feel you, my son, to know whether you are really my son Esau or not."

22 So Jacob went near to Isaac his father, who felt him and said, "The voice is Jacob's voice, but the hands are the hands of Esau."

23 And he did not recognize him, because his hands were hairy like his brother Esau's hands. So he blessed him.

24 He said, "Are you really my son Esau?" He answered, "I am."

25 Then he said, "Bring it near to me, that I may eat of my son's game and bless you." So he brought it near to him, and he ate; and he brought him wine, and he drank.

26 Then his father Isaac said to him, "Come near and kiss me, my son."

27 So he came near and kissed him. And Isaac smelled the smell of his garments and blessed him and said, "See, the smell of my son is as the smell of a field that the Lord has blessed!

28 May God give you of the dew of heaven and of the fatness of the earth and plenty of grain and wine.

29 Let peoples serve you, and nations bow down to you. Be lord over your brothers, and may your mother's sons bow down to you. Cursed be everyone who curses you, and blessed be everyone who blesses you!"

30 As soon as Isaac had finished blessing Jacob, when Jacob had scarcely gone out from the presence of Isaac his father, Esau his brother came in from his hunting.

31 He also prepared delicious food and brought it to his father. And he said to his father, "Let my father arise and eat of his son's game, that you may bless me."

32 His father Isaac said to him, "Who are you?" He answered, "I am your son, your firstborn, Esau."

33 Then Isaac trembled very violently and said, "Who was it then that hunted game and brought it to me, and I ate it all before you came, and I have blessed him? Yes, and he shall be blessed."

34 As soon as Esau heard the words of his father, he cried out with an exceedingly great and bitter cry and said to his father, "Bless me, even me also, O my father!"

35 But he said, "Your brother came deceitfully, and he has taken away your blessing."

36 Esau said, "Is he not rightly named Jacob? For he has cheated me these two times. He took away my birthright, and behold, now he has taken away my blessing." Then he said, "Have you not reserved a blessing for me?"

37 Isaac answered and said to Esau, "Behold, I have made him lord over you, and all his brothers I have given to him for servants, and with grain and wine I have sustained him. What then can I do for you, my son?"

38 Esau said to his father, "Have you but one blessing, my father? Bless me, even me also, O my father." And Esau lifted up his voice and wept.

39 Then Isaac his father answered and said to him: "Behold, away from the fatness of the earth shall your dwelling be, and away from the dew of heaven on high.

40 By your sword you shall live, and you shall serve your brother; but when you grow restless you shall break his yoke from your neck."

41 Now Esau hated Jacob because of the blessing with which his father had blessed him, and Esau said to himself, "The days of mourning for my father are approaching; then I will kill my brother Jacob."

42 But the words of Esau her older son were told to Rebekah. So she sent and called Jacob her younger son and said to him, "Behold, your brother Esau comforts himself about you by planning to kill you.

43 Now therefore, my son, obey my voice. Arise, flee to Laban my brother in Haran

44 and stay with him a while, until your brother's fury turns away—

45 until your brother's anger turns away from you, and he forgets what you have done to him. Then I will send and bring you from there. Why should I be bereft of you both in one day?"

46 Then Rebekah said to Isaac, "I loathe my life because of the Hittite women. If Jacob marries one of the Hittite women like these, one of the women of the land, what good will my life be to me?"

Genesis 28

English Standard Version

Jacob Sent to Laban

1 Then Isaac called Jacob and blessed him and directed him, "You must not take a wife from the Canaanite women.

2 Arise, go to Paddan-aram to the house of Bethuel your mother's father, and take as your wife from there one of the daughters of Laban your mother's brother.

3 God Almighty bless you and make you fruitful and multiply you, that you may become a company of peoples.

4 May he give the blessing of Abraham to you and to your offspring with you, that you may take possession of the land of your sojournings that God gave to Abraham!"

5 Thus Isaac sent Jacob away. And he went to Paddan-aram, to Laban, the son of Bethuel the Aramean, the brother of Rebekah, Jacob's and Esau's mother.

Esau Marries an Ishmaelite

6 Now Esau saw that Isaac had blessed Jacob and sent him away to Paddan-aram to take a wife from there, and that as he blessed him he directed him, "You must not take a wife from the Canaanite women,"

7 and that Jacob had obeyed his father and his mother and gone to Paddan-aram.

8 So when Esau saw that the Canaanite women did not please Isaac his father,

9 Esau went to Ishmael and took as his wife, besides the wives he had, Mahalath the daughter of Ishmael, Abraham's son, the sister of Nebaioth.

Jacob's Dream

10 Jacob left Beersheba and went toward Haran.

11 And he came to a certain place and stayed there that night, because the sun had set. Taking one of the stones of the place, he put it under his head and lay down in that place to sleep.

12 And he dreamed, and behold, there was a ladder set up on the earth, and the top of it reached to heaven. And behold, the angels of God were ascending and descending on it!

13 And behold, the Lord stood above it and said, "I am the Lord, the God of Abraham your father and the God of Isaac. The land on which you lie I will give to you and to your offspring.

14 Your offspring shall be like the dust of the earth, and you shall spread abroad to the west and to the east and to the north and to the south, and in you and your offspring shall all the families of the earth be blessed.

15 Behold, I am with you and will keep you wherever you go, and will bring you back to this land. For I will not leave you until I have done what I have promised you."

16 Then Jacob awoke from his sleep and said, "Surely the Lord is in this place, and I did not know it."

17 And he was afraid and said, "How awesome is this place! This is none other than the house of God, and this is the gate of heaven."

18 So early in the morning Jacob took the stone that he had put under his head and set it up for a pillar and poured oil on the top of it.

19 He called the name of that place Bethel, but the name of the city was Luz at the first.

20 Then Jacob made a vow, saying, "If God will be with me and will keep me in this way that I go, and will give me bread to eat and clothing to wear,

21 so that I come again to my father's house in peace, then the Lord shall be my God,

22 and this stone, which I have set up for a pillar, shall be God's house. And of all that you give me I will give a full tenth to you."

Genesis 29

English Standard Version

Jacob Marries Leah and Rachel

1 Then Jacob went on his journey and came to the land of the people of the east.

2 As he looked, he saw a well in the field, and behold, three flocks of sheep lying beside it, for out of that well the flocks were watered. The stone on the well's mouth was large,

3 and when all the flocks were gathered there, the shepherds would roll the stone from the mouth of the well and water the sheep, and put the stone back in its place over the mouth of the well.

4 Jacob said to them, "My brothers, where do you come from?" They said, "We are from Haran."

5 He said to them, "Do you know Laban the son of Nahor?" They said, "We know him."

6 He said to them, "Is it well with him?" They said, "It is well; and see, Rachel his daughter is coming with the sheep!"

7 He said, "Behold, it is still high day; it is not time for the livestock to be gathered together. Water the sheep and go, pasture them."

8 But they said, "We cannot until all the flocks are gathered together and the stone is rolled from the mouth of the well; then we water the sheep."

9 While he was still speaking with them, Rachel came with her father's sheep, for she was a shepherdess.

10 Now as soon as Jacob saw Rachel the daughter of Laban his mother's brother, and the sheep of Laban his mother's brother, Jacob came near and rolled the stone from the well's mouth and watered the flock of Laban his mother's brother.

11 Then Jacob kissed Rachel and wept aloud.

12 And Jacob told Rachel that he was her father's kinsman, and that he was Rebekah's son, and she ran and told her father.

13 As soon as Laban heard the news about Jacob, his sister's son, he ran to meet him and embraced him and kissed him and brought him to his house. Jacob told Laban all these things,

14 and Laban said to him, "Surely you are my bone and my flesh!" And he stayed with him a month.

15 Then Laban said to Jacob, "Because you are my kinsman, should you therefore serve me for nothing? Tell me, what shall your wages be?"

16 Now Laban had two daughters. The name of the older was Leah, and the name of the younger was Rachel.

17 Leah's eyes were weak, but Rachel was beautiful in form and appearance.

18 Jacob loved Rachel. And he said, "I will serve you seven years for your younger daughter Rachel."

19 Laban said, "It is better that I give her to you than that I should give her to any other man; stay with me."

20 So Jacob served seven years for Rachel, and they seemed to him but a few days because of the love he had for her.

21 Then Jacob said to Laban, "Give me my wife that I may go in to her, for my time is completed."

22 So Laban gathered together all the people of the place and made a feast.

23 But in the evening he took his daughter Leah and brought her to Jacob, and he went in to her.

24 (Laban gave his female servant Zilpah to his daughter Leah to be her servant.)

25 And in the morning, behold, it was Leah! And Jacob said to Laban, "What is this you have done to me? Did I not serve with you for Rachel? Why then have you deceived me?"

26 Laban said, "It is not so done in our country, to give the younger before the firstborn.

27 Complete the week of this one, and we will give you the other also in return for serving me another seven years."

28 Jacob did so, and completed her week. Then Laban gave him his daughter Rachel to be his wife.

29 (Laban gave his female servant Bilhah to his daughter Rachel to be her servant.)

30 So Jacob went in to Rachel also, and he loved Rachel more than Leah, and served Laban for another seven years.

Jacob's Children

31 When the Lord saw that Leah was hated, he opened her womb, but Rachel was barren.

32 And Leah conceived and bore a son, and she called his name Reuben, for she said, "Because the Lord has looked upon my affliction; for now my husband will love me."

33 She conceived again and bore a son, and said, "Because the Lord has heard that I am hated, he has given me this son also." And she called his name Simeon.

34 Again she conceived and bore a son, and said, "Now this time my husband will be attached to me, because I have borne him three sons." Therefore his name was called Levi.

35 And she conceived again and bore a son, and said, "This time I will praise the Lord." Therefore she called his name Judah. Then she ceased bearing.

Genesis 30

English Standard Version

1 When Rachel saw that she bore Jacob no children, she envied her sister. She said to Jacob, "Give me children, or I shall die!"

2 Jacob's anger was kindled against Rachel, and he said, "Am I in the place of God, who has withheld from you the fruit of the womb?"

3 Then she said, "Here is my servant Bilhah; go in to her, so that she may give birth on my behalf, that even I may have children through her."

4 So she gave him her servant Bilhah as a wife, and Jacob went in to her.

5 And Bilhah conceived and bore Jacob a son.

6 Then Rachel said, "God has judged me, and has also heard my voice and given me a son." Therefore she called his name Dan.

7 Rachel's servant Bilhah conceived again and bore Jacob a second son.

8 Then Rachel said, "With mighty wrestlings I have wrestled with my sister and have prevailed." So she called his name Naphtali.

9 When Leah saw that she had ceased bearing children, she took her servant Zilpah and gave her to Jacob as a wife.

10 Then Leah's servant Zilpah bore Jacob a son.

11 And Leah said, "Good fortune has come!" so she called his name Gad.

12 Leah's servant Zilpah bore Jacob a second son.

13 And Leah said, "Happy am I! For women have called me happy." So she called his name Asher.

14 In the days of wheat harvest Reuben went and found mandrakes in the field and brought them to his mother Leah. Then Rachel said to Leah, "Please give me some of your son's mandrakes."

15 But she said to her, "Is it a small matter that you have taken away my husband? Would you take away my son's mandrakes also?" Rachel said, "Then he may lie with you tonight in exchange for your son's mandrakes."

16 When Jacob came from the field in the evening, Leah went out to meet him and said, "You must come in to me, for I have hired you with my son's mandrakes." So he lay with her that night.

17 And God listened to Leah, and she conceived and bore Jacob a fifth son.

18 Leah said, "God has given me my wages because I gave my servant to my husband." So she called his name Issachar.

19 And Leah conceived again, and she bore Jacob a sixth son.

20 Then Leah said, "God has endowed me with a good endowment; now my husband will honor me, because I have borne him six sons." So she called his name Zebulun.

21 Afterward she bore a daughter and called her name Dinah.

22 Then God remembered Rachel, and God listened to her and opened her womb.

23 She conceived and bore a son and said, "God has taken away my reproach."

24 And she called his name Joseph, saying, "May the Lord add to me another son!"

Jacob's Prosperity

25 As soon as Rachel had borne Joseph, Jacob said to Laban, "Send me away, that I may go to my own home and country.

26 Give me my wives and my children for whom I have served you, that I may go, for you know the service that I have given you."

27 But Laban said to him, "If I have found favor in your sight, I have learned by divination that the Lord has blessed me because of you.

28 Name your wages, and I will give it."

29 Jacob said to him, "You yourself know how I have served you, and how your livestock has fared with me.

30 For you had little before I came, and it has increased abundantly, and the Lord has blessed you wherever I turned. But now when shall I provide for my own household also?"

31 He said, "What shall I give you?" Jacob said, "You shall not give me anything. If you will do this for me, I will again pasture your flock and keep it:

32 let me pass through all your flock today, removing from it every speckled and spotted sheep and every black lamb, and the spotted and speckled among the goats, and they shall be my wages.

33 So my honesty will answer for me later, when you come to look into my wages with you. Every one that is not speckled and spotted among the goats and black among the lambs, if found with me, shall be counted stolen."

34 Laban said, "Good! Let it be as you have said."

35 But that day Laban removed the male goats that were striped and spotted, and all the female goats that were speckled and spotted, every one

that had white on it, and every lamb that was black, and put them in the charge of his sons.

36 And he set a distance of three days' journey between himself and Jacob, and Jacob pastured the rest of Laban's flock.

37 Then Jacob took fresh sticks of poplar and almond and plane trees, and peeled white streaks in them, exposing the white of the sticks.

38 He set the sticks that he had peeled in front of the flocks in the troughs, that is, the watering places, where the flocks came to drink. And since they bred when they came to drink,

39 the flocks bred in front of the sticks and so the flocks brought forth striped, speckled, and spotted.

40 And Jacob separated the lambs and set the faces of the flocks toward the striped and all the black in the flock of Laban. He put his own droves apart and did not put them with Laban's flock.

41 Whenever the stronger of the flock were breeding, Jacob would lay the sticks in the troughs before the eyes of the flock, that they might breed among the sticks,

42 but for the feebler of the flock he would not lay them there. So the feebler would be Laban's, and the stronger Jacob's.

43 Thus the man increased greatly and had large flocks, female servants and male servants, and camels and donkeys.

Genesis 31

English Standard Version

Jacob Flees from Laban

1 Now Jacob heard that the sons of Laban were saying, "Jacob has taken all that was our father's, and from what was our father's he has gained all this wealth."

2 And Jacob saw that Laban did not regard him with favor as before.

3 Then the Lord said to Jacob, "Return to the land of your fathers and to your kindred, and I will be with you."

4 So Jacob sent and called Rachel and Leah into the field where his flock was

5 and said to them, "I see that your father does not regard me with favor as he did before. But the God of my father has been with me.

6 You know that I have served your father with all my strength,

7 yet your father has cheated me and changed my wages ten times. But God did not permit him to harm me.

8 If he said, 'The spotted shall be your wages,' then all the flock bore spotted; and if he said, 'The striped shall be your wages,' then all the flock bore striped.

9 Thus God has taken away the livestock of your father and given them to me.

10 In the breeding season of the flock I lifted up my eyes and saw in a dream that the goats that mated with the flock were striped, spotted, and mottled.

11 Then the angel of God said to me in the dream, 'Jacob,' and I said, 'Here I am!'

12 And he said, 'Lift up your eyes and see, all the goats that mate with the flock are striped, spotted, and mottled, for I have seen all that Laban is doing to you.

13 I am the God of Bethel, where you anointed a pillar and made a vow to me. Now arise, go out from this land and return to the land of your kindred.'"

14 Then Rachel and Leah answered and said to him, "Is there any portion or inheritance left to us in our father's house?

15 Are we not regarded by him as foreigners? For he has sold us, and he has indeed devoured our money.

16 All the wealth that God has taken away from our father belongs to us and to our children. Now then, whatever God has said to you, do."

17 So Jacob arose and set his sons and his wives on camels.

18 He drove away all his livestock, all his property that he had gained, the livestock in his possession that he had acquired in Paddan-aram, to go to the land of Canaan to his father Isaac.

19 Laban had gone to shear his sheep, and Rachel stole her father's household gods.

20 And Jacob tricked[a] Laban the Aramean, by not telling him that he intended to flee.

21 He fled with all that he had and arose and crossed the Euphrates, and set his face toward the hill country of Gilead.

22 When it was told Laban on the third day that Jacob had fled,

23 he took his kinsmen with him and pursued him for seven days and followed close after him into the hill country of Gilead.

24 But God came to Laban the Aramean in a dream by night and said to him, "Be careful not to say anything to Jacob, either good or bad."

25 And Laban overtook Jacob. Now Jacob had pitched his tent in the hill country, and Laban with his kinsmen pitched tents in the hill country of Gilead.

26 And Laban said to Jacob, "What have you done, that you have tricked me and driven away my daughters like captives of the sword?

27 Why did you flee secretly and trick me, and did not tell me, so that I might have sent you away with mirth and songs, with tambourine and lyre?

28 And why did you not permit me to kiss my sons and my daughters farewell? Now you have done foolishly.

29 It is in my power to do you harm. But the God of your father spoke to me last night, saying, 'Be careful not to say anything to Jacob, either good or bad.'

30 And now you have gone away because you longed greatly for your father's house, but why did you steal my gods?"

31 Jacob answered and said to Laban, "Because I was afraid, for I thought that you would take your daughters from me by force.

32 Anyone with whom you find your gods shall not live. In the presence of our kinsmen point out what I have that is yours, and take it." Now Jacob did not know that Rachel had stolen them.

33 So Laban went into Jacob's tent and into Leah's tent and into the tent of the two female servants, but he did not find them. And he went out of Leah's tent and entered Rachel's.

34 Now Rachel had taken the household gods and put them in the camel's saddle and sat on them. Laban felt all about the tent, but did not find them.

35 And she said to her father, "Let not my lord be angry that I cannot rise before you, for the way of women is upon me." So he searched but did not find the household gods.

36 Then Jacob became angry and berated Laban. Jacob said to Laban, "What is my offense? What is my sin, that you have hotly pursued me?

37 For you have felt through all my goods; what have you found of all your household goods? Set it here before my kinsmen and your kinsmen, that they may decide between us two.

38 These twenty years I have been with you. Your ewes and your female goats have not miscarried, and I have not eaten the rams of your flocks.

39 What was torn by wild beasts I did not bring to you. I bore the loss of it myself. From my hand you required it, whether stolen by day or stolen by night.

40 There I was: by day the heat consumed me, and the cold by night, and my sleep fled from my eyes.

41 These twenty years I have been in your house. I served you fourteen years for your two daughters, and six years for your flock, and you have changed my wages ten times.

42 If the God of my father, the God of Abraham and the Fear of Isaac, had not been on my side, surely now you would have sent me away empty-

handed. God saw my affliction and the labor of my hands and rebuked you last night."

43 Then Laban answered and said to Jacob, "The daughters are my daughters, the children are my children, the flocks are my flocks, and all that you see is mine. But what can I do this day for these my daughters or for their children whom they have borne?

44 Come now, let us make a covenant, you and I. And let it be a witness between you and me."

45 So Jacob took a stone and set it up as a pillar.

46 And Jacob said to his kinsmen, "Gather stones." And they took stones and made a heap, and they ate there by the heap.

47 Laban called it Jegar-sahadutha, but Jacob called it Galeed.

48 Laban said, "This heap is a witness between you and me today." Therefore he named it Galeed,

49 and Mizpah, for he said, "The Lord watch between you and me, when we are out of one another's sight.

50 If you oppress my daughters, or if you take wives besides my daughters, although no one is with us, see, God is witness between you and me."

51 Then Laban said to Jacob, "See this heap and the pillar, which I have set between you and me.

52 This heap is a witness, and the pillar is a witness, that I will not pass over this heap to you, and you will not pass over this heap and this pillar to me, to do harm.

53 The God of Abraham and the God of Nahor, the God of their father, judge between us." So Jacob swore by the Fear of his father Isaac,

54 and Jacob offered a sacrifice in the hill country and called his kinsmen to eat bread. They ate bread and spent the night in the hill country.

Genesis 31

55 Early in the morning Laban arose and kissed his grandchildren and his daughters and blessed them. Then Laban departed and returned home.

Genesis 32

English Standard Version

Jacob Fears Esau

1 Jacob went on his way, and the angels of God met him.

2 And when Jacob saw them he said, "This is God's camp!" So he called the name of that place Mahanaim.

3 And Jacob sent messengers before him to Esau his brother in the land of Seir, the country of Edom,

4 instructing them, "Thus you shall say to my lord Esau: Thus says your servant Jacob, 'I have sojourned with Laban and stayed until now.

5 I have oxen, donkeys, flocks, male servants, and female servants. I have sent to tell my lord, in order that I may find favor in your sight.'"

6 And the messengers returned to Jacob, saying, "We came to your brother Esau, and he is coming to meet you, and there are four hundred men with him."

7 Then Jacob was greatly afraid and distressed. He divided the people who were with him, and the flocks and herds and camels, into two camps,

Genesis 32

8 thinking, "If Esau comes to the one camp and attacks it, then the camp that is left will escape."

9 And Jacob said, "O God of my father Abraham and God of my father Isaac, O Lord who said to me, 'Return to your country and to your kindred, that I may do you good,'

10 I am not worthy of the least of all the deeds of steadfast love and all the faithfulness that you have shown to your servant, for with only my staff I crossed this Jordan, and now I have become two camps.

11 Please deliver me from the hand of my brother, from the hand of Esau, for I fear him, that he may come and attack me, the mothers with the children.

12 But you said, 'I will surely do you good, and make your offspring as the sand of the sea, which cannot be numbered for multitude.'"

13 So he stayed there that night, and from what he had with him he took a present for his brother Esau,

14 two hundred female goats and twenty male goats, two hundred ewes and twenty rams,

15 thirty milking camels and their calves, forty cows and ten bulls, twenty female donkeys and ten male donkeys.

16 These he handed over to his servants, every drove by itself, and said to his servants, "Pass on ahead of me and put a space between drove and drove."

17 He instructed the first, "When Esau my brother meets you and asks you, 'To whom do you belong? Where are you going? And whose are these ahead of you?'

18 then you shall say, 'They belong to your servant Jacob. They are a present sent to my lord Esau. And moreover, he is behind us.'"

19 He likewise instructed the second and the third and all who followed the droves, "You shall say the same thing to Esau when you find him,

20 and you shall say, 'Moreover, your servant Jacob is behind us.'" For he thought, "I may appease him with the present that goes ahead of me, and afterward I shall see his face. Perhaps he will accept me."

21 So the present passed on ahead of him, and he himself stayed that night in the camp.

Jacob Wrestles with God

22 The same night he arose and took his two wives, his two female servants, and his eleven children, and crossed the ford of the Jabbok.

23 He took them and sent them across the stream, and everything else that he had.

24 And Jacob was left alone. And a man wrestled with him until the breaking of the day.

25 When the man saw that he did not prevail against Jacob, he touched his hip socket, and Jacob's hip was put out of joint as he wrestled with him.

26 Then he said, "Let me go, for the day has broken." But Jacob said, "I will not let you go unless you bless me."

27 And he said to him, "What is your name?" And he said, "Jacob."

28 Then he said, "Your name shall no longer be called Jacob, but Israel, for you have striven with God and with men, and have prevailed."

29 Then Jacob asked him, "Please tell me your name." But he said, "Why is it that you ask my name?" And there he blessed him.

30 So Jacob called the name of the place Peniel, saying, "For I have seen God face to face, and yet my life has been delivered."

31 The sun rose upon him as he passed Penuel, limping because of his hip.

Genesis 32

32 Therefore to this day the people of Israel do not eat the sinew of the thigh that is on the hip socket, because he touched the socket of Jacob's hip on the sinew of the thigh.

Genesis 33

English Standard Version

Jacob Meets Esau

1 And Jacob lifted up his eyes and looked, and behold, Esau was coming, and four hundred men with him. So he divided the children among Leah and Rachel and the two female servants.

2 And he put the servants with their children in front, then Leah with her children, and Rachel and Joseph last of all.

3 He himself went on before them, bowing himself to the ground seven times, until he came near to his brother.

4 But Esau ran to meet him and embraced him and fell on his neck and kissed him, and they wept.

5 And when Esau lifted up his eyes and saw the women and children, he said, "Who are these with you?" Jacob said, "The children whom God has graciously given your servant."

6 Then the servants drew near, they and their children, and bowed down.

7 Leah likewise and her children drew near and bowed down. And last Joseph and Rachel drew near, and they bowed down.

8 Esau said, "What do you mean by all this company that I met?" Jacob answered, "To find favor in the sight of my lord."

9 But Esau said, "I have enough, my brother; keep what you have for yourself."

10 Jacob said, "No, please, if I have found favor in your sight, then accept my present from my hand. For I have seen your face, which is like seeing the face of God, and you have accepted me.

11 Please accept my blessing that is brought to you, because God has dealt graciously with me, and because I have enough." Thus he urged him, and he took it.

12 Then Esau said, "Let us journey on our way, and I will go ahead of you."

13 But Jacob said to him, "My lord knows that the children are frail, and that the nursing flocks and herds are a care to me. If they are driven hard for one day, all the flocks will die.

14 Let my lord pass on ahead of his servant, and I will lead on slowly, at the pace of the livestock that are ahead of me and at the pace of the children, until I come to my lord in Seir."

15 So Esau said, "Let me leave with you some of the people who are with me." But he said, "What need is there? Let me find favor in the sight of my lord."

16 So Esau returned that day on his way to Seir.

17 But Jacob journeyed to Succoth, and built himself a house and made booths for his livestock. Therefore the name of the place is called Succoth.

18 And Jacob came safely to the city of Shechem, which is in the land of Canaan, on his way from Paddan-aram, and he camped before the city.

19 And from the sons of Hamor, Shechem's father, he bought for a hundred pieces of money the piece of land on which he had pitched his tent.

20 There he erected an altar and called it El-Elohe-Israel.

Genesis 34

English Standard Version

The Defiling of Dinah

1 Now Dinah the daughter of Leah, whom she had borne to Jacob, went out to see the women of the land.

2 And when Shechem the son of Hamor the Hivite, the prince of the land, saw her, he seized her and lay with her and humiliated her.

3 And his soul was drawn to Dinah the daughter of Jacob. He loved the young woman and spoke tenderly to her.

4 So Shechem spoke to his father Hamor, saying, "Get me this girl for my wife."

5 Now Jacob heard that he had defiled his daughter Dinah. But his sons were with his livestock in the field, so Jacob held his peace until they came.

6 And Hamor the father of Shechem went out to Jacob to speak with him.

7 The sons of Jacob had come in from the field as soon as they heard of it, and the men were indignant and very angry, because he had done an outrageous thing in Israel by lying with Jacob's daughter, for such a thing must not be done.

8 But Hamor spoke with them, saying, "The soul of my son Shechem longs for your daughter. Please give her to him to be his wife.

9 Make marriages with us. Give your daughters to us, and take our daughters for yourselves.

10 You shall dwell with us, and the land shall be open to you. Dwell and trade in it, and get property in it."

11 Shechem also said to her father and to her brothers, "Let me find favor in your eyes, and whatever you say to me I will give.

12 Ask me for as great a bride-price and gift as you will, and I will give whatever you say to me. Only give me the young woman to be my wife."

13 The sons of Jacob answered Shechem and his father Hamor deceitfully, because he had defiled their sister Dinah.

14 They said to them, "We cannot do this thing, to give our sister to one who is uncircumcised, for that would be a disgrace to us.

15 Only on this condition will we agree with you—that you will become as we are by every male among you being circumcised.

16 Then we will give our daughters to you, and we will take your daughters to ourselves, and we will dwell with you and become one people.

17 But if you will not listen to us and be circumcised, then we will take our daughter, and we will be gone."

18 Their words pleased Hamor and Hamor's son Shechem.

19 And the young man did not delay to do the thing, because he delighted in Jacob's daughter. Now he was the most honored of all his father's house.

20 So Hamor and his son Shechem came to the gate of their city and spoke to the men of their city, saying,

21 "These men are at peace with us; let them dwell in the land and trade in it, for behold, the land is large enough for them. Let us take their daughters as wives, and let us give them our daughters.

22 Only on this condition will the men agree to dwell with us to become one people—when every male among us is circumcised as they are circumcised.

23 Will not their livestock, their property and all their beasts be ours? Only let us agree with them, and they will dwell with us."

24 And all who went out of the gate of his city listened to Hamor and his son Shechem, and every male was circumcised, all who went out of the gate of his city.

25 On the third day, when they were sore, two of the sons of Jacob, Simeon and Levi, Dinah's brothers, took their swords and came against the city while it felt secure and killed all the males.

26 They killed Hamor and his son Shechem with the sword and took Dinah out of Shechem's house and went away.

27 The sons of Jacob came upon the slain and plundered the city, because they had defiled their sister.

28 They took their flocks and their herds, their donkeys, and whatever was in the city and in the field.

29 All their wealth, all their little ones and their wives, all that was in the houses, they captured and plundered.

30 Then Jacob said to Simeon and Levi, "You have brought trouble on me by making me stink to the inhabitants of the land, the Canaanites and the Perizzites. My numbers are few, and if they gather themselves against me and attack me, I shall be destroyed, both I and my household."

31 But they said, "Should he treat our sister like a prostitute?"

Genesis 35

English Standard Version

God Blesses and Renames Jacob

1 God said to Jacob, "Arise, go up to Bethel and dwell there. Make an altar there to the God who appeared to you when you fled from your brother Esau."

2 So Jacob said to his household and to all who were with him, "Put away the foreign gods that are among you and purify yourselves and change your garments.

3 Then let us arise and go up to Bethel, so that I may make there an altar to the God who answers me in the day of my distress and has been with me wherever I have gone."

4 So they gave to Jacob all the foreign gods that they had, and the rings that were in their ears. Jacob hid them under the terebinth tree that was near Shechem.

5 And as they journeyed, a terror from God fell upon the cities that were around them, so that they did not pursue the sons of Jacob.

6 And Jacob came to Luz (that is, Bethel), which is in the land of Canaan, he and all the people who were with him,

7 and there he built an altar and called the place El-bethel, because there God had revealed himself to him when he fled from his brother.

8 And Deborah, Rebekah's nurse, died, and she was buried under an oak below Bethel. So he called its name Allon-bacuth.

9 God appeared to Jacob again, when he came from Paddan-aram, and blessed him.

10 And God said to him, "Your name is Jacob; no longer shall your name be called Jacob, but Israel shall be your name." So he called his name Israel.

11 And God said to him, "I am God Almighty: be fruitful and multiply. A nation and a company of nations shall come from you, and kings shall come from your own body.

12 The land that I gave to Abraham and Isaac I will give to you, and I will give the land to your offspring after you."

13 Then God went up from him in the place where he had spoken with him.

14 And Jacob set up a pillar in the place where he had spoken with him, a pillar of stone. He poured out a drink offering on it and poured oil on it.

15 So Jacob called the name of the place where God had spoken with him Bethel.

The Deaths of Rachel and Isaac

16 Then they journeyed from Bethel. When they were still some distance from Ephrath, Rachel went into labor, and she had hard labor.

17 And when her labor was at its hardest, the midwife said to her, "Do not fear, for you have another son."

18 And as her soul was departing (for she was dying), she called his name Ben-oni; but his father called him Benjamin.

19 So Rachel died, and she was buried on the way to Ephrath (that is, Bethlehem),

20 and Jacob set up a pillar over her tomb. It is the pillar of Rachel's tomb, which is there to this day.

21 Israel journeyed on and pitched his tent beyond the tower of Eder.

22 While Israel lived in that land, Reuben went and lay with Bilhah his father's concubine. And Israel heard of it. Now the sons of Jacob were twelve.

23 The sons of Leah: Reuben (Jacob's firstborn), Simeon, Levi, Judah, Issachar, and Zebulun.

24 The sons of Rachel: Joseph and Benjamin.

25 The sons of Bilhah, Rachel's servant: Dan and Naphtali.

26 The sons of Zilpah, Leah's servant: Gad and Asher. These were the sons of Jacob who were born to him in Paddan-aram.

27 And Jacob came to his father Isaac at Mamre, or Kiriath-arba (that is, Hebron), where Abraham and Isaac had sojourned.

28 Now the days of Isaac were 180 years.

29 And Isaac breathed his last, and he died and was gathered to his people, old and full of days. And his sons Esau and Jacob buried him.

Genesis 36

English Standard Version

Esau's Descendants

1 These are the generations of Esau (that is, Edom).

2 Esau took his wives from the Canaanites: Adah the daughter of Elon the Hittite, Oholibamah the daughter of Anah the daughter of Zibeon the Hivite,

3 and Basemath, Ishmael's daughter, the sister of Nebaioth.

4 And Adah bore to Esau, Eliphaz; Basemath bore Reuel;

5 and Oholibamah bore Jeush, Jalam, and Korah. These are the sons of Esau who were born to him in the land of Canaan.

6 Then Esau took his wives, his sons, his daughters, and all the members of his household, his livestock, all his beasts, and all his property that he had acquired in the land of Canaan. He went into a land away from his brother Jacob.

7 For their possessions were too great for them to dwell together. The land of their sojournings could not support them because of their livestock.

8 So Esau settled in the hill country of Seir. (Esau is Edom.)

9 These are the generations of Esau the father of the Edomites in the hill country of Seir.

10 These are the names of Esau's sons: Eliphaz the son of Adah the wife of Esau, Reuel the son of Basemath the wife of Esau.

11 The sons of Eliphaz were Teman, Omar, Zepho, Gatam, and Kenaz.

12 (Timna was a concubine of Eliphaz, Esau's son; she bore Amalek to Eliphaz.) These are the sons of Adah, Esau's wife.

13 These are the sons of Reuel: Nahath, Zerah, Shammah, and Mizzah. These are the sons of Basemath, Esau's wife.

14 These are the sons of Oholibamah the daughter of Anah the daughter of Zibeon, Esau's wife: she bore to Esau Jeush, Jalam, and Korah.

15 These are the chiefs of the sons of Esau. The sons of Eliphaz the firstborn of Esau: the chiefs Teman, Omar, Zepho, Kenaz,

16 Korah, Gatam, and Amalek; these are the chiefs of Eliphaz in the land of Edom; these are the sons of Adah.

17 These are the sons of Reuel, Esau's son: the chiefs Nahath, Zerah, Shammah, and Mizzah; these are the chiefs of Reuel in the land of Edom; these are the sons of Basemath, Esau's wife.

18 These are the sons of Oholibamah, Esau's wife: the chiefs Jeush, Jalam, and Korah; these are the chiefs born of Oholibamah the daughter of Anah, Esau's wife.

19 These are the sons of Esau (that is, Edom), and these are their chiefs.

20 These are the sons of Seir the Horite, the inhabitants of the land: Lotan, Shobal, Zibeon, Anah,

21 Dishon, Ezer, and Dishan; these are the chiefs of the Horites, the sons of Seir in the land of Edom.

Genesis 36

22 The sons of Lotan were Hori and Hemam; and Lotan's sister was Timna.

23 These are the sons of Shobal: Alvan, Manahath, Ebal, Shepho, and Onam.

24 These are the sons of Zibeon: Aiah and Anah; he is the Anah who found the hot springs in the wilderness, as he pastured the donkeys of Zibeon his father.

25 These are the children of Anah: Dishon and Oholibamah the daughter of Anah.

26 These are the sons of Dishon: Hemdan, Eshban, Ithran, and Cheran.

27 These are the sons of Ezer: Bilhan, Zaavan, and Akan.

28 These are the sons of Dishan: Uz and Aran.

29 These are the chiefs of the Horites: the chiefs Lotan, Shobal, Zibeon, Anah,

30 Dishon, Ezer, and Dishan; these are the chiefs of the Horites, chief by chief in the land of Seir.

31 These are the kings who reigned in the land of Edom, before any king reigned over the Israelites.

32 Bela the son of Beor reigned in Edom, the name of his city being Dinhabah.

33 Bela died, and Jobab the son of Zerah of Bozrah reigned in his place. 3

4 Jobab died, and Husham of the land of the Temanites reigned in his place.

35 Husham died, and Hadad the son of Bedad, who defeated Midian in the country of Moab, reigned in his place, the name of his city being Avith.

36 Hadad died, and Samlah of Masrekah reigned in his place.

37 Samlah died, and Shaul of Rehoboth on the Euphrates reigned in his place.

38 Shaul died, and Baal-hanan the son of Achbor reigned in his place.

39 Baal-hanan the son of Achbor died, and Hadar reigned in his place, the name of his city being Pau; his wife's name was Mehetabel, the daughter of Matred, daughter of Mezahab.

40 These are the names of the chiefs of Esau, according to their clans and their dwelling places, by their names: the chiefs Timna, Alvah, Jetheth,

41 Oholibamah, Elah, Pinon,

42 Kenaz, Teman, Mibzar,

43 Magdiel, and Iram; these are the chiefs of Edom (that is, Esau, the father of Edom), according to their dwelling places in the land of their possession.

Genesis 37

English Standard Version

Joseph's Dreams

1 Jacob lived in the land of his father's sojournings, in the land of Canaan.

2 These are the generations of Jacob. Joseph, being seventeen years old, was pasturing the flock with his brothers. He was a boy with the sons of Bilhah and Zilpah, his father's wives. And Joseph brought a bad report of them to their father.

3 Now Israel loved Joseph more than any other of his sons, because he was the son of his old age. And he made him a robe of many colors.

4 But when his brothers saw that their father loved him more than all his brothers, they hated him and could not speak peacefully to him.

5 Now Joseph had a dream, and when he told it to his brothers they hated him even more.

6 He said to them, "Hear this dream that I have dreamed:

7 Behold, we were binding sheaves in the field, and behold, my sheaf arose and stood upright. And behold, your sheaves gathered around it and bowed down to my sheaf."

8 His brothers said to him, "Are you indeed to reign over us? Or are you indeed to rule over us?" So they hated him even more for his dreams and for his words.

9 Then he dreamed another dream and told it to his brothers and said, "Behold, I have dreamed another dream. Behold, the sun, the moon, and eleven stars were bowing down to me."

10 But when he told it to his father and to his brothers, his father rebuked him and said to him, "What is this dream that you have dreamed? Shall I and your mother and your brothers indeed come to bow ourselves to the ground before you?"

11 And his brothers were jealous of him, but his father kept the saying in mind.

Joseph Sold by His Brothers

12 Now his brothers went to pasture their father's flock near Shechem.

13 And Israel said to Joseph, "Are not your brothers pasturing the flock at Shechem? Come, I will send you to them." And he said to him, "Here I am."

14 So he said to him, "Go now, see if it is well with your brothers and with the flock, and bring me word." So he sent him from the Valley of Hebron, and he came to Shechem.

15 And a man found him wandering in the fields. And the man asked him, "What are you seeking?"

16 "I am seeking my brothers," he said. "Tell me, please, where they are pasturing the flock."

17 And the man said, "They have gone away, for I heard them say, 'Let us go to Dothan.'" So Joseph went after his brothers and found them at Dothan.

18 They saw him from afar, and before he came near to them they conspired against him to kill him.

19 They said to one another, "Here comes this dreamer.

20 Come now, let us kill him and throw him into one of the pits. Then we will say that a fierce animal has devoured him, and we will see what will become of his dreams."

21 But when Reuben heard it, he rescued him out of their hands, saying, "Let us not take his life."

22 And Reuben said to them, "Shed no blood; throw him into this pit here in the wilderness, but do not lay a hand on him"—that he might rescue him out of their hand to restore him to his father.

23 So when Joseph came to his brothers, they stripped him of his robe, the robe of many colors that he wore.

24 And they took him and threw him into a pit. The pit was empty; there was no water in it.

25 Then they sat down to eat. And looking up they saw a caravan of Ishmaelites coming from Gilead, with their camels bearing gum, balm, and myrrh, on their way to carry it down to Egypt.

26 Then Judah said to his brothers, "What profit is it if we kill our brother and conceal his blood?

27 Come, let us sell him to the Ishmaelites, and let not our hand be upon him, for he is our brother, our own flesh." And his brothers listened to him.

28 Then Midianite traders passed by. And they drew Joseph up and lifted him out of the pit, and sold him to the Ishmaelites for twenty shekels[c] of silver. They took Joseph to Egypt.

29 When Reuben returned to the pit and saw that Joseph was not in the pit, he tore his clothes

30 and returned to his brothers and said, "The boy is gone, and I, where shall I go?"

31 Then they took Joseph's robe and slaughtered a goat and dipped the robe in the blood.

32 And they sent the robe of many colors and brought it to their father and said, "This we have found; please identify whether it is your son's robe or not."

33 And he identified it and said, "It is my son's robe. A fierce animal has devoured him. Joseph is without doubt torn to pieces."

34 Then Jacob tore his garments and put sackcloth on his loins and mourned for his son many days.

35 All his sons and all his daughters rose up to comfort him, but he refused to be comforted and said, "No, I shall go down to Sheol to my son, mourning." Thus his father wept for him.

36 Meanwhile the Midianites had sold him in Egypt to Potiphar, an officer of Pharaoh, the captain of the guard.

Genesis 38

English Standard Version

Judah and Tamar

1 It happened at that time that Judah went down from his brothers and turned aside to a certain Adullamite, whose name was Hirah.

2 There Judah saw the daughter of a certain Canaanite whose name was Shua. He took her and went in to her,

3 and she conceived and bore a son, and he called his name Er.

4 She conceived again and bore a son, and she called his name Onan.

5 Yet again she bore a son, and she called his name Shelah. Judah was in Chezib when she bore him.

6 And Judah took a wife for Er his firstborn, and her name was Tamar.

7 But Er, Judah's firstborn, was wicked in the sight of the Lord, and the Lord put him to death.

8 Then Judah said to Onan, "Go in to your brother's wife and perform the duty of a brother-in-law to her, and raise up offspring for your brother."

9 But Onan knew that the offspring would not be his. So whenever he went in to his brother's wife he would waste the semen on the ground, so as not to give offspring to his brother.

10 And what he did was wicked in the sight of the Lord, and he put him to death also.

11 Then Judah said to Tamar his daughter-in-law, "Remain a widow in your father's house, till Shelah my son grows up"—for he feared that he would die, like his brothers. So Tamar went and remained in her father's house.

12 In the course of time the wife of Judah, Shua's daughter, died. When Judah was comforted, he went up to Timnah to his sheepshearers, he and his friend Hirah the Adullamite.

13 And when Tamar was told, "Your father-in-law is going up to Timnah to shear his sheep,"

14 she took off her widow's garments and covered herself with a veil, wrapping herself up, and sat at the entrance to Enaim, which is on the road to Timnah. For she saw that Shelah was grown up, and she had not been given to him in marriage.

15 When Judah saw her, he thought she was a prostitute, for she had covered her face.

16 He turned to her at the roadside and said, "Come, let me come in to you," for he did not know that she was his daughter-in-law. She said, "What will you give me, that you may come in to me?"

17 He answered, "I will send you a young goat from the flock." And she said, "If you give me a pledge, until you send it—"

18 He said, "What pledge shall I give you?" She replied, "Your signet and your cord and your staff that is in your hand." So he gave them to her and went in to her, and she conceived by him.

19 Then she arose and went away, and taking off her veil she put on the garments of her widowhood.

20 When Judah sent the young goat by his friend the Adullamite to take back the pledge from the woman's hand, he did not find her.

21 And he asked the men of the place, "Where is the cult prostitute who was at Enaim at the roadside?" And they said, "No cult prostitute has been here."

22 So he returned to Judah and said, "I have not found her. Also, the men of the place said, 'No cult prostitute has been here.'"

23 And Judah replied, "Let her keep the things as her own, or we shall be laughed at. You see, I sent this young goat, and you did not find her."

24 About three months later Judah was told, "Tamar your daughter-in-law has been immoral. Moreover, she is pregnant by immorality." And Judah said, "Bring her out, and let her be burned."

25 As she was being brought out, she sent word to her father-in-law, "By the man to whom these belong, I am pregnant." And she said, "Please identify whose these are, the signet and the cord and the staff."

26 Then Judah identified them and said, "She is more righteous than I, since I did not give her to my son Shelah." And he did not know her again.

27 When the time of her labor came, there were twins in her womb.

28 And when she was in labor, one put out a hand, and the midwife took and tied a scarlet thread on his hand, saying, "This one came out first."

29 But as he drew back his hand, behold, his brother came out. And she said, "What a breach you have made for yourself!" Therefore his name was called Perez.

30 Afterward his brother came out with the scarlet thread on his hand, and his name was called Zerah.

Genesis 39

English Standard Version

Joseph and Potiphar's Wife

1 Now Joseph had been brought down to Egypt, and Potiphar, an officer of Pharaoh, the captain of the guard, an Egyptian, had bought him from the Ishmaelites who had brought him down there.

2 The Lord was with Joseph, and he became a successful man, and he was in the house of his Egyptian master.

3 His master saw that the Lord was with him and that the Lord caused all that he did to succeed in his hands.

4 So Joseph found favor in his sight and attended him, and he made him overseer of his house and put him in charge of all that he had.

5 From the time that he made him overseer in his house and over all that he had, the Lord blessed the Egyptian's house for Joseph's sake; the blessing of the Lord was on all that he had, in house and field.

6 So he left all that he had in Joseph's charge, and because of him he had no concern about anything but the food he ate. Now Joseph was handsome in form and appearance.

7 And after a time his master's wife cast her eyes on Joseph and said, "Lie with me."

8 But he refused and said to his master's wife, "Behold, because of me my master has no concern about anything in the house, and he has put everything that he has in my charge.

9 He is not greater in this house than I am, nor has he kept back anything from me except you, because you are his wife. How then can I do this great wickedness and sin against God?"

10 And as she spoke to Joseph day after day, he would not listen to her, to lie beside her or to be with her.

11 But one day, when he went into the house to do his work and none of the men of the house was there in the house,

12 she caught him by his garment, saying, "Lie with me." But he left his garment in her hand and fled and got out of the house.

13 And as soon as she saw that he had left his garment in her hand and had fled out of the house,

14 she called to the men of her household and said to them, "See, he has brought among us a Hebrew to laugh at us. He came in to me to lie with me, and I cried out with a loud voice.

15 And as soon as he heard that I lifted up my voice and cried out, he left his garment beside me and fled and got out of the house."

16 Then she laid up his garment by her until his master came home,

17 and she told him the same story, saying, "The Hebrew servant, whom you have brought among us, came in to me to laugh at me.

18 But as soon as I lifted up my voice and cried, he left his garment beside me and fled out of the house."

19 As soon as his master heard the words that his wife spoke to him, "This is the way your servant treated me," his anger was kindled.

20 And Joseph's master took him and put him into the prison, the place where the king's prisoners were confined, and he was there in prison.

21 But the Lord was with Joseph and showed him steadfast love and gave him favor in the sight of the keeper of the prison.

22 And the keeper of the prison put Joseph in charge of all the prisoners who were in the prison. Whatever was done there, he was the one who did it.

23 The keeper of the prison paid no attention to anything that was in Joseph's charge, because the Lord was with him. And whatever he did, the Lord made it succeed.

Genesis 40

English Standard Version

Joseph Interprets Two Prisoners' Dreams

1 Some time after this, the cupbearer of the king of Egypt and his baker committed an offense against their lord the king of Egypt.

2 And Pharaoh was angry with his two officers, the chief cupbearer and the chief baker,

3 and he put them in custody in the house of the captain of the guard, in the prison where Joseph was confined.

4 The captain of the guard appointed Joseph to be with them, and he attended them. They continued for some time in custody.

5 And one night they both dreamed—the cupbearer and the baker of the king of Egypt, who were confined in the prison—each his own dream, and each dream with its own interpretation.

6 When Joseph came to them in the morning, he saw that they were troubled.

7 So he asked Pharaoh's officers who were with him in custody in his master's house, "Why are your faces downcast today?"

8 They said to him, "We have had dreams, and there is no one to interpret them." And Joseph said to them, "Do not interpretations belong to God? Please tell them to me."

9 So the chief cupbearer told his dream to Joseph and said to him, "In my dream there was a vine before me,

10 and on the vine there were three branches. As soon as it budded, its blossoms shot forth, and the clusters ripened into grapes.

11 Pharaoh's cup was in my hand, and I took the grapes and pressed them into Pharaoh's cup and placed the cup in Pharaoh's hand."

12 Then Joseph said to him, "This is its interpretation: the three branches are three days.

13 In three days Pharaoh will lift up your head and restore you to your office, and you shall place Pharaoh's cup in his hand as formerly, when you were his cupbearer.

14 Only remember me, when it is well with you, and please do me the kindness to mention me to Pharaoh, and so get me out of this house.

15 For I was indeed stolen out of the land of the Hebrews, and here also I have done nothing that they should put me into the pit."

16 When the chief baker saw that the interpretation was favorable, he said to Joseph, "I also had a dream: there were three cake baskets on my head,

17 and in the uppermost basket there were all sorts of baked food for Pharaoh, but the birds were eating it out of the basket on my head."

18 And Joseph answered and said, "This is its interpretation: the three baskets are three days.

19 In three days Pharaoh will lift up your head—from you!—and hang you on a tree. And the birds will eat the flesh from you."

20 On the third day, which was Pharaoh's birthday, he made a feast for all his servants and lifted up the head of the chief cupbearer and the head of the chief baker among his servants.

21 He restored the chief cupbearer to his position, and he placed the cup in Pharaoh's hand.

22 But he hanged the chief baker, as Joseph had interpreted to them.

23 Yet the chief cupbearer did not remember Joseph, but forgot him.

Genesis 41

English Standard Version

Joseph Interprets Pharaoh's Dreams

1 After two whole years, Pharaoh dreamed that he was standing by the Nile,

2 and behold, there came up out of the Nile seven cows, attractive and plump, and they fed in the reed grass.

3 And behold, seven other cows, ugly and thin, came up out of the Nile after them, and stood by the other cows on the bank of the Nile.

4 And the ugly, thin cows ate up the seven attractive, plump cows. And Pharaoh awoke.

5 And he fell asleep and dreamed a second time. And behold, seven ears of grain, plump and good, were growing on one stalk.

6 And behold, after them sprouted seven ears, thin and blighted by the east wind.

7 And the thin ears swallowed up the seven plump, full ears. And Pharaoh awoke, and behold, it was a dream.

8 So in the morning his spirit was troubled, and he sent and called for all the magicians of Egypt and all its wise men. Pharaoh told them his dreams, but there was none who could interpret them to Pharaoh.

9 Then the chief cupbearer said to Pharaoh, "I remember my offenses today.

10 When Pharaoh was angry with his servants and put me and the chief baker in custody in the house of the captain of the guard,

11 we dreamed on the same night, he and I, each having a dream with its own interpretation.

12 A young Hebrew was there with us, a servant of the captain of the guard. When we told him, he interpreted our dreams to us, giving an interpretation to each man according to his dream.

13 And as he interpreted to us, so it came about. I was restored to my office, and the baker was hanged."

14 Then Pharaoh sent and called Joseph, and they quickly brought him out of the pit. And when he had shaved himself and changed his clothes, he came in before Pharaoh.

15 And Pharaoh said to Joseph, "I have had a dream, and there is no one who can interpret it. I have heard it said of you that when you hear a dream you can interpret it."

16 Joseph answered Pharaoh, "It is not in me; God will give Pharaoh a favorable answer."

17 Then Pharaoh said to Joseph, "Behold, in my dream I was standing on the banks of the Nile.

18 Seven cows, plump and attractive, came up out of the Nile and fed in the reed grass.

19 Seven other cows came up after them, poor and very ugly and thin, such as I had never seen in all the land of Egypt.

20 And the thin, ugly cows ate up the first seven plump cows,

21 but when they had eaten them no one would have known that they had eaten them, for they were still as ugly as at the beginning. Then I awoke.

22 I also saw in my dream seven ears growing on one stalk, full and good.

23 Seven ears, withered, thin, and blighted by the east wind, sprouted after them,

24 and the thin ears swallowed up the seven good ears. And I told it to the magicians, but there was no one who could explain it to me."

25 Then Joseph said to Pharaoh, "The dreams of Pharaoh are one; God has revealed to Pharaoh what he is about to do.

26 The seven good cows are seven years, and the seven good ears are seven years; the dreams are one.

27 The seven lean and ugly cows that came up after them are seven years, and the seven empty ears blighted by the east wind are also seven years of famine.

28 It is as I told Pharaoh; God has shown to Pharaoh what he is about to do.

29 There will come seven years of great plenty throughout all the land of Egypt,

30 but after them there will arise seven years of famine, and all the plenty will be forgotten in the land of Egypt. The famine will consume the land,

31 and the plenty will be unknown in the land by reason of the famine that will follow, for it will be very severe.

32 And the doubling of Pharaoh's dream means that the thing is fixed by God, and God will shortly bring it about.

33 Now therefore let Pharaoh select a discerning and wise man, and set him over the land of Egypt.

34 Let Pharaoh proceed to appoint overseers over the land and take one-fifth of the produce of the land of Egypt during the seven plentiful years.

35 And let them gather all the food of these good years that are coming and store up grain under the authority of Pharaoh for food in the cities, and let them keep it.

36 That food shall be a reserve for the land against the seven years of famine that are to occur in the land of Egypt, so that the land may not perish through the famine."

Joseph Rises to Power

37 This proposal pleased Pharaoh and all his servants.

38 And Pharaoh said to his servants, "Can we find a man like this, in whom is the Spirit of God?"

39 Then Pharaoh said to Joseph, "Since God has shown you all this, there is none so discerning and wise as you are.

40 You shall be over my house, and all my people shall order themselves as you command. Only as regards the throne will I be greater than you."

41 And Pharaoh said to Joseph, "See, I have set you over all the land of Egypt."

42 Then Pharaoh took his signet ring from his hand and put it on Joseph's hand, and clothed him in garments of fine linen and put a gold chain about his neck.

43 And he made him ride in his second chariot. And they called out before him, "Bow the knee!" Thus he set him over all the land of Egypt.

44 Moreover, Pharaoh said to Joseph, "I am Pharaoh, and without your consent no one shall lift up hand or foot in all the land of Egypt."

45 And Pharaoh called Joseph's name Zaphenath-paneah. And he gave him in marriage Asenath, the daughter of Potiphera priest of On. So Joseph went out over the land of Egypt.

46 Joseph was thirty years old when he entered the service of Pharaoh king of Egypt. And Joseph went out from the presence of Pharaoh and went through all the land of Egypt.

47 During the seven plentiful years the earth produced abundantly,

48 and he gathered up all the food of these seven years, which occurred in the land of Egypt, and put the food in the cities. He put in every city the food from the fields around it.

49 And Joseph stored up grain in great abundance, like the sand of the sea, until he ceased to measure it, for it could not be measured.

50 Before the year of famine came, two sons were born to Joseph. Asenath, the daughter of Potiphera priest of On, bore them to him.

51 Joseph called the name of the firstborn Manasseh. "For," he said, "God has made me forget all my hardship and all my father's house."

52 The name of the second he called Ephraim, "For God has made me fruitful in the land of my affliction."

53 The seven years of plenty that occurred in the land of Egypt came to an end,

54 and the seven years of famine began to come, as Joseph had said. There was famine in all lands, but in all the land of Egypt there was bread.

55 When all the land of Egypt was famished, the people cried to Pharaoh for bread. Pharaoh said to all the Egyptians, "Go to Joseph. What he says to you, do."

56 So when the famine had spread over all the land, Joseph opened all the storehouses and sold to the Egyptians, for the famine was severe in the land of Egypt.

57 Moreover, all the earth came to Egypt to Joseph to buy grain, because the famine was severe over all the earth.

Genesis 42

English Standard Version

Joseph's Brothers Go to Egypt

1 When Jacob learned that there was grain for sale in Egypt, he said to his sons, "Why do you look at one another?"

2 And he said, "Behold, I have heard that there is grain for sale in Egypt. Go down and buy grain for us there, that we may live and not die."

3 So ten of Joseph's brothers went down to buy grain in Egypt.

4 But Jacob did not send Benjamin, Joseph's brother, with his brothers, for he feared that harm might happen to him.

5 Thus the sons of Israel came to buy among the others who came, for the famine was in the land of Canaan.

6 Now Joseph was governor over the land. He was the one who sold to all the people of the land. And Joseph's brothers came and bowed themselves before him with their faces to the ground.

7 Joseph saw his brothers and recognized them, but he treated them like strangers and spoke roughly to them. "Where do you come from?" he said. They said, "From the land of Canaan, to buy food."

Genesis 42

8 And Joseph recognized his brothers, but they did not recognize him.

9 And Joseph remembered the dreams that he had dreamed of them. And he said to them, "You are spies; you have come to see the nakedness of the land."

10 They said to him, "No, my lord, your servants have come to buy food.

11 We are all sons of one man. We are honest men. Your servants have never been spies."

12 He said to them, "No, it is the nakedness of the land that you have come to see."

13 And they said, "We, your servants, are twelve brothers, the sons of one man in the land of Canaan, and behold, the youngest is this day with our father, and one is no more."

14 But Joseph said to them, "It is as I said to you. You are spies. 1

5 By this you shall be tested: by the life of Pharaoh, you shall not go from this place unless your youngest brother comes here.

16 Send one of you, and let him bring your brother, while you remain confined, that your words may be tested, whether there is truth in you. Or else, by the life of Pharaoh, surely you are spies."

17 And he put them all together in custody for three days.

18 On the third day Joseph said to them, "Do this and you will live, for I fear God:

19 if you are honest men, let one of your brothers remain confined where you are in custody, and let the rest go and carry grain for the famine of your households,

20 and bring your youngest brother to me. So your words will be verified, and you shall not die." And they did so.

21 Then they said to one another, "In truth we are guilty concerning our brother, in that we saw the distress of his soul, when he begged us and we did not listen. That is why this distress has come upon us."

22 And Reuben answered them, "Did I not tell you not to sin against the boy? But you did not listen. So now there comes a reckoning for his blood."

23 They did not know that Joseph understood them, for there was an interpreter between them.

24 Then he turned away from them and wept. And he returned to them and spoke to them. And he took Simeon from them and bound him before their eyes.

25 And Joseph gave orders to fill their bags with grain, and to replace every man's money in his sack, and to give them provisions for the journey. This was done for them.

26 Then they loaded their donkeys with their grain and departed.

27 And as one of them opened his sack to give his donkey fodder at the lodging place, he saw his money in the mouth of his sack.

28 He said to his brothers, "My money has been put back; here it is in the mouth of my sack!" At this their hearts failed them, and they turned trembling to one another, saying, "What is this that God has done to us?"

29 When they came to Jacob their father in the land of Canaan, they told him all that had happened to them, saying,

30 "The man, the lord of the land, spoke roughly to us and took us to be spies of the land.

31 But we said to him, 'We are honest men; we have never been spies.

32 We are twelve brothers, sons of our father. One is no more, and the youngest is this day with our father in the land of Canaan.'

33 Then the man, the lord of the land, said to us, 'By this I shall know that you are honest men: leave one of your brothers with me, and take grain for the famine of your households, and go your way.

34 Bring your youngest brother to me. Then I shall know that you are not spies but honest men, and I will deliver your brother to you, and you shall trade in the land.'"

35 As they emptied their sacks, behold, every man's bundle of money was in his sack. And when they and their father saw their bundles of money, they were afraid.

36 And Jacob their father said to them, "You have bereaved me of my children: Joseph is no more, and Simeon is no more, and now you would take Benjamin. All this has come against me."

37 Then Reuben said to his father, "Kill my two sons if I do not bring him back to you. Put him in my hands, and I will bring him back to you."

38 But he said, "My son shall not go down with you, for his brother is dead, and he is the only one left. If harm should happen to him on the journey that you are to make, you would bring down my gray hairs with sorrow to Sheol."

Genesis 43

English Standard Version

Joseph's Brothers Return to Egypt

1 Now the famine was severe in the land.

2 And when they had eaten the grain that they had brought from Egypt, their father said to them, "Go again, buy us a little food."

3 But Judah said to him, "The man solemnly warned us, saying, 'You shall not see my face unless your brother is with you.'

4 If you will send our brother with us, we will go down and buy you food.

5 But if you will not send him, we will not go down, for the man said to us, 'You shall not see my face, unless your brother is with you.'"

6 Israel said, "Why did you treat me so badly as to tell the man that you had another brother?"

7 They replied, "The man questioned us carefully about ourselves and our kindred, saying, 'Is your father still alive? Do you have another brother?' What we told him was in answer to these questions. Could we in any way know that he would say, 'Bring your brother down'?"

8 And Judah said to Israel his father, "Send the boy with me, and we will arise and go, that we may live and not die, both we and you and also our little ones.

9 I will be a pledge of his safety. From my hand you shall require him. If I do not bring him back to you and set him before you, then let me bear the blame forever.

10 If we had not delayed, we would now have returned twice."

11 Then their father Israel said to them, "If it must be so, then do this: take some of the choice fruits of the land in your bags, and carry a present down to the man, a little balm and a little honey, gum, myrrh, pistachio nuts, and almonds.

12 Take double the money with you. Carry back with you the money that was returned in the mouth of your sacks. Perhaps it was an oversight.

13 Take also your brother, and arise, go again to the man.

14 May God Almighty grant you mercy before the man, and may he send back your other brother and Benjamin. And as for me, if I am bereaved of my children, I am bereaved."

15 So the men took this present, and they took double the money with them, and Benjamin. They arose and went down to Egypt and stood before Joseph.

16 When Joseph saw Benjamin with them, he said to the steward of his house, "Bring the men into the house, and slaughter an animal and make ready, for the men are to dine with me at noon."

17 The man did as Joseph told him and brought the men to Joseph's house.

18 And the men were afraid because they were brought to Joseph's house, and they said, "It is because of the money, which was replaced in our sacks the first time, that we are brought in, so that he may assault us and fall upon us to make us servants and seize our donkeys."

19 So they went up to the steward of Joseph's house and spoke with him at the door of the house,

20 and said, "Oh, my lord, we came down the first time to buy food.

21 And when we came to the lodging place we opened our sacks, and there was each man's money in the mouth of his sack, our money in full weight. So we have brought it again with us,

22 and we have brought other money down with us to buy food. We do not know who put our money in our sacks."

23 He replied, "Peace to you, do not be afraid. Your God and the God of your father has put treasure in your sacks for you. I received your money." Then he brought Simeon out to them.

24 And when the man had brought the men into Joseph's house and given them water, and they had washed their feet, and when he had given their donkeys fodder,

25 they prepared the present for Joseph's coming at noon, for they heard that they should eat bread there.

26 When Joseph came home, they brought into the house to him the present that they had with them and bowed down to him to the ground.

27 And he inquired about their welfare and said, "Is your father well, the old man of whom you spoke? Is he still alive?"

28 They said, "Your servant our father is well; he is still alive." And they bowed their heads and prostrated themselves.

29 And he lifted up his eyes and saw his brother Benjamin, his mother's son, and said, "Is this your youngest brother, of whom you spoke to me? God be gracious to you, my son!"

30 Then Joseph hurried out, for his compassion grew warm for his brother, and he sought a place to weep. And he entered his chamber and wept there.

31 Then he washed his face and came out. And controlling himself he said, "Serve the food."

32 They served him by himself, and them by themselves, and the Egyptians who ate with him by themselves, because the Egyptians could not eat with the Hebrews, for that is an abomination to the Egyptians.

33 And they sat before him, the firstborn according to his birthright and the youngest according to his youth. And the men looked at one another in amazement.

34 Portions were taken to them from Joseph's table, but Benjamin's portion was five times as much as any of theirs. And they drank and were merry with him.

Genesis 44

English Standard Version

Joseph Tests His Brothers

1 Then he commanded the steward of his house, "Fill the men's sacks with food, as much as they can carry, and put each man's money in the mouth of his sack,

2 and put my cup, the silver cup, in the mouth of the sack of the youngest, with his money for the grain." And he did as Joseph told him.

3 As soon as the morning was light, the men were sent away with their donkeys.

4 They had gone only a short distance from the city. Now Joseph said to his steward, "Up, follow after the men, and when you overtake them, say to them, 'Why have you repaid evil for good?

5 Is it not from this that my lord drinks, and by this that he practices divination? You have done evil in doing this.'"

6 When he overtook them, he spoke to them these words.

7 They said to him, "Why does my lord speak such words as these? Far be it from your servants to do such a thing!

Genesis 44

8 Behold, the money that we found in the mouths of our sacks we brought back to you from the land of Canaan. How then could we steal silver or gold from your lord's house?

9 Whichever of your servants is found with it shall die, and we also will be my lord's servants."

10 He said, "Let it be as you say: he who is found with it shall be my servant, and the rest of you shall be innocent."

11 Then each man quickly lowered his sack to the ground, and each man opened his sack.

12 And he searched, beginning with the eldest and ending with the youngest. And the cup was found in Benjamin's sack.

13 Then they tore their clothes, and every man loaded his donkey, and they returned to the city.

14 When Judah and his brothers came to Joseph's house, he was still there. They fell before him to the ground.

15 Joseph said to them, "What deed is this that you have done? Do you not know that a man like me can indeed practice divination?"

16 And Judah said, "What shall we say to my lord? What shall we speak? Or how can we clear ourselves? God has found out the guilt of your servants; behold, we are my lord's servants, both we and he also in whose hand the cup has been found."

17 But he said, "Far be it from me that I should do so! Only the man in whose hand the cup was found shall be my servant. But as for you, go up in peace to your father."

18 Then Judah went up to him and said, "Oh, my lord, please let your servant speak a word in my lord's ears, and let not your anger burn against your servant, for you are like Pharaoh himself.

19 My lord asked his servants, saying, 'Have you a father, or a brother?'

20 And we said to my lord, 'We have a father, an old man, and a young brother, the child of his old age. His brother is dead, and he alone is left of his mother's children, and his father loves him.'

21 Then you said to your servants, 'Bring him down to me, that I may set my eyes on him.'

22 We said to my lord, 'The boy cannot leave his father, for if he should leave his father, his father would die.'

23 Then you said to your servants, 'Unless your youngest brother comes down with you, you shall not see my face again.'

24 "When we went back to your servant my father, we told him the words of my lord.

25 And when our father said, 'Go again, buy us a little food,'

26 we said, 'We cannot go down. If our youngest brother goes with us, then we will go down. For we cannot see the man's face unless our youngest brother is with us.'

27 Then your servant my father said to us, 'You know that my wife bore me two sons.

28 One left me, and I said, "Surely he has been torn to pieces," and I have never seen him since.

29 If you take this one also from me, and harm happens to him, you will bring down my gray hairs in evil to Sheol.'

30 "Now therefore, as soon as I come to your servant my father, and the boy is not with us, then, as his life is bound up in the boy's life,

31 as soon as he sees that the boy is not with us, he will die, and your servants will bring down the gray hairs of your servant our father with sorrow to Sheol.

32 For your servant became a pledge of safety for the boy to my father, saying, 'If I do not bring him back to you, then I shall bear the blame before my father all my life.'

33 Now therefore, please let your servant remain instead of the boy as a servant to my lord, and let the boy go back with his brothers.

34 For how can I go back to my father if the boy is not with me? I fear to see the evil that would find my father."

Genesis 45

English Standard Version

Joseph Provides for His Brothers and Family

1 Then Joseph could not control himself before all those who stood by him. He cried, "Make everyone go out from me." So no one stayed with him when Joseph made himself known to his brothers.

2 And he wept aloud, so that the Egyptians heard it, and the household of Pharaoh heard it.

3 And Joseph said to his brothers, "I am Joseph! Is my father still alive?" But his brothers could not answer him, for they were dismayed at his presence.

4 So Joseph said to his brothers, "Come near to me, please." And they came near. And he said, "I am your brother, Joseph, whom you sold into Egypt.

5 And now do not be distressed or angry with yourselves because you sold me here, for God sent me before you to preserve life.

6 For the famine has been in the land these two years, and there are yet five years in which there will be neither plowing nor harvest.

7 And God sent me before you to preserve for you a remnant on earth, and to keep alive for you many survivors.

8 So it was not you who sent me here, but God. He has made me a father to Pharaoh, and lord of all his house and ruler over all the land of Egypt.

9 Hurry and go up to my father and say to him, 'Thus says your son Joseph, God has made me lord of all Egypt. Come down to me; do not tarry.

10 You shall dwell in the land of Goshen, and you shall be near me, you and your children and your children's children, and your flocks, your herds, and all that you have.

11 There I will provide for you, for there are yet five years of famine to come, so that you and your household, and all that you have, do not come to poverty.'

12 And now your eyes see, and the eyes of my brother Benjamin see, that it is my mouth that speaks to you.

13 You must tell my father of all my honor in Egypt, and of all that you have seen. Hurry and bring my father down here."

14 Then he fell upon his brother Benjamin's neck and wept, and Benjamin wept upon his neck. 15 And he kissed all his brothers and wept upon them. After that his brothers talked with him.

16 When the report was heard in Pharaoh's house, "Joseph's brothers have come," it pleased Pharaoh and his servants.

17 And Pharaoh said to Joseph, "Say to your brothers, 'Do this: load your beasts and go back to the land of Canaan,

18 and take your father and your households, and come to me, and I will give you the best of the land of Egypt, and you shall eat the fat of the land.'

19 And you, Joseph, are commanded to say, 'Do this: take wagons from the land of Egypt for your little ones and for your wives, and bring your father, and come. 20 Have no concern for your goods, for the best of all the land of Egypt is yours.'"

21 The sons of Israel did so: and Joseph gave them wagons, according to the command of Pharaoh, and gave them provisions for the journey.

22 To each and all of them he gave a change of clothes, but to Benjamin he gave three hundred shekels of silver and five changes of clothes.

23 To his father he sent as follows: ten donkeys loaded with the good things of Egypt, and ten female donkeys loaded with grain, bread, and provision for his father on the journey.

24 Then he sent his brothers away, and as they departed, he said to them, "Do not quarrel on the way."

25 So they went up out of Egypt and came to the land of Canaan to their father Jacob.

26 And they told him, "Joseph is still alive, and he is ruler over all the land of Egypt." And his heart became numb, for he did not believe them.

27 But when they told him all the words of Joseph, which he had said to them, and when he saw the wagons that Joseph had sent to carry him, the spirit of their father Jacob revived.

28 And Israel said, "It is enough; Joseph my son is still alive. I will go and see him before I die."

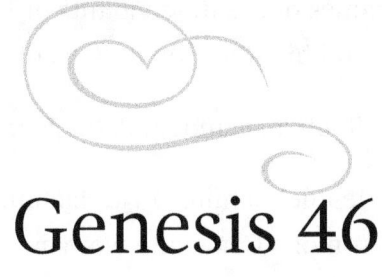

Genesis 46

English Standard Version

Joseph Brings His Family to Egypt

1 So Israel took his journey with all that he had and came to Beersheba, and offered sacrifices to the God of his father Isaac.

2 And God spoke to Israel in visions of the night and said, "Jacob, Jacob." And he said, "Here I am."

3 Then he said, "I am God, the God of your father. Do not be afraid to go down to Egypt, for there I will make you into a great nation.

4 I myself will go down with you to Egypt, and I will also bring you up again, and Joseph's hand shall close your eyes."

5 Then Jacob set out from Beersheba. The sons of Israel carried Jacob their father, their little ones, and their wives, in the wagons that Pharaoh had sent to carry him.

6 They also took their livestock and their goods, which they had gained in the land of Canaan, and came into Egypt, Jacob and all his offspring with him,

7 his sons, and his sons' sons with him, his daughters, and his sons' daughters. All his offspring he brought with him into Egypt.

8 Now these are the names of the descendants of Israel, who came into Egypt, Jacob and his sons. Reuben, Jacob's firstborn,

9 and the sons of Reuben: Hanoch, Pallu, Hezron, and Carmi.

10 The sons of Simeon: Jemuel, Jamin, Ohad, Jachin, Zohar, and Shaul, the son of a Canaanite woman.

11 The sons of Levi: Gershon, Kohath, and Merari.

12 The sons of Judah: Er, Onan, Shelah, Perez, and Zerah (but Er and Onan died in the land of Canaan); and the sons of Perez were Hezron and Hamul.

13 The sons of Issachar: Tola, Puvah, Yob, and Shimron.

14 The sons of Zebulun: Sered, Elon, and Jahleel.

15 These are the sons of Leah, whom she bore to Jacob in Paddan-aram, together with his daughter Dinah; altogether his sons and his daughters numbered thirty-three.

16 The sons of Gad: Ziphion, Haggi, Shuni, Ezbon, Eri, Arodi, and Areli.

17 The sons of Asher: Imnah, Ishvah, Ishvi, Beriah, with Serah their sister. And the sons of Beriah: Heber and Malchiel.

18 These are the sons of Zilpah, whom Laban gave to Leah his daughter; and these she bore to Jacob—sixteen persons.

19 The sons of Rachel, Jacob's wife: Joseph and Benjamin.

20 And to Joseph in the land of Egypt were born Manasseh and Ephraim, whom Asenath, the daughter of Potiphera the priest of On, bore to him.

21 And the sons of Benjamin: Bela, Becher, Ashbel, Gera, Naaman, Ehi, Rosh, Muppim, Huppim, and Ard.

22 These are the sons of Rachel, who were born to Jacob—fourteen persons in all.

23 The son of Dan: Hushim.

24 The sons of Naphtali: Jahzeel, Guni, Jezer, and Shillem.

25 These are the sons of Bilhah, whom Laban gave to Rachel his daughter, and these she bore to Jacob—seven persons in all.

26 All the persons belonging to Jacob who came into Egypt, who were his own descendants, not including Jacob's sons' wives, were sixty-six persons in all.

27 And the sons of Joseph, who were born to him in Egypt, were two. All the persons of the house of Jacob who came into Egypt were seventy.

Jacob and Joseph Reunited

28 He had sent Judah ahead of him to Joseph to show the way before him in Goshen, and they came into the land of Goshen.

29 Then Joseph prepared his chariot and went up to meet Israel his father in Goshen. He presented himself to him and fell on his neck and wept on his neck a good while.

30 Israel said to Joseph, "Now let me die, since I have seen your face and know that you are still alive."

31 Joseph said to his brothers and to his father's household, "I will go up and tell Pharaoh and will say to him, 'My brothers and my father's household, who were in the land of Canaan, have come to me.

32 And the men are shepherds, for they have been keepers of livestock, and they have brought their flocks and their herds and all that they have.'

33 When Pharaoh calls you and says, 'What is your occupation?'

34 you shall say, 'Your servants have been keepers of livestock from our youth even until now, both we and our fathers,' in order that you may dwell in the land of Goshen, for every shepherd is an abomination to the Egyptians

Genesis 47

English Standard Version

Jacob's Family Settles in Goshen

1 So Joseph went in and told Pharaoh, "My father and my brothers, with their flocks and herds and all that they possess, have come from the land of Canaan. They are now in the land of Goshen."

2 And from among his brothers he took five men and presented them to Pharaoh.

3 Pharaoh said to his brothers, "What is your occupation?" And they said to Pharaoh, "Your servants are shepherds, as our fathers were."

4 They said to Pharaoh, "We have come to sojourn in the land, for there is no pasture for your servants' flocks, for the famine is severe in the land of Canaan. And now, please let your servants dwell in the land of Goshen."

5 Then Pharaoh said to Joseph, "Your father and your brothers have come to you.

6 The land of Egypt is before you. Settle your father and your brothers in the best of the land. Let them settle in the land of Goshen, and if you know any able men among them, put them in charge of my livestock."

7 Then Joseph brought in Jacob his father and stood him before Pharaoh, and Jacob blessed Pharaoh.

8 And Pharaoh said to Jacob, "How many are the days of the years of your life?"

9 And Jacob said to Pharaoh, "The days of the years of my sojourning are 130 years. Few and evil have been the days of the years of my life, and they have not attained to the days of the years of the life of my fathers in the days of their sojourning."

10 And Jacob blessed Pharaoh and went out from the presence of Pharaoh.

11 Then Joseph settled his father and his brothers and gave them a possession in the land of Egypt, in the best of the land, in the land of Rameses, as Pharaoh had commanded.

12 And Joseph provided his father, his brothers, and all his father's household with food, according to the number of their dependents.

Joseph and the Famine

13 Now there was no food in all the land, for the famine was very severe, so that the land of Egypt and the land of Canaan languished by reason of the famine.

14 And Joseph gathered up all the money that was found in the land of Egypt and in the land of Canaan, in exchange for the grain that they bought. And Joseph brought the money into Pharaoh's house.

15 And when the money was all spent in the land of Egypt and in the land of Canaan, all the Egyptians came to Joseph and said, "Give us food. Why should we die before your eyes? For our money is gone."

16 And Joseph answered, "Give your livestock, and I will give you food in exchange for your livestock, if your money is gone."

17 So they brought their livestock to Joseph, and Joseph gave them food in exchange for the horses, the flocks, the herds, and the donkeys. He supplied them with food in exchange for all their livestock that year.

18 And when that year was ended, they came to him the following year and said to him, "We will not hide from my lord that our money is all spent. The herds of livestock are my lord's. There is nothing left in the sight of my lord but our bodies and our land.

19 Why should we die before your eyes, both we and our land? Buy us and our land for food, and we with our land will be servants to Pharaoh. And give us seed that we may live and not die, and that the land may not be desolate."

20 So Joseph bought all the land of Egypt for Pharaoh, for all the Egyptians sold their fields, because the famine was severe on them. The land became Pharaoh's.

21 As for the people, he made servants of them from one end of Egypt to the other.

22 Only the land of the priests he did not buy, for the priests had a fixed allowance from Pharaoh and lived on the allowance that Pharaoh gave them; therefore they did not sell their land.

23 Then Joseph said to the people, "Behold, I have this day bought you and your land for Pharaoh. Now here is seed for you, and you shall sow the land.

24 And at the harvests you shall give a fifth to Pharaoh, and four fifths shall be your own, as seed for the field and as food for yourselves and your households, and as food for your little ones."

25 And they said, "You have saved our lives; may it please my lord, we will be servants to Pharaoh."

26 So Joseph made it a statute concerning the land of Egypt, and it stands to this day, that Pharaoh should have the fifth; the land of the priests alone did not become Pharaoh's.

27 Thus Israel settled in the land of Egypt, in the land of Goshen. And they gained possessions in it, and were fruitful and multiplied greatly.

28 And Jacob lived in the land of Egypt seventeen years. So the days of Jacob, the years of his life, were 147 years.

29 And when the time drew near that Israel must die, he called his son Joseph and said to him, "If now I have found favor in your sight, put your hand under my thigh and promise to deal kindly and truly with me. Do not bury me in Egypt,

30 but let me lie with my fathers. Carry me out of Egypt and bury me in their burying place." He answered, "I will do as you have said."

31 And he said, "Swear to me"; and he swore to him. Then Israel bowed himself upon the head of his bed.

Genesis 48

English Standard Version

Jacob Blesses Ephraim and Manasseh

1 After this, Joseph was told, "Behold, your father is ill." So he took with him his two sons, Manasseh and Ephraim.

2 And it was told to Jacob, "Your son Joseph has come to you." Then Israel summoned his strength and sat up in bed.

3 And Jacob said to Joseph, "God Almighty appeared to me at Luz in the land of Canaan and blessed me,

4 and said to me, 'Behold, I will make you fruitful and multiply you, and I will make of you a company of peoples and will give this land to your offspring after you for an everlasting possession.'

5 And now your two sons, who were born to you in the land of Egypt before I came to you in Egypt, are mine; Ephraim and Manasseh shall be mine, as Reuben and Simeon are.

6 And the children that you fathered after them shall be yours. They shall be called by the name of their brothers in their inheritance.

Genesis 48

7 As for me, when I came from Paddan, to my sorrow Rachel died in the land of Canaan on the way, when there was still some distance to go to Ephrath, and I buried her there on the way to Ephrath (that is, Bethlehem)."

8 When Israel saw Joseph's sons, he said, "Who are these?"

9 Joseph said to his father, "They are my sons, whom God has given me here." And he said, "Bring them to me, please, that I may bless them."

10 Now the eyes of Israel were dim with age, so that he could not see. So Joseph brought them near him, and he kissed them and embraced them.

11 And Israel said to Joseph, "I never expected to see your face; and behold, God has let me see your offspring also."

12 Then Joseph removed them from his knees, and he bowed himself with his face to the earth.

13 And Joseph took them both, Ephraim in his right hand toward Israel's left hand, and Manasseh in his left hand toward Israel's right hand, and brought them near him.

14 And Israel stretched out his right hand and laid it on the head of Ephraim, who was the younger, and his left hand on the head of Manasseh, crossing his hands (for Manasseh was the firstborn).

15 And he blessed Joseph and said, "The God before whom my fathers Abraham and Isaac walked, the God who has been my shepherd all my life long to this day,

16 the angel who has redeemed me from all evil, bless the boys; and in them let my name be carried on, and the name of my fathers Abraham and Isaac; and let them grow into a multitude[c] in the midst of the earth."

17 When Joseph saw that his father laid his right hand on the head of Ephraim, it displeased him, and he took his father's hand to move it from Ephraim's head to Manasseh's head. 18 And Joseph said to his father, "Not

this way, my father; since this one is the firstborn, put your right hand on his head."

19 But his father refused and said, "I know, my son, I know. He also shall become a people, and he also shall be great. Nevertheless, his younger brother shall be greater than he, and his offspring shall become a multitude of nations."

20 So he blessed them that day, saying, "By you Israel will pronounce blessings, saying, 'God make you as Ephraim and as Manasseh.'" Thus he put Ephraim before Manasseh.

21 Then Israel said to Joseph, "Behold, I am about to die, but God will be with you and will bring you again to the land of your fathers.

22 Moreover, I have given to you rather than to your brothers one mountain slope that I took from the hand of the Amorites with my sword and with my bow."

Genesis 49

English Standard Version

Jacob Blesses His Sons

1 Then Jacob called his sons and said, "Gather yourselves together, that I may tell you what shall happen to you in days to come.

2 "Assemble and listen, O sons of Jacob, listen to Israel your father.

3 "Reuben, you are my firstborn, my might, and the firstfruits of my strength, preeminent in dignity and preeminent in power.

4 Unstable as water, you shall not have preeminence, because you went up to your father's bed; then you defiled it—he went up to my couch!

5 "Simeon and Levi are brothers; weapons of violence are their swords.

6 Let my soul come not into their council; O my glory, be not joined to their company. For in their anger they killed men, and in their willfulness they hamstrung oxen.

7 Cursed be their anger, for it is fierce, and their wrath, for it is cruel! I will divide them in Jacob and scatter them in Israel.

8 "Judah, your brothers shall praise you; your hand shall be on the neck of your enemies; your father's sons shall bow down before you.

9 Judah is a lion's cub; from the prey, my son, you have gone up. He stooped down; he crouched as a lion and as a lioness; who dares rouse him?

10 The scepter shall not depart from Judah, nor the ruler's staff from between his feet, until tribute comes to him; and to him shall be the obedience of the peoples.

11 Binding his foal to the vine and his donkey's colt to the choice vine, he has washed his garments in wine and his vesture in the blood of grapes.

12 His eyes are darker than wine, and his teeth whiter than milk.

13 "Zebulun shall dwell at the shore of the sea; he shall become a haven for ships, and his border shall be at Sidon.

14 "Issachar is a strong donkey, crouching between the sheepfolds.

15 He saw that a resting place was good, and that the land was pleasant, so he bowed his shoulder to bear, and became a servant at forced labor.

16 "Dan shall judge his people as one of the tribes of Israel.

17 Dan shall be a serpent in the way, a viper by the path, that bites the horse's heels so that his rider falls backward.

18 I wait for your salvation, O Lord.

19 "Raiders shall raid Gad, but he shall raid at their heels.

20 "Asher's food shall be rich, and he shall yield royal delicacies.

21 "Naphtali is a doe let loose that bears beautiful fawns.

22 "Joseph is a fruitful bough, a fruitful bough by a spring; his branches run over the wall.

23 The archers bitterly attacked him, shot at him, and harassed him severely,

24 yet his bow remained unmoved; his arms were made agile by the hands of the Mighty One of Jacob (from there is the Shepherd, the Stone of Israel),

25 by the God of your father who will help you, by the Almighty[h] who will bless you with blessings of heaven above, blessings of the deep that crouches beneath, blessings of the breasts and of the womb.

26 The blessings of your father are mighty beyond the blessings of my parents, up to the bounties of the everlasting hills. May they be on the head of Joseph, and on the brow of him who was set apart from his brothers.

27 "Benjamin is a ravenous wolf, in the morning devouring the prey and at evening dividing the spoil."

Jacob's Death and Burial

28 All these are the twelve tribes of Israel. This is what their father said to them as he blessed them, blessing each with the blessing suitable to him.

29 Then he commanded them and said to them, "I am to be gathered to my people; bury me with my fathers in the cave that is in the field of Ephron the Hittite,

30 in the cave that is in the field at Machpelah, to the east of Mamre, in the land of Canaan, which Abraham bought with the field from Ephron the Hittite to possess as a burying place.

31 There they buried Abraham and Sarah his wife. There they buried Isaac and Rebekah his wife, and there I buried Leah—

32 the field and the cave that is in it were bought from the Hittites."

33 When Jacob finished commanding his sons, he drew up his feet into the bed and breathed his last and was gathered to his people.

Genesis 50

English Standard Version

1 Then Joseph fell on his father's face and wept over him and kissed him.

2 And Joseph commanded his servants the physicians to embalm his father. So the physicians embalmed Israel.

3 Forty days were required for it, for that is how many are required for embalming. And the Egyptians wept for him seventy days.

4 And when the days of weeping for him were past, Joseph spoke to the household of Pharaoh, saying, "If now I have found favor in your eyes, please speak in the ears of Pharaoh, saying,

5 'My father made me swear, saying, "I am about to die: in my tomb that I hewed out for myself in the land of Canaan, there shall you bury me." Now therefore, let me please go up and bury my father. Then I will return.'"

6 And Pharaoh answered, "Go up, and bury your father, as he made you swear."

7 So Joseph went up to bury his father. With him went up all the servants of Pharaoh, the elders of his household, and all the elders of the land of Egypt,

8 as well as all the household of Joseph, his brothers, and his father's household. Only their children, their flocks, and their herds were left in the land of Goshen.

9 And there went up with him both chariots and horsemen. It was a very great company.

10 When they came to the threshing floor of Atad, which is beyond the Jordan, they lamented there with a very great and grievous lamentation, and he made a mourning for his father seven days.

11 When the inhabitants of the land, the Canaanites, saw the mourning on the threshing floor of Atad, they said, "This is a grievous mourning by the Egyptians." Therefore the place was named Abel-mizraim; it is beyond the Jordan.

12 Thus his sons did for him as he had commanded them,

13 for his sons carried him to the land of Canaan and buried him in the cave of the field at Machpelah, to the east of Mamre, which Abraham bought with the field from Ephron the Hittite to possess as a burying place.

14 After he had buried his father, Joseph returned to Egypt with his brothers and all who had gone up with him to bury his father.

God's Good Purposes

15 When Joseph's brothers saw that their father was dead, they said, "It may be that Joseph will hate us and pay us back for all the evil that we did to him."

16 So they sent a message to Joseph, saying, "Your father gave this command before he died:

17 'Say to Joseph, "Please forgive the transgression of your brothers and their sin, because they did evil to you."' And now, please forgive the transgression of the servants of the God of your father." Joseph wept when

they spoke to him. 18 His brothers also came and fell down before him and said, "Behold, we are your servants."

19 But Joseph said to them, "Do not fear, for am I in the place of God?

20 As for you, you meant evil against me, but God meant it for good, to bring it about that many people should be kept alive, as they are today.

21 So do not fear; I will provide for you and your little ones." Thus he comforted them and spoke kindly to them.

The Death of Joseph

22 So Joseph remained in Egypt, he and his father's house. Joseph lived 110 years.

23 And Joseph saw Ephraim's children of the third generation. The children also of Machir the son of Manasseh were counted as Joseph's own.

24 And Joseph said to his brothers, "I am about to die, but God will visit you and bring you up out of this land to the land that he swore to Abraham, to Isaac, and to Jacob."

25 Then Joseph made the sons of Israel swear, saying, "God will surely visit you, and you shall carry up my bones from here."

26 So Joseph died, being 110 years old. They embalmed him, and he was put in a coffin in Egypt.

Exodus 1

English Standard Version

Israel Increases Greatly in Egypt

1 These are the names of the sons of Israel who came to Egypt with Jacob, each with his household:

2 Reuben, Simeon, Levi, and Judah,

3 Issachar, Zebulun, and Benjamin,

4 Dan and Naphtali, Gad and Asher.

5 All the descendants of Jacob were seventy persons; Joseph was already in Egypt.

6 Then Joseph died, and all his brothers and all that generation.

7 But the people of Israel were fruitful and increased greatly; they multiplied and grew exceedingly strong, so that the land was filled with them.

Pharaoh Oppresses Israel

8 Now there arose a new king over Egypt, who did not know Joseph.

Pearls of Wisdom

9 And he said to his people, "Behold, the people of Israel are too many and too mighty for us.

10 Come, let us deal shrewdly with them, lest they multiply, and, if war breaks out, they join our enemies and fight against us and escape from the land."

11 Therefore they set taskmasters over them to afflict them with heavy burdens. They built for Pharaoh store cities, Pithom and Raamses.

12 But the more they were oppressed, the more they multiplied and the more they spread abroad. And the Egyptians were in dread of the people of Israel.

13 So they ruthlessly made the people of Israel work as slaves

14 and made their lives bitter with hard service, in mortar and brick, and in all kinds of work in the field. In all their work they ruthlessly made them work as slaves.

15 Then the king of Egypt said to the Hebrew midwives, one of whom was named Shiphrah and the other Puah,

16 "When you serve as midwife to the Hebrew women and see them on the birthstool, if it is a son, you shall kill him, but if it is a daughter, she shall live."

17 But the midwives feared God and did not do as the king of Egypt commanded them, but let the male children live.

18 So the king of Egypt called the midwives and said to them, "Why have you done this, and let the male children live?"

19 The midwives said to Pharaoh, "Because the Hebrew women are not like the Egyptian women, for they are vigorous and give birth before the midwife comes to them."

Exodus 1

20 So God dealt well with the midwives. And the people multiplied and grew very strong.

21 And because the midwives feared God, he gave them families.

22 Then Pharaoh commanded all his people, "Every son that is born to the Hebrews you shall cast into the Nile, but you shall let every daughter live."

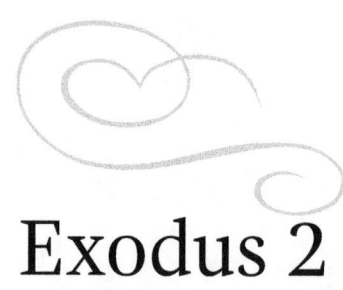

Exodus 2

English Standard Version

The Birth of Moses

1 Now a man from the house of Levi went and took as his wife a Levite woman.

2 The woman conceived and bore a son, and when she saw that he was a fine child, she hid him three months.

3 When she could hide him no longer, she took for him a basket made of bulrushes and daubed it with bitumen and pitch. She put the child in it and placed it among the reeds by the river bank.

4 And his sister stood at a distance to know what would be done to him.

5 Now the daughter of Pharaoh came down to bathe at the river, while her young women walked beside the river. She saw the basket among the reeds and sent her servant woman, and she took it.

6 When she opened it, she saw the child, and behold, the baby was crying. She took pity on him and said, "This is one of the Hebrews' children."

7 Then his sister said to Pharaoh's daughter, "Shall I go and call you a nurse from the Hebrew women to nurse the child for you?"

8 And Pharaoh's daughter said to her, "Go." So the girl went and called the child's mother.

9 And Pharaoh's daughter said to her, "Take this child away and nurse him for me, and I will give you your wages." So the woman took the child and nursed him.

10 When the child grew older, she brought him to Pharaoh's daughter, and he became her son. She named him Moses, "Because," she said, "I drew him out of the water."

Moses Flees to Midian

11 One day, when Moses had grown up, he went out to his people and looked on their burdens, and he saw an Egyptian beating a Hebrew, one of his people.

12 He looked this way and that, and seeing no one, he struck down the Egyptian and hid him in the sand.

13 When he went out the next day, behold, two Hebrews were struggling together. And he said to the man in the wrong, "Why do you strike your companion?"

14 He answered, "Who made you a prince and a judge over us? Do you mean to kill me as you killed the Egyptian?" Then Moses was afraid, and thought, "Surely the thing is known."

15 When Pharaoh heard of it, he sought to kill Moses. But Moses fled from Pharaoh and stayed in the land of Midian. And he sat down by a well.

16 Now the priest of Midian had seven daughters, and they came and drew water and filled the troughs to water their father's flock.

17 The shepherds came and drove them away, but Moses stood up and saved them, and watered their flock.

18 When they came home to their father Reuel, he said, "How is it that you have come home so soon today?"

19 They said, "An Egyptian delivered us out of the hand of the shepherds and even drew water for us and watered the flock."

20 He said to his daughters, "Then where is he? Why have you left the man? Call him, that he may eat bread."

21 And Moses was content to dwell with the man, and he gave Moses his daughter Zipporah.

22 She gave birth to a son, and he called his name Gershom, for he said, "I have been a sojourner in a foreign land."

God Hears Israel's Groaning

23 During those many days the king of Egypt died, and the people of Israel groaned because of their slavery and cried out for help. Their cry for rescue from slavery came up to God.

24 And God heard their groaning, and God remembered his covenant with Abraham, with Isaac, and with Jacob.

25 God saw the people of Israel—and God knew.

Exodus 3

English Standard Version

The Burning Bush

1 Now Moses was keeping the flock of his father-in-law, Jethro, the priest of Midian, and he led his flock to the west side of the wilderness and came to Horeb, the mountain of God.

2 And the angel of the Lord appeared to him in a flame of fire out of the midst of a bush. He looked, and behold, the bush was burning, yet it was not consumed.

3 And Moses said, "I will turn aside to see this great sight, why the bush is not burned."

4 When the Lord saw that he turned aside to see, God called to him out of the bush, "Moses, Moses!" And he said, "Here I am."

5 Then he said, "Do not come near; take your sandals off your feet, for the place on which you are standing is holy ground."

6 And he said, "I am the God of your father, the God of Abraham, the God of Isaac, and the God of Jacob." And Moses hid his face, for he was afraid to look at God.

7 Then the Lord said, "I have surely seen the affliction of my people who are in Egypt and have heard their cry because of their taskmasters. I know their sufferings,

8 and I have come down to deliver them out of the hand of the Egyptians and to bring them up out of that land to a good and broad land, a land flowing with milk and honey, to the place of the Canaanites, the Hittites, the Amorites, the Perizzites, the Hivites, and the Jebusites.

9 And now, behold, the cry of the people of Israel has come to me, and I have also seen the oppression with which the Egyptians oppress them.

10 Come, I will send you to Pharaoh that you may bring my people, the children of Israel, out of Egypt."

11 But Moses said to God, "Who am I that I should go to Pharaoh and bring the children of Israel out of Egypt?"

12 He said, "But I will be with you, and this shall be the sign for you, that I have sent you: when you have brought the people out of Egypt, you shall serve God on this mountain."

13 Then Moses said to God, "If I come to the people of Israel and say to them, 'The God of your fathers has sent me to you,' and they ask me, 'What is his name?' what shall I say to them?"

14 God said to Moses, "I am who I am." And he said, "Say this to the people of Israel: 'I am has sent me to you.'"

15 God also said to Moses, "Say this to the people of Israel: 'The Lord, the God of your fathers, the God of Abraham, the God of Isaac, and the God of Jacob, has sent me to you.' This is my name forever, and thus I am to be remembered throughout all generations.

16 Go and gather the elders of Israel together and say to them, 'The Lord, the God of your fathers, the God of Abraham, of Isaac, and of Jacob, has

appeared to me, saying, "I have observed you and what has been done to you in Egypt,

17 and I promise that I will bring you up out of the affliction of Egypt to the land of the Canaanites, the Hittites, the Amorites, the Perizzites, the Hivites, and the Jebusites, a land flowing with milk and honey."'

18 And they will listen to your voice, and you and the elders of Israel shall go to the king of Egypt and say to him, 'The Lord, the God of the Hebrews, has met with us; and now, please let us go a three days' journey into the wilderness, that we may sacrifice to the Lord our God.'

19 But I know that the king of Egypt will not let you go unless compelled by a mighty hand.

20 So I will stretch out my hand and strike Egypt with all the wonders that I will do in it; after that he will let you go.

21 And I will give this people favor in the sight of the Egyptians; and when you go, you shall not go empty,

22 but each woman shall ask of her neighbor, and any woman who lives in her house, for silver and gold jewelry, and for clothing. You shall put them on your sons and on your daughters. So you shall plunder the Egyptians."

Exodus 4

English Standard Version

Moses Given Powerful Signs

1 Then Moses answered, "But behold, they will not believe me or listen to my voice, for they will say, 'The Lord did not appear to you.'"

2 The Lord said to him, "What is that in your hand?" He said, "A staff."

3 And he said, "Throw it on the ground." So he threw it on the ground, and it became a serpent, and Moses ran from it.

4 But the Lord said to Moses, "Put out your hand and catch it by the tail"—so he put out his hand and caught it, and it became a staff in his hand—

5 "that they may believe that the Lord, the God of their fathers, the God of Abraham, the God of Isaac, and the God of Jacob, has appeared to you."

6 Again, the Lord said to him, "Put your hand inside your cloak." And he put his hand inside his cloak, and when he took it out, behold, his hand was leprous like snow.

7 Then God said, "Put your hand back inside your cloak." So he put his hand back inside his cloak, and when he took it out, behold, it was restored like the rest of his flesh.

8 "If they will not believe you," God said, "or listen to the first sign, they may believe the latter sign.

9 If they will not believe even these two signs or listen to your voice, you shall take some water from the Nile and pour it on the dry ground, and the water that you shall take from the Nile will become blood on the dry ground."

10 But Moses said to the Lord, "Oh, my Lord, I am not eloquent, either in the past or since you have spoken to your servant, but I am slow of speech and of tongue."

11 Then the Lord said to him, "Who has made man's mouth? Who makes him mute, or deaf, or seeing, or blind? Is it not I, the Lord?

12 Now therefore go, and I will be with your mouth and teach you what you shall speak."

13 But he said, "Oh, my Lord, please send someone else."

14 Then the anger of the Lord was kindled against Moses and he said, "Is there not Aaron, your brother, the Levite? I know that he can speak well. Behold, he is coming out to meet you, and when he sees you, he will be glad in his heart.

15 You shall speak to him and put the words in his mouth, and I will be with your mouth and with his mouth and will teach you both what to do.

16 He shall speak for you to the people, and he shall be your mouth, and you shall be as God to him.

17 And take in your hand this staff, with which you shall do the signs."

Moses Returns to Egypt

18 Moses went back to Jethro his father-in-law and said to him, "Please let me go back to my brothers in Egypt to see whether they are still alive." And Jethro said to Moses, "Go in peace."

19 And the Lord said to Moses in Midian, "Go back to Egypt, for all the men who were seeking your life are dead."

20 So Moses took his wife and his sons and had them ride on a donkey, and went back to the land of Egypt. And Moses took the staff of God in his hand.

21 And the Lord said to Moses, "When you go back to Egypt, see that you do before Pharaoh all the miracles that I have put in your power. But I will harden his heart, so that he will not let the people go.

22 Then you shall say to Pharaoh, 'Thus says the Lord, Israel is my firstborn son,

23 and I say to you, "Let my son go that he may serve me." If you refuse to let him go, behold, I will kill your firstborn son.'"

24 At a lodging place on the way the Lord met him and sought to put him to death.

25 Then Zipporah took a flint and cut off her son's foreskin and touched Moses' feet with it and said, "Surely you are a bridegroom of blood to me!" 26 So he let him alone. It was then that she said, "A bridegroom of blood," because of the circumcision.

27 The Lord said to Aaron, "Go into the wilderness to meet Moses." So he went and met him at the mountain of God and kissed him.

28 And Moses told Aaron all the words of the Lord with which he had sent him to speak, and all the signs that he had commanded him to do.

29 Then Moses and Aaron went and gathered together all the elders of the people of Israel.

30 Aaron spoke all the words that the Lord had spoken to Moses and did the signs in the sight of the people.

31 And the people believed; and when they heard that the Lord had visited the people of Israel and that he had seen their affliction, they bowed their heads and worshiped.

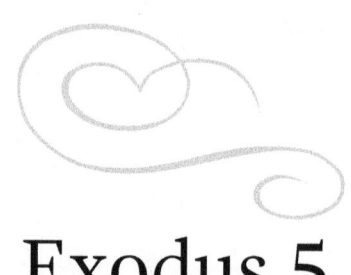

Exodus 5

English Standard Version

Making Bricks Without Straw

1 Afterward Moses and Aaron went and said to Pharaoh, "Thus says the Lord, the God of Israel, 'Let my people go, that they may hold a feast to me in the wilderness.'"

2 But Pharaoh said, "Who is the Lord, that I should obey his voice and let Israel go? I do not know the Lord, and moreover, I will not let Israel go."

3 Then they said, "The God of the Hebrews has met with us. Please let us go a three days' journey into the wilderness that we may sacrifice to the Lord our God, lest he fall upon us with pestilence or with the sword."

4 But the king of Egypt said to them, "Moses and Aaron, why do you take the people away from their work? Get back to your burdens."

5 And Pharaoh said, "Behold, the people of the land are now many, and you make them rest from their burdens!"

6 The same day Pharaoh commanded the taskmasters of the people and their foremen,

7 "You shall no longer give the people straw to make bricks, as in the past; let them go and gather straw for themselves.

8 But the number of bricks that they made in the past you shall impose on them, you shall by no means reduce it, for they are idle. Therefore they cry, 'Let us go and offer sacrifice to our God.'

9 Let heavier work be laid on the men that they may labor at it and pay no regard to lying words."

10 So the taskmasters and the foremen of the people went out and said to the people, "Thus says Pharaoh, 'I will not give you straw.

11 Go and get your straw yourselves wherever you can find it, but your work will not be reduced in the least.'"

12 So the people were scattered throughout all the land of Egypt to gather stubble for straw.

13 The taskmasters were urgent, saying, "Complete your work, your daily task each day, as when there was straw."

14 And the foremen of the people of Israel, whom Pharaoh's taskmasters had set over them, were beaten and were asked, "Why have you not done all your task of making bricks today and yesterday, as in the past?"

15 Then the foremen of the people of Israel came and cried to Pharaoh, "Why do you treat your servants like this?

16 No straw is given to your servants, yet they say to us, 'Make bricks!' And behold, your servants are beaten; but the fault is in your own people."

17 But he said, "You are idle, you are idle; that is why you say, 'Let us go and sacrifice to the Lord.'

18 Go now and work. No straw will be given you, but you must still deliver the same number of bricks."

19 The foremen of the people of Israel saw that they were in trouble when they said, "You shall by no means reduce your number of bricks, your daily task each day."

20 They met Moses and Aaron, who were waiting for them, as they came out from Pharaoh;

21 and they said to them, "The Lord look on you and judge, because you have made us stink in the sight of Pharaoh and his servants, and have put a sword in their hand to kill us."

22 Then Moses turned to the Lord and said, "O Lord, why have you done evil to this people? Why did you ever send me?

23 For since I came to Pharaoh to speak in your name, he has done evil to this people, and you have not delivered your people at all."

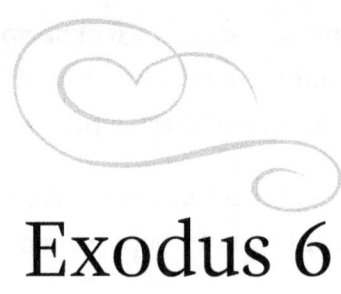

Exodus 6

English Standard Version

God Promises Deliverance

1 But the Lord said to Moses, "Now you shall see what I will do to Pharaoh; for with a strong hand he will send them out, and with a strong hand he will drive them out of his land."

2 God spoke to Moses and said to him, "I am the Lord.

3 I appeared to Abraham, to Isaac, and to Jacob, as God Almighty, but by my name the Lord I did not make myself known to them.

4 I also established my covenant with them to give them the land of Canaan, the land in which they lived as sojourners.

5 Moreover, I have heard the groaning of the people of Israel whom the Egyptians hold as slaves, and I have remembered my covenant.

6 Say therefore to the people of Israel, 'I am the Lord, and I will bring you out from under the burdens of the Egyptians, and I will deliver you from slavery to them, and I will redeem you with an outstretched arm and with great acts of judgment.

7 I will take you to be my people, and I will be your God, and you shall know that I am the Lord your God, who has brought you out from under the burdens of the Egyptians.

8 I will bring you into the land that I swore to give to Abraham, to Isaac, and to Jacob. I will give it to you for a possession. I am the Lord.'"

9 Moses spoke thus to the people of Israel, but they did not listen to Moses, because of their broken spirit and harsh slavery.

10 So the Lord said to Moses,

11 "Go in, tell Pharaoh king of Egypt to let the people of Israel go out of his land."

12 But Moses said to the Lord, "Behold, the people of Israel have not listened to me. How then shall Pharaoh listen to me, for I am of uncircumcised lips?"

13 But the Lord spoke to Moses and Aaron and gave them a charge about the people of Israel and about Pharaoh king of Egypt: to bring the people of Israel out of the land of Egypt.

The Genealogy of Moses and Aaron

14 These are the heads of their fathers' houses: the sons of Reuben, the firstborn of Israel: Hanoch, Pallu, Hezron, and Carmi; these are the clans of Reuben.

15 The sons of Simeon: Jemuel, Jamin, Ohad, Jachin, Zohar, and Shaul, the son of a Canaanite woman; these are the clans of Simeon.

16 These are the names of the sons of Levi according to their generations: Gershon, Kohath, and Merari, the years of the life of Levi being 137 years.

17 The sons of Gershon: Libni and Shimei, by their clans.

18 The sons of Kohath: Amram, Izhar, Hebron, and Uzziel, the years of the life of Kohath being 133 years.

19 The sons of Merari: Mahli and Mushi. These are the clans of the Levites according to their generations.

20 Amram took as his wife Jochebed his father's sister, and she bore him Aaron and Moses, the years of the life of Amram being 137 years.

21 The sons of Izhar: Korah, Nepheg, and Zichri.

22 The sons of Uzziel: Mishael, Elzaphan, and Sithri.

23 Aaron took as his wife Elisheba, the daughter of Amminadab and the sister of Nahshon, and she bore him Nadab, Abihu, Eleazar, and Ithamar.

24 The sons of Korah: Assir, Elkanah, and Abiasaph; these are the clans of the Korahites.

25 Eleazar, Aaron's son, took as his wife one of the daughters of Putiel, and she bore him Phinehas. These are the heads of the fathers' houses of the Levites by their clans.

26 These are the Aaron and Moses to whom the Lord said: "Bring out the people of Israel from the land of Egypt by their hosts."

27 It was they who spoke to Pharaoh king of Egypt about bringing out the people of Israel from Egypt, this Moses and this Aaron.

28 On the day when the Lord spoke to Moses in the land of Egypt,

29 the Lord said to Moses, "I am the Lord; tell Pharaoh king of Egypt all that I say to you."

30 But Moses said to the Lord, "Behold, I am of uncircumcised lips. How will Pharaoh listen to me?"

Exodus 7

English Standard Version

Moses and Aaron Before Pharaoh

1 And the Lord said to Moses, "See, I have made you like God to Pharaoh, and your brother Aaron shall be your prophet.

2 You shall speak all that I command you, and your brother Aaron shall tell Pharaoh to let the people of Israel go out of his land.

3 But I will harden Pharaoh's heart, and though I multiply my signs and wonders in the land of Egypt,

4 Pharaoh will not listen to you. Then I will lay my hand on Egypt and bring my hosts, my people the children of Israel, out of the land of Egypt by great acts of judgment.

5 The Egyptians shall know that I am the Lord, when I stretch out my hand against Egypt and bring out the people of Israel from among them."

6 Moses and Aaron did so; they did just as the Lord commanded them.

7 Now Moses was eighty years old, and Aaron eighty-three years old, when they spoke to Pharaoh.

8 Then the Lord said to Moses and Aaron,

9 "When Pharaoh says to you, 'Prove yourselves by working a miracle,' then you shall say to Aaron, 'Take your staff and cast it down before Pharaoh, that it may become a serpent.'"

10 So Moses and Aaron went to Pharaoh and did just as the Lord commanded. Aaron cast down his staff before Pharaoh and his servants, and it became a serpent.

11 Then Pharaoh summoned the wise men and the sorcerers, and they, the magicians of Egypt, also did the same by their secret arts.

12 For each man cast down his staff, and they became serpents. But Aaron's staff swallowed up their staffs.

13 Still Pharaoh's heart was hardened, and he would not listen to them, as the Lord had said.

The First Plague: Water Turned to Blood

14 Then the Lord said to Moses, "Pharaoh's heart is hardened; he refuses to let the people go.

15 Go to Pharaoh in the morning, as he is going out to the water. Stand on the bank of the Nile to meet him, and take in your hand the staff that turned into a serpent.

16 And you shall say to him, 'The Lord, the God of the Hebrews, sent me to you, saying, "Let my people go, that they may serve me in the wilderness." But so far, you have not obeyed.

17 Thus says the Lord, "By this you shall know that I am the Lord: behold, with the staff that is in my hand I will strike the water that is in the Nile, and it shall turn into blood.

18 The fish in the Nile shall die, and the Nile will stink, and the Egyptians will grow weary of drinking water from the Nile."'"

19 And the Lord said to Moses, "Say to Aaron, 'Take your staff and stretch out your hand over the waters of Egypt, over their rivers, their canals, and their ponds, and all their pools of water, so that they may become blood, and there shall be blood throughout all the land of Egypt, even in vessels of wood and in vessels of stone.'"

20 Moses and Aaron did as the Lord commanded. In the sight of Pharaoh and in the sight of his servants he lifted up the staff and struck the water in the Nile, and all the water in the Nile turned into blood.

21 And the fish in the Nile died, and the Nile stank, so that the Egyptians could not drink water from the Nile. There was blood throughout all the land of Egypt.

22 But the magicians of Egypt did the same by their secret arts. So Pharaoh's heart remained hardened, and he would not listen to them, as the Lord had said.

23 Pharaoh turned and went into his house, and he did not take even this to heart.

24 And all the Egyptians dug along the Nile for water to drink, for they could not drink the water of the Nile.

25 Seven full days passed after the Lord had struck the Nile.

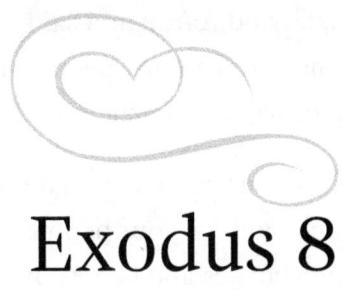

Exodus 8

English Standard Version

The Second Plague: Frogs

1 Then the Lord said to Moses, "Go in to Pharaoh and say to him, 'Thus says the Lord, "Let my people go, that they may serve me.

2 But if you refuse to let them go, behold, I will plague all your country with frogs.

3 The Nile shall swarm with frogs that shall come up into your house and into your bedroom and on your bed and into the houses of your servants and your people, and into your ovens and your kneading bowls.

4 The frogs shall come up on you and on your people and on all your servants."'"

5 And the Lord said to Moses, "Say to Aaron, 'Stretch out your hand with your staff over the rivers, over the canals and over the pools, and make frogs come up on the land of Egypt!'"

6 So Aaron stretched out his hand over the waters of Egypt, and the frogs came up and covered the land of Egypt.

7 But the magicians did the same by their secret arts and made frogs come up on the land of Egypt.

8 Then Pharaoh called Moses and Aaron and said, "Plead with the Lord to take away the frogs from me and from my people, and I will let the people go to sacrifice to the Lord."

9 Moses said to Pharaoh, "Be pleased to command me when I am to plead for you and for your servants and for your people, that the frogs be cut off from you and your houses and be left only in the Nile."

10 And he said, "Tomorrow." Moses said, "Be it as you say, so that you may know that there is no one like the Lord our God.

11 The frogs shall go away from you and your houses and your servants and your people. They shall be left only in the Nile."

12 So Moses and Aaron went out from Pharaoh, and Moses cried to the Lord about the frogs, as he had agreed with Pharaoh.

13 And the Lord did according to the word of Moses. The frogs died out in the houses, the courtyards, and the fields.

14 And they gathered them together in heaps, and the land stank.

15 But when Pharaoh saw that there was a respite, he hardened his heart and would not listen to them, as the Lord had said.

The Third Plague: Gnats

16 Then the Lord said to Moses, "Say to Aaron, 'Stretch out your staff and strike the dust of the earth, so that it may become gnats in all the land of Egypt.'"

17 And they did so. Aaron stretched out his hand with his staff and struck the dust of the earth, and there were gnats on man and beast. All the dust of the earth became gnats in all the land of Egypt.

18 The magicians tried by their secret arts to produce gnats, but they could not. So there were gnats on man and beast.

19 Then the magicians said to Pharaoh, "This is the finger of God." But Pharaoh's heart was hardened, and he would not listen to them, as the Lord had said.

The Fourth Plague: Flies

20 Then the Lord said to Moses, "Rise up early in the morning and present yourself to Pharaoh, as he goes out to the water, and say to him, 'Thus says the Lord, "Let my people go, that they may serve me.

21 Or else, if you will not let my people go, behold, I will send swarms of flies on you and your servants and your people, and into your houses. And the houses of the Egyptians shall be filled with swarms of flies, and also the ground on which they stand.

22 But on that day I will set apart the land of Goshen, where my people dwell, so that no swarms of flies shall be there, that you may know that I am the Lord in the midst of the earth.

23 Thus I will put a division between my people and your people. Tomorrow this sign shall happen."'"

24 And the Lord did so. There came great swarms of flies into the house of Pharaoh and into his servants' houses. Throughout all the land of Egypt the land was ruined by the swarms of flies.

25 Then Pharaoh called Moses and Aaron and said, "Go, sacrifice to your God within the land."

26 But Moses said, "It would not be right to do so, for the offerings we shall sacrifice to the Lord our God are an abomination to the Egyptians. If we sacrifice offerings abominable to the Egyptians before their eyes, will they not stone us?

27 We must go three days' journey into the wilderness and sacrifice to the Lord our God as he tells us."

28 So Pharaoh said, "I will let you go to sacrifice to the Lord your God in the wilderness; only you must not go very far away. Plead for me."

29 Then Moses said, "Behold, I am going out from you and I will plead with the Lord that the swarms of flies may depart from Pharaoh, from his servants, and from his people, tomorrow. Only let not Pharaoh cheat again by not letting the people go to sacrifice to the Lord."

30 So Moses went out from Pharaoh and prayed to the Lord.

31 And the Lord did as Moses asked, and removed the swarms of flies from Pharaoh, from his servants, and from his people; not one remained.

32 But Pharaoh hardened his heart this time also, and did not let the people go

Exodus 9

English Standard Version

The Fifth Plague: Egyptian Livestock Die

1 Then the Lord said to Moses, "Go in to Pharaoh and say to him, 'Thus says the Lord, the God of the Hebrews, "Let my people go, that they may serve me.

2 For if you refuse to let them go and still hold them,

3 behold, the hand of the Lord will fall with a very severe plague upon your livestock that are in the field, the horses, the donkeys, the camels, the herds, and the flocks.

4 But the Lord will make a distinction between the livestock of Israel and the livestock of Egypt, so that nothing of all that belongs to the people of Israel shall die."'"

5 And the Lord set a time, saying, "Tomorrow the Lord will do this thing in the land."

6 And the next day the Lord did this thing. All the livestock of the Egyptians died, but not one of the livestock of the people of Israel died.

7 And Pharaoh sent, and behold, not one of the livestock of Israel was dead. But the heart of Pharaoh was hardened, and he did not let the people go.

The Sixth Plague: Boils

8 And the Lord said to Moses and Aaron, "Take handfuls of soot from the kiln, and let Moses throw them in the air in the sight of Pharaoh.

9 It shall become fine dust over all the land of Egypt, and become boils breaking out in sores on man and beast throughout all the land of Egypt."

10 So they took soot from the kiln and stood before Pharaoh. And Moses threw it in the air, and it became boils breaking out in sores on man and beast.

11 And the magicians could not stand before Moses because of the boils, for the boils came upon the magicians and upon all the Egyptians.

12 But the Lord hardened the heart of Pharaoh, and he did not listen to them, as the Lord had spoken to Moses.

The Seventh Plague: Hail

13 Then the Lord said to Moses, "Rise up early in the morning and present yourself before Pharaoh and say to him, 'Thus says the Lord, the God of the Hebrews, "Let my people go, that they may serve me.

14 For this time I will send all my plagues on you yourself, and on your servants and your people, so that you may know that there is none like me in all the earth.

15 For by now I could have put out my hand and struck you and your people with pestilence, and you would have been cut off from the earth.

16 But for this purpose I have raised you up, to show you my power, so that my name may be proclaimed in all the earth.

17 You are still exalting yourself against my people and will not let them go.

18 Behold, about this time tomorrow I will cause very heavy hail to fall, such as never has been in Egypt from the day it was founded until now.

19 Now therefore send, get your livestock and all that you have in the field into safe shelter, for every man and beast that is in the field and is not brought home will die when the hail falls on them.""

20 Then whoever feared the word of the Lord among the servants of Pharaoh hurried his slaves and his livestock into the houses,

21 but whoever did not pay attention to the word of the Lord left his slaves and his livestock in the field.

22 Then the Lord said to Moses, "Stretch out your hand toward heaven, so that there may be hail in all the land of Egypt, on man and beast and every plant of the field, in the land of Egypt."

23 Then Moses stretched out his staff toward heaven, and the Lord sent thunder and hail, and fire ran down to the earth. And the Lord rained hail upon the land of Egypt.

24 There was hail and fire flashing continually in the midst of the hail, very heavy hail, such as had never been in all the land of Egypt since it became a nation.

25 The hail struck down everything that was in the field in all the land of Egypt, both man and beast. And the hail struck down every plant of the field and broke every tree of the field.

26 Only in the land of Goshen, where the people of Israel were, was there no hail.

27 Then Pharaoh sent and called Moses and Aaron and said to them, "This time I have sinned; the Lord is in the right, and I and my people are in the wrong.

28 Plead with the Lord, for there has been enough of God's thunder and hail. I will let you go, and you shall stay no longer."

29 Moses said to him, "As soon as I have gone out of the city, I will stretch out my hands to the Lord. The thunder will cease, and there will be no more hail, so that you may know that the earth is the Lord's.

30 But as for you and your servants, I know that you do not yet fear the Lord God."

31 (The flax and the barley were struck down, for the barley was in the ear and the flax was in bud.

32 But the wheat and the emmer were not struck down, for they are late in coming up.)

33 So Moses went out of the city from Pharaoh and stretched out his hands to the Lord, and the thunder and the hail ceased, and the rain no longer poured upon the earth.

34 But when Pharaoh saw that the rain and the hail and the thunder had ceased, he sinned yet again and hardened his heart, he and his servants.

35 So the heart of Pharaoh was hardened, and he did not let the people of Israel go, just as the Lord had spoken through Moses..

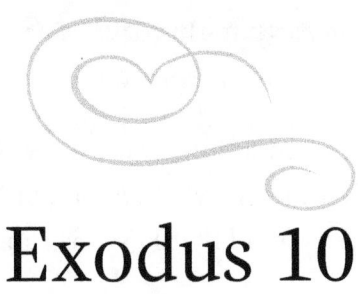

Exodus 10

English Standard Version

The Eighth Plague: Locusts

1 Then the Lord said to Moses, "Go in to Pharaoh, for I have hardened his heart and the heart of his servants, that I may show these signs of mine among them,

2 and that you may tell in the hearing of your son and of your grandson how I have dealt harshly with the Egyptians and what signs I have done among them, that you may know that I am the Lord."

3 So Moses and Aaron went in to Pharaoh and said to him, "Thus says the Lord, the God of the Hebrews, 'How long will you refuse to humble yourself before me? Let my people go, that they may serve me.

4 For if you refuse to let my people go, behold, tomorrow I will bring locusts into your country,

5 and they shall cover the face of the land, so that no one can see the land. And they shall eat what is left to you after the hail, and they shall eat every tree of yours that grows in the field,

6 and they shall fill your houses and the houses of all your servants and of all the Egyptians, as neither your fathers nor your grandfathers have seen,

from the day they came on earth to this day.'" Then he turned and went out from Pharaoh.

7 Then Pharaoh's servants said to him, "How long shall this man be a snare to us? Let the men go, that they may serve the Lord their God. Do you not yet understand that Egypt is ruined?"

8 So Moses and Aaron were brought back to Pharaoh. And he said to them, "Go, serve the Lord your God. But which ones are to go?"

9 Moses said, "We will go with our young and our old. We will go with our sons and daughters and with our flocks and herds, for we must hold a feast to the Lord."

10 But he said to them, "The Lord be with you, if ever I let you and your little ones go! Look, you have some evil purpose in mind.

11 No! Go, the men among you, and serve the Lord, for that is what you are asking." And they were driven out from Pharaoh's presence.

12 Then the Lord said to Moses, "Stretch out your hand over the land of Egypt for the locusts, so that they may come upon the land of Egypt and eat every plant in the land, all that the hail has left."

13 So Moses stretched out his staff over the land of Egypt, and the Lord brought an east wind upon the land all that day and all that night. When it was morning, the east wind had brought the locusts.

14 The locusts came up over all the land of Egypt and settled on the whole country of Egypt, such a dense swarm of locusts as had never been before, nor ever will be again.

15 They covered the face of the whole land, so that the land was darkened, and they ate all the plants in the land and all the fruit of the trees that the hail had left. Not a green thing remained, neither tree nor plant of the field, through all the land of Egypt.

16 Then Pharaoh hastily called Moses and Aaron and said, "I have sinned against the Lord your God, and against you.

17 Now therefore, forgive my sin, please, only this once, and plead with the Lord your God only to remove this death from me."

18 So he went out from Pharaoh and pleaded with the Lord.

19 And the Lord turned the wind into a very strong west wind, which lifted the locusts and drove them into the Red Sea. Not a single locust was left in all the country of Egypt.

20 But the Lord hardened Pharaoh's heart, and he did not let the people of Israel go.

The Ninth Plague: Darkness

21 Then the Lord said to Moses, "Stretch out your hand toward heaven, that there may be darkness over the land of Egypt, a darkness to be felt." 22 So Moses stretched out his hand toward heaven, and there was pitch darkness in all the land of Egypt three days.

23 They did not see one another, nor did anyone rise from his place for three days, but all the people of Israel had light where they lived.

24 Then Pharaoh called Moses and said, "Go, serve the Lord; your little ones also may go with you; only let your flocks and your herds remain behind."

25 But Moses said, "You must also let us have sacrifices and burnt offerings, that we may sacrifice to the Lord our God.

26 Our livestock also must go with us; not a hoof shall be left behind, for we must take of them to serve the Lord our God, and we do not know with what we must serve the Lord until we arrive there."

27 But the Lord hardened Pharaoh's heart, and he would not let them go.

28 Then Pharaoh said to him, "Get away from me; take care never to see my face again, for on the day you see my face you shall die."

29 Moses said, "As you say! I will not see your face again."

Exodus 11

English Standard Version

A Final Plague Threatened

1 The Lord said to Moses, "Yet one plague more I will bring upon Pharaoh and upon Egypt. Afterward he will let you go from here. When he lets you go, he will drive you away completely.

2 Speak now in the hearing of the people, that they ask, every man of his neighbor and every woman of her neighbor, for silver and gold jewelry."

3 And the Lord gave the people favor in the sight of the Egyptians. Moreover, the man Moses was very great in the land of Egypt, in the sight of Pharaoh's servants and in the sight of the people.

4 So Moses said, "Thus says the Lord: 'About midnight I will go out in the midst of Egypt,

5 and every firstborn in the land of Egypt shall die, from the firstborn of Pharaoh who sits on his throne, even to the firstborn of the slave girl who is behind the handmill, and all the firstborn of the cattle.

6 There shall be a great cry throughout all the land of Egypt, such as there has never been, nor ever will be again.

7 But not a dog shall growl against any of the people of Israel, either man or beast, that you may know that the Lord makes a distinction between Egypt and Israel.'

8 And all these your servants shall come down to me and bow down to me, saying, 'Get out, you and all the people who follow you.' And after that I will go out." And he went out from Pharaoh in hot anger.

9 Then the Lord said to Moses, "Pharaoh will not listen to you, that my wonders may be multiplied in the land of Egypt."

10 Moses and Aaron did all these wonders before Pharaoh, and the Lord hardened Pharaoh's heart, and he did not let the people of Israel go out of his land.

Exodus 12

English Standard Version

The Passover

1 The Lord said to Moses and Aaron in the land of Egypt,

2 "This month shall be for you the beginning of months. It shall be the first month of the year for you.

3 Tell all the congregation of Israel that on the tenth day of this month every man shall take a lamb according to their fathers' houses, a lamb for a household.

4 And if the household is too small for a lamb, then he and his nearest neighbor shall take according to the number of persons; according to what each can eat you shall make your count for the lamb.

5 Your lamb shall be without blemish, a male a year old. You may take it from the sheep or from the goats,

6 and you shall keep it until the fourteenth day of this month, when the whole assembly of the congregation of Israel shall kill their lambs at twilight.

7 "Then they shall take some of the blood and put it on the two doorposts and the lintel of the houses in which they eat it.

8 They shall eat the flesh that night, roasted on the fire; with unleavened bread and bitter herbs they shall eat it.

9 Do not eat any of it raw or boiled in water, but roasted, its head with its legs and its inner parts.

10 And you shall let none of it remain until the morning; anything that remains until the morning you shall burn.

11 In this manner you shall eat it: with your belt fastened, your sandals on your feet, and your staff in your hand. And you shall eat it in haste. It is the Lord's Passover.

12 For I will pass through the land of Egypt that night, and I will strike all the firstborn in the land of Egypt, both man and beast; and on all the gods of Egypt I will execute judgments: I am the Lord.

13 The blood shall be a sign for you, on the houses where you are. And when I see the blood, I will pass over you, and no plague will befall you to destroy you, when I strike the land of Egypt.

14 "This day shall be for you a memorial day, and you shall keep it as a feast to the Lord; throughout your generations, as a statute forever, you shall keep it as a feast.

15 Seven days you shall eat unleavened bread. On the first day you shall remove leaven out of your houses, for if anyone eats what is leavened, from the first day until the seventh day, that person shall be cut off from Israel.

16 On the first day you shall hold a holy assembly, and on the seventh day a holy assembly. No work shall be done on those days. But what everyone needs to eat, that alone may be prepared by you.

17 And you shall observe the Feast of Unleavened Bread, for on this very day I brought your hosts out of the land of Egypt. Therefore you shall observe this day, throughout your generations, as a statute forever.

Exodus 12

18 In the first month, from the fourteenth day of the month at evening, you shall eat unleavened bread until the twenty-first day of the month at evening.

19 For seven days no leaven is to be found in your houses. If anyone eats what is leavened, that person will be cut off from the congregation of Israel, whether he is a sojourner or a native of the land.

20 You shall eat nothing leavened; in all your dwelling places you shall eat unleavened bread."

21 Then Moses called all the elders of Israel and said to them, "Go and select lambs for yourselves according to your clans, and kill the Passover lamb.

22 Take a bunch of hyssop and dip it in the blood that is in the basin, and touch the lintel and the two doorposts with the blood that is in the basin. None of you shall go out of the door of his house until the morning.

23 For the Lord will pass through to strike the Egyptians, and when he sees the blood on the lintel and on the two doorposts, the Lord will pass over the door and will not allow the destroyer to enter your houses to strike you.

24 You shall observe this rite as a statute for you and for your sons forever.

25 And when you come to the land that the Lord will give you, as he has promised, you shall keep this service.

26 And when your children say to you, 'What do you mean by this service?'

27 you shall say, 'It is the sacrifice of the Lord's Passover, for he passed over the houses of the people of Israel in Egypt, when he struck the Egyptians but spared our houses.'" And the people bowed their heads and worshiped.

28 Then the people of Israel went and did so; as the Lord had commanded Moses and Aaron, so they did.

The Tenth Plague: Death of the Firstborn

29 At midnight the Lord struck down all the firstborn in the land of Egypt, from the firstborn of Pharaoh who sat on his throne to the firstborn of the captive who was in the dungeon, and all the firstborn of the livestock.

30 And Pharaoh rose up in the night, he and all his servants and all the Egyptians. And there was a great cry in Egypt, for there was not a house where someone was not dead.

31 Then he summoned Moses and Aaron by night and said, "Up, go out from among my people, both you and the people of Israel; and go, serve the Lord, as you have said.

32 Take your flocks and your herds, as you have said, and be gone, and bless me also!"

The Exodus

33 The Egyptians were urgent with the people to send them out of the land in haste. For they said, "We shall all be dead."

34 So the people took their dough before it was leavened, their kneading bowls being bound up in their cloaks on their shoulders.

35 The people of Israel had also done as Moses told them, for they had asked the Egyptians for silver and gold jewelry and for clothing.

36 And the Lord had given the people favor in the sight of the Egyptians, so that they let them have what they asked. Thus they plundered the Egyptians.

37 And the people of Israel journeyed from Rameses to Succoth, about six hundred thousand men on foot, besides women and children.

38 A mixed multitude also went up with them, and very much livestock, both flocks and herds.

39 And they baked unleavened cakes of the dough that they had brought out of Egypt, for it was not leavened, because they were thrust out of Egypt and could not wait, nor had they prepared any provisions for themselves.

40 The time that the people of Israel lived in Egypt was 430 years.

41 At the end of 430 years, on that very day, all the hosts of the Lord went out from the land of Egypt.

42 It was a night of watching by the Lord, to bring them out of the land of Egypt; so this same night is a night of watching kept to the Lord by all the people of Israel throughout their generations.

Institution of the Passover

43 And the Lord said to Moses and Aaron, "This is the statute of the Passover: no foreigner shall eat of it,

44 but every slave that is bought for money may eat of it after you have circumcised him.

45 No foreigner or hired worker may eat of it.

46 It shall be eaten in one house; you shall not take any of the flesh outside the house, and you shall not break any of its bones.

47 All the congregation of Israel shall keep it.

48 If a stranger shall sojourn with you and would keep the Passover to the Lord, let all his males be circumcised. Then he may come near and keep it; he shall be as a native of the land. But no uncircumcised person shall eat of it.

49 There shall be one law for the native and for the stranger who sojourns among you."

50 All the people of Israel did just as the Lord commanded Moses and Aaron.

51 And on that very day the Lord brought the people of Israel out of the land of Egypt by their hosts.

Exodus 13

English Standard Version

Consecration of the Firstborn

1 The Lord said to Moses,

2 "Consecrate to me all the firstborn. Whatever is the first to open the womb among the people of Israel, both of man and of beast, is mine."

The Feast of Unleavened Bread

3 Then Moses said to the people, "Remember this day in which you came out from Egypt, out of the house of slavery, for by a strong hand the Lord brought you out from this place. No leavened bread shall be eaten.

4 Today, in the month of Abib, you are going out.

5 And when the Lord brings you into the land of the Canaanites, the Hittites, the Amorites, the Hivites, and the Jebusites, which he swore to your fathers to give you, a land flowing with milk and honey, you shall keep this service in this month.

6 Seven days you shall eat unleavened bread, and on the seventh day there shall be a feast to the Lord.

7 Unleavened bread shall be eaten for seven days; no leavened bread shall be seen with you, and no leaven shall be seen with you in all your territory.

8 You shall tell your son on that day, 'It is because of what the Lord did for me when I came out of Egypt.'

9 And it shall be to you as a sign on your hand and as a memorial between your eyes, that the law of the Lord may be in your mouth. For with a strong hand the Lord has brought you out of Egypt.

10 You shall therefore keep this statute at its appointed time from year to year.

11 "When the Lord brings you into the land of the Canaanites, as he swore to you and your fathers, and shall give it to you,

12 you shall set apart to the Lord all that first opens the womb. All the firstborn of your animals that are males shall be the Lord's.

13 Every firstborn of a donkey you shall redeem with a lamb, or if you will not redeem it you shall break its neck. Every firstborn of man among your sons you shall redeem.

14 And when in time to come your son asks you, 'What does this mean?' you shall say to him, 'By a strong hand the Lord brought us out of Egypt, from the house of slavery.

15 For when Pharaoh stubbornly refused to let us go, the Lord killed all the firstborn in the land of Egypt, both the firstborn of man and the firstborn of animals. Therefore I sacrifice to the Lord all the males that first open the womb, but all the firstborn of my sons I redeem.'

16 It shall be as a mark on your hand or frontlets between your eyes, for by a strong hand the Lord brought us out of Egypt."

Pillars of Cloud and Fire

17 When Pharaoh let the people go, God did not lead them by way of the land of the Philistines, although that was near. For God said, "Lest the people change their minds when they see war and return to Egypt."

18 But God led the people around by the way of the wilderness toward the Red Sea. And the people of Israel went up out of the land of Egypt equipped for battle.

19 Moses took the bones of Joseph with him, for Joseph[a] had made the sons of Israel solemnly swear, saying, "God will surely visit you, and you shall carry up my bones with you from here."

20 And they moved on from Succoth and encamped at Etham, on the edge of the wilderness.

21 And the Lord went before them by day in a pillar of cloud to lead them along the way, and by night in a pillar of fire to give them light, that they might travel by day and by night.

22 The pillar of cloud by day and the pillar of fire by night did not depart from before the people.

Exodus 14

English Standard Version

Crossing the Red Sea

1 Then the Lord said to Moses,

2 "Tell the people of Israel to turn back and encamp in front of Pi-hahiroth, between Migdol and the sea, in front of Baal-zephon; you shall encamp facing it, by the sea.

3 For Pharaoh will say of the people of Israel, 'They are wandering in the land; the wilderness has shut them in.'

4 And I will harden Pharaoh's heart, and he will pursue them, and I will get glory over Pharaoh and all his host, and the Egyptians shall know that I am the Lord." And they did so.

5 When the king of Egypt was told that the people had fled, the mind of Pharaoh and his servants was changed toward the people, and they said, "What is this we have done, that we have let Israel go from serving us?"

6 So he made ready his chariot and took his army with him,

7 and took six hundred chosen chariots and all the other chariots of Egypt with officers over all of them.

Exodus 14

8 And the Lord hardened the heart of Pharaoh king of Egypt, and he pursued the people of Israel while the people of Israel were going out defiantly.

9 The Egyptians pursued them, all Pharaoh's horses and chariots and his horsemen and his army, and overtook them encamped at the sea, by Pi-hahiroth, in front of Baal-zephon.

10 When Pharaoh drew near, the people of Israel lifted up their eyes, and behold, the Egyptians were marching after them, and they feared greatly. And the people of Israel cried out to the Lord.

11 They said to Moses, "Is it because there are no graves in Egypt that you have taken us away to die in the wilderness? What have you done to us in bringing us out of Egypt?

12 Is not this what we said to you in Egypt: 'Leave us alone that we may serve the Egyptians'? For it would have been better for us to serve the Egyptians than to die in the wilderness."

13 And Moses said to the people, "Fear not, stand firm, and see the salvation of the Lord, which he will work for you today. For the Egyptians whom you see today, you shall never see again.

14 The Lord will fight for you, and you have only to be silent."

15 The Lord said to Moses, "Why do you cry to me? Tell the people of Israel to go forward.

16 Lift up your staff, and stretch out your hand over the sea and divide it, that the people of Israel may go through the sea on dry ground.

17 And I will harden the hearts of the Egyptians so that they shall go in after them, and I will get glory over Pharaoh and all his host, his chariots, and his horsemen.

18 And the Egyptians shall know that I am the Lord, when I have gotten glory over Pharaoh, his chariots, and his horsemen."

19 Then the angel of God who was going before the host of Israel moved and went behind them, and the pillar of cloud moved from before them and stood behind them,

20 coming between the host of Egypt and the host of Israel. And there was the cloud and the darkness. And it lit up the night without one coming near the other all night.

21 Then Moses stretched out his hand over the sea, and the Lord drove the sea back by a strong east wind all night and made the sea dry land, and the waters were divided.

22 And the people of Israel went into the midst of the sea on dry ground, the waters being a wall to them on their right hand and on their left.

23 The Egyptians pursued and went in after them into the midst of the sea, all Pharaoh's horses, his chariots, and his horsemen.

24 And in the morning watch the Lord in the pillar of fire and of cloud looked down on the Egyptian forces and threw the Egyptian forces into a panic,

25 clogging their chariot wheels so that they drove heavily. And the Egyptians said, "Let us flee from before Israel, for the Lord fights for them against the Egyptians."

26 Then the Lord said to Moses, "Stretch out your hand over the sea, that the water may come back upon the Egyptians, upon their chariots, and upon their horsemen."

27 So Moses stretched out his hand over the sea, and the sea returned to its normal course when the morning appeared. And as the Egyptians fled into it, the Lord threw the Egyptians into the midst of the sea.

28 The waters returned and covered the chariots and the horsemen; of all the host of Pharaoh that had followed them into the sea, not one of them remained.

Exodus 14

29 But the people of Israel walked on dry ground through the sea, the waters being a wall to them on their right hand and on their left.

30 Thus the Lord saved Israel that day from the hand of the Egyptians, and Israel saw the Egyptians dead on the seashore.

31 Israel saw the great power that the Lord used against the Egyptians, so the people feared the Lord, and they believed in the Lord and in his servant Moses.

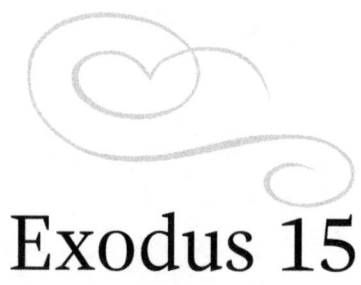

Exodus 15

English Standard Version

The Song of Moses

15 Then Moses and the people of Israel sang this song to the Lord, saying, "I will sing to the Lord, for he has triumphed gloriously; the horse and his rider he has thrown into the sea.

2 The Lord is my strength and my song, and he has become my salvation; this is my God, and I will praise him, my father's God, and I will exalt him.

3 The Lord is a man of war; the Lord is his name.

4 "Pharaoh's chariots and his host he cast into the sea, and his chosen officers were sunk in the Red Sea.

5 The floods covered them; they went down into the depths like a stone.

6 Your right hand, O Lord, glorious in power, your right hand, O Lord, shatters the enemy.

7 In the greatness of your majesty you overthrow your adversaries; you send out your fury; it consumes them like stubble.

8 At the blast of your nostrils the waters piled up; the floods stood up in a heap; the deeps congealed in the heart of the sea.

Exodus 15

9 The enemy said, 'I will pursue, I will overtake, I will divide the spoil, my desire shall have its fill of them. I will draw my sword; my hand shall destroy them.'

10 You blew with your wind; the sea covered them; they sank like lead in the mighty waters.

11 "Who is like you, O Lord, among the gods? Who is like you, majestic in holiness, awesome in glorious deeds, doing wonders?

12 You stretched out your right hand; the earth swallowed them.

13 "You have led in your steadfast love the people whom you have redeemed; you have guided them by your strength to your holy abode.

14 The peoples have heard; they tremble; pangs have seized the inhabitants of Philistia.

15 Now are the chiefs of Edom dismayed; trembling seizes the leaders of Moab; all the inhabitants of Canaan have melted away.

16 Terror and dread fall upon them; because of the greatness of your arm, they are still as a stone, till your people, O Lord, pass by, till the people pass by whom you have purchased.

17 You will bring them in and plant them on your own mountain, the place, O Lord, which you have made for your abode, the sanctuary, O Lord, which your hands have established.

18 The Lord will reign forever and ever."

19 For when the horses of Pharaoh with his chariots and his horsemen went into the sea, the Lord brought back the waters of the sea upon them, but the people of Israel walked on dry ground in the midst of the sea.

20 Then Miriam the prophetess, the sister of Aaron, took a tambourine in her hand, and all the women went out after her with tambourines and dancing.

21 And Miriam sang to them: "Sing to the Lord, for he has triumphed gloriously; the horse and his rider he has thrown into the sea."

Bitter Water Made Sweet

22 Then Moses made Israel set out from the Red Sea, and they went into the wilderness of Shur. They went three days in the wilderness and found no water.

23 When they came to Marah, they could not drink the water of Marah because it was bitter; therefore it was named Marah.

24 And the people grumbled against Moses, saying, "What shall we drink?"

25 And he cried to the Lord, and the Lord showed him a log, and he threw it into the water, and the water became sweet. There the Lord made for them a statute and a rule, and there he tested them,

26 saying, "If you will diligently listen to the voice of the Lord your God, and do that which is right in his eyes, and give ear to his commandments and keep all his statutes, I will put none of the diseases on you that I put on the Egyptians, for I am the Lord, your healer."

27 Then they came to Elim, where there were twelve springs of water and seventy palm trees, and they encamped there by the water.

Exodus 16

English Standard Version

Bread from Heaven

1 They set out from Elim, and all the congregation of the people of Israel came to the wilderness of Sin, which is between Elim and Sinai, on the fifteenth day of the second month after they had departed from the land of Egypt.

2 And the whole congregation of the people of Israel grumbled against Moses and Aaron in the wilderness,

3 and the people of Israel said to them, "Would that we had died by the hand of the Lord in the land of Egypt, when we sat by the meat pots and ate bread to the full, for you have brought us out into this wilderness to kill this whole assembly with hunger."

4 Then the Lord said to Moses, "Behold, I am about to rain bread from heaven for you, and the people shall go out and gather a day's portion every day, that I may test them, whether they will walk in my law or not.

5 On the sixth day, when they prepare what they bring in, it will be twice as much as they gather daily."

6 So Moses and Aaron said to all the people of Israel, "At evening you shall know that it was the Lord who brought you out of the land of Egypt,

7 and in the morning you shall see the glory of the Lord, because he has heard your grumbling against the Lord. For what are we, that you grumble against us?"

8 And Moses said, "When the Lord gives you in the evening meat to eat and in the morning bread to the full, because the Lord has heard your grumbling that you grumble against him—what are we? Your grumbling is not against us but against the Lord."

9 Then Moses said to Aaron, "Say to the whole congregation of the people of Israel, 'Come near before the Lord, for he has heard your grumbling.'"

10 And as soon as Aaron spoke to the whole congregation of the people of Israel, they looked toward the wilderness, and behold, the glory of the Lord appeared in the cloud.

11 And the Lord said to Moses,

12 "I have heard the grumbling of the people of Israel. Say to them, 'At twilight you shall eat meat, and in the morning you shall be filled with bread. Then you shall know that I am the Lord your God.'"

13 In the evening quail came up and covered the camp, and in the morning dew lay around the camp.

14 And when the dew had gone up, there was on the face of the wilderness a fine, flake-like thing, fine as frost on the ground.

15 When the people of Israel saw it, they said to one another, "What is it?" For they did not know what it was. And Moses said to them, "It is the bread that the Lord has given you to eat.

16 This is what the Lord has commanded: 'Gather of it, each one of you, as much as he can eat. You shall each take an omer, according to the number of the persons that each of you has in his tent.'"

17 And the people of Israel did so. They gathered, some more, some less.

18 But when they measured it with an omer, whoever gathered much had nothing left over, and whoever gathered little had no lack. Each of them gathered as much as he could eat.

19 And Moses said to them, "Let no one leave any of it over till the morning."

20 But they did not listen to Moses. Some left part of it till the morning, and it bred worms and stank. And Moses was angry with them.

21 Morning by morning they gathered it, each as much as he could eat; but when the sun grew hot, it melted.

22 On the sixth day they gathered twice as much bread, two omers each. And when all the leaders of the congregation came and told Moses,

23 he said to them, "This is what the Lord has commanded: 'Tomorrow is a day of solemn rest, a holy Sabbath to the Lord; bake what you will bake and boil what you will boil, and all that is left over lay aside to be kept till the morning.'"

24 So they laid it aside till the morning, as Moses commanded them, and it did not stink, and there were no worms in it.

25 Moses said, "Eat it today, for today is a Sabbath to the Lord; today you will not find it in the field.

26 Six days you shall gather it, but on the seventh day, which is a Sabbath, there will be none."

27 On the seventh day some of the people went out to gather, but they found none.

28 And the Lord said to Moses, "How long will you refuse to keep my commandments and my laws?

29 See! The Lord has given you the Sabbath; therefore on the sixth day he gives you bread for two days. Remain each of you in his place; let no one go out of his place on the seventh day."

30 So the people rested on the seventh day.

31 Now the house of Israel called its name manna. It was like coriander seed, white, and the taste of it was like wafers made with honey.

32 Moses said, "This is what the Lord has commanded: 'Let an omer of it be kept throughout your generations, so that they may see the bread with which I fed you in the wilderness, when I brought you out of the land of Egypt.'"

33 And Moses said to Aaron, "Take a jar, and put an omer of manna in it, and place it before the Lord to be kept throughout your generations."

34 As the Lord commanded Moses, so Aaron placed it before the testimony to be kept.

35 The people of Israel ate the manna forty years, till they came to a habitable land. They ate the manna till they came to the border of the land of Canaan.

36 (An omer is the tenth part of an ephah.)

Exodus 17

English Standard Version

Water from the Rock

1 All the congregation of the people of Israel moved on from the wilderness of Sin by stages, according to the commandment of the Lord, and camped at Rephidim, but there was no water for the people to drink.

2 Therefore the people quarreled with Moses and said, "Give us water to drink." And Moses said to them, "Why do you quarrel with me? Why do you test the Lord?"

3 But the people thirsted there for water, and the people grumbled against Moses and said, "Why did you bring us up out of Egypt, to kill us and our children and our livestock with thirst?"

4 So Moses cried to the Lord, "What shall I do with this people? They are almost ready to stone me."

5 And the Lord said to Moses, "Pass on before the people, taking with you some of the elders of Israel, and take in your hand the staff with which you struck the Nile, and go.

6 Behold, I will stand before you there on the rock at Horeb, and you shall strike the rock, and water shall come out of it, and the people will drink." And Moses did so, in the sight of the elders of Israel.

7 And he called the name of the place Massah and Meribah, because of the quarreling of the people of Israel, and because they tested the Lord by saying, "Is the Lord among us or not?"

Israel Defeats Amalek

8 Then Amalek came and fought with Israel at Rephidim.

9 So Moses said to Joshua, "Choose for us men, and go out and fight with Amalek. Tomorrow I will stand on the top of the hill with the staff of God in my hand."

10 So Joshua did as Moses told him, and fought with Amalek, while Moses, Aaron, and Hur went up to the top of the hill.

11 Whenever Moses held up his hand, Israel prevailed, and whenever he lowered his hand, Amalek prevailed.

12 But Moses' hands grew weary, so they took a stone and put it under him, and he sat on it, while Aaron and Hur held up his hands, one on one side, and the other on the other side. So his hands were steady until the going down of the sun.

13 And Joshua overwhelmed Amalek and his people with the sword.

14 Then the Lord said to Moses, "Write this as a memorial in a book and recite it in the ears of Joshua, that I will utterly blot out the memory of Amalek from under heaven."

15 And Moses built an altar and called the name of it, The Lord Is My Banner,

16 saying, "A hand upon the throne of the Lord! The Lord will have war with Amalek from generation to generation."

Exodus 18

English Standard Version

Jethro's Advice

1 Jethro, the priest of Midian, Moses' father-in-law, heard of all that God had done for Moses and for Israel his people, how the Lord had brought Israel out of Egypt.

2 Now Jethro, Moses' father-in-law, had taken Zipporah, Moses' wife, after he had sent her home,

3 along with her two sons. The name of the one was Gershom (for he said, "I have been a sojourner in a foreign land"),

4 and the name of the other, Eliezer (for he said, "The God of my father was my help, and delivered me from the sword of Pharaoh").

5 Jethro, Moses' father-in-law, came with his sons and his wife to Moses in the wilderness where he was encamped at the mountain of God.

6 And when he sent word to Moses, "I, your father-in-law Jethro, am coming to you with your wife and her two sons with her,"

7 Moses went out to meet his father-in-law and bowed down and kissed him. And they asked each other of their welfare and went into the tent.

8 Then Moses told his father-in-law all that the Lord had done to Pharaoh and to the Egyptians for Israel's sake, all the hardship that had come upon them in the way, and how the Lord had delivered them.

9 And Jethro rejoiced for all the good that the Lord had done to Israel, in that he had delivered them out of the hand of the Egyptians.

10 Jethro said, "Blessed be the Lord, who has delivered you out of the hand of the Egyptians and out of the hand of Pharaoh and has delivered the people from under the hand of the Egyptians.

11 Now I know that the Lord is greater than all gods, because in this affair they dealt arrogantly with the people."

12 And Jethro, Moses' father-in-law, brought a burnt offering and sacrifices to God; and Aaron came with all the elders of Israel to eat bread with Moses' father-in-law before God.

13 The next day Moses sat to judge the people, and the people stood around Moses from morning till evening.

14 When Moses' father-in-law saw all that he was doing for the people, he said, "What is this that you are doing for the people? Why do you sit alone, and all the people stand around you from morning till evening?"

15 And Moses said to his father-in-law, "Because the people come to me to inquire of God;

16 when they have a dispute, they come to me and I decide between one person and another, and I make them know the statutes of God and his laws."

17 Moses' father-in-law said to him, "What you are doing is not good.

18 You and the people with you will certainly wear yourselves out, for the thing is too heavy for you. You are not able to do it alone.

19 Now obey my voice; I will give you advice, and God be with you! You shall represent the people before God and bring their cases to God,

20 and you shall warn them about the statutes and the laws, and make them know the way in which they must walk and what they must do.

21 Moreover, look for able men from all the people, men who fear God, who are trustworthy and hate a bribe, and place such men over the people as chiefs of thousands, of hundreds, of fifties, and of tens.

22 And let them judge the people at all times. Every great matter they shall bring to you, but any small matter they shall decide themselves. So it will be easier for you, and they will bear the burden with you.

23 If you do this, God will direct you, you will be able to endure, and all this people also will go to their place in peace."

24 So Moses listened to the voice of his father-in-law and did all that he had said.

25 Moses chose able men out of all Israel and made them heads over the people, chiefs of thousands, of hundreds, of fifties, and of tens.

26 And they judged the people at all times. Any hard case they brought to Moses, but any small matter they decided themselves.

27 Then Moses let his father-in-law depart, and he went away to his own country.

Exodus 19

English Standard Version

Israel at Mount Sinai

1 On the third new moon after the people of Israel had gone out of the land of Egypt, on that day they came into the wilderness of Sinai.

2 They set out from Rephidim and came into the wilderness of Sinai, and they encamped in the wilderness. There Israel encamped before the mountain,

3 while Moses went up to God. The Lord called to him out of the mountain, saying, "Thus you shall say to the house of Jacob, and tell the people of Israel:

4 'You yourselves have seen what I did to the Egyptians, and how I bore you on eagles' wings and brought you to myself.

5 Now therefore, if you will indeed obey my voice and keep my covenant, you shall be my treasured possession among all peoples, for all the earth is mine;

6 and you shall be to me a kingdom of priests and a holy nation.' These are the words that you shall speak to the people of Israel."

Exodus 19

7 So Moses came and called the elders of the people and set before them all these words that the Lord had commanded him.

8 All the people answered together and said, "All that the Lord has spoken we will do." And Moses reported the words of the people to the Lord.

9 And the Lord said to Moses, "Behold, I am coming to you in a thick cloud, that the people may hear when I speak with you, and may also believe you forever." When Moses told the words of the people to the Lord,

10 the Lord said to Moses, "Go to the people and consecrate them today and tomorrow, and let them wash their garments

11 and be ready for the third day. For on the third day the Lord will come down on Mount Sinai in the sight of all the people.

12 And you shall set limits for the people all around, saying, 'Take care not to go up into the mountain or touch the edge of it. Whoever touches the mountain shall be put to death.

13 No hand shall touch him, but he shall be stoned or shot; whether beast or man, he shall not live.' When the trumpet sounds a long blast, they shall come up to the mountain."

14 So Moses went down from the mountain to the people and consecrated the people; and they washed their garments.

15 And he said to the people, "Be ready for the third day; do not go near a woman."

16 On the morning of the third day there were thunders and lightnings and a thick cloud on the mountain and a very loud trumpet blast, so that all the people in the camp trembled.

17 Then Moses brought the people out of the camp to meet God, and they took their stand at the foot of the mountain.

18 Now Mount Sinai was wrapped in smoke because the Lord had descended on it in fire. The smoke of it went up like the smoke of a kiln, and the whole mountain trembled greatly.

19 And as the sound of the trumpet grew louder and louder, Moses spoke, and God answered him in thunder.

20 The Lord came down on Mount Sinai, to the top of the mountain. And the Lord called Moses to the top of the mountain, and Moses went up.

21 And the Lord said to Moses, "Go down and warn the people, lest they break through to the Lord to look and many of them perish.

22 Also let the priests who come near to the Lord consecrate themselves, lest the Lord break out against them."

23 And Moses said to the Lord, "The people cannot come up to Mount Sinai, for you yourself warned us, saying, 'Set limits around the mountain and consecrate it.'"

24 And the Lord said to him, "Go down, and come up bringing Aaron with you. But do not let the priests and the people break through to come up to the Lord, lest he break out against them."

25 So Moses went down to the people and told them.

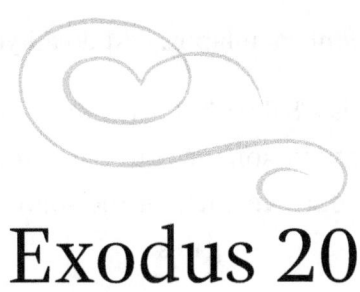

Exodus 20

English Standard Version

The Ten Commandments

1 And God spoke all these words, saying,

2 "I am the Lord your God, who brought you out of the land of Egypt, out of the house of slavery.

3 "You shall have no other gods before me.

4 "You shall not make for yourself a carved image, or any likeness of anything that is in heaven above, or that is in the earth beneath, or that is in the water under the earth.

5 You shall not bow down to them or serve them, for I the Lord your God am a jealous God, visiting the iniquity of the fathers on the children to the third and the fourth generation of those who hate me,

6 but showing steadfast love to thousands of those who love me and keep my commandments.

7 "You shall not take the name of the Lord your God in vain, for the Lord will not hold him guiltless who takes his name in vain.

8 "Remember the Sabbath day, to keep it holy.

9 Six days you shall labor, and do all your work,

10 but the seventh day is a Sabbath to the Lord your God. On it you shall not do any work, you, or your son, or your daughter, your male servant, or your female servant, or your livestock, or the sojourner who is within your gates.

11 For in six days the Lord made heaven and earth, the sea, and all that is in them, and rested on the seventh day. Therefore the Lord blessed the Sabbath day and made it holy.

12 "Honor your father and your mother, that your days may be long in the land that the Lord your God is giving you.

13 "You shall not murder.

14 "You shall not commit adultery.

15 "You shall not steal.

16 "You shall not bear false witness against your neighbor.

17 "You shall not covet your neighbor's house; you shall not covet your neighbor's wife, or his male servant, or his female servant, or his ox, or his donkey, or anything that is your neighbor's."

18 Now when all the people saw the thunder and the flashes of lightning and the sound of the trumpet and the mountain smoking, the people were afraid and trembled, and they stood far off

19 and said to Moses, "You speak to us, and we will listen; but do not let God speak to us, lest we die."

20 Moses said to the people, "Do not fear, for God has come to test you, that the fear of him may be before you, that you may not sin."

21 The people stood far off, while Moses drew near to the thick darkness where God was.

Exodus 20

Laws About Altars

22 And the Lord said to Moses, "Thus you shall say to the people of Israel: 'You have seen for yourselves that I have talked with you from heaven.

23 You shall not make gods of silver to be with me, nor shall you make for yourselves gods of gold.

24 An altar of earth you shall make for me and sacrifice on it your burnt offerings and your peace offerings, your sheep and your oxen. In every place where I cause my name to be remembered I will come to you and bless you.

25 If you make me an altar of stone, you shall not build it of hewn stones, for if you wield your tool on it you profane it.

26 And you shall not go up by steps to my altar, that your nakedness be not exposed on it.'

Exodus 21

English Standard Version

Laws About Slaves

1 "Now these are the rules that you shall set before them.

2 When you buy a Hebrew slave, he shall serve six years, and in the seventh he shall go out free, for nothing.

3 If he comes in single, he shall go out single; if he comes in married, then his wife shall go out with him.

4 If his master gives him a wife and she bears him sons or daughters, the wife and her children shall be her master's, and he shall go out alone.

5 But if the slave plainly says, 'I love my master, my wife, and my children; I will not go out free,'

6 then his master shall bring him to God, and he shall bring him to the door or the doorpost. And his master shall bore his ear through with an awl, and he shall be his slave forever.

7 "When a man sells his daughter as a slave, she shall not go out as the male slaves do.

8 If she does not please her master, who has designated her for himself, then he shall let her be redeemed. He shall have no right to sell her to a foreign people, since he has broken faith with her.

9 If he designates her for his son, he shall deal with her as with a daughter.

10 If he takes another wife to himself, he shall not diminish her food, her clothing, or her marital rights.

11 And if he does not do these three things for her, she shall go out for nothing, without payment of money.

12 "Whoever strikes a man so that he dies shall be put to death.

13 But if he did not lie in wait for him, but God let him fall into his hand, then I will appoint for you a place to which he may flee.

14 But if a man willfully attacks another to kill him by cunning, you shall take him from my altar, that he may die.

15 "Whoever strikes his father or his mother shall be put to death.

16 "Whoever steals a man and sells him, and anyone found in possession of him, shall be put to death.

17 "Whoever curses his father or his mother shall be put to death.

18 "When men quarrel and one strikes the other with a stone or with his fist and the man does not die but takes to his bed,

19 then if the man rises again and walks outdoors with his staff, he who struck him shall be clear; only he shall pay for the loss of his time, and shall have him thoroughly healed.

20 "When a man strikes his slave, male or female, with a rod and the slave dies under his hand, he shall be avenged.

21 But if the slave survives a day or two, he is not to be avenged, for the slave is his money.

22 "When men strive together and hit a pregnant woman, so that her children come out, but there is no harm, the one who hit her shall surely be fined, as the woman's husband shall impose on him, and he shall pay as the judges determine.

23 But if there is harm, then you shall pay life for life,

24 eye for eye, tooth for tooth, hand for hand, foot for foot,

25 burn for burn, wound for wound, stripe for stripe.

26 "When a man strikes the eye of his slave, male or female, and destroys it, he shall let the slave go free because of his eye.

27 If he knocks out the tooth of his slave, male or female, he shall let the slave go free because of his tooth.

28 "When an ox gores a man or a woman to death, the ox shall be stoned, and its flesh shall not be eaten, but the owner of the ox shall not be liable.

29 But if the ox has been accustomed to gore in the past, and its owner has been warned but has not kept it in, and it kills a man or a woman, the ox shall be stoned, and its owner also shall be put to death.

30 If a ransom is imposed on him, then he shall give for the redemption of his life whatever is imposed on him.

31 If it gores a man's son or daughter, he shall be dealt with according to this same rule.

32 If the ox gores a slave, male or female, the owner shall give to their master thirty shekels of silver, and the ox shall be stoned.

Laws About Restitution

33 "When a man opens a pit, or when a man digs a pit and does not cover it, and an ox or a donkey falls into it,

34 the owner of the pit shall make restoration. He shall give money to its owner, and the dead beast shall be his.

35 "When one man's ox butts another's, so that it dies, then they shall sell the live ox and share its price, and the dead beast also they shall share.

36 Or if it is known that the ox has been accustomed to gore in the past, and its owner has not kept it in, he shall repay ox for ox, and the dead beast shall be his.

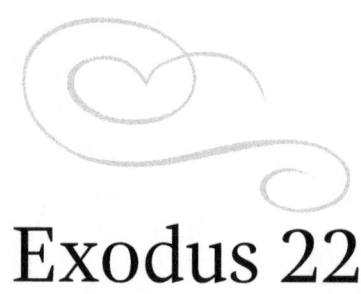

Exodus 22

English Standard Version

22 "If a man steals an ox or a sheep, and kills it or sells it, he shall repay five oxen for an ox, and four sheep for a sheep.

2 If a thief is found breaking in and is struck so that he dies, there shall be no bloodguilt for him,

3 but if the sun has risen on him, there shall be bloodguilt for him. He shall surely pay. If he has nothing, then he shall be sold for his theft.

4 If the stolen beast is found alive in his possession, whether it is an ox or a donkey or a sheep, he shall pay double.

5 "If a man causes a field or vineyard to be grazed over, or lets his beast loose and it feeds in another man's field, he shall make restitution from the best in his own field and in his own vineyard.

6 "If fire breaks out and catches in thorns so that the stacked grain or the standing grain or the field is consumed, he who started the fire shall make full restitution.

7 "If a man gives to his neighbor money or goods to keep safe, and it is stolen from the man's house, then, if the thief is found, he shall pay double.

8 If the thief is not found, the owner of the house shall come near to God to show whether or not he has put his hand to his neighbor's property.

9 For every breach of trust, whether it is for an ox, for a donkey, for a sheep, for a cloak, or for any kind of lost thing, of which one says, 'This is it,' the case of both parties shall come before God. The one whom God condemns shall pay double to his neighbor.

10 "If a man gives to his neighbor a donkey or an ox or a sheep or any beast to keep safe, and it dies or is injured or is driven away, without anyone seeing it,

11 an oath by the Lord shall be between them both to see whether or not he has put his hand to his neighbor's property. The owner shall accept the oath, and he shall not make restitution.

12 But if it is stolen from him, he shall make restitution to its owner.

13 If it is torn by beasts, let him bring it as evidence. He shall not make restitution for what has been torn.

14 "If a man borrows anything of his neighbor, and it is injured or dies, the owner not being with it, he shall make full restitution.

15 If the owner was with it, he shall not make restitution; if it was hired, it came for its hiring fee.

Laws About Social Justice

16 "If a man seduces a virgin who is not betrothed and lies with her, he shall give the bride-price for her and make her his wife.

17 If her father utterly refuses to give her to him, he shall pay money equal to the bride-price for virgins.

18 "You shall not permit a sorceress to live.

19 "Whoever lies with an animal shall be put to death.

20 "Whoever sacrifices to any god, other than the Lord alone, shall be devoted to destruction.

21 "You shall not wrong a sojourner or oppress him, for you were sojourners in the land of Egypt.

22 You shall not mistreat any widow or fatherless child.

23 If you do mistreat them, and they cry out to me, I will surely hear their cry,

24 and my wrath will burn, and I will kill you with the sword, and your wives shall become widows and your children fatherless.

25 "If you lend money to any of my people with you who is poor, you shall not be like a moneylender to him, and you shall not exact interest from him.

26 If ever you take your neighbor's cloak in pledge, you shall return it to him before the sun goes down,

27 for that is his only covering, and it is his cloak for his body; in what else shall he sleep? And if he cries to me, I will hear, for I am compassionate.

28 "You shall not revile God, nor curse a ruler of your people.

29 "You shall not delay to offer from the fullness of your harvest and from the outflow of your presses. The firstborn of your sons you shall give to me.

30 You shall do the same with your oxen and with your sheep: seven days it shall be with its mother; on the eighth day you shall give it to me.

31 "You shall be consecrated to me. Therefore you shall not eat any flesh that is torn by beasts in the field; you shall throw it to the dogs.

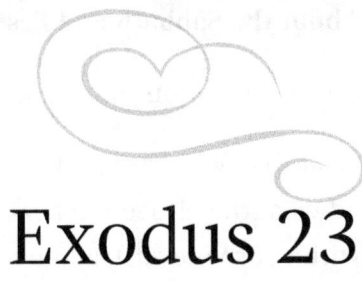

Exodus 23

English Standard Version

1 "You shall not spread a false report. You shall not join hands with a wicked man to be a malicious witness.

2 You shall not fall in with the many to do evil, nor shall you bear witness in a lawsuit, siding with the many, so as to pervert justice,

3 nor shall you be partial to a poor man in his lawsuit.

4 "If you meet your enemy's ox or his donkey going astray, you shall bring it back to him.

5 If you see the donkey of one who hates you lying down under its burden, you shall refrain from leaving him with it; you shall rescue it with him.

6 "You shall not pervert the justice due to your poor in his lawsuit.

7 Keep far from a false charge, and do not kill the innocent and righteous, for I will not acquit the wicked.

8 And you shall take no bribe, for a bribe blinds the clear-sighted and subverts the cause of those who are in the right.

9 "You shall not oppress a sojourner. You know the heart of a sojourner, for you were sojourners in the land of Egypt.

Laws About the Sabbath and Festivals

10 "For six years you shall sow your land and gather in its yield,

11 but the seventh year you shall let it rest and lie fallow, that the poor of your people may eat; and what they leave the beasts of the field may eat. You shall do likewise with your vineyard, and with your olive orchard.

12 "Six days you shall do your work, but on the seventh day you shall rest; that your ox and your donkey may have rest, and the son of your servant woman, and the alien, may be refreshed.

13 "Pay attention to all that I have said to you, and make no mention of the names of other gods, nor let it be heard on your lips.

14 "Three times in the year you shall keep a feast to me.

15 You shall keep the Feast of Unleavened Bread. As I commanded you, you shall eat unleavened bread for seven days at the appointed time in the month of Abib, for in it you came out of Egypt. None shall appear before me empty-handed.

16 You shall keep the Feast of Harvest, of the firstfruits of your labor, of what you sow in the field. You shall keep the Feast of Ingathering at the end of the year, when you gather in from the field the fruit of your labor.

17 Three times in the year shall all your males appear before the Lord God.

18 "You shall not offer the blood of my sacrifice with anything leavened, or let the fat of my feast remain until the morning.

19 "The best of the firstfruits of your ground you shall bring into the house of the Lord your God. "You shall not boil a young goat in its mother's milk.

Conquest of Canaan Promised

20 "Behold, I send an angel before you to guard you on the way and to bring you to the place that I have prepared.

Exodus 23

21 Pay careful attention to him and obey his voice; do not rebel against him, for he will not pardon your transgression, for my name is in him.

22 "But if you carefully obey his voice and do all that I say, then I will be an enemy to your enemies and an adversary to your adversaries.

23 "When my angel goes before you and brings you to the Amorites and the Hittites and the Perizzites and the Canaanites, the Hivites and the Jebusites, and I blot them out,

24 you shall not bow down to their gods nor serve them, nor do as they do, but you shall utterly overthrow them and break their pillars in pieces.

25 You shall serve the Lord your God, and he will bless your bread and your water, and I will take sickness away from among you.

26 None shall miscarry or be barren in your land; I will fulfill the number of your days.

27 I will send my terror before you and will throw into confusion all the people against whom you shall come, and I will make all your enemies turn their backs to you.

28 And I will send hornets before you, which shall drive out the Hivites, the Canaanites, and the Hittites from before you.

29 I will not drive them out from before you in one year, lest the land become desolate and the wild beasts multiply against you.

30 Little by little I will drive them out from before you, until you have increased and possess the land.

31 And I will set your border from the Red Sea to the Sea of the Philistines, and from the wilderness to the Euphrates, for I will give the inhabitants of the land into your hand, and you shall drive them out before you.

32 You shall make no covenant with them and their gods.

33 They shall not dwell in your land, lest they make you sin against me; for if you serve their gods, it will surely be a snare to you."

Exodus 24

English Standard Version

The Covenant Confirmed

1 Then he said to Moses, "Come up to the Lord, you and Aaron, Nadab, and Abihu, and seventy of the elders of Israel, and worship from afar.

2 Moses alone shall come near to the Lord, but the others shall not come near, and the people shall not come up with him."

3 Moses came and told the people all the words of the Lord and all the rules. And all the people answered with one voice and said, "All the words that the Lord has spoken we will do."

4 And Moses wrote down all the words of the Lord. He rose early in the morning and built an altar at the foot of the mountain, and twelve pillars, according to the twelve tribes of Israel.

5 And he sent young men of the people of Israel, who offered burnt offerings and sacrificed peace offerings of oxen to the Lord.

6 And Moses took half of the blood and put it in basins, and half of the blood he threw against the altar.

7 Then he took the Book of the Covenant and read it in the hearing of the people. And they said, "All that the Lord has spoken we will do, and we will

be obedient." 8 And Moses took the blood and threw it on the people and said, "Behold the blood of the covenant that the Lord has made with you in accordance with all these words."

9 Then Moses and Aaron, Nadab, and Abihu, and seventy of the elders of Israel went up,

10 and they saw the God of Israel. There was under his feet as it were a pavement of sapphire stone, like the very heaven for clearness.

11 And he did not lay his hand on the chief men of the people of Israel; they beheld God, and ate and drank.

12 The Lord said to Moses, "Come up to me on the mountain and wait there, that I may give you the tablets of stone, with the law and the commandment, which I have written for their instruction."

13 So Moses rose with his assistant Joshua, and Moses went up into the mountain of God.

14 And he said to the elders, "Wait here for us until we return to you. And behold, Aaron and Hur are with you. Whoever has a dispute, let him go to them."

15 Then Moses went up on the mountain, and the cloud covered the mountain.

16 The glory of the Lord dwelt on Mount Sinai, and the cloud covered it six days. And on the seventh day he called to Moses out of the midst of the cloud.

17 Now the appearance of the glory of the Lord was like a devouring fire on the top of the mountain in the sight of the people of Israel.

18 Moses entered the cloud and went up on the mountain. And Moses was on the mountain forty days and forty nights.

Exodus 25

English Standard Version

Contributions for the Sanctuary

1 The Lord said to Moses,

2 "Speak to the people of Israel, that they take for me a contribution. From every man whose heart moves him you shall receive the contribution for me.

3 And this is the contribution that you shall receive from them: gold, silver, and bronze,

4 blue and purple and scarlet yarns and fine twined linen, goats' hair,

5 tanned rams' skins, goatskins, acacia wood,

6 oil for the lamps, spices for the anointing oil and for the fragrant incense,

7 onyx stones, and stones for setting, for the ephod and for the breastpiece.

8 And let them make me a sanctuary, that I may dwell in their midst.

9 Exactly as I show you concerning the pattern of the tabernacle, and of all its furniture, so you shall make it.

The Ark of the Covenant

10 "They shall make an ark of acacia wood. Two cubits and a half shall be its length, a cubit and a half its breadth, and a cubit and a half its height.

11 You shall overlay it with pure gold, inside and outside shall you overlay it, and you shall make on it a molding of gold around it.

12 You shall cast four rings of gold for it and put them on its four feet, two rings on the one side of it, and two rings on the other side of it.

13 You shall make poles of acacia wood and overlay them with gold.

14 And you shall put the poles into the rings on the sides of the ark to carry the ark by them.

15 The poles shall remain in the rings of the ark; they shall not be taken from it.

16 And you shall put into the ark the testimony that I shall give you.

17 "You shall make a mercy seat of pure gold. Two cubits and a half shall be its length, and a cubit and a half its breadth.

18 And you shall make two cherubim of gold; of hammered work shall you make them, on the two ends of the mercy seat.

19 Make one cherub on the one end, and one cherub on the other end. Of one piece with the mercy seat shall you make the cherubim on its two ends.

20 The cherubim shall spread out their wings above, overshadowing the mercy seat with their wings, their faces one to another; toward the mercy seat shall the faces of the cherubim be.

21 And you shall put the mercy seat on the top of the ark, and in the ark you shall put the testimony that I shall give you.

22 There I will meet with you, and from above the mercy seat, from between the two cherubim that are on the ark of the testimony, I will speak with you about all that I will give you in commandment for the people of Israel.

The Table for Bread

23 "You shall make a table of acacia wood. Two cubits shall be its length, a cubit its breadth, and a cubit and a half its height.

24 You shall overlay it with pure gold and make a molding of gold around it.

25 And you shall make a rim around it a handbreadth wide, and a molding of gold around the rim. 26 And you shall make for it four rings of gold, and fasten the rings to the four corners at its four legs.

27 Close to the frame the rings shall lie, as holders for the poles to carry the table.

28 You shall make the poles of acacia wood, and overlay them with gold, and the table shall be carried with these.

29 And you shall make its plates and dishes for incense, and its flagons and bowls with which to pour drink offerings; you shall make them of pure gold. 30 And you shall set the bread of the Presence on the table before me regularly.

The Golden Lampstand

31 "You shall make a lampstand of pure gold. The lampstand shall be made of hammered work: its base, its stem, its cups, its calyxes, and its flowers shall be of one piece with it.

32 And there shall be six branches going out of its sides, three branches of the lampstand out of one side of it and three branches of the lampstand out of the other side of it;

33 three cups made like almond blossoms, each with calyx and flower, on one branch, and three cups made like almond blossoms, each with calyx and flower, on the other branch—so for the six branches going out of the lampstand.

34 And on the lampstand itself there shall be four cups made like almond blossoms, with their calyxes and flowers,

35 and a calyx of one piece with it under each pair of the six branches going out from the lampstand.

36 Their calyxes and their branches shall be of one piece with it, the whole of it a single piece of hammered work of pure gold.

37 You shall make seven lamps for it. And the lamps shall be set up so as to give light on the space in front of it.

38 Its tongs and their trays shall be of pure gold.

39 It shall be made, with all these utensils, out of a talent of pure gold.

40 And see that you make them after the pattern for them, which is being shown you on the mountain.

Exodus 26

English Standard Version

The Tabernacle

1 "Moreover, you shall make the tabernacle with ten curtains of fine twined linen and blue and purple and scarlet yarns; you shall make them with cherubim skillfully worked into them.

2 The length of each curtain shall be twenty-eight cubits, and the breadth of each curtain four cubits; all the curtains shall be the same size.

3 Five curtains shall be coupled to one another, and the other five curtains shall be coupled to one another.

4 And you shall make loops of blue on the edge of the outermost curtain in the first set. Likewise you shall make loops on the edge of the outermost curtain in the second set.

5 Fifty loops you shall make on the one curtain, and fifty loops you shall make on the edge of the curtain that is in the second set; the loops shall be opposite one another.

6 And you shall make fifty clasps of gold, and couple the curtains one to the other with the clasps, so that the tabernacle may be a single whole.

7 "You shall also make curtains of goats' hair for a tent over the tabernacle; eleven curtains shall you make.

8 The length of each curtain shall be thirty cubits, and the breadth of each curtain four cubits. The eleven curtains shall be the same size.

9 You shall couple five curtains by themselves, and six curtains by themselves, and the sixth curtain you shall double over at the front of the tent.

10 You shall make fifty loops on the edge of the curtain that is outermost in one set, and fifty loops on the edge of the curtain that is outermost in the second set.

11 "You shall make fifty clasps of bronze, and put the clasps into the loops, and couple the tent together that it may be a single whole.

12 And the part that remains of the curtains of the tent, the half curtain that remains, shall hang over the back of the tabernacle.

13 And the extra that remains in the length of the curtains, the cubit on the one side, and the cubit on the other side, shall hang over the sides of the tabernacle, on this side and that side, to cover it.

14 And you shall make for the tent a covering of tanned rams' skins and a covering of goatskins on top.

15 "You shall make upright frames for the tabernacle of acacia wood.

16 Ten cubits shall be the length of a frame, and a cubit and a half the breadth of each frame.

17 There shall be two tenons in each frame, for fitting together. So shall you do for all the frames of the tabernacle.

18 You shall make the frames for the tabernacle: twenty frames for the south side;

19 and forty bases of silver you shall make under the twenty frames, two bases under one frame for its two tenons, and two bases under the next frame for its two tenons;

20 and for the second side of the tabernacle, on the north side twenty frames,

21 and their forty bases of silver, two bases under one frame, and two bases under the next frame.

22 And for the rear of the tabernacle westward you shall make six frames.

23 And you shall make two frames for corners of the tabernacle in the rear;

24 they shall be separate beneath, but joined at the top, at the first ring. Thus shall it be with both of them; they shall form the two corners.

25 And there shall be eight frames, with their bases of silver, sixteen bases; two bases under one frame, and two bases under another frame.

26 "You shall make bars of acacia wood, five for the frames of the one side of the tabernacle,

27 and five bars for the frames of the other side of the tabernacle, and five bars for the frames of the side of the tabernacle at the rear westward.

28 The middle bar, halfway up the frames, shall run from end to end.

29 You shall overlay the frames with gold and shall make their rings of gold for holders for the bars, and you shall overlay the bars with gold.

30 Then you shall erect the tabernacle according to the plan for it that you were shown on the mountain.

31 "And you shall make a veil of blue and purple and scarlet yarns and fine twined linen. It shall be made with cherubim skillfully worked into it.

32 And you shall hang it on four pillars of acacia overlaid with gold, with hooks of gold, on four bases of silver.

33 And you shall hang the veil from the clasps, and bring the ark of the testimony in there within the veil. And the veil shall separate for you the Holy Place from the Most Holy.

34 You shall put the mercy seat on the ark of the testimony in the Most Holy Place.

35 And you shall set the table outside the veil, and the lampstand on the south side of the tabernacle opposite the table, and you shall put the table on the north side.

36 "You shall make a screen for the entrance of the tent, of blue and purple and scarlet yarns and fine twined linen, embroidered with needlework.

37 And you shall make for the screen five pillars of acacia, and overlay them with gold. Their hooks shall be of gold, and you shall cast five bases of bronze for them.

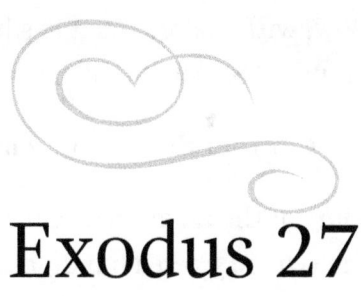

Exodus 27

English Standard Version

The Bronze Altar

1 "You shall make the altar of acacia wood, five cubits long and five cubits broad. The altar shall be square, and its height shall be three cubits.

2 And you shall make horns for it on its four corners; its horns shall be of one piece with it, and you shall overlay it with bronze.

3 You shall make pots for it to receive its ashes, and shovels and basins and forks and fire pans. You shall make all its utensils of bronze.

4 You shall also make for it a grating, a network of bronze, and on the net you shall make four bronze rings at its four corners.

5 And you shall set it under the ledge of the altar so that the net extends halfway down the altar.

6 And you shall make poles for the altar, poles of acacia wood, and overlay them with bronze.

7 And the poles shall be put through the rings, so that the poles are on the two sides of the altar when it is carried.

8 You shall make it hollow, with boards. As it has been shown you on the mountain, so shall it be made.

The Court of the Tabernacle

9 "You shall make the court of the tabernacle. On the south side the court shall have hangings of fine twined linen a hundred cubits long for one side.

10 Its twenty pillars and their twenty bases shall be of bronze, but the hooks of the pillars and their fillets shall be of silver.

11 And likewise for its length on the north side there shall be hangings a hundred cubits long, its pillars twenty and their bases twenty, of bronze, but the hooks of the pillars and their fillets shall be of silver.

12 And for the breadth of the court on the west side there shall be hangings for fifty cubits, with ten pillars and ten bases.

13 The breadth of the court on the front to the east shall be fifty cubits.

14 The hangings for the one side of the gate shall be fifteen cubits, with their three pillars and three bases.

15 On the other side the hangings shall be fifteen cubits, with their three pillars and three bases.

16 For the gate of the court there shall be a screen twenty cubits long, of blue and purple and scarlet yarns and fine twined linen, embroidered with needlework. It shall have four pillars and with them four bases.

17 All the pillars around the court shall be filleted with silver. Their hooks shall be of silver, and their bases of bronze.

18 The length of the court shall be a hundred cubits, the breadth fifty, and the height five cubits, with hangings of fine twined linen and bases of bronze.

19 All the utensils of the tabernacle for every use, and all its pegs and all the pegs of the court, shall be of bronze.

Exodus 27

Oil for the Lamp

20 "You shall command the people of Israel that they bring to you pure beaten olive oil for the light, that a lamp may regularly be set up to burn.

21 In the tent of meeting, outside the veil that is before the testimony, Aaron and his sons shall tend it from evening to morning before the Lord. It shall be a statute forever to be observed throughout their generations by the people of Israel.

Exodus 28

English Standard Version

The Priests' Garments

1 "Then bring near to you Aaron your brother, and his sons with him, from among the people of Israel, to serve me as priests—Aaron and Aaron's sons, Nadab and Abihu, Eleazar and Ithamar.

2 And you shall make holy garments for Aaron your brother, for glory and for beauty.

3 You shall speak to all the skillful, whom I have filled with a spirit of skill, that they make Aaron's garments to consecrate him for my priesthood.

4 These are the garments that they shall make: a breastpiece, an ephod, a robe, a coat of checker work, a turban, and a sash. They shall make holy garments for Aaron your brother and his sons to serve me as priests.

5 They shall receive gold, blue and purple and scarlet yarns, and fine twined linen.

6 "And they shall make the ephod of gold, of blue and purple and scarlet yarns, and of fine twined linen, skillfully worked.

7 It shall have two shoulder pieces attached to its two edges, so that it may be joined together.

8 And the skillfully woven band on it shall be made like it and be of one piece with it, of gold, blue and purple and scarlet yarns, and fine twined linen.

9 You shall take two onyx stones, and engrave on them the names of the sons of Israel,

10 six of their names on the one stone, and the names of the remaining six on the other stone, in the order of their birth.

11 As a jeweler engraves signets, so shall you engrave the two stones with the names of the sons of Israel. You shall enclose them in settings of gold filigree.

12 And you shall set the two stones on the shoulder pieces of the ephod, as stones of remembrance for the sons of Israel. And Aaron shall bear their names before the Lord on his two shoulders for remembrance.

13 You shall make settings of gold filigree,

14 and two chains of pure gold, twisted like cords; and you shall attach the corded chains to the settings.

15 "You shall make a breastpiece of judgment, in skilled work. In the style of the ephod you shall make it—of gold, blue and purple and scarlet yarns, and fine twined linen shall you make it.

16 It shall be square and doubled, a span its length and a span its breadth.

17 You shall set in it four rows of stones. A row of sardius, topaz, and carbuncle shall be the first row;

18 and the second row an emerald, a sapphire, and a diamond;

19 and the third row a jacinth, an agate, and an amethyst;

20 and the fourth row a beryl, an onyx, and a jasper. They shall be set in gold filigree.

21 There shall be twelve stones with their names according to the names of the sons of Israel. They shall be like signets, each engraved with its name, for the twelve tribes.

22 You shall make for the breastpiece twisted chains like cords, of pure gold.

23 And you shall make for the breastpiece two rings of gold, and put the two rings on the two edges of the breastpiece.

24 And you shall put the two cords of gold in the two rings at the edges of the breastpiece.

25 The two ends of the two cords you shall attach to the two settings of filigree, and so attach it in front to the shoulder pieces of the ephod.

26 You shall make two rings of gold, and put them at the two ends of the breastpiece, on its inside edge next to the ephod.

27 And you shall make two rings of gold, and attach them in front to the lower part of the two shoulder pieces of the ephod, at its seam above the skillfully woven band of the ephod.

28 And they shall bind the breastpiece by its rings to the rings of the ephod with a lace of blue, so that it may lie on the skillfully woven band of the ephod, so that the breastpiece shall not come loose from the ephod.

29 So Aaron shall bear the names of the sons of Israel in the breastpiece of judgment on his heart, when he goes into the Holy Place, to bring them to regular remembrance before the Lord.

30 And in the breastpiece of judgment you shall put the Urim and the Thummim, and they shall be on Aaron's heart, when he goes in before the Lord. Thus Aaron shall bear the judgment of the people of Israel on his heart before the Lord regularly.

31 "You shall make the robe of the ephod all of blue.

Exodus 28

32 It shall have an opening for the head in the middle of it, with a woven binding around the opening, like the opening in a garment, so that it may not tear.

33 On its hem you shall make pomegranates of blue and purple and scarlet yarns, around its hem, with bells of gold between them,

34 a golden bell and a pomegranate, a golden bell and a pomegranate, around the hem of the robe.

35 And it shall be on Aaron when he ministers, and its sound shall be heard when he goes into the Holy Place before the Lord, and when he comes out, so that he does not die.

36 "You shall make a plate of pure gold and engrave on it, like the engraving of a signet, 'Holy to the Lord.'

37 And you shall fasten it on the turban by a cord of blue. It shall be on the front of the turban.

38 It shall be on Aaron's forehead, and Aaron shall bear any guilt from the holy things that the people of Israel consecrate as their holy gifts. It shall regularly be on his forehead, that they may be accepted before the Lord.

39 "You shall weave the coat in checker work of fine linen, and you shall make a turban of fine linen, and you shall make a sash embroidered with needlework.

40 "For Aaron's sons you shall make coats and sashes and caps. You shall make them for glory and beauty.

41 And you shall put them on Aaron your brother, and on his sons with him, and shall anoint them and ordain them and consecrate them, that they may serve me as priests.

42 You shall make for them linen undergarments to cover their naked flesh. They shall reach from the hips to the thighs;

43 and they shall be on Aaron and on his sons when they go into the tent of meeting or when they come near the altar to minister in the Holy Place, lest they bear guilt and die. This shall be a statute forever for him and for his offspring after him.

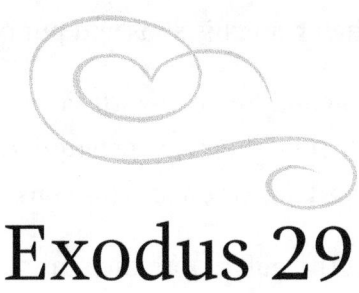

Exodus 29

English Standard Version

Consecration of the Priests

1 "Now this is what you shall do to them to consecrate them, that they may serve me as priests. Take one bull of the herd and two rams without blemish,

2 and unleavened bread, unleavened cakes mixed with oil, and unleavened wafers smeared with oil. You shall make them of fine wheat flour.

3 You shall put them in one basket and bring them in the basket, and bring the bull and the two rams.

4 You shall bring Aaron and his sons to the entrance of the tent of meeting and wash them with water.

5 Then you shall take the garments, and put on Aaron the coat and the robe of the ephod, and the ephod, and the breastpiece, and gird him with the skillfully woven band of the ephod.

6 And you shall set the turban on his head and put the holy crown on the turban.

7 You shall take the anointing oil and pour it on his head and anoint him.

8 Then you shall bring his sons and put coats on them,

9 and you shall gird Aaron and his sons with sashes and bind caps on them. And the priesthood shall be theirs by a statute forever. Thus you shall ordain Aaron and his sons.

10 "Then you shall bring the bull before the tent of meeting. Aaron and his sons shall lay their hands on the head of the bull.

11 Then you shall kill the bull before the Lord at the entrance of the tent of meeting,

12 and shall take part of the blood of the bull and put it on the horns of the altar with your finger, and the rest of the blood you shall pour out at the base of the altar.

13 And you shall take all the fat that covers the entrails, and the long lobe of the liver, and the two kidneys with the fat that is on them, and burn them on the altar.

14 But the flesh of the bull and its skin and its dung you shall burn with fire outside the camp; it is a sin offering.

15 "Then you shall take one of the rams, and Aaron and his sons shall lay their hands on the head of the ram,

16 and you shall kill the ram and shall take its blood and throw it against the sides of the altar.

17 Then you shall cut the ram into pieces, and wash its entrails and its legs, and put them with its pieces and its head,

18 and burn the whole ram on the altar. It is a burnt offering to the Lord. It is a pleasing aroma, a food offering to the Lord.

19 "You shall take the other ram, and Aaron and his sons shall lay their hands on the head of the ram,

Exodus 29

20 and you shall kill the ram and take part of its blood and put it on the tip of the right ear of Aaron and on the tips of the right ears of his sons, and on the thumbs of their right hands and on the great toes of their right feet, and throw the rest of the blood against the sides of the altar.

21 Then you shall take part of the blood that is on the altar, and of the anointing oil, and sprinkle it on Aaron and his garments, and on his sons and his sons' garments with him. He and his garments shall be holy, and his sons and his sons' garments with him.

22 "You shall also take the fat from the ram and the fat tail and the fat that covers the entrails, and the long lobe of the liver and the two kidneys with the fat that is on them, and the right thigh (for it is a ram of ordination),

23 and one loaf of bread and one cake of bread made with oil, and one wafer out of the basket of unleavened bread that is before the Lord.

24 You shall put all these on the palms of Aaron and on the palms of his sons, and wave them for a wave offering before the Lord.

25 Then you shall take them from their hands and burn them on the altar on top of the burnt offering, as a pleasing aroma before the Lord. It is a food offering to the Lord.

26 "You shall take the breast of the ram of Aaron's ordination and wave it for a wave offering before the Lord, and it shall be your portion.

27 And you shall consecrate the breast of the wave offering that is waved and the thigh of the priests' portion that is contributed from the ram of ordination, from what was Aaron's and his sons'.

28 It shall be for Aaron and his sons as a perpetual due from the people of Israel, for it is a contribution. It shall be a contribution from the people of Israel from their peace offerings, their contribution to the Lord.

29 "The holy garments of Aaron shall be for his sons after him; they shall be anointed in them and ordained in them.

30 The son who succeeds him as priest, who comes into the tent of meeting to minister in the Holy Place, shall wear them seven days.

31 "You shall take the ram of ordination and boil its flesh in a holy place.

32 And Aaron and his sons shall eat the flesh of the ram and the bread that is in the basket in the entrance of the tent of meeting.

33 They shall eat those things with which atonement was made at their ordination and consecration, but an outsider shall not eat of them, because they are holy.

34 And if any of the flesh for the ordination or of the bread remain until the morning, then you shall burn the remainder with fire. It shall not be eaten, because it is holy.

35 "Thus you shall do to Aaron and to his sons, according to all that I have commanded you. Through seven days shall you ordain them,

36 and every day you shall offer a bull as a sin offering for atonement. Also you shall purify the altar, when you make atonement for it, and shall anoint it to consecrate it.

37 Seven days you shall make atonement for the altar and consecrate it, and the altar shall be most holy. Whatever touches the altar shall become holy.

38 "Now this is what you shall offer on the altar: two lambs a year old day by day regularly.

39 One lamb you shall offer in the morning, and the other lamb you shall offer at twilight.

40 And with the first lamb a tenth measure of fine flour mingled with a fourth of a hin of beaten oil, and a fourth of a hin of wine for a drink offering.

41 The other lamb you shall offer at twilight, and shall offer with it a grain offering and its drink offering, as in the morning, for a pleasing aroma, a food offering to the Lord.

42 It shall be a regular burnt offering throughout your generations at the entrance of the tent of meeting before the Lord, where I will meet with you, to speak to you there.

43 There I will meet with the people of Israel, and it shall be sanctified by my glory.

44 I will consecrate the tent of meeting and the altar. Aaron also and his sons I will consecrate to serve me as priests.

45 I will dwell among the people of Israel and will be their God.

46 And they shall know that I am the Lord their God, who brought them out of the land of Egypt that I might dwell among them. I am the Lord their God.

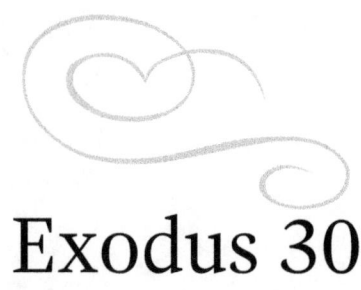

Exodus 30

English Standard Version

The Altar of Incense

1 "You shall make an altar on which to burn incense; you shall make it of acacia wood.

2 A cubit shall be its length, and a cubit its breadth. It shall be square, and two cubits shall be its height. Its horns shall be of one piece with it.

3 You shall overlay it with pure gold, its top and around its sides and its horns. And you shall make a molding of gold around it.

4 And you shall make two golden rings for it. Under its molding on two opposite sides of it you shall make them, and they shall be holders for poles with which to carry it.

5 You shall make the poles of acacia wood and overlay them with gold.

6 And you shall put it in front of the veil that is above the ark of the testimony, in front of the mercy seat that is above the testimony, where I will meet with you.

7 And Aaron shall burn fragrant incense on it. Every morning when he dresses the lamps he shall burn it,

8 and when Aaron sets up the lamps at twilight, he shall burn it, a regular incense offering before the Lord throughout your generations.

9 You shall not offer unauthorized incense on it, or a burnt offering, or a grain offering, and you shall not pour a drink offering on it.

10 Aaron shall make atonement on its horns once a year. With the blood of the sin offering of atonement he shall make atonement for it once in the year throughout your generations. It is most holy to the Lord."

The Census Tax

11 The Lord said to Moses,

12 "When you take the census of the people of Israel, then each shall give a ransom for his life to the Lord when you number them, that there be no plague among them when you number them.

13 Each one who is numbered in the census shall give this: half a shekel according to the shekel of the sanctuary (the shekel is twenty gerahs), half a shekel as an offering to the Lord.

14 Everyone who is numbered in the census, from twenty years old and upward, shall give the Lord's offering.

15 The rich shall not give more, and the poor shall not give less, than the half shekel, when you give the Lord's offering to make atonement for your lives.

16 You shall take the atonement money from the people of Israel and shall give it for the service of the tent of meeting, that it may bring the people of Israel to remembrance before the Lord, so as to make atonement for your lives."

The Bronze Basin

17 The Lord said to Moses,

18 "You shall also make a basin of bronze, with its stand of bronze, for washing. You shall put it between the tent of meeting and the altar, and you shall put water in it,

19 with which Aaron and his sons shall wash their hands and their feet.

20 When they go into the tent of meeting, or when they come near the altar to minister, to burn a food offering to the Lord, they shall wash with water, so that they may not die.

21 They shall wash their hands and their feet, so that they may not die. It shall be a statute forever to them, even to him and to his offspring throughout their generations."

The Anointing Oil and Incense

22 The Lord said to Moses,

23 "Take the finest spices: of liquid myrrh 500 shekels, and of sweet-smelling cinnamon half as much, that is, 250, and 250 of aromatic cane,

24 and 500 of cassia, according to the shekel of the sanctuary, and a hin of olive oil.

25 And you shall make of these a sacred anointing oil blended as by the perfumer; it shall be a holy anointing oil.

26 With it you shall anoint the tent of meeting and the ark of the testimony,

27 and the table and all its utensils, and the lampstand and its utensils, and the altar of incense,

28 and the altar of burnt offering with all its utensils and the basin and its stand.

29 You shall consecrate them, that they may be most holy. Whatever touches them will become holy.

Exodus 30

30 You shall anoint Aaron and his sons, and consecrate them, that they may serve me as priests.

31 And you shall say to the people of Israel, 'This shall be my holy anointing oil throughout your generations.

32 It shall not be poured on the body of an ordinary person, and you shall make no other like it in composition. It is holy, and it shall be holy to you.

33 Whoever compounds any like it or whoever puts any of it on an outsider shall be cut off from his people.'"

34 The Lord said to Moses, "Take sweet spices, stacte, and onycha, and galbanum, sweet spices with pure frankincense (of each shall there be an equal part),

35 and make an incense blended as by the perfumer, seasoned with salt, pure and holy.

36 You shall beat some of it very small, and put part of it before the testimony in the tent of meeting where I shall meet with you. It shall be most holy for you.

37 And the incense that you shall make according to its composition, you shall not make for yourselves. It shall be for you holy to the Lord.

38 Whoever makes any like it to use as perfume shall be cut off from his people."

Exodus 31

English Standard Version

Oholiab and Bezalel

1 The Lord said to Moses,

2 "See, I have called by name Bezalel the son of Uri, son of Hur, of the tribe of Judah,

3 and I have filled him with the Spirit of God, with ability and intelligence, with knowledge and all craftsmanship,

4 to devise artistic designs, to work in gold, silver, and bronze,

5 in cutting stones for setting, and in carving wood, to work in every craft.

6 And behold, I have appointed with him Oholiab, the son of Ahisamach, of the tribe of Dan. And I have given to all able men ability, that they may make all that I have commanded you:

7 the tent of meeting, and the ark of the testimony, and the mercy seat that is on it, and all the furnishings of the tent,

8 the table and its utensils, and the pure lampstand with all its utensils, and the altar of incense,

9 and the altar of burnt offering with all its utensils, and the basin and its stand,

10 and the finely worked garments, the holy garments for Aaron the priest and the garments of his sons, for their service as priests,

11 and the anointing oil and the fragrant incense for the Holy Place. According to all that I have commanded you, they shall do."

The Sabbath

12 And the Lord said to Moses,

13 "You are to speak to the people of Israel and say, 'Above all you shall keep my Sabbaths, for this is a sign between me and you throughout your generations, that you may know that I, the Lord, sanctify you.

14 You shall keep the Sabbath, because it is holy for you. Everyone who profanes it shall be put to death. Whoever does any work on it, that soul shall be cut off from among his people.

15 Six days shall work be done, but the seventh day is a Sabbath of solemn rest, holy to the Lord. Whoever does any work on the Sabbath day shall be put to death.

16 Therefore the people of Israel shall keep the Sabbath, observing the Sabbath throughout their generations, as a covenant forever.

17 It is a sign forever between me and the people of Israel that in six days the Lord made heaven and earth, and on the seventh day he rested and was refreshed.'"

18 And he gave to Moses, when he had finished speaking with him on Mount Sinai, the two tablets of the testimony, tablets of stone, written with the finger of God.

Exodus 32

English Standard Version

The Golden Calf

1 When the people saw that Moses delayed to come down from the mountain, the people gathered themselves together to Aaron and said to him, "Up, make us gods who shall go before us. As for this Moses, the man who brought us up out of the land of Egypt, we do not know what has become of him."

2 So Aaron said to them, "Take off the rings of gold that are in the ears of your wives, your sons, and your daughters, and bring them to me."

3 So all the people took off the rings of gold that were in their ears and brought them to Aaron.

4 And he received the gold from their hand and fashioned it with a graving tool and made a golden calf. And they said, "These are your gods, O Israel, who brought you up out of the land of Egypt!"

5 When Aaron saw this, he built an altar before it. And Aaron made a proclamation and said, "Tomorrow shall be a feast to the Lord."

Exodus 32

6 And they rose up early the next day and offered burnt offerings and brought peace offerings. And the people sat down to eat and drink and rose up to play.

7 And the Lord said to Moses, "Go down, for your people, whom you brought up out of the land of Egypt, have corrupted themselves.

8 They have turned aside quickly out of the way that I commanded them. They have made for themselves a golden calf and have worshiped it and sacrificed to it and said, 'These are your gods, O Israel, who brought you up out of the land of Egypt!'"

9 And the Lord said to Moses, "I have seen this people, and behold, it is a stiff-necked people.

10 Now therefore let me alone, that my wrath may burn hot against them and I may consume them, in order that I may make a great nation of you."

11 But Moses implored the Lord his God and said, "O Lord, why does your wrath burn hot against your people, whom you have brought out of the land of Egypt with great power and with a mighty hand?

12 Why should the Egyptians say, 'With evil intent did he bring them out, to kill them in the mountains and to consume them from the face of the earth'? Turn from your burning anger and relent from this disaster against your people.

13 Remember Abraham, Isaac, and Israel, your servants, to whom you swore by your own self, and said to them, 'I will multiply your offspring as the stars of heaven, and all this land that I have promised I will give to your offspring, and they shall inherit it forever.'"

14 And the Lord relented from the disaster that he had spoken of bringing on his people.

15 Then Moses turned and went down from the mountain with the two tablets of the testimony in his hand, tablets that were written on both sides; on the front and on the back they were written.

16 The tablets were the work of God, and the writing was the writing of God, engraved on the tablets.

17 When Joshua heard the noise of the people as they shouted, he said to Moses, "There is a noise of war in the camp."

18 But he said, "It is not the sound of shouting for victory, or the sound of the cry of defeat, but the sound of singing that I hear."

19 And as soon as he came near the camp and saw the calf and the dancing, Moses' anger burned hot, and he threw the tablets out of his hands and broke them at the foot of the mountain.

20 He took the calf that they had made and burned it with fire and ground it to powder and scattered it on the water and made the people of Israel drink it.

21 And Moses said to Aaron, "What did this people do to you that you have brought such a great sin upon them?"

22 And Aaron said, "Let not the anger of my lord burn hot. You know the people, that they are set on evil.

23 For they said to me, 'Make us gods who shall go before us. As for this Moses, the man who brought us up out of the land of Egypt, we do not know what has become of him.'

24 So I said to them, 'Let any who have gold take it off.' So they gave it to me, and I threw it into the fire, and out came this calf."

25 And when Moses saw that the people had broken loose (for Aaron had let them break loose, to the derision of their enemies),

26 then Moses stood in the gate of the camp and said, "Who is on the Lord's side? Come to me." And all the sons of Levi gathered around him.

27 And he said to them, "Thus says the Lord God of Israel, 'Put your sword on your side each of you, and go to and fro from gate to gate throughout the camp, and each of you kill his brother and his companion and his neighbor.'"

28 And the sons of Levi did according to the word of Moses. And that day about three thousand men of the people fell.

29 And Moses said, "Today you have been ordained for the service of the Lord, each one at the cost of his son and of his brother, so that he might bestow a blessing upon you this day."

30 The next day Moses said to the people, "You have sinned a great sin. And now I will go up to the Lord; perhaps I can make atonement for your sin."

31 So Moses returned to the Lord and said, "Alas, this people has sinned a great sin. They have made for themselves gods of gold.

32 But now, if you will forgive their sin—but if not, please blot me out of your book that you have written."

33 But the Lord said to Moses, "Whoever has sinned against me, I will blot out of my book.

34 But now go, lead the people to the place about which I have spoken to you; behold, my angel shall go before you. Nevertheless, in the day when I visit, I will visit their sin upon them."

35 Then the Lord sent a plague on the people, because they made the calf, the one that Aaron made.

Exodus 33

English Standard Version

The Command to Leave Sinai

1 The Lord said to Moses, "Depart; go up from here, you and the people whom you have brought up out of the land of Egypt, to the land of which I swore to Abraham, Isaac, and Jacob, saying, 'To your offspring I will give it.'

2 I will send an angel before you, and I will drive out the Canaanites, the Amorites, the Hittites, the Perizzites, the Hivites, and the Jebusites.

3 Go up to a land flowing with milk and honey; but I will not go up among you, lest I consume you on the way, for you are a stiff-necked people."

4 When the people heard this disastrous word, they mourned, and no one put on his ornaments.

5 For the Lord had said to Moses, "Say to the people of Israel, 'You are a stiff-necked people; if for a single moment I should go up among you, I would consume you. So now take off your ornaments, that I may know what to do with you.'"

6 Therefore the people of Israel stripped themselves of their ornaments, from Mount Horeb onward.

The Tent of Meeting

7 Now Moses used to take the tent and pitch it outside the camp, far off from the camp, and he called it the tent of meeting. And everyone who sought the Lord would go out to the tent of meeting, which was outside the camp.

8 Whenever Moses went out to the tent, all the people would rise up, and each would stand at his tent door, and watch Moses until he had gone into the tent.

9 When Moses entered the tent, the pillar of cloud would descend and stand at the entrance of the tent, and the Lord would speak with Moses.

10 And when all the people saw the pillar of cloud standing at the entrance of the tent, all the people would rise up and worship, each at his tent door.

11 Thus the Lord used to speak to Moses face to face, as a man speaks to his friend. When Moses turned again into the camp, his assistant Joshua the son of Nun, a young man, would not depart from the tent.

Moses' Intercession

12 Moses said to the Lord, "See, you say to me, 'Bring up this people,' but you have not let me know whom you will send with me. Yet you have said, 'I know you by name, and you have also found favor in my sight.'

13 Now therefore, if I have found favor in your sight, please show me now your ways, that I may know you in order to find favor in your sight. Consider too that this nation is your people."

14 And he said, "My presence will go with you, and I will give you rest."

15 And he said to him, "If your presence will not go with me, do not bring us up from here.

16 For how shall it be known that I have found favor in your sight, I and your people? Is it not in your going with us, so that we are distinct, I and your people, from every other people on the face of the earth?"

17 And the Lord said to Moses, "This very thing that you have spoken I will do, for you have found favor in my sight, and I know you by name."

18 Moses said, "Please show me your glory."

19 And he said, "I will make all my goodness pass before you and will proclaim before you my name 'The Lord.' And I will be gracious to whom I will be gracious, and will show mercy on whom I will show mercy.

20 But," he said, "you cannot see my face, for man shall not see me and live."

21 And the Lord said, "Behold, there is a place by me where you shall stand on the rock,

22 and while my glory passes by I will put you in a cleft of the rock, and I will cover you with my hand until I have passed by.

23 Then I will take away my hand, and you shall see my back, but my face shall not be seen."

Exodus 34

English Standard Version

Moses Makes New Tablets

1 The Lord said to Moses, "Cut for yourself two tablets of stone like the first, and I will write on the tablets the words that were on the first tablets, which you broke.

2 Be ready by the morning, and come up in the morning to Mount Sinai, and present yourself there to me on the top of the mountain.

3 No one shall come up with you, and let no one be seen throughout all the mountain. Let no flocks or herds graze opposite that mountain."

4 So Moses cut two tablets of stone like the first. And he rose early in the morning and went up on Mount Sinai, as the Lord had commanded him, and took in his hand two tablets of stone.

5 The Lord descended in the cloud and stood with him there, and proclaimed the name of the Lord.

6 The Lord passed before him and proclaimed, "The Lord, the Lord, a God merciful and gracious, slow to anger, and abounding in steadfast love and faithfulness,

7 keeping steadfast love for thousands, forgiving iniquity and transgression and sin, but who will by no means clear the guilty, visiting the iniquity of the fathers on the children and the children's children, to the third and the fourth generation."

8 And Moses quickly bowed his head toward the earth and worshiped.

9 And he said, "If now I have found favor in your sight, O Lord, please let the Lord go in the midst of us, for it is a stiff-necked people, and pardon our iniquity and our sin, and take us for your inheritance."

The Covenant Renewed

10 And he said, "Behold, I am making a covenant. Before all your people I will do marvels, such as have not been created in all the earth or in any nation. And all the people among whom you are shall see the work of the Lord, for it is an awesome thing that I will do with you.

11 "Observe what I command you this day. Behold, I will drive out before you the Amorites, the Canaanites, the Hittites, the Perizzites, the Hivites, and the Jebusites.

12 Take care, lest you make a covenant with the inhabitants of the land to which you go, lest it become a snare in your midst.

13 You shall tear down their altars and break their pillars and cut down their Asherim

14 (for you shall worship no other god, for the Lord, whose name is Jealous, is a jealous God),

15 lest you make a covenant with the inhabitants of the land, and when they whore after their gods and sacrifice to their gods and you are invited, you eat of his sacrifice,

16 and you take of their daughters for your sons, and their daughters whore after their gods and make your sons whore after their gods.

17 "You shall not make for yourself any gods of cast metal.

18 "You shall keep the Feast of Unleavened Bread. Seven days you shall eat unleavened bread, as I commanded you, at the time appointed in the month Abib, for in the month Abib you came out from Egypt.

19 All that open the womb are mine, all your male livestock, the firstborn of cow and sheep.

20 The firstborn of a donkey you shall redeem with a lamb, or if you will not redeem it you shall break its neck. All the firstborn of your sons you shall redeem. And none shall appear before me empty-handed.

21 "Six days you shall work, but on the seventh day you shall rest. In plowing time and in harvest you shall rest.

22 You shall observe the Feast of Weeks, the firstfruits of wheat harvest, and the Feast of Ingathering at the year's end.

23 Three times in the year shall all your males appear before the Lord God, the God of Israel.

24 For I will cast out nations before you and enlarge your borders; no one shall covet your land, when you go up to appear before the Lord your God three times in the year.

25 "You shall not offer the blood of my sacrifice with anything leavened, or let the sacrifice of the Feast of the Passover remain until the morning.

26 The best of the firstfruits of your ground you shall bring to the house of the Lord your God. You shall not boil a young goat in its mother's milk."

27 And the Lord said to Moses, "Write these words, for in accordance with these words I have made a covenant with you and with Israel."

28 So he was there with the Lord forty days and forty nights. He neither ate bread nor drank water. And he wrote on the tablets the words of the covenant, the Ten Commandments.

Pearls of Wisdom

The Shining Face of Moses

29 When Moses came down from Mount Sinai, with the two tablets of the testimony in his hand as he came down from the mountain, Moses did not know that the skin of his face shone because he had been talking with God.

30 Aaron and all the people of Israel saw Moses, and behold, the skin of his face shone, and they were afraid to come near him.

31 But Moses called to them, and Aaron and all the leaders of the congregation returned to him, and Moses talked with them.

32 Afterward all the people of Israel came near, and he commanded them all that the Lord had spoken with him in Mount Sinai.

33 And when Moses had finished speaking with them, he put a veil over his face.

34 Whenever Moses went in before the Lord to speak with him, he would remove the veil, until he came out. And when he came out and told the people of Israel what he was commanded,

35 the people of Israel would see the face of Moses, that the skin of Moses' face was shining. And Moses would put the veil over his face again, until he went in to speak with him.

Exodus 35

English Standard Version

Sabbath Regulations

1 Moses assembled all the congregation of the people of Israel and said to them, "These are the things that the Lord has commanded you to do.

2 Six days work shall be done, but on the seventh day you shall have a Sabbath of solemn rest, holy to the Lord. Whoever does any work on it shall be put to death.

3 You shall kindle no fire in all your dwelling places on the Sabbath day."

Contributions for the Tabernacle

4 Moses said to all the congregation of the people of Israel, "This is the thing that the Lord has commanded.

5 Take from among you a contribution to the Lord. Whoever is of a generous heart, let him bring the Lord's contribution: gold, silver, and bronze;

6 blue and purple and scarlet yarns and fine twined linen; goats' hair,

7 tanned rams' skins, and goatskins; acacia wood,

8 oil for the light, spices for the anointing oil and for the fragrant incense,

9 and onyx stones and stones for setting, for the ephod and for the breastpiece.

10 "Let every skillful craftsman among you come and make all that the Lord has commanded:

11 the tabernacle, its tent and its covering, its hooks and its frames, its bars, its pillars, and its bases;

12 the ark with its poles, the mercy seat, and the veil of the screen;

13 the table with its poles and all its utensils, and the bread of the Presence;

14 the lampstand also for the light, with its utensils and its lamps, and the oil for the light;

15 and the altar of incense, with its poles, and the anointing oil and the fragrant incense, and the screen for the door, at the door of the tabernacle;

16 the altar of burnt offering, with its grating of bronze, its poles, and all its utensils, the basin and its stand;

17 the hangings of the court, its pillars and its bases, and the screen for the gate of the court;

18 the pegs of the tabernacle and the pegs of the court, and their cords;

19 the finely worked garments for ministering in the Holy Place, the holy garments for Aaron the priest, and the garments of his sons, for their service as priests."

20 Then all the congregation of the people of Israel departed from the presence of Moses.

21 And they came, everyone whose heart stirred him, and everyone whose spirit moved him, and brought the Lord's contribution to be used for the tent of meeting, and for all its service, and for the holy garments.

Exodus 35

22 So they came, both men and women. All who were of a willing heart brought brooches and earrings and signet rings and armlets, all sorts of gold objects, every man dedicating an offering of gold to the Lord.

23 And every one who possessed blue or purple or scarlet yarns or fine linen or goats' hair or tanned rams' skins or goatskins brought them.

24 Everyone who could make a contribution of silver or bronze brought it as the Lord's contribution. And every one who possessed acacia wood of any use in the work brought it.

25 And every skillful woman spun with her hands, and they all brought what they had spun in blue and purple and scarlet yarns and fine twined linen.

26 All the women whose hearts stirred them to use their skill spun the goats' hair.

27 And the leaders brought onyx stones and stones to be set, for the ephod and for the breastpiece,

28 and spices and oil for the light, and for the anointing oil, and for the fragrant incense.

29 All the men and women, the people of Israel, whose heart moved them to bring anything for the work that the Lord had commanded by Moses to be done brought it as a freewill offering to the Lord.

Construction of the Tabernacle

30 Then Moses said to the people of Israel, "See, the Lord has called by name Bezalel the son of Uri, son of Hur, of the tribe of Judah;

31 and he has filled him with the Spirit of God, with skill, with intelligence, with knowledge, and with all craftsmanship,

32 to devise artistic designs, to work in gold and silver and bronze, 33 in cutting stones for setting, and in carving wood, for work in every skilled craft.

34 And he has inspired him to teach, both him and Oholiab the son of Ahisamach of the tribe of Dan.

35 He has filled them with skill to do every sort of work done by an engraver or by a designer or by an embroiderer in blue and purple and scarlet yarns and fine twined linen, or by a weaver—by any sort of workman or skilled designer.

Exodus 36

English Standard Version

1 "Bezalel and Oholiab and every craftsman in whom the Lord has put skill and intelligence to know how to do any work in the construction of the sanctuary shall work in accordance with all that the Lord has commanded."

2 And Moses called Bezalel and Oholiab and every craftsman in whose mind the Lord had put skill, everyone whose heart stirred him up to come to do the work.

3 And they received from Moses all the contribution that the people of Israel had brought for doing the work on the sanctuary. They still kept bringing him freewill offerings every morning,

4 so that all the craftsmen who were doing every sort of task on the sanctuary came, each from the task that he was doing,

5 and said to Moses, "The people bring much more than enough for doing the work that the Lord has commanded us to do."

6 So Moses gave command, and word was proclaimed throughout the camp, "Let no man or woman do anything more for the contribution for the sanctuary." So the people were restrained from bringing,

7 for the material they had was sufficient to do all the work, and more.

8 And all the craftsmen among the workmen made the tabernacle with ten curtains. They were made of fine twined linen and blue and purple and scarlet yarns, with cherubim skillfully worked.

9 The length of each curtain was twenty-eight cubits, and the breadth of each curtain four cubits. All the curtains were the same size.

10 He coupled five curtains to one another, and the other five curtains he coupled to one another.

11 He made loops of blue on the edge of the outermost curtain of the first set. Likewise he made them on the edge of the outermost curtain of the second set.

12 He made fifty loops on the one curtain, and he made fifty loops on the edge of the curtain that was in the second set. The loops were opposite one another.

13 And he made fifty clasps of gold, and coupled the curtains one to the other with clasps. So the tabernacle was a single whole.

14 He also made curtains of goats' hair for a tent over the tabernacle. He made eleven curtains.

15 The length of each curtain was thirty cubits, and the breadth of each curtain four cubits. The eleven curtains were the same size.

16 He coupled five curtains by themselves, and six curtains by themselves.

17 And he made fifty loops on the edge of the outermost curtain of the one set, and fifty loops on the edge of the other connecting curtain.

18 And he made fifty clasps of bronze to couple the tent together that it might be a single whole.

19 And he made for the tent a covering of tanned rams' skins and goatskins.

20 Then he made the upright frames for the tabernacle of acacia wood.

21 Ten cubits was the length of a frame, and a cubit and a half the breadth of each frame.

22 Each frame had two tenons for fitting together. He did this for all the frames of the tabernacle.

23 The frames for the tabernacle he made thus: twenty frames for the south side.

24 And he made forty bases of silver under the twenty frames, two bases under one frame for its two tenons, and two bases under the next frame for its two tenons.

25 For the second side of the tabernacle, on the north side, he made twenty frames

26 and their forty bases of silver, two bases under one frame and two bases under the next frame.

27 For the rear of the tabernacle westward he made six frames.

28 He made two frames for corners of the tabernacle in the rear.

29 And they were separate beneath but joined at the top, at the first ring. He made two of them this way for the two corners.

30 There were eight frames with their bases of silver: sixteen bases, under every frame two bases.

31 He made bars of acacia wood, five for the frames of the one side of the tabernacle,

32 and five bars for the frames of the other side of the tabernacle, and five bars for the frames of the tabernacle at the rear westward.

33 And he made the middle bar to run from end to end halfway up the frames.

34 And he overlaid the frames with gold, and made their rings of gold for holders for the bars, and overlaid the bars with gold.

35 He made the veil of blue and purple and scarlet yarns and fine twined linen; with cherubim skillfully worked into it he made it.

36 And for it he made four pillars of acacia and overlaid them with gold. Their hooks were of gold, and he cast for them four bases of silver.

37 He also made a screen for the entrance of the tent, of blue and purple and scarlet yarns and fine twined linen, embroidered with needlework,

38 and its five pillars with their hooks. He overlaid their capitals, and their fillets were of gold, but their five bases were of bronze.

Exodus 37

English Standard Version

Making the Ark

1 Bezalel made the ark of acacia wood. Two cubits and a half was its length, a cubit and a half its breadth, and a cubit and a half its height.

2 And he overlaid it with pure gold inside and outside, and made a molding of gold around it.

3 And he cast for it four rings of gold for its four feet, two rings on its one side and two rings on its other side.

4 And he made poles of acacia wood and overlaid them with gold

5 and put the poles into the rings on the sides of the ark to carry the ark.

6 And he made a mercy seat of pure gold. Two cubits and a half was its length, and a cubit and a half its breadth.

7 And he made two cherubim of gold. He made them of hammered work on the two ends of the mercy seat,

8 one cherub on the one end, and one cherub on the other end. Of one piece with the mercy seat he made the cherubim on its two ends.

9 The cherubim spread out their wings above, overshadowing the mercy seat with their wings, with their faces one to another; toward the mercy seat were the faces of the cherubim.

Making the Table

10 He also made the table of acacia wood. Two cubits was its length, a cubit its breadth, and a cubit and a half its height.

11 And he overlaid it with pure gold, and made a molding of gold around it.

12 And he made a rim around it a handbreadth wide, and made a molding of gold around the rim.

13 He cast for it four rings of gold and fastened the rings to the four corners at its four legs.

14 Close to the frame were the rings, as holders for the poles to carry the table.

15 He made the poles of acacia wood to carry the table, and overlaid them with gold.

16 And he made the vessels of pure gold that were to be on the table, its plates and dishes for incense, and its bowls and flagons with which to pour drink offerings.

Making the Lampstand

17 He also made the lampstand of pure gold. He made the lampstand of hammered work. Its base, its stem, its cups, its calyxes, and its flowers were of one piece with it.

18 And there were six branches going out of its sides, three branches of the lampstand out of one side of it and three branches of the lampstand out of the other side of it;

19 three cups made like almond blossoms, each with calyx and flower, on one branch, and three cups made like almond blossoms, each with calyx

Exodus 37

and flower, on the other branch—so for the six branches going out of the lampstand.

20 And on the lampstand itself were four cups made like almond blossoms, with their calyxes and flowers,

21 and a calyx of one piece with it under each pair of the six branches going out of it.

22 Their calyxes and their branches were of one piece with it. The whole of it was a single piece of hammered work of pure gold.

23 And he made its seven lamps and its tongs and its trays of pure gold.

24 He made it and all its utensils out of a talent of pure gold.

Making the Altar of Incense

25 He made the altar of incense of acacia wood. Its length was a cubit, and its breadth was a cubit. It was square, and two cubits was its height. Its horns were of one piece with it.

26 He overlaid it with pure gold, its top and around its sides and its horns. And he made a molding of gold around it,

27 and made two rings of gold on it under its molding, on two opposite sides of it, as holders for the poles with which to carry it.

28 And he made the poles of acacia wood and overlaid them with gold.

29 He made the holy anointing oil also, and the pure fragrant incense, blended as by the perfumer.

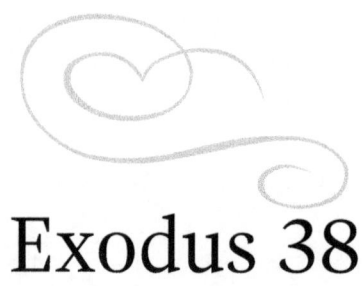

Exodus 38

English Standard Version

Making the Altar of Burnt Offering

1 He made the altar of burnt offering of acacia wood. Five cubits was its length, and five cubits its breadth. It was square, and three cubits was its height.

2 He made horns for it on its four corners. Its horns were of one piece with it, and he overlaid it with bronze.

3 And he made all the utensils of the altar, the pots, the shovels, the basins, the forks, and the fire pans. He made all its utensils of bronze.

4 And he made for the altar a grating, a network of bronze, under its ledge, extending halfway down.

5 He cast four rings on the four corners of the bronze grating as holders for the poles.

6 He made the poles of acacia wood and overlaid them with bronze.

7 And he put the poles through the rings on the sides of the altar to carry it with them. He made it hollow, with boards.

Making the Bronze Basin

8 He made the basin of bronze and its stand of bronze, from the mirrors of the ministering women who ministered in the entrance of the tent of meeting.

Making the Court

9 And he made the court. For the south side the hangings of the court were of fine twined linen, a hundred cubits;

10 their twenty pillars and their twenty bases were of bronze, but the hooks of the pillars and their fillets were of silver.

11 And for the north side there were hangings of a hundred cubits; their twenty pillars and their twenty bases were of bronze, but the hooks of the pillars and their fillets were of silver.

12 And for the west side were hangings of fifty cubits, their ten pillars, and their ten bases; the hooks of the pillars and their fillets were of silver.

13 And for the front to the east, fifty cubits.

14 The hangings for one side of the gate were fifteen cubits, with their three pillars and three bases.

15 And so for the other side. On both sides of the gate of the court were hangings of fifteen cubits, with their three pillars and their three bases.

16 All the hangings around the court were of fine twined linen.

17 And the bases for the pillars were of bronze, but the hooks of the pillars and their fillets were of silver. The overlaying of their capitals was also of silver, and all the pillars of the court were filleted with silver.

18 And the screen for the gate of the court was embroidered with needlework in blue and purple and scarlet yarns and fine twined linen. It was twenty cubits long and five cubits high in its breadth, corresponding to the hangings of the court.

19 And their pillars were four in number. Their four bases were of bronze, their hooks of silver, and the overlaying of their capitals and their fillets of silver.

20 And all the pegs for the tabernacle and for the court all around were of bronze.

Materials for the Tabernacle

21 These are the records of the tabernacle, the tabernacle of the testimony, as they were recorded at the commandment of Moses, the responsibility of the Levites under the direction of Ithamar the son of Aaron the priest.

22 Bezalel the son of Uri, son of Hur, of the tribe of Judah, made all that the Lord commanded Moses;

23 and with him was Oholiab the son of Ahisamach, of the tribe of Dan, an engraver and designer and embroiderer in blue and purple and scarlet yarns and fine twined linen.

24 All the gold that was used for the work, in all the construction of the sanctuary, the gold from the offering, was twenty-nine talents and 730 shekels, by the shekel of the sanctuary.

25 The silver from those of the congregation who were recorded was a hundred talents and 1,775 shekels, by the shekel of the sanctuary:

26 a beka a head (that is, half a shekel, by the shekel of the sanctuary), for everyone who was listed in the records, from twenty years old and upward, for 603,550 men.

27 The hundred talents of silver were for casting the bases of the sanctuary and the bases of the veil; a hundred bases for the hundred talents, a talent a base.

28 And of the 1,775 shekels he made hooks for the pillars and overlaid their capitals and made fillets for them.

Exodus 38

29 The bronze that was offered was seventy talents and 2,400 shekels;

30 with it he made the bases for the entrance of the tent of meeting, the bronze altar and the bronze grating for it and all the utensils of the altar,

31 the bases around the court, and the bases of the gate of the court, all the pegs of the tabernacle, and all the pegs around the court.

Exodus 39

English Standard Version

Making the Priestly Garments

1 From the blue and purple and scarlet yarns they made finely woven garments, for ministering in the Holy Place. They made the holy garments for Aaron, as the Lord had commanded Moses.

2 He made the ephod of gold, blue and purple and scarlet yarns, and fine twined linen.

3 And they hammered out gold leaf, and he cut it into threads to work into the blue and purple and the scarlet yarns, and into the fine twined linen, in skilled design.

4 They made for the ephod attaching shoulder pieces, joined to it at its two edges.

5 And the skillfully woven band on it was of one piece with it and made like it, of gold, blue and purple and scarlet yarns, and fine twined linen, as the Lord had commanded Moses.

6 They made the onyx stones, enclosed in settings of gold filigree, and engraved like the engravings of a signet, according to the names of the sons of Israel.

Exodus 39

7 And he set them on the shoulder pieces of the ephod to be stones of remembrance for the sons of Israel, as the Lord had commanded Moses.

8 He made the breastpiece, in skilled work, in the style of the ephod, of gold, blue and purple and scarlet yarns, and fine twined linen.

9 It was square. They made the breastpiece doubled, a span its length and a span its breadth when doubled.

10 And they set in it four rows of stones. A row of sardius, topaz, and carbuncle was the first row;

11 and the second row, an emerald, a sapphire, and a diamond;

12 and the third row, a jacinth, an agate, and an amethyst;

13 and the fourth row, a beryl, an onyx, and a jasper. They were enclosed in settings of gold filigree. 1

4 There were twelve stones with their names according to the names of the sons of Israel. They were like signets, each engraved with its name, for the twelve tribes.

15 And they made on the breastpiece twisted chains like cords, of pure gold.

16 And they made two settings of gold filigree and two gold rings, and put the two rings on the two edges of the breastpiece.

17 And they put the two cords of gold in the two rings at the edges of the breastpiece.

18 They attached the two ends of the two cords to the two settings of filigree. Thus they attached it in front to the shoulder pieces of the ephod.

19 Then they made two rings of gold, and put them at the two ends of the breastpiece, on its inside edge next to the ephod.

20 And they made two rings of gold, and attached them in front to the lower part of the two shoulder pieces of the ephod, at its seam above the skillfully woven band of the ephod.

21 And they bound the breastpiece by its rings to the rings of the ephod with a lace of blue, so that it should lie on the skillfully woven band of the ephod, and that the breastpiece should not come loose from the ephod, as the Lord had commanded Moses.

22 He also made the robe of the ephod woven all of blue,

23 and the opening of the robe in it was like the opening in a garment, with a binding around the opening, so that it might not tear.

24 On the hem of the robe they made pomegranates of blue and purple and scarlet yarns and fine twined linen.

25 They also made bells of pure gold, and put the bells between the pomegranates all around the hem of the robe, between the pomegranates—

26 a bell and a pomegranate, a bell and a pomegranate around the hem of the robe for ministering, as the Lord had commanded Moses.

27 They also made the coats, woven of fine linen, for Aaron and his sons,

28 and the turban of fine linen, and the caps of fine linen, and the linen undergarments of fine twined linen,

29 and the sash of fine twined linen and of blue and purple and scarlet yarns, embroidered with needlework, as the Lord had commanded Moses.

30 They made the plate of the holy crown of pure gold, and wrote on it an inscription, like the engraving of a signet, "Holy to the Lord."

31 And they tied to it a cord of blue to fasten it on the turban above, as the Lord had commanded Moses.

32 Thus all the work of the tabernacle of the tent of meeting was finished, and the people of Israel did according to all that the Lord had commanded Moses; so they did.

33 Then they brought the tabernacle to Moses, the tent and all its utensils, its hooks, its frames, its bars, its pillars, and its bases;

34 the covering of tanned rams' skins and goatskins, and the veil of the screen;

35 the ark of the testimony with its poles and the mercy seat;

36 the table with all its utensils, and the bread of the Presence;

37 the lampstand of pure gold and its lamps with the lamps set and all its utensils, and the oil for the light;

38 the golden altar, the anointing oil and the fragrant incense, and the screen for the entrance of the tent;

39 the bronze altar, and its grating of bronze, its poles, and all its utensils; the basin and its stand;

40 the hangings of the court, its pillars, and its bases, and the screen for the gate of the court, its cords, and its pegs; and all the utensils for the service of the tabernacle, for the tent of meeting;

41 the finely worked garments for ministering in the Holy Place, the holy garments for Aaron the priest, and the garments of his sons for their service as priests.

42 According to all that the Lord had commanded Moses, so the people of Israel had done all the work.

43 And Moses saw all the work, and behold, they had done it; as the Lord had commanded, so had they done it. Then Moses blessed them.

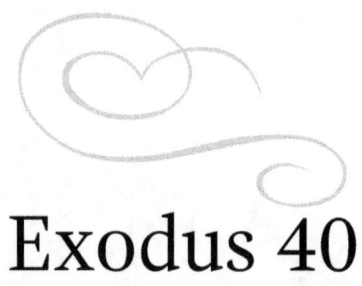

Exodus 40

English Standard Version

The Tabernacle Erected

1 The Lord spoke to Moses, saying,

2 "On the first day of the first month you shall erect the tabernacle of the tent of meeting.

3 And you shall put in it the ark of the testimony, and you shall screen the ark with the veil.

4 And you shall bring in the table and arrange it, and you shall bring in the lampstand and set up its lamps.

5 And you shall put the golden altar for incense before the ark of the testimony, and set up the screen for the door of the tabernacle.

6 You shall set the altar of burnt offering before the door of the tabernacle of the tent of meeting,

7 and place the basin between the tent of meeting and the altar, and put water in it. 8 And you shall set up the court all around, and hang up the screen for the gate of the court.

9 "Then you shall take the anointing oil and anoint the tabernacle and all that is in it, and consecrate it and all its furniture, so that it may become holy.

10 You shall also anoint the altar of burnt offering and all its utensils, and consecrate the altar, so that the altar may become most holy.

11 You shall also anoint the basin and its stand, and consecrate it.

12 Then you shall bring Aaron and his sons to the entrance of the tent of meeting and shall wash them with water

13 and put on Aaron the holy garments. And you shall anoint him and consecrate him, that he may serve me as priest.

14 You shall bring his sons also and put coats on them,

15 and anoint them, as you anointed their father, that they may serve me as priests. And their anointing shall admit them to a perpetual priesthood throughout their generations."

16 This Moses did; according to all that the Lord commanded him, so he did.

17 In the first month in the second year, on the first day of the month, the tabernacle was erected.

18 Moses erected the tabernacle. He laid its bases, and set up its frames, and put in its poles, and raised up its pillars.

19 And he spread the tent over the tabernacle and put the covering of the tent over it, as the Lord had commanded Moses.

20 He took the testimony and put it into the ark, and put the poles on the ark and set the mercy seat above on the ark.

21 And he brought the ark into the tabernacle and set up the veil of the screen, and screened the ark of the testimony, as the Lord had commanded Moses.

22 He put the table in the tent of meeting, on the north side of the tabernacle, outside the veil,

23 and arranged the bread on it before the Lord, as the Lord had commanded Moses.

24 He put the lampstand in the tent of meeting, opposite the table on the south side of the tabernacle,

25 and set up the lamps before the Lord, as the Lord had commanded Moses.

26 He put the golden altar in the tent of meeting before the veil,

27 and burned fragrant incense on it, as the Lord had commanded Moses.

28 He put in place the screen for the door of the tabernacle.

29 And he set the altar of burnt offering at the entrance of the tabernacle of the tent of meeting, and offered on it the burnt offering and the grain offering, as the Lord had commanded Moses.

30 He set the basin between the tent of meeting and the altar, and put water in it for washing,

31 with which Moses and Aaron and his sons washed their hands and their feet.

32 When they went into the tent of meeting, and when they approached the altar, they washed, as the Lord commanded Moses.

33 And he erected the court around the tabernacle and the altar, and set up the screen of the gate of the court. So Moses finished the work.

The Glory of the Lord

34 Then the cloud covered the tent of meeting, and the glory of the Lord filled the tabernacle.

35 And Moses was not able to enter the tent of meeting because the cloud settled on it, and the glory of the Lord filled the tabernacle.

36 Throughout all their journeys, whenever the cloud was taken up from over the tabernacle, the people of Israel would set out.

37 But if the cloud was not taken up, then they did not set out till the day that it was taken up.

38 For the cloud of the Lord was on the tabernacle by day, and fire was in it by night, in the sight of all the house of Israel throughout all their journeys.

Leviticus 1

English Standard Version

Laws for Burnt Offerings

1 The Lord called Moses and spoke to him from the tent of meeting, saying,

2 "Speak to the people of Israel and say to them, When any one of you brings an offering to the Lord, you shall bring your offering of livestock from the herd or from the flock.

3 "If his offering is a burnt offering from the herd, he shall offer a male without blemish. He shall bring it to the entrance of the tent of meeting, that he may be accepted before the Lord.

4 He shall lay his hand on the head of the burnt offering, and it shall be accepted for him to make atonement for him.

5 Then he shall kill the bull before the Lord, and Aaron's sons the priests shall bring the blood and throw the blood against the sides of the altar that is at the entrance of the tent of meeting.

6 Then he shall flay the burnt offering and cut it into pieces,

7 and the sons of Aaron the priest shall put fire on the altar and arrange wood on the fire.

Leviticus 1

8 And Aaron's sons the priests shall arrange the pieces, the head, and the fat, on the wood that is on the fire on the altar;

9 but its entrails and its legs he shall wash with water. And the priest shall burn all of it on the altar, as a burnt offering, a food offering with a pleasing aroma to the Lord.

10 "If his gift for a burnt offering is from the flock, from the sheep or goats, he shall bring a male without blemish,

11 and he shall kill it on the north side of the altar before the Lord, and Aaron's sons the priests shall throw its blood against the sides of the altar.

12 And he shall cut it into pieces, with its head and its fat, and the priest shall arrange them on the wood that is on the fire on the altar,

13 but the entrails and the legs he shall wash with water. And the priest shall offer all of it and burn it on the altar; it is a burnt offering, a food offering with a pleasing aroma to the Lord.

14 "If his offering to the Lord is a burnt offering of birds, then he shall bring his offering of turtledoves or pigeons.

15 And the priest shall bring it to the altar and wring off its head and burn it on the altar. Its blood shall be drained out on the side of the altar.

16 He shall remove its crop with its contents and cast it beside the altar on the east side, in the place for ashes.

17 He shall tear it open by its wings, but shall not sever it completely. And the priest shall burn it on the altar, on the wood that is on the fire. It is a burnt offering, a food offering with a pleasing aroma to the Lord.

Leviticus 2

English Standard Version

Laws for Grain Offerings

1 "When anyone brings a grain offering as an offering to the Lord, his offering shall be of fine flour. He shall pour oil on it and put frankincense on it

2 and bring it to Aaron's sons the priests. And he shall take from it a handful of the fine flour and oil, with all of its frankincense, and the priest shall burn this as its memorial portion on the altar, a food offering with a pleasing aroma to the Lord.

3 But the rest of the grain offering shall be for Aaron and his sons; it is a most holy part of the Lord's food offerings.

4 "When you bring a grain offering baked in the oven as an offering, it shall be unleavened loaves of fine flour mixed with oil or unleavened wafers smeared with oil.

5 And if your offering is a grain offering baked on a griddle, it shall be of fine flour unleavened, mixed with oil.

6 You shall break it in pieces and pour oil on it; it is a grain offering.

7 And if your offering is a grain offering cooked in a pan, it shall be made of fine flour with oil.

8 And you shall bring the grain offering that is made of these things to the Lord, and when it is presented to the priest, he shall bring it to the altar.

9 And the priest shall take from the grain offering its memorial portion and burn this on the altar, a food offering with a pleasing aroma to the Lord.

10 But the rest of the grain offering shall be for Aaron and his sons; it is a most holy part of the Lord's food offerings.

11 "No grain offering that you bring to the Lord shall be made with leaven, for you shall burn no leaven nor any honey as a food offering to the Lord.

12 As an offering of firstfruits you may bring them to the Lord, but they shall not be offered on the altar for a pleasing aroma.

13 You shall season all your grain offerings with salt. You shall not let the salt of the covenant with your God be missing from your grain offering; with all your offerings you shall offer salt.

14 "If you offer a grain offering of firstfruits to the Lord, you shall offer for the grain offering of your firstfruits fresh ears, roasted with fire, crushed new grain.

15 And you shall put oil on it and lay frankincense on it; it is a grain offering.

16 And the priest shall burn as its memorial portion some of the crushed grain and some of the oil with all of its frankincense; it is a food offering to the Lord.

Leviticus 3

English Standard Version

Laws for Peace Offerings

1 "If his offering is a sacrifice of peace offering, if he offers an animal from the herd, male or female, he shall offer it without blemish before the Lord.

2 And he shall lay his hand on the head of his offering and kill it at the entrance of the tent of meeting, and Aaron's sons the priests shall throw the blood against the sides of the altar.

3 And from the sacrifice of the peace offering, as a food offering to the Lord, he shall offer the fat covering the entrails and all the fat that is on the entrails,

4 and the two kidneys with the fat that is on them at the loins, and the long lobe of the liver that he shall remove with the kidneys.

5 Then Aaron's sons shall burn it on the altar on top of the burnt offering, which is on the wood on the fire; it is a food offering with a pleasing aroma to the Lord.

6 "If his offering for a sacrifice of peace offering to the Lord is an animal from the flock, male or female, he shall offer it without blemish.

7 If he offers a lamb for his offering, then he shall offer it before the Lord,

Leviticus 3

8 lay his hand on the head of his offering, and kill it in front of the tent of meeting; and Aaron's sons shall throw its blood against the sides of the altar.

9 Then from the sacrifice of the peace offering he shall offer as a food offering to the Lord its fat; he shall remove the whole fat tail, cut off close to the backbone, and the fat that covers the entrails and all the fat that is on the entrails

10 and the two kidneys with the fat that is on them at the loins and the long lobe of the liver that he shall remove with the kidneys.

11 And the priest shall burn it on the altar as a food offering to the Lord.

12 "If his offering is a goat, then he shall offer it before the Lord

13 and lay his hand on its head and kill it in front of the tent of meeting, and the sons of Aaron shall throw its blood against the sides of the altar.

14 Then he shall offer from it, as his offering for a food offering to the Lord, the fat covering the entrails and all the fat that is on the entrails

15 and the two kidneys with the fat that is on them at the loins and the long lobe of the liver that he shall remove with the kidneys.

16 And the priest shall burn them on the altar as a food offering with a pleasing aroma. All fat is the Lord's.

17 It shall be a statute forever throughout your generations, in all your dwelling places, that you eat neither fat nor blood."

Leviticus 4

English Standard Version

Laws for Sin Offerings

1 And the Lord spoke to Moses, saying,

2 "Speak to the people of Israel, saying, If anyone sins unintentionally in any of the Lord's commandments about things not to be done, and does any one of them,

3 if it is the anointed priest who sins, thus bringing guilt on the people, then he shall offer for the sin that he has committed a bull from the herd without blemish to the Lord for a sin offering.

4 He shall bring the bull to the entrance of the tent of meeting before the Lord and lay his hand on the head of the bull and kill the bull before the Lord.

5 And the anointed priest shall take some of the blood of the bull and bring it into the tent of meeting,

6 and the priest shall dip his finger in the blood and sprinkle part of the blood seven times before the Lord in front of the veil of the sanctuary.

7 And the priest shall put some of the blood on the horns of the altar of fragrant incense before the Lord that is in the tent of meeting, and all the

Leviticus 4

rest of the blood of the bull he shall pour out at the base of the altar of burnt offering that is at the entrance of the tent of meeting.

8 And all the fat of the bull of the sin offering he shall remove from it, the fat that covers the entrails and all the fat that is on the entrails

9 and the two kidneys with the fat that is on them at the loins and the long lobe of the liver that he shall remove with the kidneys

10 (just as these are taken from the ox of the sacrifice of the peace offerings); and the priest shall burn them on the altar of burnt offering.

11 But the skin of the bull and all its flesh, with its head, its legs, its entrails, and its dung—

12 all the rest of the bull—he shall carry outside the camp to a clean place, to the ash heap, and shall burn it up on a fire of wood. On the ash heap it shall be burned up.

13 "If the whole congregation of Israel sins unintentionally and the thing is hidden from the eyes of the assembly, and they do any one of the things that by the Lord's commandments ought not to be done, and they realize their guilt,

14 when the sin which they have committed becomes known, the assembly shall offer a bull from the herd for a sin offering and bring it in front of the tent of meeting.

15 And the elders of the congregation shall lay their hands on the head of the bull before the Lord, and the bull shall be killed before the Lord.

16 Then the anointed priest shall bring some of the blood of the bull into the tent of meeting,

17 and the priest shall dip his finger in the blood and sprinkle it seven times before the Lord in front of the veil.

18 And he shall put some of the blood on the horns of the altar that is in the tent of meeting before the Lord, and the rest of the blood he shall pour out at the base of the altar of burnt offering that is at the entrance of the tent of meeting.

19 And all its fat he shall take from it and burn on the altar.

20 Thus shall he do with the bull. As he did with the bull of the sin offering, so shall he do with this. And the priest shall make atonement for them, and they shall be forgiven.

21 And he shall carry the bull outside the camp and burn it up as he burned the first bull; it is the sin offering for the assembly.

22 "When a leader sins, doing unintentionally any one of all the things that by the commandments of the Lord his God ought not to be done, and realizes his guilt,

23 or the sin which he has committed is made known to him, he shall bring as his offering a goat, a male without blemish,

24 and shall lay his hand on the head of the goat and kill it in the place where they kill the burnt offering before the Lord; it is a sin offering.

25 Then the priest shall take some of the blood of the sin offering with his finger and put it on the horns of the altar of burnt offering and pour out the rest of its blood at the base of the altar of burnt offering.

26 And all its fat he shall burn on the altar, like the fat of the sacrifice of peace offerings. So the priest shall make atonement for him for his sin, and he shall be forgiven.

27 "If anyone of the common people sins unintentionally in doing any one of the things that by the Lord's commandments ought not to be done, and realizes his guilt,

28 or the sin which he has committed is made known to him, he shall bring for his offering a goat, a female without blemish, for his sin which he has committed.

29 And he shall lay his hand on the head of the sin offering and kill the sin offering in the place of burnt offering.

30 And the priest shall take some of its blood with his finger and put it on the horns of the altar of burnt offering and pour out all the rest of its blood at the base of the altar.

31 And all its fat he shall remove, as the fat is removed from the peace offerings, and the priest shall burn it on the altar for a pleasing aroma to the Lord. And the priest shall make atonement for him, and he shall be forgiven.

32 "If he brings a lamb as his offering for a sin offering, he shall bring a female without blemish

33 and lay his hand on the head of the sin offering and kill it for a sin offering in the place where they kill the burnt offering.

34 Then the priest shall take some of the blood of the sin offering with his finger and put it on the horns of the altar of burnt offering and pour out all the rest of its blood at the base of the altar.

35 And all its fat he shall remove as the fat of the lamb is removed from the sacrifice of peace offerings, and the priest shall burn it on the altar, on top of the Lord's food offerings. And the priest shall make atonement for him for the sin which he has committed, and he shall be forgiven.

Leviticus 5

English Standard Version

1 "If anyone sins in that he hears a public adjuration to testify, and though he is a witness, whether he has seen or come to know the matter, yet does not speak, he shall bear his iniquity;

2 or if anyone touches an unclean thing, whether a carcass of an unclean wild animal or a carcass of unclean livestock or a carcass of unclean swarming things, and it is hidden from him and he has become unclean, and he realizes his guilt;

3 or if he touches human uncleanness, of whatever sort the uncleanness may be with which one becomes unclean, and it is hidden from him, when he comes to know it, and realizes his guilt;

4 or if anyone utters with his lips a rash oath to do evil or to do good, any sort of rash oath that people swear, and it is hidden from him, when he comes to know it, and he realizes his guilt in any of these;

5 when he realizes his guilt in any of these and confesses the sin he has committed,

6 he shall bring to the Lord as his compensation for the sin that he has committed, a female from the flock, a lamb or a goat, for a sin offering. And the priest shall make atonement for him for his sin.

7 "But if he cannot afford a lamb, then he shall bring to the Lord as his compensation for the sin that he has committed two turtledoves or two pigeons, one for a sin offering and the other for a burnt offering.

8 He shall bring them to the priest, who shall offer first the one for the sin offering. He shall wring its head from its neck but shall not sever it completely,

9 and he shall sprinkle some of the blood of the sin offering on the side of the altar, while the rest of the blood shall be drained out at the base of the altar; it is a sin offering.

10 Then he shall offer the second for a burnt offering according to the rule. And the priest shall make atonement for him for the sin that he has committed, and he shall be forgiven.

11 "But if he cannot afford two turtledoves or two pigeons, then he shall bring as his offering for the sin that he has committed a tenth of an ephah of fine flour for a sin offering. He shall put no oil on it and shall put no frankincense on it, for it is a sin offering.

12 And he shall bring it to the priest, and the priest shall take a handful of it as its memorial portion and burn this on the altar, on the Lord's food offerings; it is a sin offering.

13 Thus the priest shall make atonement for him for the sin which he has committed in any one of these things, and he shall be forgiven. And the remainder shall be for the priest, as in the grain offering."

Laws for Guilt Offerings

14 The Lord spoke to Moses, saying,

15 "If anyone commits a breach of faith and sins unintentionally in any of the holy things of the Lord, he shall bring to the Lord as his compensation, a ram without blemish out of the flock, valued in silver shekels, according to the shekel of the sanctuary, for a guilt offering.

16 He shall also make restitution for what he has done amiss in the holy thing and shall add a fifth to it and give it to the priest. And the priest shall make atonement for him with the ram of the guilt offering, and he shall be forgiven.

17 "If anyone sins, doing any of the things that by the Lord's commandments ought not to be done, though he did not know it, then realizes his guilt, he shall bear his iniquity.

18 He shall bring to the priest a ram without blemish out of the flock, or its equivalent, for a guilt offering, and the priest shall make atonement for him for the mistake that he made unintentionally, and he shall be forgiven.

19 It is a guilt offering; he has indeed incurred guilt before the Lord."

Leviticus 6

English Standard Version

1 The Lord spoke to Moses, saying,

2 "If anyone sins and commits a breach of faith against the Lord by deceiving his neighbor in a matter of deposit or security, or through robbery, or if he has oppressed his neighbor

3 or has found something lost and lied about it, swearing falsely—in any of all the things that people do and sin thereby—

4 if he has sinned and has realized his guilt and will restore what he took by robbery or what he got by oppression or the deposit that was committed to him or the lost thing that he found

5 or anything about which he has sworn falsely, he shall restore it in full and shall add a fifth to it, and give it to him to whom it belongs on the day he realizes his guilt.

6 And he shall bring to the priest as his compensation to the Lord a ram without blemish out of the flock, or its equivalent, for a guilt offering.

7 And the priest shall make atonement for him before the Lord, and he shall be forgiven for any of the things that one may do and thereby become guilty."

The Priests and the Offerings

8 The Lord spoke to Moses, saying,

9 "Command Aaron and his sons, saying, This is the law of the burnt offering. The burnt offering shall be on the hearth on the altar all night until the morning, and the fire of the altar shall be kept burning on it.

10 And the priest shall put on his linen garment and put his linen undergarment on his body, and he shall take up the ashes to which the fire has reduced the burnt offering on the altar and put them beside the altar.

11 Then he shall take off his garments and put on other garments and carry the ashes outside the camp to a clean place.

12 The fire on the altar shall be kept burning on it; it shall not go out. The priest shall burn wood on it every morning, and he shall arrange the burnt offering on it and shall burn on it the fat of the peace offerings.

13 Fire shall be kept burning on the altar continually; it shall not go out.

14 "And this is the law of the grain offering. The sons of Aaron shall offer it before the Lord in front of the altar.

15 And one shall take from it a handful of the fine flour of the grain offering and its oil and all the frankincense that is on the grain offering and burn this as its memorial portion on the altar, a pleasing aroma to the Lord.

16 And the rest of it Aaron and his sons shall eat. It shall be eaten unleavened in a holy place. In the court of the tent of meeting they shall eat it.

17 It shall not be baked with leaven. I have given it as their portion of my food offerings. It is a thing most holy, like the sin offering and the guilt offering.

Leviticus 6

18 Every male among the children of Aaron may eat of it, as decreed forever throughout your generations, from the Lord's food offerings. Whatever touches them shall become holy."

19 The Lord spoke to Moses, saying,

20 "This is the offering that Aaron and his sons shall offer to the Lord on the day when he is anointed: a tenth of an ephah of fine flour as a regular grain offering, half of it in the morning and half in the evening.

21 It shall be made with oil on a griddle. You shall bring it well mixed, in baked pieces like a grain offering, and offer it for a pleasing aroma to the Lord.

22 The priest from among Aaron's sons, who is anointed to succeed him, shall offer it to the Lord as decreed forever. The whole of it shall be burned.

23 Every grain offering of a priest shall be wholly burned. It shall not be eaten."

24 The Lord spoke to Moses, saying,

25 "Speak to Aaron and his sons, saying, This is the law of the sin offering. In the place where the burnt offering is killed shall the sin offering be killed before the Lord; it is most holy. 26 The priest who offers it for sin shall eat it. In a holy place it shall be eaten, in the court of the tent of meeting.

27 Whatever touches its flesh shall be holy, and when any of its blood is splashed on a garment, you shall wash that on which it was splashed in a holy place.

28 And the earthenware vessel in which it is boiled shall be broken. But if it is boiled in a bronze vessel, that shall be scoured and rinsed in water.

29 Every male among the priests may eat of it; it is most holy.

30 But no sin offering shall be eaten from which any blood is brought into the tent of meeting to make atonement in the Holy Place; it shall be burned up with fire.

Leviticus 7

English Standard Version

1 "This is the law of the guilt offering. It is most holy.

2 In the place where they kill the burnt offering they shall kill the guilt offering, and its blood shall be thrown against the sides of the altar.

3 And all its fat shall be offered, the fat tail, the fat that covers the entrails,

4 the two kidneys with the fat that is on them at the loins, and the long lobe of the liver that he shall remove with the kidneys.

5 The priest shall burn them on the altar as a food offering to the Lord; it is a guilt offering.

6 Every male among the priests may eat of it. It shall be eaten in a holy place. It is most holy.

7 The guilt offering is just like the sin offering; there is one law for them. The priest who makes atonement with it shall have it.

8 And the priest who offers any man's burnt offering shall have for himself the skin of the burnt offering that he has offered.

9 And every grain offering baked in the oven and all that is prepared on a pan or a griddle shall belong to the priest who offers it.

10 And every grain offering, mixed with oil or dry, shall be shared equally among all the sons of Aaron.

11 "And this is the law of the sacrifice of peace offerings that one may offer to the Lord.

12 If he offers it for a thanksgiving, then he shall offer with the thanksgiving sacrifice unleavened loaves mixed with oil, unleavened wafers smeared with oil, and loaves of fine flour well mixed with oil.

13 With the sacrifice of his peace offerings for thanksgiving he shall bring his offering with loaves of leavened bread.

14 And from it he shall offer one loaf from each offering, as a gift to the Lord. It shall belong to the priest who throws the blood of the peace offerings.

15 And the flesh of the sacrifice of his peace offerings for thanksgiving shall be eaten on the day of his offering. He shall not leave any of it until the morning.

16 But if the sacrifice of his offering is a vow offering or a freewill offering, it shall be eaten on the day that he offers his sacrifice, and on the next day what remains of it shall be eaten.

17 But what remains of the flesh of the sacrifice on the third day shall be burned up with fire.

18 If any of the flesh of the sacrifice of his peace offering is eaten on the third day, he who offers it shall not be accepted, neither shall it be credited to him. It is tainted, and he who eats of it shall bear his iniquity.

19 "Flesh that touches any unclean thing shall not be eaten. It shall be burned up with fire. All who are clean may eat flesh,

20 but the person who eats of the flesh of the sacrifice of the Lord's peace offerings while an uncleanness is on him, that person shall be cut off from his people.

21 And if anyone touches an unclean thing, whether human uncleanness or an unclean beast or any unclean detestable creature, and then eats some flesh from the sacrifice of the Lord's peace offerings, that person shall be cut off from his people."

22 The Lord spoke to Moses, saying,

23 "Speak to the people of Israel, saying, You shall eat no fat, of ox or sheep or goat.

24 The fat of an animal that dies of itself and the fat of one that is torn by beasts may be put to any other use, but on no account shall you eat it.

25 For every person who eats of the fat of an animal of which a food offering may be made to the Lord shall be cut off from his people.

26 Moreover, you shall eat no blood whatever, whether of fowl or of animal, in any of your dwelling places.

27 Whoever eats any blood, that person shall be cut off from his people."

28 The Lord spoke to Moses, saying,

29 "Speak to the people of Israel, saying, Whoever offers the sacrifice of his peace offerings to the Lord shall bring his offering to the Lord from the sacrifice of his peace offerings.

30 His own hands shall bring the Lord's food offerings. He shall bring the fat with the breast, that the breast may be waved as a wave offering before the Lord.

31 The priest shall burn the fat on the altar, but the breast shall be for Aaron and his sons.

32 And the right thigh you shall give to the priest as a contribution from the sacrifice of your peace offerings.

33 Whoever among the sons of Aaron offers the blood of the peace offerings and the fat shall have the right thigh for a portion.

34 For the breast that is waved and the thigh that is contributed I have taken from the people of Israel, out of the sacrifices of their peace offerings, and have given them to Aaron the priest and to his sons, as a perpetual due from the people of Israel.

35 This is the portion of Aaron and of his sons from the Lord's food offerings, from the day they were presented to serve as priests of the Lord.

36 The Lord commanded this to be given them by the people of Israel, from the day that he anointed them. It is a perpetual due throughout their generations."

37 This is the law of the burnt offering, of the grain offering, of the sin offering, of the guilt offering, of the ordination offering, and of the peace offering,

38 which the Lord commanded Moses on Mount Sinai, on the day that he commanded the people of Israel to bring their offerings to the Lord, in the wilderness of Sinai.

Leviticus 8

English Standard Version

Consecration of Aaron and His Sons

1 The Lord spoke to Moses, saying,

2 "Take Aaron and his sons with him, and the garments and the anointing oil and the bull of the sin offering and the two rams and the basket of unleavened bread.

3 And assemble all the congregation at the entrance of the tent of meeting."

4 And Moses did as the Lord commanded him, and the congregation was assembled at the entrance of the tent of meeting.

5 And Moses said to the congregation, "This is the thing that the Lord has commanded to be done."

6 And Moses brought Aaron and his sons and washed them with water.

7 And he put the coat on him and tied the sash around his waist and clothed him with the robe and put the ephod on him and tied the skillfully woven band of the ephod around him, binding it to him with the band.

8 And he placed the breastpiece on him, and in the breastpiece he put the Urim and the Thummim.

9 And he set the turban on his head, and on the turban, in front, he set the golden plate, the holy crown, as the Lord commanded Moses.

10 Then Moses took the anointing oil and anointed the tabernacle and all that was in it, and consecrated them.

11 And he sprinkled some of it on the altar seven times, and anointed the altar and all its utensils and the basin and its stand, to consecrate them.

12 And he poured some of the anointing oil on Aaron's head and anointed him to consecrate him.

13 And Moses brought Aaron's sons and clothed them with coats and tied sashes around their waists and bound caps on them, as the Lord commanded Moses.

14 Then he brought the bull of the sin offering, and Aaron and his sons laid their hands on the head of the bull of the sin offering.

15 And he killed it, and Moses took the blood, and with his finger put it on the horns of the altar around it and purified the altar and poured out the blood at the base of the altar and consecrated it to make atonement for it.

16 And he took all the fat that was on the entrails and the long lobe of the liver and the two kidneys with their fat, and Moses burned them on the altar.

17 But the bull and its skin and its flesh and its dung he burned up with fire outside the camp, as the Lord commanded Moses.

18 Then he presented the ram of the burnt offering, and Aaron and his sons laid their hands on the head of the ram.

19 And he killed it, and Moses threw the blood against the sides of the altar.

20 He cut the ram into pieces, and Moses burned the head and the pieces and the fat.

Leviticus 8

21 He washed the entrails and the legs with water, and Moses burned the whole ram on the altar. It was a burnt offering with a pleasing aroma, a food offering for the Lord, as the Lord commanded Moses.

22 Then he presented the other ram, the ram of ordination, and Aaron and his sons laid their hands on the head of the ram.

23 And he killed it, and Moses took some of its blood and put it on the lobe of Aaron's right ear and on the thumb of his right hand and on the big toe of his right foot.

24 Then he presented Aaron's sons, and Moses put some of the blood on the lobes of their right ears and on the thumbs of their right hands and on the big toes of their right feet. And Moses threw the blood against the sides of the altar.

25 Then he took the fat and the fat tail and all the fat that was on the entrails and the long lobe of the liver and the two kidneys with their fat and the right thigh,

26 and out of the basket of unleavened bread that was before the Lord he took one unleavened loaf and one loaf of bread with oil and one wafer and placed them on the pieces of fat and on the right thigh.

27 And he put all these in the hands of Aaron and in the hands of his sons and waved them as a wave offering before the Lord.

28 Then Moses took them from their hands and burned them on the altar with the burnt offering. This was an ordination offering with a pleasing aroma, a food offering to the Lord.

29 And Moses took the breast and waved it for a wave offering before the Lord. It was Moses' portion of the ram of ordination, as the Lord commanded Moses.

30 Then Moses took some of the anointing oil and of the blood that was on the altar and sprinkled it on Aaron and his garments, and also on his sons

and his sons' garments. So he consecrated Aaron and his garments, and his sons and his sons' garments with him.

31 And Moses said to Aaron and his sons, "Boil the flesh at the entrance of the tent of meeting, and there eat it and the bread that is in the basket of ordination offerings, as I commanded, saying, 'Aaron and his sons shall eat it.'

32 And what remains of the flesh and the bread you shall burn up with fire.

33 And you shall not go outside the entrance of the tent of meeting for seven days, until the days of your ordination are completed, for it will take seven days to ordain you.

34 As has been done today, the Lord has commanded to be done to make atonement for you.

35 At the entrance of the tent of meeting you shall remain day and night for seven days, performing what the Lord has charged, so that you do not die, for so I have been commanded."

36 And Aaron and his sons did all the things that the Lord commanded by Moses.

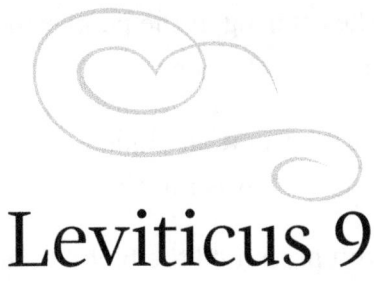

Leviticus 9

English Standard Version

The Lord Accepts Aaron's Offering

1 On the eighth day Moses called Aaron and his sons and the elders of Israel,

2 and he said to Aaron, "Take for yourself a bull calf for a sin offering and a ram for a burnt offering, both without blemish, and offer them before the Lord.

3 And say to the people of Israel, 'Take a male goat for a sin offering, and a calf and a lamb, both a year old without blemish, for a burnt offering,

4 and an ox and a ram for peace offerings, to sacrifice before the Lord, and a grain offering mixed with oil, for today the Lord will appear to you.'"

5 And they brought what Moses commanded in front of the tent of meeting, and all the congregation drew near and stood before the Lord.

6 And Moses said, "This is the thing that the Lord commanded you to do, that the glory of the Lord may appear to you."

7 Then Moses said to Aaron, "Draw near to the altar and offer your sin offering and your burnt offering and make atonement for yourself and for

the people, and bring the offering of the people and make atonement for them, as the Lord has commanded."

8 So Aaron drew near to the altar and killed the calf of the sin offering, which was for himself.'

9 And the sons of Aaron presented the blood to him, and he dipped his finger in the blood and put it on the horns of the altar and poured out the blood at the base of the altar.

10 But the fat and the kidneys and the long lobe of the liver from the sin offering he burned on the altar, as the Lord commanded Moses.

11 The flesh and the skin he burned up with fire outside the camp.

12 Then he killed the burnt offering, and Aaron's sons handed him the blood, and he threw it against the sides of the altar.

13 And they handed the burnt offering to him, piece by piece, and the head, and he burned them on the altar.

14 And he washed the entrails and the legs and burned them with the burnt offering on the altar.

15 Then he presented the people's offering and took the goat of the sin offering that was for the people and killed it and offered it as a sin offering, like the first one.

16 And he presented the burnt offering and offered it according to the rule.

17 And he presented the grain offering, took a handful of it, and burned it on the altar, besides the burnt offering of the morning.

18 Then he killed the ox and the ram, the sacrifice of peace offerings for the people. And Aaron's sons handed him the blood, and he threw it against the sides of the altar.

19 But the fat pieces of the ox and of the ram, the fat tail and that which covers the entrails and the kidneys and the long lobe of the liver—

Leviticus 9

20 they put the fat pieces on the breasts, and he burned the fat pieces on the altar, 21 but the breasts and the right thigh Aaron waved for a wave offering before the Lord, as Moses commanded.

22 Then Aaron lifted up his hands toward the people and blessed them, and he came down from offering the sin offering and the burnt offering and the peace offerings.

23 And Moses and Aaron went into the tent of meeting, and when they came out they blessed the people, and the glory of the Lord appeared to all the people.

24 And fire came out from before the Lord and consumed the burnt offering and the pieces of fat on the altar, and when all the people saw it, they shouted and fell on their faces.

Leviticus 10

English Standard Version

The Death of Nadab and Abihu

1 Now Nadab and Abihu, the sons of Aaron, each took his censer and put fire in it and laid incense on it and offered unauthorized fire before the Lord, which he had not commanded them.

2 And fire came out from before the Lord and consumed them, and they died before the Lord.

3 Then Moses said to Aaron, "This is what the Lord has said: 'Among those who are near me I will be sanctified, and before all the people I will be glorified.'" And Aaron held his peace.

4 And Moses called Mishael and Elzaphan, the sons of Uzziel the uncle of Aaron, and said to them, "Come near; carry your brothers away from the front of the sanctuary and out of the camp."

5 So they came near and carried them in their coats out of the camp, as Moses had said.

6 And Moses said to Aaron and to Eleazar and Ithamar his sons, "Do not let the hair of your heads hang loose, and do not tear your clothes, lest you die,

and wrath come upon all the congregation; but let your brothers, the whole house of Israel, bewail the burning that the Lord has kindled.

7 And do not go outside the entrance of the tent of meeting, lest you die, for the anointing oil of the Lord is upon you." And they did according to the word of Moses.

8 And the Lord spoke to Aaron, saying,

9 "Drink no wine or strong drink, you or your sons with you, when you go into the tent of meeting, lest you die. It shall be a statute forever throughout your generations.

10 You are to distinguish between the holy and the common, and between the unclean and the clean,

11 and you are to teach the people of Israel all the statutes that the Lord has spoken to them by Moses."

12 Moses spoke to Aaron and to Eleazar and Ithamar, his surviving sons: "Take the grain offering that is left of the Lord's food offerings, and eat it unleavened beside the altar, for it is most holy.

13 You shall eat it in a holy place, because it is your due and your sons' due, from the Lord's food offerings, for so I am commanded.

14 But the breast that is waved and the thigh that is contributed you shall eat in a clean place, you and your sons and your daughters with you, for they are given as your due and your sons' due from the sacrifices of the peace offerings of the people of Israel.

15 The thigh that is contributed and the breast that is waved they shall bring with the food offerings of the fat pieces to wave for a wave offering before the Lord, and it shall be yours and your sons' with you as a due forever, as the Lord has commanded."

16 Now Moses diligently inquired about the goat of the sin offering, and behold, it was burned up! And he was angry with Eleazar and Ithamar, the surviving sons of Aaron, saying,

17 "Why have you not eaten the sin offering in the place of the sanctuary, since it is a thing most holy and has been given to you that you may bear the iniquity of the congregation, to make atonement for them before the Lord?

18 Behold, its blood was not brought into the inner part of the sanctuary. You certainly ought to have eaten it in the sanctuary, as I commanded."

19 And Aaron said to Moses, "Behold, today they have offered their sin offering and their burnt offering before the Lord, and yet such things as these have happened to me! If I had eaten the sin offering today, would the Lord have approved?"

20 And when Moses heard that, he approved.

Leviticus 11

English Standard Version

Clean and Unclean Animals

1 And the Lord spoke to Moses and Aaron, saying to them,

2 "Speak to the people of Israel, saying, These are the living things that you may eat among all the animals that are on the earth.

3 Whatever parts the hoof and is cloven-footed and chews the cud, among the animals, you may eat.

4 Nevertheless, among those that chew the cud or part the hoof, you shall not eat these: The camel, because it chews the cud but does not part the hoof, is unclean to you.

5 And the rock badger, because it chews the cud but does not part the hoof, is unclean to you.

6 And the hare, because it chews the cud but does not part the hoof, is unclean to you.

7 And the pig, because it parts the hoof and is cloven-footed but does not chew the cud, is unclean to you.

Pearls of Wisdom

8 You shall not eat any of their flesh, and you shall not touch their carcasses; they are unclean to you.

9 "These you may eat, of all that are in the waters. Everything in the waters that has fins and scales, whether in the seas or in the rivers, you may eat.

10 But anything in the seas or the rivers that does not have fins and scales, of the swarming creatures in the waters and of the living creatures that are in the waters, is detestable to you.

11 You shall regard them as detestable; you shall not eat any of their flesh, and you shall detest their carcasses.

12 Everything in the waters that does not have fins and scales is detestable to you.

13 "And these you shall detest among the birds; they shall not be eaten; they are detestable: the eagle, the bearded vulture, the black vulture,

14 the kite, the falcon of any kind,

15 every raven of any kind,

16 the ostrich, the nighthawk, the sea gull, the hawk of any kind,

17 the little owl, the cormorant, the short-eared owl,

18 the barn owl, the tawny owl, the carrion vulture,

19 the stork, the heron of any kind, the hoopoe, and the bat.

20 "All winged insects that go on all fours are detestable to you.

21 Yet among the winged insects that go on all fours you may eat those that have jointed legs above their feet, with which to hop on the ground.

22 Of them you may eat: the locust of any kind, the bald locust of any kind, the cricket of any kind, and the grasshopper of any kind.

23 But all other winged insects that have four feet are detestable to you.

Leviticus 11

24 "And by these you shall become unclean. Whoever touches their carcass shall be unclean until the evening,

25 and whoever carries any part of their carcass shall wash his clothes and be unclean until the evening.

26 Every animal that parts the hoof but is not cloven-footed or does not chew the cud is unclean to you. Everyone who touches them shall be unclean.

27 And all that walk on their paws, among the animals that go on all fours, are unclean to you. Whoever touches their carcass shall be unclean until the evening,

28 and he who carries their carcass shall wash his clothes and be unclean until the evening; they are unclean to you.

29 "And these are unclean to you among the swarming things that swarm on the ground: the mole rat, the mouse, the great lizard of any kind,

30 the gecko, the monitor lizard, the lizard, the sand lizard, and the chameleon.

31 These are unclean to you among all that swarm. Whoever touches them when they are dead shall be unclean until the evening.

32 And anything on which any of them falls when they are dead shall be unclean, whether it is an article of wood or a garment or a skin or a sack, any article that is used for any purpose. It must be put into water, and it shall be unclean until the evening; then it shall be clean.

33 And if any of them falls into any earthenware vessel, all that is in it shall be unclean, and you shall break it.

34 Any food in it that could be eaten, on which water comes, shall be unclean. And all drink that could be drunk from every such vessel shall be unclean.

35 And everything on which any part of their carcass falls shall be unclean. Whether oven or stove, it shall be broken in pieces. They are unclean and shall remain unclean for you.

36 Nevertheless, a spring or a cistern holding water shall be clean, but whoever touches a carcass in them shall be unclean.

37 And if any part of their carcass falls upon any seed grain that is to be sown, it is clean,

38 but if water is put on the seed and any part of their carcass falls on it, it is unclean to you.

39 "And if any animal which you may eat dies, whoever touches its carcass shall be unclean until the evening,

40 and whoever eats of its carcass shall wash his clothes and be unclean until the evening. And whoever carries the carcass shall wash his clothes and be unclean until the evening.

41 "Every swarming thing that swarms on the ground is detestable; it shall not be eaten.

42 Whatever goes on its belly, and whatever goes on all fours, or whatever has many feet, any swarming thing that swarms on the ground, you shall not eat, for they are detestable.

43 You shall not make yourselves detestable with any swarming thing that swarms, and you shall not defile yourselves with them, and become unclean through them.

44 For I am the Lord your God. Consecrate yourselves therefore, and be holy, for I am holy. You shall not defile yourselves with any swarming thing that crawls on the ground.

45 For I am the Lord who brought you up out of the land of Egypt to be your God. You shall therefore be holy, for I am holy."

Leviticus 11

46 This is the law about beast and bird and every living creature that moves through the waters and every creature that swarms on the ground,

47 to make a distinction between the unclean and the clean and between the living creature that may be eaten and the living creature that may not be eaten.

Leviticus 12

English Standard Version

Purification After Childbirth

1 The Lord spoke to Moses, saying,

2 "Speak to the people of Israel, saying, If a woman conceives and bears a male child, then she shall be unclean seven days. As at the time of her menstruation, she shall be unclean.

3 And on the eighth day the flesh of his foreskin shall be circumcised.

4 Then she shall continue for thirty-three days in the blood of her purifying. She shall not touch anything holy, nor come into the sanctuary, until the days of her purifying are completed.

5 But if she bears a female child, then she shall be unclean two weeks, as in her menstruation. And she shall continue in the blood of her purifying for sixty-six days.

6 "And when the days of her purifying are completed, whether for a son or for a daughter, she shall bring to the priest at the entrance of the tent of meeting a lamb a year old for a burnt offering, and a pigeon or a turtledove for a sin offering,

7 and he shall offer it before the Lord and make atonement for her. Then she shall be clean from the flow of her blood. This is the law for her who bears a child, either male or female.

8 And if she cannot afford a lamb, then she shall take two turtledoves or two pigeons, one for a burnt offering and the other for a sin offering. And the priest shall make atonement for her, and she shall be clean."

Leviticus 13

English Standard Version

Laws About Leprosy

1 The Lord spoke to Moses and Aaron, saying,

2 "When a person has on the skin of his body a swelling or an eruption or a spot, and it turns into a case of leprous disease on the skin of his body, then he shall be brought to Aaron the priest or to one of his sons the priests,

3 and the priest shall examine the diseased area on the skin of his body. And if the hair in the diseased area has turned white and the disease appears to be deeper than the skin of his body, it is a case of leprous disease. When the priest has examined him, he shall pronounce him unclean.

4 But if the spot is white in the skin of his body and appears no deeper than the skin, and the hair in it has not turned white, the priest shall shut up the diseased person for seven days.

5 And the priest shall examine him on the seventh day, and if in his eyes the disease is checked and the disease has not spread in the skin, then the priest shall shut him up for another seven days.

Leviticus 13

6 And the priest shall examine him again on the seventh day, and if the diseased area has faded and the disease has not spread in the skin, then the priest shall pronounce him clean; it is only an eruption. And he shall wash his clothes and be clean.

7 But if the eruption spreads in the skin, after he has shown himself to the priest for his cleansing, he shall appear again before the priest.

8 And the priest shall look, and if the eruption has spread in the skin, then the priest shall pronounce him unclean; it is a leprous disease.

9 "When a man is afflicted with a leprous disease, he shall be brought to the priest,

10 and the priest shall look. And if there is a white swelling in the skin that has turned the hair white, and there is raw flesh in the swelling,

11 it is a chronic leprous disease in the skin of his body, and the priest shall pronounce him unclean. He shall not shut him up, for he is unclean.

12 And if the leprous disease breaks out in the skin, so that the leprous disease covers all the skin of the diseased person from head to foot, so far as the priest can see,

13 then the priest shall look, and if the leprous disease has covered all his body, he shall pronounce him clean of the disease; it has all turned white, and he is clean.

14 But when raw flesh appears on him, he shall be unclean. 15 And the priest shall examine the raw flesh and pronounce him unclean. Raw flesh is unclean, for it is a leprous disease. 16 But if the raw flesh recovers and turns white again, then he shall come to the priest, 17 and the priest shall examine him, and if the disease has turned white, then the priest shall pronounce the diseased person clean; he is clean.

18 "If there is in the skin of one's body a boil and it heals, 19 and in the place of the boil there comes a white swelling or a reddish-white spot, then it shall be shown to the priest.

20 And the priest shall look, and if it appears deeper than the skin and its hair has turned white, then the priest shall pronounce him unclean. It is a case of leprous disease that has broken out in the boil.

21 But if the priest examines it and there is no white hair in it and it is not deeper than the skin, but has faded, then the priest shall shut him up seven days.

22 And if it spreads in the skin, then the priest shall pronounce him unclean; it is a disease.

23 But if the spot remains in one place and does not spread, it is the scar of the boil, and the priest shall pronounce him clean.

24 "Or, when the body has a burn on its skin and the raw flesh of the burn becomes a spot, reddish-white or white,

25 the priest shall examine it, and if the hair in the spot has turned white and it appears deeper than the skin, then it is a leprous disease. It has broken out in the burn, and the priest shall pronounce him unclean; it is a case of leprous disease.

26 But if the priest examines it and there is no white hair in the spot and it is no deeper than the skin, but has faded, the priest shall shut him up seven days,

27 and the priest shall examine him the seventh day. If it is spreading in the skin, then the priest shall pronounce him unclean; it is a case of leprous disease.

28 But if the spot remains in one place and does not spread in the skin, but has faded, it is a swelling from the burn, and the priest shall pronounce him clean, for it is the scar of the burn.

Leviticus 13

29 "When a man or woman has a disease on the head or the beard,

30 the priest shall examine the disease. And if it appears deeper than the skin, and the hair in it is yellow and thin, then the priest shall pronounce him unclean. It is an itch, a leprous disease of the head or the beard.

31 And if the priest examines the itching disease and it appears no deeper than the skin and there is no black hair in it, then the priest shall shut up the person with the itching disease for seven days,

32 and on the seventh day the priest shall examine the disease. If the itch has not spread, and there is in it no yellow hair, and the itch appears to be no deeper than the skin,

33 then he shall shave himself, but the itch he shall not shave; and the priest shall shut up the person with the itching disease for another seven days.

34 And on the seventh day the priest shall examine the itch, and if the itch has not spread in the skin and it appears to be no deeper than the skin, then the priest shall pronounce him clean. And he shall wash his clothes and be clean.

35 But if the itch spreads in the skin after his cleansing,

36 then the priest shall examine him, and if the itch has spread in the skin, the priest need not seek for the yellow hair; he is unclean.

37 But if in his eyes the itch is unchanged and black hair has grown in it, the itch is healed and he is clean, and the priest shall pronounce him clean.

38 "When a man or a woman has spots on the skin of the body, white spots,

39 the priest shall look, and if the spots on the skin of the body are of a dull white, it is leukoderma that has broken out in the skin; he is clean.

40 "If a man's hair falls out from his head, he is bald; he is clean.

41 And if a man's hair falls out from his forehead, he has baldness of the forehead; he is clean. 42 But if there is on the bald head or the bald forehead

a reddish-white diseased area, it is a leprous disease breaking out on his bald head or his bald forehead.

43 Then the priest shall examine him, and if the diseased swelling is reddish-white on his bald head or on his bald forehead, like the appearance of leprous disease in the skin of the body,

44 he is a leprous man, he is unclean. The priest must pronounce him unclean; his disease is on his head.

45 "The leprous person who has the disease shall wear torn clothes and let the hair of his head hang loose, and he shall cover his upper lip[b] and cry out, 'Unclean, unclean.'

46 He shall remain unclean as long as he has the disease. He is unclean. He shall live alone. His dwelling shall be outside the camp.

47 "When there is a case of leprous disease in a garment, whether a woolen or a linen garment,

48 in warp or woof of linen or wool, or in a skin or in anything made of skin,

49 if the disease is greenish or reddish in the garment, or in the skin or in the warp or the woof or in any article made of skin, it is a case of leprous disease, and it shall be shown to the priest.

50 And the priest shall examine the disease and shut up that which has the disease for seven days.

51 Then he shall examine the disease on the seventh day. If the disease has spread in the garment, in the warp or the woof, or in the skin, whatever be the use of the skin, the disease is a persistent leprous disease; it is unclean.

52 And he shall burn the garment, or the warp or the woof, the wool or the linen, or any article made of skin that is diseased, for it is a persistent leprous disease. It shall be burned in the fire.

Leviticus 13

53 "And if the priest examines, and if the disease has not spread in the garment, in the warp or the woof or in any article made of skin,

54 then the priest shall command that they wash the thing in which is the disease, and he shall shut it up for another seven days.

55 And the priest shall examine the diseased thing after it has been washed. And if the appearance of the diseased area has not changed, though the disease has not spread, it is unclean. You shall burn it in the fire, whether the rot is on the back or on the front.

56 "But if the priest examines, and if the diseased area has faded after it has been washed, he shall tear it out of the garment or the skin or the warp or the woof.

57 Then if it appears again in the garment, in the warp or the woof, or in any article made of skin, it is spreading. You shall burn with fire whatever has the disease.

58 But the garment, or the warp or the woof, or any article made of skin from which the disease departs when you have washed it, shall then be washed a second time, and be clean."

59 This is the law for a case of leprous disease in a garment of wool or linen, either in the warp or the woof, or in any article made of skin, to determine whether it is clean or unclean.

Leviticus 14

English Standard Version

Laws for Cleansing Lepers

1 The Lord spoke to Moses, saying,

2 "This shall be the law of the leprous person for the day of his cleansing. He shall be brought to the priest,

3 and the priest shall go out of the camp, and the priest shall look. Then, if the case of leprous disease is healed in the leprous person,

4 the priest shall command them to take for him who is to be cleansed two live clean birds and cedarwood and scarlet yarn and hyssop.

5 And the priest shall command them to kill one of the birds in an earthenware vessel over fresh water.

6 He shall take the live bird with the cedarwood and the scarlet yarn and the hyssop, and dip them and the live bird in the blood of the bird that was killed over the fresh water.

7 And he shall sprinkle it seven times on him who is to be cleansed of the leprous disease. Then he shall pronounce him clean and shall let the living bird go into the open field.

Leviticus 14

8 And he who is to be cleansed shall wash his clothes and shave off all his hair and bathe himself in water, and he shall be clean. And after that he may come into the camp, but live outside his tent seven days.

9 And on the seventh day he shall shave off all his hair from his head, his beard, and his eyebrows. He shall shave off all his hair, and then he shall wash his clothes and bathe his body in water, and he shall be clean.

10 "And on the eighth day he shall take two male lambs without blemish, and one ewe lamb a year old without blemish, and a grain offering of three tenths of an ephah of fine flour mixed with oil, and one log of oil.

11 And the priest who cleanses him shall set the man who is to be cleansed and these things before the Lord, at the entrance of the tent of meeting.

12 And the priest shall take one of the male lambs and offer it for a guilt offering, along with the log of oil, and wave them for a wave offering before the Lord.

13 And he shall kill the lamb in the place where they kill the sin offering and the burnt offering, in the place of the sanctuary. For the guilt offering, like the sin offering, belongs to the priest; it is most holy.

14 The priest shall take some of the blood of the guilt offering, and the priest shall put it on the lobe of the right ear of him who is to be cleansed and on the thumb of his right hand and on the big toe of his right foot.

15 Then the priest shall take some of the log of oil and pour it into the palm of his own left hand

16 and dip his right finger in the oil that is in his left hand and sprinkle some oil with his finger seven times before the Lord.

17 And some of the oil that remains in his hand the priest shall put on the lobe of the right ear of him who is to be cleansed and on the thumb of his right hand and on the big toe of his right foot, on top of the blood of the guilt offering.

18 And the rest of the oil that is in the priest's hand he shall put on the head of him who is to be cleansed. Then the priest shall make atonement for him before the Lord.

19 The priest shall offer the sin offering, to make atonement for him who is to be cleansed from his uncleanness. And afterward he shall kill the burnt offering.

20 And the priest shall offer the burnt offering and the grain offering on the altar. Thus the priest shall make atonement for him, and he shall be clean.

21 "But if he is poor and cannot afford so much, then he shall take one male lamb for a guilt offering to be waved, to make atonement for him, and a tenth of an ephah of fine flour mixed with oil for a grain offering, and a log of oil;

22 also two turtledoves or two pigeons, whichever he can afford. The one shall be a sin offering and the other a burnt offering.

23 And on the eighth day he shall bring them for his cleansing to the priest, to the entrance of the tent of meeting, before the Lord.

24 And the priest shall take the lamb of the guilt offering and the log of oil, and the priest shall wave them for a wave offering before the Lord.

25 And he shall kill the lamb of the guilt offering. And the priest shall take some of the blood of the guilt offering and put it on the lobe of the right ear of him who is to be cleansed, and on the thumb of his right hand and on the big toe of his right foot.

26 And the priest shall pour some of the oil into the palm of his own left hand,

27 and shall sprinkle with his right finger some of the oil that is in his left hand seven times before the Lord.

28 And the priest shall put some of the oil that is in his hand on the lobe of the right ear of him who is to be cleansed and on the thumb of his right

hand and on the big toe of his right foot, in the place where the blood of the guilt offering was put.

29 And the rest of the oil that is in the priest's hand he shall put on the head of him who is to be cleansed, to make atonement for him before the Lord.

30 And he shall offer, of the turtledoves or pigeons, whichever he can afford,

31 one for a sin offering and the other for a burnt offering, along with a grain offering. And the priest shall make atonement before the Lord for him who is being cleansed.

32 This is the law for him in whom is a case of leprous disease, who cannot afford the offerings for his cleansing."

Laws for Cleansing Houses

33 The Lord spoke to Moses and Aaron, saying,

34 "When you come into the land of Canaan, which I give you for a possession, and I put a case of leprous disease in a house in the land of your possession,

35 then he who owns the house shall come and tell the priest, 'There seems to me to be some case of disease in my house.'

36 Then the priest shall command that they empty the house before the priest goes to examine the disease, lest all that is in the house be declared unclean. And afterward the priest shall go in to see the house.

37 And he shall examine the disease. And if the disease is in the walls of the house with greenish or reddish spots, and if it appears to be deeper than the surface,

38 then the priest shall go out of the house to the door of the house and shut up the house seven days.

39 And the priest shall come again on the seventh day, and look. If the disease has spread in the walls of the house,

40 then the priest shall command that they take out the stones in which is the disease and throw them into an unclean place outside the city.

41 And he shall have the inside of the house scraped all around, and the plaster that they scrape off they shall pour out in an unclean place outside the city.

42 Then they shall take other stones and put them in the place of those stones, and he shall take other plaster and plaster the house.

43 "If the disease breaks out again in the house, after he has taken out the stones and scraped the house and plastered it,

44 then the priest shall go and look. And if the disease has spread in the house, it is a persistent leprous disease in the house; it is unclean.

45 And he shall break down the house, its stones and timber and all the plaster of the house, and he shall carry them out of the city to an unclean place.

46 Moreover, whoever enters the house while it is shut up shall be unclean until the evening,

47 and whoever sleeps in the house shall wash his clothes, and whoever eats in the house shall wash his clothes.

48 "But if the priest comes and looks, and if the disease has not spread in the house after the house was plastered, then the priest shall pronounce the house clean, for the disease is healed.

49 And for the cleansing of the house he shall take two small birds, with cedarwood and scarlet yarn and hyssop,

50 and shall kill one of the birds in an earthenware vessel over fresh water

51 and shall take the cedarwood and the hyssop and the scarlet yarn, along with the live bird, and dip them in the blood of the bird that was killed and in the fresh water and sprinkle the house seven times.

52 Thus he shall cleanse the house with the blood of the bird and with the fresh water and with the live bird and with the cedarwood and hyssop and scarlet yarn.

53 And he shall let the live bird go out of the city into the open country. So he shall make atonement for the house, and it shall be clean."

54 This is the law for any case of leprous disease: for an itch, 55 for leprous disease in a garment or in a house,

56 and for a swelling or an eruption or a spot,

57 to show when it is unclean and when it is clean. This is the law for leprous disease.

Leviticus 15

English Standard Version

Laws About Bodily Discharges

1 The Lord spoke to Moses and Aaron, saying,

2 "Speak to the people of Israel and say to them, When any man has a discharge from his body, his discharge is unclean.

3 And this is the law of his uncleanness for a discharge: whether his body runs with his discharge, or his body is blocked up by his discharge, it is his uncleanness.

4 Every bed on which the one with the discharge lies shall be unclean, and everything on which he sits shall be unclean.

5 And anyone who touches his bed shall wash his clothes and bathe himself in water and be unclean until the evening.

6 And whoever sits on anything on which the one with the discharge has sat shall wash his clothes and bathe himself in water and be unclean until the evening.

7 And whoever touches the body of the one with the discharge shall wash his clothes and bathe himself in water and be unclean until the evening.

Leviticus 15

8 And if the one with the discharge spits on someone who is clean, then he shall wash his clothes and bathe himself in water and be unclean until the evening.

9 And any saddle on which the one with the discharge rides shall be unclean.

10 And whoever touches anything that was under him shall be unclean until the evening. And whoever carries such things shall wash his clothes and bathe himself in water and be unclean until the evening.

11 Anyone whom the one with the discharge touches without having rinsed his hands in water shall wash his clothes and bathe himself in water and be unclean until the evening.

12 And an earthenware vessel that the one with the discharge touches shall be broken, and every vessel of wood shall be rinsed in water.

13 "And when the one with a discharge is cleansed of his discharge, then he shall count for himself seven days for his cleansing, and wash his clothes. And he shall bathe his body in fresh water and shall be clean.

14 And on the eighth day he shall take two turtledoves or two pigeons and come before the Lord to the entrance of the tent of meeting and give them to the priest.

15 And the priest shall use them, one for a sin offering and the other for a burnt offering. And the priest shall make atonement for him before the Lord for his discharge.

16 "If a man has an emission of semen, he shall bathe his whole body in water and be unclean until the evening.

17 And every garment and every skin on which the semen comes shall be washed with water and be unclean until the evening.

18 If a man lies with a woman and has an emission of semen, both of them shall bathe themselves in water and be unclean until the evening.

19 "When a woman has a discharge, and the discharge in her body is blood, she shall be in her menstrual impurity for seven days, and whoever touches her shall be unclean until the evening.

20 And everything on which she lies during her menstrual impurity shall be unclean. Everything also on which she sits shall be unclean.

21 And whoever touches her bed shall wash his clothes and bathe himself in water and be unclean until the evening.

22 And whoever touches anything on which she sits shall wash his clothes and bathe himself in water and be unclean until the evening.

23 Whether it is the bed or anything on which she sits, when he touches it he shall be unclean until the evening.

24 And if any man lies with her and her menstrual impurity comes upon him, he shall be unclean seven days, and every bed on which he lies shall be unclean.

25 "If a woman has a discharge of blood for many days, not at the time of her menstrual impurity, or if she has a discharge beyond the time of her impurity, all the days of the discharge she shall continue in uncleanness. As in the days of her impurity, she shall be unclean.

26 Every bed on which she lies, all the days of her discharge, shall be to her as the bed of her impurity. And everything on which she sits shall be unclean, as in the uncleanness of her menstrual impurity.

27 And whoever touches these things shall be unclean, and shall wash his clothes and bathe himself in water and be unclean until the evening.

28 But if she is cleansed of her discharge, she shall count for herself seven days, and after that she shall be clean.

29 And on the eighth day she shall take two turtledoves or two pigeons and bring them to the priest, to the entrance of the tent of meeting.

Leviticus 15

30 And the priest shall use one for a sin offering and the other for a burnt offering. And the priest shall make atonement for her before the Lord for her unclean discharge.

31 "Thus you shall keep the people of Israel separate from their uncleanness, lest they die in their uncleanness by defiling my tabernacle that is in their midst."

32 This is the law for him who has a discharge and for him who has an emission of semen, becoming unclean thereby;

33 also for her who is unwell with her menstrual impurity, that is, for anyone, male or female, who has a discharge, and for the man who lies with a woman who is unclean.

Leviticus 16

English Standard Version

The Day of Atonement

1 The Lord spoke to Moses after the death of the two sons of Aaron, when they drew near before the Lord and died,

2 and the Lord said to Moses, "Tell Aaron your brother not to come at any time into the Holy Place inside the veil, before the mercy seat that is on the ark, so that he may not die. For I will appear in the cloud over the mercy seat.

3 But in this way Aaron shall come into the Holy Place: with a bull from the herd for a sin offering and a ram for a burnt offering.

4 He shall put on the holy linen coat and shall have the linen undergarment on his body, and he shall tie the linen sash around his waist, and wear the linen turban; these are the holy garments. He shall bathe his body in water and then put them on.

5 And he shall take from the congregation of the people of Israel two male goats for a sin offering, and one ram for a burnt offering.

6 "Aaron shall offer the bull as a sin offering for himself and shall make atonement for himself and for his house.

Leviticus 16

7 Then he shall take the two goats and set them before the Lord at the entrance of the tent of meeting. 8 And Aaron shall cast lots over the two goats, one lot for the Lord and the other lot for Azazel.

9 And Aaron shall present the goat on which the lot fell for the Lord and use it as a sin offering,

10 but the goat on which the lot fell for Azazel shall be presented alive before the Lord to make atonement over it, that it may be sent away into the wilderness to Azazel.

11 "Aaron shall present the bull as a sin offering for himself, and shall make atonement for himself and for his house. He shall kill the bull as a sin offering for himself.

12 And he shall take a censer full of coals of fire from the altar before the Lord, and two handfuls of sweet incense beaten small, and he shall bring it inside the veil

13 and put the incense on the fire before the Lord, that the cloud of the incense may cover the mercy seat that is over the testimony, so that he does not die.

14 And he shall take some of the blood of the bull and sprinkle it with his finger on the front of the mercy seat on the east side, and in front of the mercy seat he shall sprinkle some of the blood with his finger seven times.

15 "Then he shall kill the goat of the sin offering that is for the people and bring its blood inside the veil and do with its blood as he did with the blood of the bull, sprinkling it over the mercy seat and in front of the mercy seat.

16 Thus he shall make atonement for the Holy Place, because of the uncleannesses of the people of Israel and because of their transgressions, all their sins. And so he shall do for the tent of meeting, which dwells with them in the midst of their uncleannesses.

17 No one may be in the tent of meeting from the time he enters to make atonement in the Holy Place until he comes out and has made atonement for himself and for his house and for all the assembly of Israel.

18 Then he shall go out to the altar that is before the Lord and make atonement for it, and shall take some of the blood of the bull and some of the blood of the goat, and put it on the horns of the altar all around.

19 And he shall sprinkle some of the blood on it with his finger seven times, and cleanse it and consecrate it from the uncleannesses of the people of Israel.

20 "And when he has made an end of atoning for the Holy Place and the tent of meeting and the altar, he shall present the live goat.

21 And Aaron shall lay both his hands on the head of the live goat, and confess over it all the iniquities of the people of Israel, and all their transgressions, all their sins. And he shall put them on the head of the goat and send it away into the wilderness by the hand of a man who is in readiness.

22 The goat shall bear all their iniquities on itself to a remote area, and he shall let the goat go free in the wilderness.

23 "Then Aaron shall come into the tent of meeting and shall take off the linen garments that he put on when he went into the Holy Place and shall leave them there.

24 And he shall bathe his body in water in a holy place and put on his garments and come out and offer his burnt offering and the burnt offering of the people and make atonement for himself and for the people.

25 And the fat of the sin offering he shall burn on the altar.

26 And he who lets the goat go to Azazel shall wash his clothes and bathe his body in water, and afterward he may come into the camp.

Leviticus 16

27 And the bull for the sin offering and the goat for the sin offering, whose blood was brought in to make atonement in the Holy Place, shall be carried outside the camp. Their skin and their flesh and their dung shall be burned up with fire.

28 And he who burns them shall wash his clothes and bathe his body in water, and afterward he may come into the camp.

29 "And it shall be a statute to you forever that in the seventh month, on the tenth day of the month, you shall afflict yourselves and shall do no work, either the native or the stranger who sojourns among you.

30 For on this day shall atonement be made for you to cleanse you. You shall be clean before the Lord from all your sins.

31 It is a Sabbath of solemn rest to you, and you shall afflict yourselves; it is a statute forever.

32 And the priest who is anointed and consecrated as priest in his father's place shall make atonement, wearing the holy linen garments.

33 He shall make atonement for the holy sanctuary, and he shall make atonement for the tent of meeting and for the altar, and he shall make atonement for the priests and for all the people of the assembly.

34 And this shall be a statute forever for you, that atonement may be made for the people of Israel once in the year because of all their sins." And Aaron did as the Lord commanded Moses.

Leviticus 17

English Standard Version

The Place of Sacrifice

1 And the Lord spoke to Moses, saying,

2 "Speak to Aaron and his sons and to all the people of Israel and say to them, This is the thing that the Lord has commanded.

3 If any one of the house of Israel kills an ox or a lamb or a goat in the camp, or kills it outside the camp,

4 and does not bring it to the entrance of the tent of meeting to offer it as a gift to the Lord in front of the tabernacle of the Lord, bloodguilt shall be imputed to that man. He has shed blood, and that man shall be cut off from among his people.

5 This is to the end that the people of Israel may bring their sacrifices that they sacrifice in the open field, that they may bring them to the Lord, to the priest at the entrance of the tent of meeting, and sacrifice them as sacrifices of peace offerings to the Lord.

6 And the priest shall throw the blood on the altar of the Lord at the entrance of the tent of meeting and burn the fat for a pleasing aroma to the Lord.

7 So they shall no more sacrifice their sacrifices to goat demons, after whom they whore. This shall be a statute forever for them throughout their generations.

8 "And you shall say to them, Any one of the house of Israel, or of the strangers who sojourn among them, who offers a burnt offering or sacrifice

9 and does not bring it to the entrance of the tent of meeting to offer it to the Lord, that man shall be cut off from his people.

Laws Against Eating Blood

10 "If any one of the house of Israel or of the strangers who sojourn among them eats any blood, I will set my face against that person who eats blood and will cut him off from among his people.

11 For the life of the flesh is in the blood, and I have given it for you on the altar to make atonement for your souls, for it is the blood that makes atonement by the life.

12 Therefore I have said to the people of Israel, No person among you shall eat blood, neither shall any stranger who sojourns among you eat blood.

13 "Any one also of the people of Israel, or of the strangers who sojourn among them, who takes in hunting any beast or bird that may be eaten shall pour out its blood and cover it with earth.

14 For the life of every creature is its blood: its blood is its life. Therefore I have said to the people of Israel, You shall not eat the blood of any creature, for the life of every creature is its blood. Whoever eats it shall be cut off.

15 And every person who eats what dies of itself or what is torn by beasts, whether he is a native or a sojourner, shall wash his clothes and bathe himself in water and be unclean until the evening; then he shall be clean. 16 But if he does not wash them or bathe his flesh, he shall bear his iniquity."

Leviticus 18

English Standard Version

Unlawful Sexual Relations

1 And the Lord spoke to Moses, saying,

2 "Speak to the people of Israel and say to them, I am the Lord your God.

3 You shall not do as they do in the land of Egypt, where you lived, and you shall not do as they do in the land of Canaan, to which I am bringing you. You shall not walk in their statutes.

4 You shall follow my rules and keep my statutes and walk in them. I am the Lord your God.

5 You shall therefore keep my statutes and my rules; if a person does them, he shall live by them: I am the Lord.

6 "None of you shall approach any one of his close relatives to uncover nakedness. I am the Lord.

7 You shall not uncover the nakedness of your father, which is the nakedness of your mother; she is your mother, you shall not uncover her nakedness.

Leviticus 18

8 You shall not uncover the nakedness of your father's wife; it is your father's nakedness.

9 You shall not uncover the nakedness of your sister, your father's daughter or your mother's daughter, whether brought up in the family or in another home.

10 You shall not uncover the nakedness of your son's daughter or of your daughter's daughter, for their nakedness is your own nakedness.

11 You shall not uncover the nakedness of your father's wife's daughter, brought up in your father's family, since she is your sister.

12 You shall not uncover the nakedness of your father's sister; she is your father's relative.

13 You shall not uncover the nakedness of your mother's sister, for she is your mother's relative. 1

4 You shall not uncover the nakedness of your father's brother, that is, you shall not approach his wife; she is your aunt.

15 You shall not uncover the nakedness of your daughter-in-law; she is your son's wife, you shall not uncover her nakedness.

16 You shall not uncover the nakedness of your brother's wife; it is your brother's nakedness.

17 You shall not uncover the nakedness of a woman and of her daughter, and you shall not take her son's daughter or her daughter's daughter to uncover her nakedness; they are relatives; it is depravity.

18 And you shall not take a woman as a rival wife to her sister, uncovering her nakedness while her sister is still alive.

19 "You shall not approach a woman to uncover her nakedness while she is in her menstrual uncleanness.

20 And you shall not lie sexually with your neighbor's wife and so make yourself unclean with her.

21 You shall not give any of your children to offer them to Molech, and so profane the name of your God: I am the Lord.

22 You shall not lie with a male as with a woman; it is an abomination.

23 And you shall not lie with any animal and so make yourself unclean with it, neither shall any woman give herself to an animal to lie with it: it is perversion.

24 "Do not make yourselves unclean by any of these things, for by all these the nations I am driving out before you have become unclean,

25 and the land became unclean, so that I punished its iniquity, and the land vomited out its inhabitants.

26 But you shall keep my statutes and my rules and do none of these abominations, either the native or the stranger who sojourns among you

27 (for the people of the land, who were before you, did all of these abominations, so that the land became unclean),

28 lest the land vomit you out when you make it unclean, as it vomited out the nation that was before you.

29 For everyone who does any of these abominations, the persons who do them shall be cut off from among their people.

30 So keep my charge never to practice any of these abominable customs that were practiced before you, and never to make yourselves unclean by them: I am the Lord your God."

Leviticus 19

English Standard Version

The Lord Is Holy

1 And the Lord spoke to Moses, saying,

2 "Speak to all the congregation of the people of Israel and say to them, You shall be holy, for I the Lord your God am holy.

3 Every one of you shall revere his mother and his father, and you shall keep my Sabbaths: I am the Lord your God.

4 Do not turn to idols or make for yourselves any gods of cast metal: I am the Lord your God.

5 "When you offer a sacrifice of peace offerings to the Lord, you shall offer it so that you may be accepted.

6 It shall be eaten the same day you offer it or on the day after, and anything left over until the third day shall be burned up with fire.

7 If it is eaten at all on the third day, it is tainted; it will not be accepted,

8 and everyone who eats it shall bear his iniquity, because he has profaned what is holy to the Lord, and that person shall be cut off from his people.

Love Your Neighbor as Yourself

9 "When you reap the harvest of your land, you shall not reap your field right up to its edge, neither shall you gather the gleanings after your harvest.

10 And you shall not strip your vineyard bare, neither shall you gather the fallen grapes of your vineyard. You shall leave them for the poor and for the sojourner: I am the Lord your God.

11 "You shall not steal; you shall not deal falsely; you shall not lie to one another.

12 You shall not swear by my name falsely, and so profane the name of your God: I am the Lord.

13 "You shall not oppress your neighbor or rob him. The wages of a hired worker shall not remain with you all night until the morning.

14 You shall not curse the deaf or put a stumbling block before the blind, but you shall fear your God: I am the Lord.

15 "You shall do no injustice in court. You shall not be partial to the poor or defer to the great, but in righteousness shall you judge your neighbor.

16 You shall not go around as a slanderer among your people, and you shall not stand up against the life of your neighbor: I am the Lord.

17 "You shall not hate your brother in your heart, but you shall reason frankly with your neighbor, lest you incur sin because of him.

18 You shall not take vengeance or bear a grudge against the sons of your own people, but you shall love your neighbor as yourself: I am the Lord.

You Shall Keep My Statutes

19 "You shall keep my statutes. You shall not let your cattle breed with a different kind. You shall not sow your field with two kinds of seed, nor shall you wear a garment of cloth made of two kinds of material.

Leviticus 19

20 "If a man lies sexually with a woman who is a slave, assigned to another man and not yet ransomed or given her freedom, a distinction shall be made. They shall not be put to death, because she was not free;

21 but he shall bring his compensation to the Lord, to the entrance of the tent of meeting, a ram for a guilt offering.

22 And the priest shall make atonement for him with the ram of the guilt offering before the Lord for his sin that he has committed, and he shall be forgiven for the sin that he has committed.

23 "When you come into the land and plant any kind of tree for food, then you shall regard its fruit as forbidden. Three years it shall be forbidden to you; it must not be eaten.

24 And in the fourth year all its fruit shall be holy, an offering of praise to the Lord.

25 But in the fifth year you may eat of its fruit, to increase its yield for you: I am the Lord your God.

26 "You shall not eat any flesh with the blood in it. You shall not interpret omens or tell fortunes.

27 You shall not round off the hair on your temples or mar the edges of your beard.

28 You shall not make any cuts on your body for the dead or tattoo yourselves: I am the Lord.

29 "Do not profane your daughter by making her a prostitute, lest the land fall into prostitution and the land become full of depravity.

30 You shall keep my Sabbaths and reverence my sanctuary: I am the Lord.

31 "Do not turn to mediums or necromancers; do not seek them out, and so make yourselves unclean by them: I am the Lord your God.

32 "You shall stand up before the gray head and honor the face of an old man, and you shall fear your God: I am the Lord.

33 "When a stranger sojourns with you in your land, you shall not do him wrong. 34 You shall treat the stranger who sojourns with you as the native among you, and you shall love him as yourself, for you were strangers in the land of Egypt: I am the Lord your God.

35 "You shall do no wrong in judgment, in measures of length or weight or quantity. 36 You shall have just balances, just weights, a just ephah, and a just hin:[c] I am the Lord your God, who brought you out of the land of Egypt. 37 And you shall observe all my statutes and all my rules, and do them: I am the Lord."

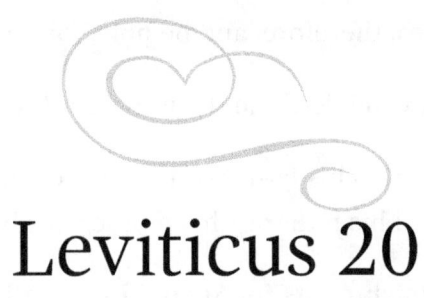

Leviticus 20

English Standard Version

Punishment for Child Sacrifice

1 The Lord spoke to Moses, saying,

2 "Say to the people of Israel, Any one of the people of Israel or of the strangers who sojourn in Israel who gives any of his children to Molech shall surely be put to death. The people of the land shall stone him with stones.

3 I myself will set my face against that man and will cut him off from among his people, because he has given one of his children to Molech, to make my sanctuary unclean and to profane my holy name.

4 And if the people of the land do at all close their eyes to that man when he gives one of his children to Molech, and do not put him to death,

5 then I will set my face against that man and against his clan and will cut them off from among their people, him and all who follow him in whoring after Molech.

6 "If a person turns to mediums and necromancers, whoring after them, I will set my face against that person and will cut him off from among his people.

7 Consecrate yourselves, therefore, and be holy, for I am the Lord your God.

8 Keep my statutes and do them; I am the Lord who sanctifies you.

9 For anyone who curses his father or his mother shall surely be put to death; he has cursed his father or his mother; his blood is upon him.

Punishments for Sexual Immorality

10 "If a man commits adultery with the wife of his neighbor, both the adulterer and the adulteress shall surely be put to death.

11 If a man lies with his father's wife, he has uncovered his father's nakedness; both of them shall surely be put to death; their blood is upon them.

12 If a man lies with his daughter-in-law, both of them shall surely be put to death; they have committed perversion; their blood is upon them.

13 If a man lies with a male as with a woman, both of them have committed an abomination; they shall surely be put to death; their blood is upon them.

14 If a man takes a woman and her mother also, it is depravity; he and they shall be burned with fire, that there may be no depravity among you.

15 If a man lies with an animal, he shall surely be put to death, and you shall kill the animal.

16 If a woman approaches any animal and lies with it, you shall kill the woman and the animal; they shall surely be put to death; their blood is upon them.

17 "If a man takes his sister, a daughter of his father or a daughter of his mother, and sees her nakedness, and she sees his nakedness, it is a disgrace, and they shall be cut off in the sight of the children of their people. He has uncovered his sister's nakedness, and he shall bear his iniquity.

18 If a man lies with a woman during her menstrual period and uncovers her nakedness, he has made naked her fountain, and she has uncovered

the fountain of her blood. Both of them shall be cut off from among their people.

19 You shall not uncover the nakedness of your mother's sister or of your father's sister, for that is to make naked one's relative; they shall bear their iniquity.

20 If a man lies with his uncle's wife, he has uncovered his uncle's nakedness; they shall bear their sin; they shall die childless.

21 If a man takes his brother's wife, it is impurity. He has uncovered his brother's nakedness; they shall be childless.

You Shall Be Holy

22 "You shall therefore keep all my statutes and all my rules and do them, that the land where I am bringing you to live may not vomit you out.

23 And you shall not walk in the customs of the nation that I am driving out before you, for they did all these things, and therefore I detested them.

24 But I have said to you, 'You shall inherit their land, and I will give it to you to possess, a land flowing with milk and honey.' I am the Lord your God, who has separated you from the peoples.

25 You shall therefore separate the clean beast from the unclean, and the unclean bird from the clean. You shall not make yourselves detestable by beast or by bird or by anything with which the ground crawls, which I have set apart for you to hold unclean.

26 You shall be holy to me, for I the Lord am holy and have separated you from the peoples, that you should be mine.

27 "A man or a woman who is a medium or a necromancer shall surely be put to death. They shall be stoned with stones; their blood shall be upon them."

Leviticus 21

English Standard Version

Holiness and the Priests

1 And the Lord said to Moses, "Speak to the priests, the sons of Aaron, and say to them, No one shall make himself unclean for the dead among his people,

2 except for his closest relatives, his mother, his father, his son, his daughter, his brother,

3 or his virgin sister (who is near to him because she has had no husband; for her he may make himself unclean).

4 He shall not make himself unclean as a husband among his people and so profane himself.

5 They shall not make bald patches on their heads, nor shave off the edges of their beards, nor make any cuts on their body.

6 They shall be holy to their God and not profane the name of their God. For they offer the Lord's food offerings, the bread of their God; therefore they shall be holy.

7 They shall not marry a prostitute or a woman who has been defiled, neither shall they marry a woman divorced from her husband, for the priest is holy to his God.

8 You shall sanctify him, for he offers the bread of your God. He shall be holy to you, for I, the Lord, who sanctify you, am holy.

9 And the daughter of any priest, if she profanes herself by whoring, profanes her father; she shall be burned with fire.

10 "The priest who is chief among his brothers, on whose head the anointing oil is poured and who has been consecrated to wear the garments, shall not let the hair of his head hang loose nor tear his clothes.

11 He shall not go in to any dead bodies nor make himself unclean, even for his father or for his mother.

12 He shall not go out of the sanctuary, lest he profane the sanctuary of his God, for the consecration of the anointing oil of his God is on him: I am the Lord.

13 And he shall take a wife in her virginity.

14 A widow, or a divorced woman, or a woman who has been defiled, or a prostitute, these he shall not marry. But he shall take as his wife a virgin of his own people,

15 that he may not profane his offspring among his people, for I am the Lord who sanctifies him."

16 And the Lord spoke to Moses, saying,

17 "Speak to Aaron, saying, None of your offspring throughout their generations who has a blemish may approach to offer the bread of his God.

18 For no one who has a blemish shall draw near, a man blind or lame, or one who has a mutilated face or a limb too long,

19 or a man who has an injured foot or an injured hand,

20 or a hunchback or a dwarf or a man with a defect in his sight or an itching disease or scabs or crushed testicles.

21 No man of the offspring of Aaron the priest who has a blemish shall come near to offer the Lord's food offerings; since he has a blemish, he shall not come near to offer the bread of his God.

22 He may eat the bread of his God, both of the most holy and of the holy things,

23 but he shall not go through the veil or approach the altar, because he has a blemish, that he may not profane my sanctuaries, for I am the Lord who sanctifies them."

24 So Moses spoke to Aaron and to his sons and to all the people of Israel.

Leviticus 22

English Standard Version

1 And the Lord spoke to Moses, saying,

2 "Speak to Aaron and his sons so that they abstain from the holy things of the people of Israel, which they dedicate to me, so that they do not profane my holy name: I am the Lord.

3 Say to them, 'If any one of all your offspring throughout your generations approaches the holy things that the people of Israel dedicate to the Lord, while he has an uncleanness, that person shall be cut off from my presence: I am the Lord.

4 None of the offspring of Aaron who has a leprous disease or a discharge may eat of the holy things until he is clean. Whoever touches anything that is unclean through contact with the dead or a man who has had an emission of semen,

5 and whoever touches a swarming thing by which he may be made unclean or a person from whom he may take uncleanness, whatever his uncleanness may be—

6 the person who touches such a thing shall be unclean until the evening and shall not eat of the holy things unless he has bathed his body in water.

7 When the sun goes down he shall be clean, and afterward he may eat of the holy things, because they are his food.

8 He shall not eat what dies of itself or is torn by beasts, and so make himself unclean by it: I am the Lord.'

9 They shall therefore keep my charge, lest they bear sin for it and die thereby when they profane it: I am the Lord who sanctifies them.

10 "A lay person shall not eat of a holy thing; no foreign guest of the priest or hired worker shall eat of a holy thing,

11 but if a priest buys a slave as his property for money, the slave may eat of it, and anyone born in his house may eat of his food.

12 If a priest's daughter marries a layman, she shall not eat of the contribution of the holy things.

13 But if a priest's daughter is widowed or divorced and has no child and returns to her father's house, as in her youth, she may eat of her father's food; yet no lay person shall eat of it.

14 And if anyone eats of a holy thing unintentionally, he shall add the fifth of its value to it and give the holy thing to the priest.

15 They shall not profane the holy things of the people of Israel, which they contribute to the Lord, 16 and so cause them to bear iniquity and guilt, by eating their holy things: for I am the Lord who sanctifies them."

Acceptable Offerings

17 And the Lord spoke to Moses, saying,

18 "Speak to Aaron and his sons and all the people of Israel and say to them, When any one of the house of Israel or of the sojourners in Israel presents a burnt offering as his offering, for any of their vows or freewill offerings that they offer to the Lord,

Leviticus 22

19 if it is to be accepted for you it shall be a male without blemish, of the bulls or the sheep or the goats.

20 You shall not offer anything that has a blemish, for it will not be acceptable for you.

21 And when anyone offers a sacrifice of peace offerings to the Lord to fulfill a vow or as a freewill offering from the herd or from the flock, to be accepted it must be perfect; there shall be no blemish in it.

22 Animals blind or disabled or mutilated or having a discharge or an itch or scabs you shall not offer to the Lord or give them to the Lord as a food offering on the altar.

23 You may present a bull or a lamb that has a part too long or too short for a freewill offering, but for a vow offering it cannot be accepted.

24 Any animal that has its testicles bruised or crushed or torn or cut you shall not offer to the Lord; you shall not do it within your land,

25 neither shall you offer as the bread of your God any such animals gotten from a foreigner. Since there is a blemish in them, because of their mutilation, they will not be accepted for you."

26 And the Lord spoke to Moses, saying,

27 "When an ox or sheep or goat is born, it shall remain seven days with its mother, and from the eighth day on it shall be acceptable as a food offering to the Lord.

28 But you shall not kill an ox or a sheep and her young in one day.

29 And when you sacrifice a sacrifice of thanksgiving to the Lord, you shall sacrifice it so that you may be accepted.

30 It shall be eaten on the same day; you shall leave none of it until morning: I am the Lord.

31 "So you shall keep my commandments and do them: I am the Lord.

32 And you shall not profane my holy name, that I may be sanctified among the people of Israel. I am the Lord who sanctifies you,

33 who brought you out of the land of Egypt to be your God: I am the Lord."

Leviticus 23

English Standard Version

Feasts of the Lord

1 The Lord spoke to Moses, saying,

2 "Speak to the people of Israel and say to them, These are the appointed feasts of the Lord that you shall proclaim as holy convocations; they are my appointed feasts.

The Sabbath

3 "Six days shall work be done, but on the seventh day is a Sabbath of solemn rest, a holy convocation. You shall do no work. It is a Sabbath to the Lord in all your dwelling places.

The Passover

4 "These are the appointed feasts of the Lord, the holy convocations, which you shall proclaim at the time appointed for them.

5 In the first month, on the fourteenth day of the month at twilight, is the Lord's Passover.

6 And on the fifteenth day of the same month is the Feast of Unleavened Bread to the Lord; for seven days you shall eat unleavened bread.

7 On the first day you shall have a holy convocation; you shall not do any ordinary work.

8 But you shall present a food offering to the Lord for seven days. On the seventh day is a holy convocation; you shall not do any ordinary work."

The Feast of Firstfruits

9 And the Lord spoke to Moses, saying,

10 "Speak to the people of Israel and say to them, When you come into the land that I give you and reap its harvest, you shall bring the sheaf of the firstfruits of your harvest to the priest,

11 and he shall wave the sheaf before the Lord, so that you may be accepted. On the day after the Sabbath the priest shall wave it.

12 And on the day when you wave the sheaf, you shall offer a male lamb a year old without blemish as a burnt offering to the Lord.

13 And the grain offering with it shall be two tenths of an ephah of fine flour mixed with oil, a food offering to the Lord with a pleasing aroma, and the drink offering with it shall be of wine, a fourth of a hin.

14 And you shall eat neither bread nor grain parched or fresh until this same day, until you have brought the offering of your God: it is a statute forever throughout your generations in all your dwellings.

The Feast of Weeks

15 "You shall count seven full weeks from the day after the Sabbath, from the day that you brought the sheaf of the wave offering.

16 You shall count fifty days to the day after the seventh Sabbath. Then you shall present a grain offering of new grain to the Lord.

17 You shall bring from your dwelling places two loaves of bread to be waved, made of two tenths of an ephah. They shall be of fine flour, and they shall be baked with leaven, as firstfruits to the Lord.

18 And you shall present with the bread seven lambs a year old without blemish, and one bull from the herd and two rams. They shall be a burnt offering to the Lord, with their grain offering and their drink offerings, a food offering with a pleasing aroma to the Lord.

19 And you shall offer one male goat for a sin offering, and two male lambs a year old as a sacrifice of peace offerings.

20 And the priest shall wave them with the bread of the firstfruits as a wave offering before the Lord, with the two lambs. They shall be holy to the Lord for the priest.

21 And you shall make a proclamation on the same day. You shall hold a holy convocation. You shall not do any ordinary work. It is a statute forever in all your dwelling places throughout your generations.

22 "And when you reap the harvest of your land, you shall not reap your field right up to its edge, nor shall you gather the gleanings after your harvest. You shall leave them for the poor and for the sojourner: I am the Lord your God."

The Feast of Trumpets

23 And the Lord spoke to Moses, saying,

24 "Speak to the people of Israel, saying, In the seventh month, on the first day of the month, you shall observe a day of solemn rest, a memorial proclaimed with blast of trumpets, a holy convocation.

25 You shall not do any ordinary work, and you shall present a food offering to the Lord."

The Day of Atonement

26 And the Lord spoke to Moses, saying,

27 "Now on the tenth day of this seventh month is the Day of Atonement. It shall be for you a time of holy convocation, and you shall afflict yourselves and present a food offering to the Lord.

28 And you shall not do any work on that very day, for it is a Day of Atonement, to make atonement for you before the Lord your God.

29 For whoever is not afflicted on that very day shall be cut off from his people.

30 And whoever does any work on that very day, that person I will destroy from among his people.

31 You shall not do any work. It is a statute forever throughout your generations in all your dwelling places.

32 It shall be to you a Sabbath of solemn rest, and you shall afflict yourselves. On the ninth day of the month beginning at evening, from evening to evening shall you keep your Sabbath."

The Feast of Booths

33 And the Lord spoke to Moses, saying,

34 "Speak to the people of Israel, saying, On the fifteenth day of this seventh month and for seven days is the Feast of Booths to the Lord.

35 On the first day shall be a holy convocation; you shall not do any ordinary work.

36 For seven days you shall present food offerings to the Lord. On the eighth day you shall hold a holy convocation and present a food offering to the Lord. It is a solemn assembly; you shall not do any ordinary work.

37 "These are the appointed feasts of the Lord, which you shall proclaim as times of holy convocation, for presenting to the Lord food offerings, burnt offerings and grain offerings, sacrifices and drink offerings, each on its proper day,

38 besides the Lord's Sabbaths and besides your gifts and besides all your vow offerings and besides all your freewill offerings, which you give to the Lord.

39 "On the fifteenth day of the seventh month, when you have gathered in the produce of the land, you shall celebrate the feast of the Lord seven days. On the first day shall be a solemn rest, and on the eighth day shall be a solemn rest.

40 And you shall take on the first day the fruit of splendid trees, branches of palm trees and boughs of leafy trees and willows of the brook, and you shall rejoice before the Lord your God seven days.

41 You shall celebrate it as a feast to the Lord for seven days in the year. It is a statute forever throughout your generations; you shall celebrate it in the seventh month.

42 You shall dwell in booths for seven days. All native Israelites shall dwell in booths,

43 that your generations may know that I made the people of Israel dwell in booths when I brought them out of the land of Egypt: I am the Lord your God."

44 Thus Moses declared to the people of Israel the appointed feasts of the Lord.

Leviticus 24

English Standard Version

The Lamps

1 The Lord spoke to Moses, saying,

2 "Command the people of Israel to bring you pure oil from beaten olives for the lamp, that a light may be kept burning regularly.

3 Outside the veil of the testimony, in the tent of meeting, Aaron shall arrange it from evening to morning before the Lord regularly. It shall be a statute forever throughout your generations.

4 He shall arrange the lamps on the lampstand of pure gold before the Lord regularly.

Bread for the Tabernacle

5 "You shall take fine flour and bake twelve loaves from it; two tenths of an ephah shall be in each loaf.

6 And you shall set them in two piles, six in a pile, on the table of pure gold before the Lord.

7 And you shall put pure frankincense on each pile, that it may go with the bread as a memorial portion as a food offering to the Lord.

Leviticus 24

8 Every Sabbath day Aaron shall arrange it before the Lord regularly; it is from the people of Israel as a covenant forever.

9 And it shall be for Aaron and his sons, and they shall eat it in a holy place, since it is for him a most holy portion out of the Lord's food offerings, a perpetual due."

Punishment for Blasphemy

10 Now an Israelite woman's son, whose father was an Egyptian, went out among the people of Israel. And the Israelite woman's son and a man of Israel fought in the camp,

11 and the Israelite woman's son blasphemed the Name, and cursed. Then they brought him to Moses. His mother's name was Shelomith, the daughter of Dibri, of the tribe of Dan.

12 And they put him in custody, till the will of the Lord should be clear to them.

13 Then the Lord spoke to Moses, saying,

14 "Bring out of the camp the one who cursed, and let all who heard him lay their hands on his head, and let all the congregation stone him.

15 And speak to the people of Israel, saying, Whoever curses his God shall bear his sin.

16 Whoever blasphemes the name of the Lord shall surely be put to death. All the congregation shall stone him. The sojourner as well as the native, when he blasphemes the Name, shall be put to death.

An Eye for an Eye

17 "Whoever takes a human life shall surely be put to death.

18 Whoever takes an animal's life shall make it good, life for life.

19 If anyone injures his neighbor, as he has done it shall be done to him,

20 fracture for fracture, eye for eye, tooth for tooth; whatever injury he has given a person shall be given to him.

21 Whoever kills an animal shall make it good, and whoever kills a person shall be put to death.

22 You shall have the same rule for the sojourner and for the native, for I am the Lord your God."

23 So Moses spoke to the people of Israel, and they brought out of the camp the one who had cursed and stoned him with stones. Thus the people of Israel did as the Lord commanded Moses.

Leviticus 25

English Standard Version

The Sabbath Year

1 The Lord spoke to Moses on Mount Sinai, saying,

2 "Speak to the people of Israel and say to them, When you come into the land that I give you, the land shall keep a Sabbath to the Lord.

3 For six years you shall sow your field, and for six years you shall prune your vineyard and gather in its fruits,

4 but in the seventh year there shall be a Sabbath of solemn rest for the land, a Sabbath to the Lord. You shall not sow your field or prune your vineyard.

5 You shall not reap what grows of itself in your harvest, or gather the grapes of your undressed vine. It shall be a year of solemn rest for the land.

6 The Sabbath of the land shall provide food for you, for yourself and for your male and female slaves and for your hired worker and the sojourner who lives with you,

7 and for your cattle and for the wild animals that are in your land: all its yield shall be for food.

Pearls of Wisdom

The Year of Jubilee

8 "You shall count seven weeks of years, seven times seven years, so that the time of the seven weeks of years shall give you forty-nine years.

9 Then you shall sound the loud trumpet on the tenth day of the seventh month. On the Day of Atonement you shall sound the trumpet throughout all your land.

10 And you shall consecrate the fiftieth year, and proclaim liberty throughout the land to all its inhabitants. It shall be a jubilee for you, when each of you shall return to his property and each of you shall return to his clan.

11 That fiftieth year shall be a jubilee for you; in it you shall neither sow nor reap what grows of itself nor gather the grapes from the undressed vines.

12 For it is a jubilee. It shall be holy to you. You may eat the produce of the field.

13 "In this year of jubilee each of you shall return to his property.

14 And if you make a sale to your neighbor or buy from your neighbor, you shall not wrong one another.

15 You shall pay your neighbor according to the number of years after the jubilee, and he shall sell to you according to the number of years for crops.

16 If the years are many, you shall increase the price, and if the years are few, you shall reduce the price, for it is the number of the crops that he is selling to you.

17 You shall not wrong one another, but you shall fear your God, for I am the Lord your God.

18 "Therefore you shall do my statutes and keep my rules and perform them, and then you will dwell in the land securely.

19 The land will yield its fruit, and you will eat your fill and dwell in it securely.

20 And if you say, 'What shall we eat in the seventh year, if we may not sow or gather in our crop?'

21 I will command my blessing on you in the sixth year, so that it will produce a crop sufficient for three years.

22 When you sow in the eighth year, you will be eating some of the old crop; you shall eat the old until the ninth year, when its crop arrives.

Redemption of Property

23 "The land shall not be sold in perpetuity, for the land is mine. For you are strangers and sojourners with me.

24 And in all the country you possess, you shall allow a redemption of the land.

25 "If your brother becomes poor and sells part of his property, then his nearest redeemer shall come and redeem what his brother has sold.

26 If a man has no one to redeem it and then himself becomes prosperous and finds sufficient means to redeem it,

27 let him calculate the years since he sold it and pay back the balance to the man to whom he sold it, and then return to his property.

28 But if he does not have sufficient means to recover it, then what he sold shall remain in the hand of the buyer until the year of jubilee. In the jubilee it shall be released, and he shall return to his property.

29 "If a man sells a dwelling house in a walled city, he may redeem it within a year of its sale. For a full year he shall have the right of redemption.

30 If it is not redeemed within a full year, then the house in the walled city shall belong in perpetuity to the buyer, throughout his generations; it shall not be released in the jubilee.

31 But the houses of the villages that have no wall around them shall be classified with the fields of the land. They may be redeemed, and they shall be released in the jubilee. 32 As for the cities of the Levites, the Levites may redeem at any time the houses in the cities they possess.

33 And if one of the Levites exercises his right of redemption, then the house that was sold in a city they possess shall be released in the jubilee. For the houses in the cities of the Levites are their possession among the people of Israel.

34 But the fields of pastureland belonging to their cities may not be sold, for that is their possession forever.

Kindness for Poor Brothers

35 "If your brother becomes poor and cannot maintain himself with you, you shall support him as though he were a stranger and a sojourner, and he shall live with you.

36 Take no interest from him or profit, but fear your God, that your brother may live beside you.

37 You shall not lend him your money at interest, nor give him your food for profit.

38 I am the Lord your God, who brought you out of the land of Egypt to give you the land of Canaan, and to be your God.

39 "If your brother becomes poor beside you and sells himself to you, you shall not make him serve as a slave:

40 he shall be with you as a hired worker and as a sojourner. He shall serve with you until the year of the jubilee.

41 Then he shall go out from you, he and his children with him, and go back to his own clan and return to the possession of his fathers.

42 For they are my servants, whom I brought out of the land of Egypt; they shall not be sold as slaves.

43 You shall not rule over him ruthlessly but shall fear your God.

44 As for your male and female slaves whom you may have: you may buy male and female slaves from among the nations that are around you.

45 You may also buy from among the strangers who sojourn with you and their clans that are with you, who have been born in your land, and they may be your property.

46 You may bequeath them to your sons after you to inherit as a possession forever. You may make slaves of them, but over your brothers the people of Israel you shall not rule, one over another ruthlessly.

Redeeming a Poor Man

47 "If a stranger or sojourner with you becomes rich, and your brother beside him becomes poor and sells himself to the stranger or sojourner with you or to a member of the stranger's clan,

48 then after he is sold he may be redeemed. One of his brothers may redeem him,

49 or his uncle or his cousin may redeem him, or a close relative from his clan may redeem him. Or if he grows rich he may redeem himself.

50 He shall calculate with his buyer from the year when he sold himself to him until the year of jubilee, and the price of his sale shall vary with the number of years. The time he was with his owner shall be rated as the time of a hired worker.

51 If there are still many years left, he shall pay proportionately for his redemption some of his sale price.

52 If there remain but a few years until the year of jubilee, he shall calculate and pay for his redemption in proportion to his years of service.

53 He shall treat him as a worker hired year by year. He shall not rule ruthlessly over him in your sight.

54 And if he is not redeemed by these means, then he and his children with him shall be released in the year of jubilee.

55 For it is to me that the people of Israel are servants. They are my servants whom I brought out of the land of Egypt: I am the Lord your God.

Leviticus 26

English Standard Version

Blessings for Obedience

1 "You shall not make idols for yourselves or erect an image or pillar, and you shall not set up a figured stone in your land to bow down to it, for I am the Lord your God.

2 You shall keep my Sabbaths and reverence my sanctuary: I am the Lord.

3 "If you walk in my statutes and observe my commandments and do them,

4 then I will give you your rains in their season, and the land shall yield its increase, and the trees of the field shall yield their fruit.

5 Your threshing shall last to the time of the grape harvest, and the grape harvest shall last to the time for sowing. And you shall eat your bread to the full and dwell in your land securely.

6 I will give peace in the land, and you shall lie down, and none shall make you afraid. And I will remove harmful beasts from the land, and the sword shall not go through your land.

7 You shall chase your enemies, and they shall fall before you by the sword.

8 Five of you shall chase a hundred, and a hundred of you shall chase ten thousand, and your enemies shall fall before you by the sword.

9 I will turn to you and make you fruitful and multiply you and will confirm my covenant with you.

10 You shall eat old store long kept, and you shall clear out the old to make way for the new.

11 I will make my dwelling among you, and my soul shall not abhor you.

12 And I will walk among you and will be your God, and you shall be my people.

13 I am the Lord your God, who brought you out of the land of Egypt, that you should not be their slaves. And I have broken the bars of your yoke and made you walk erect.

Punishment for Disobedience

14 "But if you will not listen to me and will not do all these commandments,

15 if you spurn my statutes, and if your soul abhors my rules, so that you will not do all my commandments, but break my covenant,

16 then I will do this to you: I will visit you with panic, with wasting disease and fever that consume the eyes and make the heart ache. And you shall sow your seed in vain, for your enemies shall eat it.

17 I will set my face against you, and you shall be struck down before your enemies. Those who hate you shall rule over you, and you shall flee when none pursues you.

18 And if in spite of this you will not listen to me, then I will discipline you again sevenfold for your sins,

19 and I will break the pride of your power, and I will make your heavens like iron and your earth like bronze.

Leviticus 26

20 And your strength shall be spent in vain, for your land shall not yield its increase, and the trees of the land shall not yield their fruit.

21 "Then if you walk contrary to me and will not listen to me, I will continue striking you, sevenfold for your sins.

22 And I will let loose the wild beasts against you, which shall bereave you of your children and destroy your livestock and make you few in number, so that your roads shall be deserted.

23 "And if by this discipline you are not turned to me but walk contrary to me,

24 then I also will walk contrary to you, and I myself will strike you sevenfold for your sins.

25 And I will bring a sword upon you, that shall execute vengeance for the covenant. And if you gather within your cities, I will send pestilence among you, and you shall be delivered into the hand of the enemy.

26 When I break your supply of bread, ten women shall bake your bread in a single oven and shall dole out your bread again by weight, and you shall eat and not be satisfied.

27 "But if in spite of this you will not listen to me, but walk contrary to me,

28 then I will walk contrary to you in fury, and I myself will discipline you sevenfold for your sins.

29 You shall eat the flesh of your sons, and you shall eat the flesh of your daughters.

30 And I will destroy your high places and cut down your incense altars and cast your dead bodies upon the dead bodies of your idols, and my soul will abhor you.

31 And I will lay your cities waste and will make your sanctuaries desolate, and I will not smell your pleasing aromas.

32 And I myself will devastate the land, so that your enemies who settle in it shall be appalled at it.

33 And I will scatter you among the nations, and I will unsheathe the sword after you, and your land shall be a desolation, and your cities shall be a waste.

34 "Then the land shall enjoy its Sabbaths as long as it lies desolate, while you are in your enemies' land; then the land shall rest, and enjoy its Sabbaths.

35 As long as it lies desolate it shall have rest, the rest that it did not have on your Sabbaths when you were dwelling in it.

36 And as for those of you who are left, I will send faintness into their hearts in the lands of their enemies. The sound of a driven leaf shall put them to flight, and they shall flee as one flees from the sword, and they shall fall when none pursues.

37 They shall stumble over one another, as if to escape a sword, though none pursues. And you shall have no power to stand before your enemies.

38 And you shall perish among the nations, and the land of your enemies shall eat you up.

39 And those of you who are left shall rot away in your enemies' lands because of their iniquity, and also because of the iniquities of their fathers they shall rot away like them.

40 "But if they confess their iniquity and the iniquity of their fathers in their treachery that they committed against me, and also in walking contrary to me,

41 so that I walked contrary to them and brought them into the land of their enemies—if then their uncircumcised heart is humbled and they make amends for their iniquity,

42 then I will remember my covenant with Jacob, and I will remember my covenant with Isaac and my covenant with Abraham, and I will remember the land.

43 But the land shall be abandoned by them and enjoy its Sabbaths while it lies desolate without them, and they shall make amends for their iniquity, because they spurned my rules and their soul abhorred my statutes.

44 Yet for all that, when they are in the land of their enemies, I will not spurn them, neither will I abhor them so as to destroy them utterly and break my covenant with them, for I am the Lord their God.

45 But I will for their sake remember the covenant with their forefathers, whom I brought out of the land of Egypt in the sight of the nations, that I might be their God: I am the Lord."

46 These are the statutes and rules and laws that the Lord made between himself and the people of Israel through Moses on Mount Sinai.

Leviticus 27

English Standard Version

Laws About Vows

1 The Lord spoke to Moses, saying,

2 "Speak to the people of Israel and say to them, If anyone makes a special vow to the Lord involving the valuation of persons,

3 then the valuation of a male from twenty years old up to sixty years old shall be fifty shekels of silver, according to the shekel of the sanctuary.

4 If the person is a female, the valuation shall be thirty shekels.

5 If the person is from five years old up to twenty years old, the valuation shall be for a male twenty shekels, and for a female ten shekels.

6 If the person is from a month old up to five years old, the valuation shall be for a male five shekels of silver, and for a female the valuation shall be three shekels of silver.

7 And if the person is sixty years old or over, then the valuation for a male shall be fifteen shekels, and for a female ten shekels.

Leviticus 27

8 And if someone is too poor to pay the valuation, then he shall be made to stand before the priest, and the priest shall value him; the priest shall value him according to what the vower can afford.

9 "If the vow is an animal that may be offered as an offering to the Lord, all of it that he gives to the Lord is holy.

10 He shall not exchange it or make a substitute for it, good for bad, or bad for good; and if he does in fact substitute one animal for another, then both it and the substitute shall be holy.

11 And if it is any unclean animal that may not be offered as an offering to the Lord, then he shall stand the animal before the priest,

12 and the priest shall value it as either good or bad; as the priest values it, so it shall be.

13 But if he wishes to redeem it, he shall add a fifth to the valuation.

14 "When a man dedicates his house as a holy gift to the Lord, the priest shall value it as either good or bad; as the priest values it, so it shall stand.

15 And if the donor wishes to redeem his house, he shall add a fifth to the valuation price, and it shall be his.

16 "If a man dedicates to the Lord part of the land that is his possession, then the valuation shall be in proportion to its seed. A homer of barley seed shall be valued at fifty shekels of silver.

17 If he dedicates his field from the year of jubilee, the valuation shall stand,

18 but if he dedicates his field after the jubilee, then the priest shall calculate the price according to the years that remain until the year of jubilee, and a deduction shall be made from the valuation.

19 And if he who dedicates the field wishes to redeem it, then he shall add a fifth to its valuation price, and it shall remain his.

20 But if he does not wish to redeem the field, or if he has sold the field to another man, it shall not be redeemed anymore.

21 But the field, when it is released in the jubilee, shall be a holy gift to the Lord, like a field that has been devoted. The priest shall be in possession of it.

22 If he dedicates to the Lord a field that he has bought, which is not a part of his possession,

23 then the priest shall calculate the amount of the valuation for it up to the year of jubilee, and the man shall give the valuation on that day as a holy gift to the Lord.

24 In the year of jubilee the field shall return to him from whom it was bought, to whom the land belongs as a possession.

25 Every valuation shall be according to the shekel of the sanctuary: twenty gerahs shall make a shekel.

26 "But a firstborn of animals, which as a firstborn belongs to the Lord, no man may dedicate; whether ox or sheep, it is the Lord's.

27 And if it is an unclean animal, then he shall buy it back at the valuation, and add a fifth to it; or, if it is not redeemed, it shall be sold at the valuation.

28 "But no devoted thing that a man devotes to the Lord, of anything that he has, whether man or beast, or of his inherited field, shall be sold or redeemed; every devoted thing is most holy to the Lord.

29 No one devoted, who is to be devoted for destruction from mankind, shall be ransomed; he shall surely be put to death.

30 "Every tithe of the land, whether of the seed of the land or of the fruit of the trees, is the Lord's; it is holy to the Lord.

31 If a man wishes to redeem some of his tithe, he shall add a fifth to it.

Leviticus 27

32 And every tithe of herds and flocks, every tenth animal of all that pass under the herdsman's staff, shall be holy to the Lord.

33 One shall not differentiate between good or bad, neither shall he make a substitute for it; and if he does substitute for it, then both it and the substitute shall be holy; it shall not be redeemed."

34 These are the commandments that the Lord commanded Moses for the people of Israel on Mount Sinai.

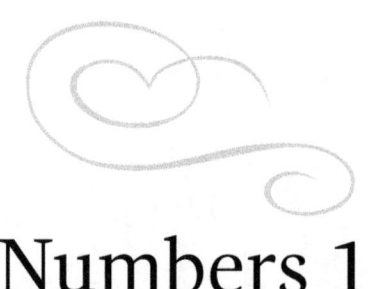

Numbers 1

English Standard Version

A Census of Israel's Warriors

1 The Lord spoke to Moses in the wilderness of Sinai, in the tent of meeting, on the first day of the second month, in the second year after they had come out of the land of Egypt, saying,

2 "Take a census of all the congregation of the people of Israel, by clans, by fathers' houses, according to the number of names, every male, head by head.

3 From twenty years old and upward, all in Israel who are able to go to war, you and Aaron shall list them, company by company.

4 And there shall be with you a man from each tribe, each man being the head of the house of his fathers.

5 And these are the names of the men who shall assist you. From Reuben, Elizur the son of Shedeur;

6 from Simeon, Shelumiel the son of Zurishaddai;

7 from Judah, Nahshon the son of Amminadab;

8 from Issachar, Nethanel the son of Zuar;

9 from Zebulun, Eliab the son of Helon;

10 from the sons of Joseph, from Ephraim, Elishama the son of Ammihud, and from Manasseh, Gamaliel the son of Pedahzur;

11 from Benjamin, Abidan the son of Gideoni;

12 from Dan, Ahiezer the son of Ammishaddai;

13 from Asher, Pagiel the son of Ochran;

14 from Gad, Eliasaph the son of Deuel;

15 from Naphtali, Ahira the son of Enan."

16 These were the ones chosen from the congregation, the chiefs of their ancestral tribes, the heads of the clans of Israel.

17 Moses and Aaron took these men who had been named,

18 and on the first day of the second month, they assembled the whole congregation together, who registered themselves by clans, by fathers' houses, according to the number of names from twenty years old and upward, head by head,

19 as the Lord commanded Moses. So he listed them in the wilderness of Sinai.

20 The people of Reuben, Israel's firstborn, their generations, by their clans, by their fathers' houses, according to the number of names, head by head, every male from twenty years old and upward, all who were able to go to war:

21 those listed of the tribe of Reuben were 46,500.

22 Of the people of Simeon, their generations, by their clans, by their fathers' houses, those of them who were listed, according to the number of names, head by head, every male from twenty years old and upward, all who were able to go to war:

Pearls of Wisdom

23 those listed of the tribe of Simeon were 59,300.

24 Of the people of Gad, their generations, by their clans, by their fathers' houses, according to the number of the names, from twenty years old and upward, all who were able to go to war:

25 those listed of the tribe of Gad were 45,650.

26 Of the people of Judah, their generations, by their clans, by their fathers' houses, according to the number of names, from twenty years old and upward, every man able to go to war:

27 those listed of the tribe of Judah were 74,600.

28 Of the people of Issachar, their generations, by their clans, by their fathers' houses, according to the number of names, from twenty years old and upward, every man able to go to war:

29 those listed of the tribe of Issachar were 54,400.

30 Of the people of Zebulun, their generations, by their clans, by their fathers' houses, according to the number of names, from twenty years old and upward, every man able to go to war:

31 those listed of the tribe of Zebulun were 57,400.

32 Of the people of Joseph, namely, of the people of Ephraim, their generations, by their clans, by their fathers' houses, according to the number of names, from twenty years old and upward, every man able to go to war:

33 those listed of the tribe of Ephraim were 40,500.

34 Of the people of Manasseh, their generations, by their clans, by their fathers' houses, according to the number of names, from twenty years old and upward, every man able to go to war:

35 those listed of the tribe of Manasseh were 32,200.

Numbers 1

36 Of the people of Benamin, their generations, by their clans, by their fathers' houses, according to the number of names, from twenty years old and upward, every man able to go to war:

37 those listed of the tribe of Benjamin were 35,400.

38 Of the people of Dan, their generations, by their clans, by their fathers' houses, according to the number of names, from twenty years old and upward, every man able to go to war:

39 those listed of the tribe of Dan were 62,700.

40 Of the people of Asher, their generations, by their clans, by their fathers' houses, according to the number of names, from twenty years old and upward, every man able to go to war:

41 those listed of the tribe of Asher were 41,500.

42 Of the people of Naphtali, their generations, by their clans, by their fathers' houses, according to the number of names, from twenty years old and upward, every man able to go to war:

43 those listed of the tribe of Naphtali were 53,400.

44 These are those who were listed, whom Moses and Aaron listed with the help of the chiefs of Israel, twelve men, each representing his fathers' house.

45 So all those listed of the people of Israel, by their fathers' houses, from twenty years old and upward, every man able to go to war in Israel—

46 all those listed were 603,550.

Levites Exempted

47 But the Levites were not listed along with them by their ancestral tribe.

48 For the Lord spoke to Moses, saying,

49 "Only the tribe of Levi you shall not list, and you shall not take a census of them among the people of Israel.

50 But appoint the Levites over the tabernacle of the testimony, and over all its furnishings, and over all that belongs to it. They are to carry the tabernacle and all its furnishings, and they shall take care of it and shall camp around the tabernacle.

51 When the tabernacle is to set out, the Levites shall take it down, and when the tabernacle is to be pitched, the Levites shall set it up. And if any outsider comes near, he shall be put to death.

52 The people of Israel shall pitch their tents by their companies, each man in his own camp and each man by his own standard.

53 But the Levites shall camp around the tabernacle of the testimony, so that there may be no wrath on the congregation of the people of Israel. And the Levites shall keep guard over the tabernacle of the testimony."

54 Thus did the people of Israel; they did according to all that the Lord commanded Moses.

Numbers 2

English Standard Version

Arrangement of the Camp

1 The Lord spoke to Moses and Aaron, saying,

2 "The people of Israel shall camp each by his own standard, with the banners of their fathers' houses. They shall camp facing the tent of meeting on every side.

3 Those to camp on the east side toward the sunrise shall be of the standard of the camp of Judah by their companies, the chief of the people of Judah being Nahshon the son of Amminadab,

4 his company as listed being 74,600.

5 Those to camp next to him shall be the tribe of Issachar, the chief of the people of Issachar being Nethanel the son of Zuar,

6 his company as listed being 54,400.

7 Then the tribe of Zebulun, the chief of the people of Zebulun being Eliab the son of Helon,

8 his company as listed being 57,400.

Pearls of Wisdom

9 All those listed of the camp of Judah, by their companies, were 186,400. They shall set out first on the march.

10 "On the south side shall be the standard of the camp of Reuben by their companies, the chief of the people of Reuben being Elizur the son of Shedeur,

11 his company as listed being 46,500.

12 And those to camp next to him shall be the tribe of Simeon, the chief of the people of Simeon being Shelumiel the son of Zurishaddai,

13 his company as listed being 59,300.

14 Then the tribe of Gad, the chief of the people of Gad being Eliasaph the son of Reuel,

15 his company as listed being 45,650.

16 All those listed of the camp of Reuben, by their companies, were 151,450. They shall set out second.

17 "Then the tent of meeting shall set out, with the camp of the Levites in the midst of the camps; as they camp, so shall they set out, each in position, standard by standard.

18 "On the west side shall be the standard of the camp of Ephraim by their companies, the chief of the people of Ephraim being Elishama the son of Ammihud,

19 his company as listed being 40,500.

20 And next to him shall be the tribe of Manasseh, the chief of the people of Manasseh being Gamaliel the son of Pedahzur,

21 his company as listed being 32,200.

22 Then the tribe of Benjamin, the chief of the people of Benjamin being Abidan the son of Gideoni,

23 his company as listed being 35,400.

24 All those listed of the camp of Ephraim, by their companies, were 108,100. They shall set out third on the march.

25 "On the north side shall be the standard of the camp of Dan by their companies, the chief of the people of Dan being Ahiezer the son of Ammishaddai,

26 his company as listed being 62,700.

27 And those to camp next to him shall be the tribe of Asher, the chief of the people of Asher being Pagiel the son of Ochran,

28 his company as listed being 41,500.

29 Then the tribe of Naphtali, the chief of the people of Naphtali being Ahira the son of Enan,

30 his company as listed being 53,400.

31 All those listed of the camp of Dan were 157,600. They shall set out last, standard by standard."

32 These are the people of Israel as listed by their fathers' houses. All those listed in the camps by their companies were 603,550.

33 But the Levites were not listed among the people of Israel, as the Lord commanded Moses.

34 Thus did the people of Israel. According to all that the Lord commanded Moses, so they camped by their standards, and so they set out, each one in his clan, according to his fathers' house

Numbers 3

English Standard Version

The Sons of Aaron

1 These are the generations of Aaron and Moses at the time when the Lord spoke with Moses on Mount Sinai.

2 These are the names of the sons of Aaron: Nadab the firstborn, and Abihu, Eleazar, and Ithamar.

3 These are the names of the sons of Aaron, the anointed priests, whom he ordained to serve as priests.

4 But Nadab and Abihu died before the Lord when they offered unauthorized fire before the Lord in the wilderness of Sinai, and they had no children. So Eleazar and Ithamar served as priests in the lifetime of Aaron their father.

Duties of the Levites

5 And the Lord spoke to Moses, saying,

6 "Bring the tribe of Levi near, and set them before Aaron the priest, that they may minister to him.

7 They shall keep guard over him and over the whole congregation before the tent of meeting, as they minister at the tabernacle.

8 They shall guard all the furnishings of the tent of meeting, and keep guard over the people of Israel as they minister at the tabernacle.

9 And you shall give the Levites to Aaron and his sons; they are wholly given to him from among the people of Israel.

10 And you shall appoint Aaron and his sons, and they shall guard their priesthood. But if any outsider comes near, he shall be put to death."

11 And the Lord spoke to Moses, saying,

12 "Behold, I have taken the Levites from among the people of Israel instead of every firstborn who opens the womb among the people of Israel. The Levites shall be mine,

13 for all the firstborn are mine. On the day that I struck down all the firstborn in the land of Egypt, I consecrated for my own all the firstborn in Israel, both of man and of beast. They shall be mine: I am the Lord."

14 And the Lord spoke to Moses in the wilderness of Sinai, saying,

15 "List the sons of Levi, by fathers' houses and by clans; every male from a month old and upward you shall list."

16 So Moses listed them according to the word of the Lord, as he was commanded.

17 And these were the sons of Levi by their names: Gershon and Kohath and Merari.

18 And these are the names of the sons of Gershon by their clans: Libni and Shimei.

19 And the sons of Kohath by their clans: Amram, Izhar, Hebron, and Uzziel.

20 And the sons of Merari by their clans: Mahli and Mushi. These are the clans of the Levites, by their fathers' houses.

21 To Gershon belonged the clan of the Libnites and the clan of the Shimeites; these were the clans of the Gershonites.

22 Their listing according to the number of all the males from a month old and upward was 7,500.

23 The clans of the Gershonites were to camp behind the tabernacle on the west,

24 with Eliasaph, the son of Lael as chief of the fathers' house of the Gershonites.

25 And the guard duty of the sons of Gershon in the tent of meeting involved the tabernacle, the tent with its covering, the screen for the entrance of the tent of meeting,

26 the hangings of the court, the screen for the door of the court that is around the tabernacle and the altar, and its cords—all the service connected with these.

27 To Kohath belonged the clan of the Amramites and the clan of the Izharites and the clan of the Hebronites and the clan of the Uzzielites; these are the clans of the Kohathites.

28 According to the number of all the males, from a month old and upward, there were 8,600, keeping guard over the sanctuary.

29 The clans of the sons of Kohath were to camp on the south side of the tabernacle,

30 with Elizaphan the son of Uzziel as chief of the fathers' house of the clans of the Kohathites.

31 And their guard duty involved the ark, the table, the lampstand, the altars, the vessels of the sanctuary with which the priests minister, and the screen; all the service connected with these.

32 And Eleazar the son of Aaron the priest was to be chief over the chiefs of the Levites, and to have oversight of those who kept guard over the sanctuary.

33 To Merari belonged the clan of the Mahlites and the clan of the Mushites: these are the clans of Merari.

34 Their listing according to the number of all the males from a month old and upward was 6,200.

35 And the chief of the fathers' house of the clans of Merari was Zuriel the son of Abihail. They were to camp on the north side of the tabernacle.

36 And the appointed guard duty of the sons of Merari involved the frames of the tabernacle, the bars, the pillars, the bases, and all their accessories; all the service connected with these;

37 also the pillars around the court, with their bases and pegs and cords.

38 Those who were to camp before the tabernacle on the east, before the tent of meeting toward the sunrise, were Moses and Aaron and his sons, guarding the sanctuary itself, to protect the people of Israel. And any outsider who came near was to be put to death.

39 All those listed among the Levites, whom Moses and Aaron listed at the commandment of the Lord, by clans, all the males from a month old and upward, were 22,000.

Redemption of the Firstborn

40 And the Lord said to Moses, "List all the firstborn males of the people of Israel, from a month old and upward, taking the number of their names.

41 And you shall take the Levites for me—I am the Lord—instead of all the firstborn among the people of Israel, and the cattle of the Levites instead of all the firstborn among the cattle of the people of Israel."

42 So Moses listed all the firstborn among the people of Israel, as the Lord commanded him.

43 And all the firstborn males, according to the number of names, from a month old and upward as listed were 22,273.

44 And the Lord spoke to Moses, saying,

45 "Take the Levites instead of all the firstborn among the people of Israel, and the cattle of the Levites instead of their cattle. The Levites shall be mine: I am the Lord.

46 And as the redemption price for the 273 of the firstborn of the people of Israel, over and above the number of the male Levites,

47 you shall take five shekels[c] per head; you shall take them according to the shekel of the sanctuary (the shekel of twenty gerahs),

48 and give the money to Aaron and his sons as the redemption price for those who are over."

49 So Moses took the redemption money from those who were over and above those redeemed by the Levites.

50 From the firstborn of the people of Israel he took the money, 1,365 shekels, by the shekel of the sanctuary.

51 And Moses gave the redemption money to Aaron and his sons, according to the word of the Lord, as the Lord commanded Moses.

Numbers 4

English Standard Version

Duties of the Kohathites, Gershonites, and Merarites

1 The Lord spoke to Moses and Aaron, saying,

2 "Take a census of the sons of Kohath from among the sons of Levi, by their clans and their fathers' houses,

3 from thirty years old up to fifty years old, all who can come on duty, to do the work in the tent of meeting.

4 This is the service of the sons of Kohath in the tent of meeting: the most holy things.

5 When the camp is to set out, Aaron and his sons shall go in and take down the veil of the screen and cover the ark of the testimony with it.

6 Then they shall put on it a covering of goatskin and spread on top of that a cloth all of blue, and shall put in its poles.

7 And over the table of the bread of the Presence they shall spread a cloth of blue and put on it the plates, the dishes for incense, the bowls, and the flagons for the drink offering; the regular showbread also shall be on it.

8 Then they shall spread over them a cloth of scarlet and cover the same with a covering of goatskin, and shall put in its poles.

9 And they shall take a cloth of blue and cover the lampstand for the light, with its lamps, its tongs, its trays, and all the vessels for oil with which it is supplied.

10 And they shall put it with all its utensils in a covering of goatskin and put it on the carrying frame.

11 And over the golden altar they shall spread a cloth of blue and cover it with a covering of goatskin, and shall put in its poles.

12 And they shall take all the vessels of the service that are used in the sanctuary and put them in a cloth of blue and cover them with a covering of goatskin and put them on the carrying frame.

13 And they shall take away the ashes from the altar and spread a purple cloth over it.

14 And they shall put on it all the utensils of the altar, which are used for the service there, the fire pans, the forks, the shovels, and the basins, all the utensils of the altar; and they shall spread on it a covering of goatskin, and shall put in its poles.

15 And when Aaron and his sons have finished covering the sanctuary and all the furnishings of the sanctuary, as the camp sets out, after that the sons of Kohath shall come to carry these, but they must not touch the holy things, lest they die. These are the things of the tent of meeting that the sons of Kohath are to carry.

16 "And Eleazar the son of Aaron the priest shall have charge of the oil for the light, the fragrant incense, the regular grain offering, and the anointing oil, with the oversight of the whole tabernacle and all that is in it, of the sanctuary and its vessels."

17 The Lord spoke to Moses and Aaron, saying,

18 "Let not the tribe of the clans of the Kohathites be destroyed from among the Levites,

19 but deal thus with them, that they may live and not die when they come near to the most holy things: Aaron and his sons shall go in and appoint them each to his task and to his burden,

20 but they shall not go in to look on the holy things even for a moment, lest they die."

21 The Lord spoke to Moses, saying,

22 "Take a census of the sons of Gershon also, by their fathers' houses and by their clans.

23 From thirty years old up to fifty years old, you shall list them, all who can come to do duty, to do service in the tent of meeting.

24 This is the service of the clans of the Gershonites, in serving and bearing burdens:

25 they shall carry the curtains of the tabernacle and the tent of meeting with its covering and the covering of goatskin that is on top of it and the screen for the entrance of the tent of meeting

26 and the hangings of the court and the screen for the entrance of the gate of the court that is around the tabernacle and the altar, and their cords and all the equipment for their service. And they shall do all that needs to be done with regard to them.

27 All the service of the sons of the Gershonites shall be at the command of Aaron and his sons, in all that they are to carry and in all that they have to do. And you shall assign to their charge all that they are to carry.

28 This is the service of the clans of the sons of the Gershonites in the tent of meeting, and their guard duty is to be under the direction of Ithamar the son of Aaron the priest.

29 "As for the sons of Merari, you shall list them by their clans and their fathers' houses.

30 From thirty years old up to fifty years old, you shall list them, everyone who can come on duty, to do the service of the tent of meeting.

31 And this is what they are charged to carry, as the whole of their service in the tent of meeting: the frames of the tabernacle, with its bars, pillars, and bases,

32 and the pillars around the court with their bases, pegs, and cords, with all their equipment and all their accessories. And you shall list by name the objects that they are required to carry.

33 This is the service of the clans of the sons of Merari, the whole of their service in the tent of meeting, under the direction of Ithamar the son of Aaron the priest."

34 And Moses and Aaron and the chiefs of the congregation listed the sons of the Kohathites, by their clans and their fathers' houses,

35 from thirty years old up to fifty years old, everyone who could come on duty, for service in the tent of meeting;

36 and those listed by clans were 2,750.

37 This was the list of the clans of the Kohathites, all who served in the tent of meeting, whom Moses and Aaron listed according to the commandment of the Lord by Moses.

38 Those listed of the sons of Gershon, by their clans and their fathers' houses,

39 from thirty years old up to fifty years old, everyone who could come on duty for service in the tent of meeting—

40 those listed by their clans and their fathers' houses were 2,630.

41 This was the list of the clans of the sons of Gershon, all who served in the tent of meeting, whom Moses and Aaron listed according to the commandment of the Lord.

42 Those listed of the clans of the sons of Merari, by their clans and their fathers' houses,

43 from thirty years old up to fifty years old, everyone who could come on duty, for service in the tent of meeting—

44 those listed by clans were 3,200.

45 This was the list of the clans of the sons of Merari, whom Moses and Aaron listed according to the commandment of the Lord by Moses.

46 All those who were listed of the Levites, whom Moses and Aaron and the chiefs of Israel listed, by their clans and their fathers' houses,

47 from thirty years old up to fifty years old, everyone who could come to do the service of ministry and the service of bearing burdens in the tent of meeting,

48 those listed were 8,580.

49 According to the commandment of the Lord through Moses they were listed, each one with his task of serving or carrying. Thus they were listed by him, as the Lord commanded Moses.

Numbers 5

English Standard Version

Unclean People

1 The Lord spoke to Moses, saying,

2 "Command the people of Israel that they put out of the camp everyone who is leprous or has a discharge and everyone who is unclean through contact with the dead.

3 You shall put out both male and female, putting them outside the camp, that they may not defile their camp, in the midst of which I dwell."

4 And the people of Israel did so, and put them outside the camp; as the Lord said to Moses, so the people of Israel did.

Confession and Restitution

5 And the Lord spoke to Moses, saying,

6 "Speak to the people of Israel, When a man or woman commits any of the sins that people commit by breaking faith with the Lord, and that person realizes his guilt,

7 he shall confess his sin that he has committed. And he shall make full restitution for his wrong, adding a fifth to it and giving it to him to whom he did the wrong.

8 But if the man has no next of kin to whom restitution may be made for the wrong, the restitution for wrong shall go to the Lord for the priest, in addition to the ram of atonement with which atonement is made for him.

9 And every contribution, all the holy donations of the people of Israel, which they bring to the priest, shall be his.

10 Each one shall keep his holy donations: whatever anyone gives to the priest shall be his."

A Test for Adultery

11 And the Lord spoke to Moses, saying,

12 "Speak to the people of Israel, If any man's wife goes astray and breaks faith with him,

13 if a man lies with her sexually, and it is hidden from the eyes of her husband, and she is undetected though she has defiled herself, and there is no witness against her, since she was not taken in the act,

14 and if the spirit of jealousy comes over him and he is jealous of his wife who has defiled herself, or if the spirit of jealousy comes over him and he is jealous of his wife, though she has not defiled herself,

15 then the man shall bring his wife to the priest and bring the offering required of her, a tenth of an ephah of barley flour. He shall pour no oil on it and put no frankincense on it, for it is a grain offering of jealousy, a grain offering of remembrance, bringing iniquity to remembrance.

16 "And the priest shall bring her near and set her before the Lord.

17 And the priest shall take holy water in an earthenware vessel and take some of the dust that is on the floor of the tabernacle and put it into the water.

18 And the priest shall set the woman before the Lord and unbind the hair of the woman's head and place in her hands the grain offering of remembrance, which is the grain offering of jealousy. And in his hand the priest shall have the water of bitterness that brings the curse.

19 Then the priest shall make her take an oath, saying, 'If no man has lain with you, and if you have not turned aside to uncleanness while you were under your husband's authority, be free from this water of bitterness that brings the curse.

20 But if you have gone astray, though you are under your husband's authority, and if you have defiled yourself, and some man other than your husband has lain with you,

21 then' (let the priest make the woman take the oath of the curse, and say to the woman) 'the Lord make you a curse and an oath among your people, when the Lord makes your thigh fall away and your body swell.

22 May this water that brings the curse pass into your bowels and make your womb swell and your thigh fall away.' And the woman shall say, 'Amen, Amen.'

23 "Then the priest shall write these curses in a book and wash them off into the water of bitterness.

24 And he shall make the woman drink the water of bitterness that brings the curse, and the water that brings the curse shall enter into her and cause bitter pain.

25 And the priest shall take the grain offering of jealousy out of the woman's hand and shall wave the grain offering before the Lord and bring it to the altar.

Numbers 5

26 And the priest shall take a handful of the grain offering, as its memorial portion, and burn it on the altar, and afterward shall make the woman drink the water.

27 And when he has made her drink the water, then, if she has defiled herself and has broken faith with her husband, the water that brings the curse shall enter into her and cause bitter pain, and her womb shall swell, and her thigh shall fall away, and the woman shall become a curse among her people.

28 But if the woman has not defiled herself and is clean, then she shall be free and shall conceive children.

29 "This is the law in cases of jealousy, when a wife, though under her husband's authority, goes astray and defiles herself,

30 or when the spirit of jealousy comes over a man and he is jealous of his wife. Then he shall set the woman before the Lord, and the priest shall carry out for her all this law.

31 The man shall be free from iniquity, but the woman shall bear her iniquity."

Numbers 6

English Standard Version

The Nazirite Vow

1 And the Lord spoke to Moses, saying,

2 "Speak to the people of Israel and say to them, When either a man or a woman makes a special vow, the vow of a Nazirite, to separate himself to the Lord,

3 he shall separate himself from wine and strong drink. He shall drink no vinegar made from wine or strong drink and shall not drink any juice of grapes or eat grapes, fresh or dried.

4 All the days of his separation he shall eat nothing that is produced by the grapevine, not even the seeds or the skins.

5 "All the days of his vow of separation, no razor shall touch his head. Until the time is completed for which he separates himself to the Lord, he shall be holy. He shall let the locks of hair of his head grow long.

6 "All the days that he separates himself to the Lord he shall not go near a dead body.

7 Not even for his father or for his mother, for brother or sister, if they die, shall he make himself unclean, because his separation to God is on his head.

Numbers 6

8 All the days of his separation he is holy to the Lord.

9 "And if any man dies very suddenly beside him and he defiles his consecrated head, then he shall shave his head on the day of his cleansing; on the seventh day he shall shave it.

10 On the eighth day he shall bring two turtledoves or two pigeons to the priest to the entrance of the tent of meeting,

11 and the priest shall offer one for a sin offering and the other for a burnt offering, and make atonement for him, because he sinned by reason of the dead body. And he shall consecrate his head that same day

12 and separate himself to the Lord for the days of his separation and bring a male lamb a year old for a guilt offering. But the previous period shall be void, because his separation was defiled.

13 "And this is the law for the Nazirite, when the time of his separation has been completed: he shall be brought to the entrance of the tent of meeting,

14 and he shall bring his gift to the Lord, one male lamb a year old without blemish for a burnt offering, and one ewe lamb a year old without blemish as a sin offering, and one ram without blemish as a peace offering,

15 and a basket of unleavened bread, loaves of fine flour mixed with oil, and unleavened wafers smeared with oil, and their grain offering and their drink offerings.

16 And the priest shall bring them before the Lord and offer his sin offering and his burnt offering,

17 and he shall offer the ram as a sacrifice of peace offering to the Lord, with the basket of unleavened bread. The priest shall offer also its grain offering and its drink offering.

18 And the Nazirite shall shave his consecrated head at the entrance of the tent of meeting and shall take the hair from his consecrated head and put it on the fire that is under the sacrifice of the peace offering.

19 And the priest shall take the shoulder of the ram, when it is boiled, and one unleavened loaf out of the basket and one unleavened wafer, and shall put them on the hands of the Nazirite, after he has shaved the hair of his consecration,

20 and the priest shall wave them for a wave offering before the Lord. They are a holy portion for the priest, together with the breast that is waved and the thigh that is contributed. And after that the Nazirite may drink wine.

21 "This is the law of the Nazirite. But if he vows an offering to the Lord above his Nazirite vow, as he can afford, in exact accordance with the vow that he takes, then he shall do in addition to the law of the Nazirite."

Aaron's Blessing

22 The Lord spoke to Moses, saying, 23 "Speak to Aaron and his sons, saying, Thus you shall bless the people of Israel: you shall say to them,

24 The Lord bless you and keep you;

25 the Lord make his face to shine upon you and be gracious to you;

26 the Lord lift up his countenance[c] upon you and give you peace.

27 "So shall they put my name upon the people of Israel, and I will bless them."

Numbers 7

English Standard Version

Offerings at the Tabernacle's Consecration

1 On the day when Moses had finished setting up the tabernacle and had anointed and consecrated it with all its furnishings and had anointed and consecrated the altar with all its utensils,

2 the chiefs of Israel, heads of their fathers' houses, who were the chiefs of the tribes, who were over those who were listed, approached

3 and brought their offerings before the Lord, six wagons and twelve oxen, a wagon for every two of the chiefs, and for each one an ox. They brought them before the tabernacle.

4 Then the Lord said to Moses,

5 "Accept these from them, that they may be used in the service of the tent of meeting, and give them to the Levites, to each man according to his service."

6 So Moses took the wagons and the oxen and gave them to the Levites.

7 Two wagons and four oxen he gave to the sons of Gershon, according to their service.

8 And four wagons and eight oxen he gave to the sons of Merari, according to their service, under the direction of Ithamar the son of Aaron the priest.

9 But to the sons of Kohath he gave none, because they were charged with the service of the holy things that had to be carried on the shoulder.

10 And the chiefs offered offerings for the dedication of the altar on the day it was anointed; and the chiefs offered their offering before the altar.

11 And the Lord said to Moses, "They shall offer their offerings, one chief each day, for the dedication of the altar."

12 He who offered his offering the first day was Nahshon the son of Amminadab, of the tribe of Judah.

13 And his offering was one silver plate whose weight was 130 shekels, one silver basin of 70 shekels, according to the shekel of the sanctuary, both of them full of fine flour mixed with oil for a grain offering;

14 one golden dish of 10 shekels, full of incense;

15 one bull from the herd, one ram, one male lamb a year old, for a burnt offering;

16 one male goat for a sin offering;

17 and for the sacrifice of peace offerings, two oxen, five rams, five male goats, and five male lambs a year old. This was the offering of Nahshon the son of Amminadab.

18 On the second day Nethanel the son of Zuar, the chief of Issachar, made an offering.

19 He offered for his offering one silver plate whose weight was 130 shekels, one silver basin of 70 shekels, according to the shekel of the sanctuary, both of them full of fine flour mixed with oil for a grain offering;

20 one golden dish of 10 shekels, full of incense;

21 one bull from the herd, one ram, one male lamb a year old, for a burnt offering;

22 one male goat for a sin offering;

23 and for the sacrifice of peace offerings, two oxen, five rams, five male goats, and five male lambs a year old. This was the offering of Nethanel the son of Zuar.

24 On the third day Eliab the son of Helon, the chief of the people of Zebulun:

25 his offering was one silver plate whose weight was 130 shekels, one silver basin of 70 shekels, according to the shekel of the sanctuary, both of them full of fine flour mixed with oil for a grain offering;

26 one golden dish of 10 shekels, full of incense;

27 one bull from the herd, one ram, one male lamb a year old, for a burnt offering;

28 one male goat for a sin offering;

29 and for the sacrifice of peace offerings, two oxen, five rams, five male goats, and five male lambs a year old. This was the offering of Eliab the son of Helon.

30 On the fourth day Elizur the son of Shedeur, the chief of the people of Reuben:

31 his offering was one silver plate whose weight was 130 shekels, one silver basin of 70 shekels, according to the shekel of the sanctuary, both of them full of fine flour mixed with oil for a grain offering;

32 one golden dish of 10 shekels, full of incense;

33 one bull from the herd, one ram, one male lamb a year old, for a burnt offering;

34 one male goat for a sin offering;

35 and for the sacrifice of peace offerings, two oxen, five rams, five male goats, and five male lambs a year old. This was the offering of Elizur the son of Shedeur.

36 On the fifth day Shelumiel the son of Zurishaddai, the chief of the people of Simeon:

37 his offering was one silver plate whose weight was 130 shekels, one silver basin of 70 shekels, according to the shekel of the sanctuary, both of them full of fine flour mixed with oil for a grain offering;

38 one golden dish of 10 shekels, full of incense;

39 one bull from the herd, one ram, one male lamb a year old, for a burnt offering;

40 one male goat for a sin offering;

41 and for the sacrifice of peace offerings, two oxen, five rams, five male goats, and five male lambs a year old. This was the offering of Shelumiel the son of Zurishaddai.

42 On the sixth day Eliasaph the son of Deuel, the chief of the people of Gad:

43 his offering was one silver plate whose weight was 130 shekels, one silver basin of 70 shekels, according to the shekel of the sanctuary, both of them full of fine flour mixed with oil for a grain offering;

44 one golden dish of 10 shekels, full of incense;

45 one bull from the herd, one ram, one male lamb a year old, for a burnt offering;

46 one male goat for a sin offering;

47 and for the sacrifice of peace offerings, two oxen, five rams, five male goats, and five male lambs a year old. This was the offering of Eliasaph the son of Deuel.

48 On the seventh day Elishama the son of Ammihud, the chief of the people of Ephraim:

49 his offering was one silver plate whose weight was 130 shekels, one silver basin of 70 shekels, according to the shekel of the sanctuary, both of them full of fine flour mixed with oil for a grain offering;

50 one golden dish of 10 shekels, full of incense;

51 one bull from the herd, one ram, one male lamb a year old, for a burnt offering;

52 one male goat for a sin offering;

53 and for the sacrifice of peace offerings, two oxen, five rams, five male goats, and five male lambs a year old. This was the offering of Elishama the son of Ammihud.

54 On the eighth day Gamaliel the son of Pedahzur, the chief of the people of Manasseh:

55 his offering was one silver plate whose weight was 130 shekels, one silver basin of 70 shekels, according to the shekel of the sanctuary, both of them full of fine flour mixed with oil for a grain offering;

56 one golden dish of 10 shekels, full of incense;

57 one bull from the herd, one ram, one male lamb a year old, for a burnt offering;

58 one male goat for a sin offering;

59 and for the sacrifice of peace offerings, two oxen, five rams, five male goats, and five male lambs a year old. This was the offering of Gamaliel the son of Pedahzur.

60 On the ninth day Abidan the son of Gideoni, the chief of the people of Benjamin:

61 his offering was one silver plate whose weight was 130 shekels, one silver basin of 70 shekels, according to the shekel of the sanctuary, both of them full of fine flour mixed with oil for a grain offering;

62 one golden dish of 10 shekels, full of incense;

63 one bull from the herd, one ram, one male lamb a year old, for a burnt offering;

64 one male goat for a sin offering;

65 and for the sacrifice of peace offerings, two oxen, five rams, five male goats, and five male lambs a year old. This was the offering of Abidan the son of Gideoni.

66 On the tenth day Ahiezer the son of Ammishaddai, the chief of the people of Dan:

67 his offering was one silver plate whose weight was 130 shekels, one silver basin of 70 shekels, according to the shekel of the sanctuary, both of them full of fine flour mixed with oil for a grain offering;

68 one golden dish of 10 shekels, full of incense;

69 one bull from the herd, one ram, one male lamb a year old, for a burnt offering;

70 one male goat for a sin offering;

71 and for the sacrifice of peace offerings, two oxen, five rams, five male goats, and five male lambs a year old. This was the offering of Ahiezer the son of Ammishaddai.

72 On the eleventh day Pagiel the son of Ochran, the chief of the people of Asher:

73 his offering was one silver plate whose weight was 130 shekels, one silver basin of 70 shekels, according to the shekel of the sanctuary, both of them full of fine flour mixed with oil for a grain offering;

74 one golden dish of 10 shekels, full of incense;

75 one bull from the herd, one ram, one male lamb a year old, for a burnt offering;

76 one male goat for a sin offering;

77 and for the sacrifice of peace offerings, two oxen, five rams, five male goats, and five male lambs a year old. This was the offering of Pagiel the son of Ochran.

78 On the twelfth day Ahira the son of Enan, the chief of the people of Naphtali:

79 his offering was one silver plate whose weight was 130 shekels, one silver basin of 70 shekels, according to the shekel of the sanctuary, both of them full of fine flour mixed with oil for a grain offering;

80 one golden dish of 10 shekels, full of incense;

81 one bull from the herd, one ram, one male lamb a year old, for a burnt offering; 82 one male goat for a sin offering;

83 and for the sacrifice of peace offerings, two oxen, five rams, five male goats, and five male lambs a year old. This was the offering of Ahira the son of Enan.

84 This was the dedication offering for the altar on the day when it was anointed, from the chiefs of Israel: twelve silver plates, twelve silver basins, twelve golden dishes,

85 each silver plate weighing 130 shekels and each basin 70, all the silver of the vessels 2,400 shekels according to the shekel of the sanctuary,

86 the twelve golden dishes, full of incense, weighing 10 shekels apiece according to the shekel of the sanctuary, all the gold of the dishes being 120 shekels;

87 all the cattle for the burnt offering twelve bulls, twelve rams, twelve male lambs a year old, with their grain offering; and twelve male goats for a sin offering;

88 and all the cattle for the sacrifice of peace offerings twenty-four bulls, the rams sixty, the male goats sixty, the male lambs a year old sixty. This was the dedication offering for the altar after it was anointed.

89 And when Moses went into the tent of meeting to speak with the Lord, he heard the voice speaking to him from above the mercy seat that was on the ark of the testimony, from between the two cherubim; and it spoke to him.

Numbers 8

English Standard Version

The Seven Lamps

1 Now the Lord spoke to Moses, saying,

2 "Speak to Aaron and say to him, When you set up the lamps, the seven lamps shall give light in front of the lampstand."

3 And Aaron did so: he set up its lamps in front of the lampstand, as the Lord commanded Moses.

4 And this was the workmanship of the lampstand, hammered work of gold. From its base to its flowers, it was hammered work; according to the pattern that the Lord had shown Moses, so he made the lampstand.

Cleansing of the Levites

5 And the Lord spoke to Moses, saying,

6 "Take the Levites from among the people of Israel and cleanse them.

7 Thus you shall do to them to cleanse them: sprinkle the water of purification upon them, and let them go with a razor over all their body, and wash their clothes and cleanse themselves.

8 Then let them take a bull from the herd and its grain offering of fine flour mixed with oil, and you shall take another bull from the herd for a sin offering.

9 And you shall bring the Levites before the tent of meeting and assemble the whole congregation of the people of Israel.

10 When you bring the Levites before the Lord, the people of Israel shall lay their hands on the Levites,

11 and Aaron shall offer the Levites before the Lord as a wave offering from the people of Israel, that they may do the service of the Lord.

12 Then the Levites shall lay their hands on the heads of the bulls, and you shall offer the one for a sin offering and the other for a burnt offering to the Lord to make atonement for the Levites.

13 And you shall set the Levites before Aaron and his sons, and shall offer them as a wave offering to the Lord.

14 "Thus you shall separate the Levites from among the people of Israel, and the Levites shall be mine.

15 And after that the Levites shall go in to serve at the tent of meeting, when you have cleansed them and offered them as a wave offering.

16 For they are wholly given to me from among the people of Israel. Instead of all who open the womb, the firstborn of all the people of Israel, I have taken them for myself.

17 For all the firstborn among the people of Israel are mine, both of man and of beast. On the day that I struck down all the firstborn in the land of Egypt I consecrated them for myself,

18 and I have taken the Levites instead of all the firstborn among the people of Israel.

19 And I have given the Levites as a gift to Aaron and his sons from among the people of Israel, to do the service for the people of Israel at the tent of meeting and to make atonement for the people of Israel, that there may be no plague among the people of Israel when the people of Israel come near the sanctuary."

20 Thus did Moses and Aaron and all the congregation of the people of Israel to the Levites. According to all that the Lord commanded Moses concerning the Levites, the people of Israel did to them.

21 And the Levites purified themselves from sin and washed their clothes, and Aaron offered them as a wave offering before the Lord, and Aaron made atonement for them to cleanse them.

22 And after that the Levites went in to do their service in the tent of meeting before Aaron and his sons; as the Lord had commanded Moses concerning the Levites, so they did to them.

Retirement of the Levites

23 And the Lord spoke to Moses, saying,

24 "This applies to the Levites: from twenty-five years old and upward they shall come to do duty in the service of the tent of meeting.

25 And from the age of fifty years they shall withdraw from the duty of the service and serve no more.

26 They minister to their brothers in the tent of meeting by keeping guard, but they shall do no service. Thus shall you do to the Levites in assigning their duties.

Numbers 9

English Standard Version

The Passover Celebrated

1 And the Lord spoke to Moses in the wilderness of Sinai, in the first month of the second year after they had come out of the land of Egypt, saying,

2 "Let the people of Israel keep the Passover at its appointed time.

3 On the fourteenth day of this month, at twilight, you shall keep it at its appointed time; according to all its statutes and all its rules you shall keep it."

4 So Moses told the people of Israel that they should keep the Passover.

5 And they kept the Passover in the first month, on the fourteenth day of the month, at twilight, in the wilderness of Sinai; according to all that the Lord commanded Moses, so the people of Israel did.

6 And there were certain men who were unclean through touching a dead body, so that they could not keep the Passover on that day, and they came before Moses and Aaron on that day.

7 And those men said to him, "We are unclean through touching a dead body. Why are we kept from bringing the Lord's offering at its appointed time among the people of Israel?"

8 And Moses said to them, "Wait, that I may hear what the Lord will command concerning you."

9 The Lord spoke to Moses, saying,

10 "Speak to the people of Israel, saying, If any one of you or of your descendants is unclean through touching a dead body, or is on a long journey, he shall still keep the Passover to the Lord.

11 In the second month on the fourteenth day at twilight they shall keep it. They shall eat it with unleavened bread and bitter herbs.

12 They shall leave none of it until the morning, nor break any of its bones; according to all the statute for the Passover they shall keep it.

13 But if anyone who is clean and is not on a journey fails to keep the Passover, that person shall be cut off from his people because he did not bring the Lord's offering at its appointed time; that man shall bear his sin.

14 And if a stranger sojourns among you and would keep the Passover to the Lord, according to the statute of the Passover and according to its rule, so shall he do. You shall have one statute, both for the sojourner and for the native."

The Cloud Covering the Tabernacle

15 On the day that the tabernacle was set up, the cloud covered the tabernacle, the tent of the testimony. And at evening it was over the tabernacle like the appearance of fire until morning.

16 So it was always: the cloud covered it by day and the appearance of fire by night.

17 And whenever the cloud lifted from over the tent, after that the people of Israel set out, and in the place where the cloud settled down, there the people of Israel camped.

18 At the command of the Lord the people of Israel set out, and at the command of the Lord they camped. As long as the cloud rested over the tabernacle, they remained in camp.

19 Even when the cloud continued over the tabernacle many days, the people of Israel kept the charge of the Lord and did not set out.

20 Sometimes the cloud was a few days over the tabernacle, and according to the command of the Lord they remained in camp; then according to the command of the Lord they set out.

21 And sometimes the cloud remained from evening until morning. And when the cloud lifted in the morning, they set out, or if it continued for a day and a night, when the cloud lifted they set out.

22 Whether it was two days, or a month, or a longer time, that the cloud continued over the tabernacle, abiding there, the people of Israel remained in camp and did not set out, but when it lifted they set out.

23 At the command of the Lord they camped, and at the command of the Lord they set out. They kept the charge of the Lord, at the command of the Lord by Moses.

Numbers 10

English Standard Version

The Silver Trumpets

1 The Lord spoke to Moses, saying,

2 "Make two silver trumpets. Of hammered work you shall make them, and you shall use them for summoning the congregation and for breaking camp.

3 And when both are blown, all the congregation shall gather themselves to you at the entrance of the tent of meeting.

4 But if they blow only one, then the chiefs, the heads of the tribes of Israel, shall gather themselves to you.

5 When you blow an alarm, the camps that are on the east side shall set out.

6 And when you blow an alarm the second time, the camps that are on the south side shall set out. An alarm is to be blown whenever they are to set out.

7 But when the assembly is to be gathered together, you shall blow a long blast, but you shall not sound an alarm.

8 And the sons of Aaron, the priests, shall blow the trumpets. The trumpets shall be to you for a perpetual statute throughout your generations.

9 And when you go to war in your land against the adversary who oppresses you, then you shall sound an alarm with the trumpets, that you may be remembered before the Lord your God, and you shall be saved from your enemies.

10 On the day of your gladness also, and at your appointed feasts and at the beginnings of your months, you shall blow the trumpets over your burnt offerings and over the sacrifices of your peace offerings. They shall be a reminder of you before your God: I am the Lord your God."

Israel Leaves Sinai

11 In the second year, in the second month, on the twentieth day of the month, the cloud lifted from over the tabernacle of the testimony,

12 and the people of Israel set out by stages from the wilderness of Sinai. And the cloud settled down in the wilderness of Paran.

13 They set out for the first time at the command of the Lord by Moses.

14 The standard of the camp of the people of Judah set out first by their companies, and over their company was Nahshon the son of Amminadab.

15 And over the company of the tribe of the people of Issachar was Nethanel the son of Zuar.

16 And over the company of the tribe of the people of Zebulun was Eliab the son of Helon.

17 And when the tabernacle was taken down, the sons of Gershon and the sons of Merari, who carried the tabernacle, set out.

18 And the standard of the camp of Reuben set out by their companies, and over their company was Elizur the son of Shedeur.

19 And over the company of the tribe of the people of Simeon was Shelumiel the son of Zurishaddai.

20 And over the company of the tribe of the people of Gad was Eliasaph the son of Deuel.

21 Then the Kohathites set out, carrying the holy things, and the tabernacle was set up before their arrival.

22 And the standard of the camp of the people of Ephraim set out by their companies, and over their company was Elishama the son of Ammihud.

23 And over the company of the tribe of the people of Manasseh was Gamaliel the son of Pedahzur.

24 And over the company of the tribe of the people of Benjamin was Abidan the son of Gideoni.

25 Then the standard of the camp of the people of Dan, acting as the rear guard of all the camps, set out by their companies, and over their company was Ahiezer the son of Ammishaddai.

26 And over the company of the tribe of the people of Asher was Pagiel the son of Ochran.

27 And over the company of the tribe of the people of Naphtali was Ahira the son of Enan.

28 This was the order of march of the people of Israel by their companies, when they set out.

29 And Moses said to Hobab the son of Reuel the Midianite, Moses' father-in-law, "We are setting out for the place of which the Lord said, 'I will give it to you.' Come with us, and we will do good to you, for the Lord has promised good to Israel."

30 But he said to him, "I will not go. I will depart to my own land and to my kindred."

31 And he said, "Please do not leave us, for you know where we should camp in the wilderness, and you will serve as eyes for us.

32 And if you do go with us, whatever good the Lord will do to us, the same will we do to you."

33 So they set out from the mount of the Lord three days' journey. And the ark of the covenant of the Lord went before them three days' journey, to seek out a resting place for them.

34 And the cloud of the Lord was over them by day, whenever they set out from the camp.

35 And whenever the ark set out, Moses said, "Arise, O Lord, and let your enemies be scattered, and let those who hate you flee before you."

36 And when it rested, he said, "Return, O Lord, to the ten thousand thousands of Israel."

Numbers 11

English Standard Version

The People Complain

1 And the people complained in the hearing of the Lord about their misfortunes, and when the Lord heard it, his anger was kindled, and the fire of the Lord burned among them and consumed some outlying parts of the camp.

2 Then the people cried out to Moses, and Moses prayed to the Lord, and the fire died down.

3 So the name of that place was called Taberah, because the fire of the Lord burned among them.

4 Now the rabble that was among them had a strong craving. And the people of Israel also wept again and said, "Oh that we had meat to eat!

5 We remember the fish we ate in Egypt that cost nothing, the cucumbers, the melons, the leeks, the onions, and the garlic.

6 But now our strength is dried up, and there is nothing at all but this manna to look at."

7 Now the manna was like coriander seed, and its appearance like that of bdellium.

8 The people went about and gathered it and ground it in handmills or beat it in mortars and boiled it in pots and made cakes of it. And the taste of it was like the taste of cakes baked with oil.

9 When the dew fell upon the camp in the night, the manna fell with it.

10 Moses heard the people weeping throughout their clans, everyone at the door of his tent. And the anger of the Lord blazed hotly, and Moses was displeased.

11 Moses said to the Lord, "Why have you dealt ill with your servant? And why have I not found favor in your sight, that you lay the burden of all this people on me?

12 Did I conceive all this people? Did I give them birth, that you should say to me, 'Carry them in your bosom, as a nurse carries a nursing child,' to the land that you swore to give their fathers?

13 Where am I to get meat to give to all this people? For they weep before me and say, 'Give us meat, that we may eat.'

14 I am not able to carry all this people alone; the burden is too heavy for me.

15 If you will treat me like this, kill me at once, if I find favor in your sight, that I may not see my wretchedness."

Elders Appointed to Aid Moses

16 Then the Lord said to Moses, "Gather for me seventy men of the elders of Israel, whom you know to be the elders of the people and officers over them, and bring them to the tent of meeting, and let them take their stand there with you.

17 And I will come down and talk with you there. And I will take some of the Spirit that is on you and put it on them, and they shall bear the burden of the people with you, so that you may not bear it yourself alone.

18 And say to the people, 'Consecrate yourselves for tomorrow, and you shall eat meat, for you have wept in the hearing of the Lord, saying, "Who will give us meat to eat? For it was better for us in Egypt." Therefore the Lord will give you meat, and you shall eat.

19 You shall not eat just one day, or two days, or five days, or ten days, or twenty days,

20 but a whole month, until it comes out at your nostrils and becomes loathsome to you, because you have rejected the Lord who is among you and have wept before him, saying, "Why did we come out of Egypt?"'"

21 But Moses said, "The people among whom I am number six hundred thousand on foot, and you have said, 'I will give them meat, that they may eat a whole month!'

22 Shall flocks and herds be slaughtered for them, and be enough for them? Or shall all the fish of the sea be gathered together for them, and be enough for them?"

23 And the Lord said to Moses, "Is the Lord's hand shortened? Now you shall see whether my word will come true for you or not."

24 So Moses went out and told the people the words of the Lord. And he gathered seventy men of the elders of the people and placed them around the tent.

25 Then the Lord came down in the cloud and spoke to him, and took some of the Spirit that was on him and put it on the seventy elders. And as soon as the Spirit rested on them, they prophesied. But they did not continue doing it.

26 Now two men remained in the camp, one named Eldad, and the other named Medad, and the Spirit rested on them. They were among those registered, but they had not gone out to the tent, and so they prophesied in the camp.

27 And a young man ran and told Moses, "Eldad and Medad are prophesying in the camp."

28 And Joshua the son of Nun, the assistant of Moses from his youth, said, "My lord Moses, stop them."

29 But Moses said to him, "Are you jealous for my sake? Would that all the Lord's people were prophets, that the Lord would put his Spirit on them!"

30 And Moses and the elders of Israel returned to the camp.

Quail and a Plague

31 Then a wind from the Lord sprang up, and it brought quail from the sea and let them fall beside the camp, about a day's journey on this side and a day's journey on the other side, around the camp, and about two cubits above the ground.

32 And the people rose all that day and all night and all the next day, and gathered the quail. Those who gathered least gathered ten homers. And they spread them out for themselves all around the camp.

33 While the meat was yet between their teeth, before it was consumed, the anger of the Lord was kindled against the people, and the Lord struck down the people with a very great plague.

34 Therefore the name of that place was called Kibroth-hattaavah, because there they buried the people who had the craving.

35 From Kibroth-hattaavah the people journeyed to Hazeroth, and they remained at Hazeroth.

Numbers 12

English Standard Version

Miriam and Aaron Oppose Moses

1 Miriam and Aaron spoke against Moses because of the Cushite woman whom he had married, for he had married a Cushite woman.

2 And they said, "Has the Lord indeed spoken only through Moses? Has he not spoken through us also?" And the Lord heard it.

3 Now the man Moses was very meek, more than all people who were on the face of the earth.

4 And suddenly the Lord said to Moses and to Aaron and Miriam, "Come out, you three, to the tent of meeting." And the three of them came out.

5 And the Lord came down in a pillar of cloud and stood at the entrance of the tent and called Aaron and Miriam, and they both came forward.

6 And he said, "Hear my words: If there is a prophet among you, I the Lord make myself known to him in a vision; I speak with him in a dream.

7 Not so with my servant Moses. He is faithful in all my house.

8 With him I speak mouth to mouth, clearly, and not in riddles, and he beholds the form of the Lord. Why then were you not afraid to speak against my servant Moses?"

9 And the anger of the Lord was kindled against them, and he departed.

10 When the cloud removed from over the tent, behold, Miriam was leprous, like snow. And Aaron turned toward Miriam, and behold, she was leprous.

11 And Aaron said to Moses, "Oh, my lord, do not punish us because we have done foolishly and have sinned.

12 Let her not be as one dead, whose flesh is half eaten away when he comes out of his mother's womb."

13 And Moses cried to the Lord, "O God, please heal her—please."

14 But the Lord said to Moses, "If her father had but spit in her face, should she not be shamed seven days? Let her be shut outside the camp seven days, and after that she may be brought in again."

15 So Miriam was shut outside the camp seven days, and the people did not set out on the march till Miriam was brought in again.

16 After that the people set out from Hazeroth, and camped in the wilderness of Paran.

Numbers 13

English Standard Version

Spies Sent into Canaan

1 The Lord spoke to Moses, saying,

2 "Send men to spy out the land of Canaan, which I am giving to the people of Israel. From each tribe of their fathers you shall send a man, every one a chief among them."

3 So Moses sent them from the wilderness of Paran, according to the command of the Lord, all of them men who were heads of the people of Israel.

4 And these were their names: From the tribe of Reuben, Shammua the son of Zaccur;

5 from the tribe of Simeon, Shaphat the son of Hori;

6 from the tribe of Judah, Caleb the son of Jephunneh;

7 from the tribe of Issachar, Igal the son of Joseph;

8 from the tribe of Ephraim, Hoshea the son of Nun;

9 from the tribe of Benjamin, Palti the son of Raphu;

10 from the tribe of Zebulun, Gaddiel the son of Sodi;

11 from the tribe of Joseph (that is, from the tribe of Manasseh), Gaddi the son of Susi;

12 from the tribe of Dan, Ammiel the son of Gemalli;

13 from the tribe of Asher, Sethur the son of Michael;

14 from the tribe of Naphtali, Nahbi the son of Vophsi;

15 from the tribe of Gad, Geuel the son of Machi.

16 These were the names of the men whom Moses sent to spy out the land. And Moses called Hoshea the son of Nun Joshua.

17 Moses sent them to spy out the land of Canaan and said to them, "Go up into the Negeb and go up into the hill country,

18 and see what the land is, and whether the people who dwell in it are strong or weak, whether they are few or many,

19 and whether the land that they dwell in is good or bad, and whether the cities that they dwell in are camps or strongholds,

20 and whether the land is rich or poor, and whether there are trees in it or not. Be of good courage and bring some of the fruit of the land." Now the time was the season of the first ripe grapes.

21 So they went up and spied out the land from the wilderness of Zin to Rehob, near Lebo-hamath.

22 They went up into the Negeb and came to Hebron. Ahiman, Sheshai, and Talmai, the descendants of Anak, were there. (Hebron was built seven years before Zoan in Egypt.)

23 And they came to the Valley of Eshcol and cut down from there a branch with a single cluster of grapes, and they carried it on a pole between two of them; they also brought some pomegranates and figs.

24 That place was called the Valley of Eshcol, because of the cluster that the people of Israel cut down from there.

Report of the Spies

25 At the end of forty days they returned from spying out the land.

26 And they came to Moses and Aaron and to all the congregation of the people of Israel in the wilderness of Paran, at Kadesh. They brought back word to them and to all the congregation, and showed them the fruit of the land.

27 And they told him, "We came to the land to which you sent us. It flows with milk and honey, and this is its fruit.

28 However, the people who dwell in the land are strong, and the cities are fortified and very large. And besides, we saw the descendants of Anak there.

29 The Amalekites dwell in the land of the Negeb. The Hittites, the Jebusites, and the Amorites dwell in the hill country. And the Canaanites dwell by the sea, and along the Jordan."

30 But Caleb quieted the people before Moses and said, "Let us go up at once and occupy it, for we are well able to overcome it."

31 Then the men who had gone up with him said, "We are not able to go up against the people, for they are stronger than we are."

32 So they brought to the people of Israel a bad report of the land that they had spied out, saying, "The land, through which we have gone to spy it out, is a land that devours its inhabitants, and all the people that we saw in it are of great height.

33 And there we saw the Nephilim (the sons of Anak, who come from the Nephilim), and we seemed to ourselves like grasshoppers, and so we seemed to them."

Numbers 14

English Standard Version

The People Rebel

1 Then all the congregation raised a loud cry, and the people wept that night.

2 And all the people of Israel grumbled against Moses and Aaron. The whole congregation said to them, "Would that we had died in the land of Egypt! Or would that we had died in this wilderness!

3 Why is the Lord bringing us into this land, to fall by the sword? Our wives and our little ones will become a prey. Would it not be better for us to go back to Egypt?"

4 And they said to one another, "Let us choose a leader and go back to Egypt."

5 Then Moses and Aaron fell on their faces before all the assembly of the congregation of the people of Israel.

6 And Joshua the son of Nun and Caleb the son of Jephunneh, who were among those who had spied out the land, tore their clothes

7 and said to all the congregation of the people of Israel, "The land, which we passed through to spy it out, is an exceedingly good land.

8 If the Lord delights in us, he will bring us into this land and give it to us, a land that flows with milk and honey.

9 Only do not rebel against the Lord. And do not fear the people of the land, for they are bread for us. Their protection is removed from them, and the Lord is with us; do not fear them."

10 Then all the congregation said to stone them with stones. But the glory of the Lord appeared at the tent of meeting to all the people of Israel.

11 And the Lord said to Moses, "How long will this people despise me? And how long will they not believe in me, in spite of all the signs that I have done among them?

12 I will strike them with the pestilence and disinherit them, and I will make of you a nation greater and mightier than they."

Moses Intercedes for the People

13 But Moses said to the Lord, "Then the Egyptians will hear of it, for you brought up this people in your might from among them,

14 and they will tell the inhabitants of this land. They have heard that you, O Lord, are in the midst of this people. For you, O Lord, are seen face to face, and your cloud stands over them and you go before them, in a pillar of cloud by day and in a pillar of fire by night.

15 Now if you kill this people as one man, then the nations who have heard your fame will say,

16 'It is because the Lord was not able to bring this people into the land that he swore to give to them that he has killed them in the wilderness.'

17 And now, please let the power of the Lord be great as you have promised, saying,

18 'The Lord is slow to anger and abounding in steadfast love, forgiving iniquity and transgression, but he will by no means clear the guilty, visiting

the iniquity of the fathers on the children, to the third and the fourth generation.'

19 Please pardon the iniquity of this people, according to the greatness of your steadfast love, just as you have forgiven this people, from Egypt until now."

God Promises Judgment

20 Then the Lord said, "I have pardoned, according to your word.

21 But truly, as I live, and as all the earth shall be filled with the glory of the Lord,

22 none of the men who have seen my glory and my signs that I did in Egypt and in the wilderness, and yet have put me to the test these ten times and have not obeyed my voice,

23 shall see the land that I swore to give to their fathers. And none of those who despised me shall see it.

24 But my servant Caleb, because he has a different spirit and has followed me fully, I will bring into the land into which he went, and his descendants shall possess it.

25 Now, since the Amalekites and the Canaanites dwell in the valleys, turn tomorrow and set out for the wilderness by the way to the Red Sea."

26 And the Lord spoke to Moses and to Aaron, saying,

27 "How long shall this wicked congregation grumble against me? I have heard the grumblings of the people of Israel, which they grumble against me.

28 Say to them, 'As I live, declares the Lord, what you have said in my hearing I will do to you:

29 your dead bodies shall fall in this wilderness, and of all your number, listed in the census from twenty years old and upward, who have grumbled against me,

30 not one shall come into the land where I swore that I would make you dwell, except Caleb the son of Jephunneh and Joshua the son of Nun.

31 But your little ones, who you said would become a prey, I will bring in, and they shall know the land that you have rejected.

32 But as for you, your dead bodies shall fall in this wilderness.

33 And your children shall be shepherds in the wilderness forty years and shall suffer for your faithlessness, until the last of your dead bodies lies in the wilderness.

34 According to the number of the days in which you spied out the land, forty days, a year for each day, you shall bear your iniquity forty years, and you shall know my displeasure.'

35 I, the Lord, have spoken. Surely this will I do to all this wicked congregation who are gathered together against me: in this wilderness they shall come to a full end, and there they shall die."

36 And the men whom Moses sent to spy out the land, who returned and made all the congregation grumble against him by bringing up a bad report about the land—

37 the men who brought up a bad report of the land—died by plague before the Lord.

38 Of those men who went to spy out the land, only Joshua the son of Nun and Caleb the son of Jephunneh remained alive.

Israel Defeated in Battle

39 When Moses told these words to all the people of Israel, the people mourned greatly.

40 And they rose early in the morning and went up to the heights of the hill country, saying, "Here we are. We will go up to the place that the Lord has promised, for we have sinned."

41 But Moses said, "Why now are you transgressing the command of the Lord, when that will not succeed?

42 Do not go up, for the Lord is not among you, lest you be struck down before your enemies.

43 For there the Amalekites and the Canaanites are facing you, and you shall fall by the sword. Because you have turned back from following the Lord, the Lord will not be with you."

44 But they presumed to go up to the heights of the hill country, although neither the ark of the covenant of the Lord nor Moses departed out of the camp.

45 Then the Amalekites and the Canaanites who lived in that hill country came down and defeated them and pursued them, even to Hormah.

Numbers 15

English Standard Version

Laws About Sacrifices

15 The Lord spoke to Moses, saying,

2 "Speak to the people of Israel and say to them, When you come into the land you are to inhabit, which I am giving you,

3 and you offer to the Lord from the herd or from the flock a food offering or a burnt offering or a sacrifice, to fulfill a vow or as a freewill offering or at your appointed feasts, to make a pleasing aroma to the Lord,

4 then he who brings his offering shall offer to the Lord a grain offering of a tenth of an ephah of fine flour, mixed with a quarter of a hin of oil;

5 and you shall offer with the burnt offering, or for the sacrifice, a quarter of a hin of wine for the drink offering for each lamb.

6 Or for a ram, you shall offer for a grain offering two tenths of an ephah of fine flour mixed with a third of a hin of oil.

7 And for the drink offering you shall offer a third of a hin of wine, a pleasing aroma to the Lord.

8 And when you offer a bull as a burnt offering or sacrifice, to fulfill a vow or for peace offerings to the Lord,

9 then one shall offer with the bull a grain offering of three tenths of an ephah of fine flour, mixed with half a hin of oil.

10 And you shall offer for the drink offering half a hin of wine, as a food offering, a pleasing aroma to the Lord.

11 "Thus it shall be done for each bull or ram, or for each lamb or young goat.

12 As many as you offer, so shall you do with each one, as many as there are.

13 Every native Israelite shall do these things in this way, in offering a food offering, with a pleasing aroma to the Lord.

14 And if a stranger is sojourning with you, or anyone is living permanently among you, and he wishes to offer a food offering, with a pleasing aroma to the Lord, he shall do as you do.

15 For the assembly, there shall be one statute for you and for the stranger who sojourns with you, a statute forever throughout your generations. You and the sojourner shall be alike before the Lord.

16 One law and one rule shall be for you and for the stranger who sojourns with you."

17 The Lord spoke to Moses, saying,

18 "Speak to the people of Israel and say to them, When you come into the land to which I bring you

19 and when you eat of the bread of the land, you shall present a contribution to the Lord.

20 Of the first of your dough you shall present a loaf as a contribution; like a contribution from the threshing floor, so shall you present it.

21 Some of the first of your dough you shall give to the Lord as a contribution throughout your generations.

Laws About Unintentional Sins

22 "But if you sin unintentionally, and do not observe all these commandments that the Lord has spoken to Moses,

23 all that the Lord has commanded you by Moses, from the day that the Lord gave commandment, and onward throughout your generations,

24 then if it was done unintentionally without the knowledge of the congregation, all the congregation shall offer one bull from the herd for a burnt offering, a pleasing aroma to the Lord, with its grain offering and its drink offering, according to the rule, and one male goat for a sin offering.

25 And the priest shall make atonement for all the congregation of the people of Israel, and they shall be forgiven, because it was a mistake, and they have brought their offering, a food offering to the Lord, and their sin offering before the Lord for their mistake.

26 And all the congregation of the people of Israel shall be forgiven, and the stranger who sojourns among them, because the whole population was involved in the mistake.

27 "If one person sins unintentionally, he shall offer a female goat a year old for a sin offering.

28 And the priest shall make atonement before the Lord for the person who makes a mistake, when he sins unintentionally, to make atonement for him, and he shall be forgiven.

29 You shall have one law for him who does anything unintentionally, for him who is native among the people of Israel and for the stranger who sojourns among them.

30 But the person who does anything with a high hand, whether he is native or a sojourner, reviles the Lord, and that person shall be cut off from among his people.

31 Because he has despised the word of the Lord and has broken his commandment, that person shall be utterly cut off; his iniquity shall be on him."

A Sabbathbreaker Executed

32 While the people of Israel were in the wilderness, they found a man gathering sticks on the Sabbath day.

33 And those who found him gathering sticks brought him to Moses and Aaron and to all the congregation.

34 They put him in custody, because it had not been made clear what should be done to him.

35 And the Lord said to Moses, "The man shall be put to death; all the congregation shall stone him with stones outside the camp."

36 And all the congregation brought him outside the camp and stoned him to death with stones, as the Lord commanded Moses.

Tassels on Garments

37 The Lord said to Moses,

38 "Speak to the people of Israel, and tell them to make tassels on the corners of their garments throughout their generations, and to put a cord of blue on the tassel of each corner.

39 And it shall be a tassel for you to look at and remember all the commandments of the Lord, to do them, not to follow after your own heart and your own eyes, which you are inclined to whore after.

40 So you shall remember and do all my commandments, and be holy to your God.

41 I am the Lord your God, who brought you out of the land of Egypt to be your God: I am the Lord your God."

Numbers 16

English Standard Version

Korah's Rebellion

1 Now Korah the son of Izhar, son of Kohath, son of Levi, and Dathan and Abiram the sons of Eliab, and On the son of Peleth, sons of Reuben, took men.

2 And they rose up before Moses, with a number of the people of Israel, 250 chiefs of the congregation, chosen from the assembly, well-known men.

3 They assembled themselves together against Moses and against Aaron and said to them, "You have gone too far! For all in the congregation are holy, every one of them, and the Lord is among them. Why then do you exalt yourselves above the assembly of the Lord?"

4 When Moses heard it, he fell on his face,

5 and he said to Korah and all his company, "In the morning the Lord will show who is his, and who is holy, and will bring him near to him. The one whom he chooses he will bring near to him.

6 Do this: take censers, Korah and all his company;

7 put fire in them and put incense on them before the Lord tomorrow, and the man whom the Lord chooses shall be the holy one. You have gone too far, sons of Levi!"

8 And Moses said to Korah, "Hear now, you sons of Levi:

9 is it too small a thing for you that the God of Israel has separated you from the congregation of Israel, to bring you near to himself, to do service in the tabernacle of the Lord and to stand before the congregation to minister to them,

10 and that he has brought you near him, and all your brothers the sons of Levi with you? And would you seek the priesthood also?

11 Therefore it is against the Lord that you and all your company have gathered together. What is Aaron that you grumble against him?"

12 And Moses sent to call Dathan and Abiram the sons of Eliab, and they said, "We will not come up.

13 Is it a small thing that you have brought us up out of a land flowing with milk and honey, to kill us in the wilderness, that you must also make yourself a prince over us?

14 Moreover, you have not brought us into a land flowing with milk and honey, nor given us inheritance of fields and vineyards. Will you put out the eyes of these men? We will not come up."

15 And Moses was very angry and said to the Lord, "Do not respect their offering. I have not taken one donkey from them, and I have not harmed one of them."

16 And Moses said to Korah, "Be present, you and all your company, before the Lord, you and they, and Aaron, tomorrow.

17 And let every one of you take his censer and put incense on it, and every one of you bring before the Lord his censer, 250 censers; you also, and Aaron, each his censer."

18 So every man took his censer and put fire in them and laid incense on them and stood at the entrance of the tent of meeting with Moses and Aaron.

19 Then Korah assembled all the congregation against them at the entrance of the tent of meeting. And the glory of the Lord appeared to all the congregation.

20 And the Lord spoke to Moses and to Aaron, saying,

21 "Separate yourselves from among this congregation, that I may consume them in a moment."

22 And they fell on their faces and said, "O God, the God of the spirits of all flesh, shall one man sin, and will you be angry with all the congregation?"

23 And the Lord spoke to Moses, saying,

24 "Say to the congregation, Get away from the dwelling of Korah, Dathan, and Abiram."

25 Then Moses rose and went to Dathan and Abiram, and the elders of Israel followed him.

26 And he spoke to the congregation, saying, "Depart, please, from the tents of these wicked men, and touch nothing of theirs, lest you be swept away with all their sins."

27 So they got away from the dwelling of Korah, Dathan, and Abiram. And Dathan and Abiram came out and stood at the door of their tents, together with their wives, their sons, and their little ones.

28 And Moses said, "Hereby you shall know that the Lord has sent me to do all these works, and that it has not been of my own accord.

29 If these men die as all men die, or if they are visited by the fate of all mankind, then the Lord has not sent me.

30 But if the Lord creates something new, and the ground opens its mouth and swallows them up with all that belongs to them, and they go down alive into Sheol, then you shall know that these men have despised the Lord."

31 And as soon as he had finished speaking all these words, the ground under them split apart.

32 And the earth opened its mouth and swallowed them up, with their households and all the people who belonged to Korah and all their goods.

33 So they and all that belonged to them went down alive into Sheol, and the earth closed over them, and they perished from the midst of the assembly.

34 And all Israel who were around them fled at their cry, for they said, "Lest the earth swallow us up!"

35 And fire came out from the Lord and consumed the 250 men offering the incense.

36 Then the Lord spoke to Moses, saying,

37 "Tell Eleazar the son of Aaron the priest to take up the censers out of the blaze. Then scatter the fire far and wide, for they have become holy.

38 As for the censers of these men who have sinned at the cost of their lives, let them be made into hammered plates as a covering for the altar, for they offered them before the Lord, and they became holy. Thus they shall be a sign to the people of Israel."

39 So Eleazar the priest took the bronze censers, which those who were burned had offered, and they were hammered out as a covering for the altar,

40 to be a reminder to the people of Israel, so that no outsider, who is not of the descendants of Aaron, should draw near to burn incense before the Lord, lest he become like Korah and his company—as the Lord said to him through Moses.

41 But on the next day all the congregation of the people of Israel grumbled against Moses and against Aaron, saying, "You have killed the people of the Lord."

42 And when the congregation had assembled against Moses and against Aaron, they turned toward the tent of meeting. And behold, the cloud covered it, and the glory of the Lord appeared.

43 And Moses and Aaron came to the front of the tent of meeting,

44 and the Lord spoke to Moses, saying,

45 "Get away from the midst of this congregation, that I may consume them in a moment." And they fell on their faces.

46 And Moses said to Aaron, "Take your censer, and put fire on it from off the altar and lay incense on it and carry it quickly to the congregation and make atonement for them, for wrath has gone out from the Lord; the plague has begun."

47 So Aaron took it as Moses said and ran into the midst of the assembly. And behold, the plague had already begun among the people. And he put on the incense and made atonement for the people.

48 And he stood between the dead and the living, and the plague was stopped.

49 Now those who died in the plague were 14,700, besides those who died in the affair of Korah.

50 And Aaron returned to Moses at the entrance of the tent of meeting, when the plague was stopped.

Numbers 17

English Standard Version

Aaron's Staff Buds

1 The Lord spoke to Moses, saying,

2 "Speak to the people of Israel, and get from them staffs, one for each fathers' house, from all their chiefs according to their fathers' houses, twelve staffs. Write each man's name on his staff,

3 and write Aaron's name on the staff of Levi. For there shall be one staff for the head of each fathers' house.

4 Then you shall deposit them in the tent of meeting before the testimony, where I meet with you.

5 And the staff of the man whom I choose shall sprout. Thus I will make to cease from me the grumblings of the people of Israel, which they grumble against you."

6 Moses spoke to the people of Israel. And all their chiefs gave him staffs, one for each chief, according to their fathers' houses, twelve staffs. And the staff of Aaron was among their staffs.

7 And Moses deposited the staffs before the Lord in the tent of the testimony.

8 On the next day Moses went into the tent of the testimony, and behold, the staff of Aaron for the house of Levi had sprouted and put forth buds and produced blossoms, and it bore ripe almonds.

9 Then Moses brought out all the staffs from before the Lord to all the people of Israel. And they looked, and each man took his staff.

10 And the Lord said to Moses, "Put back the staff of Aaron before the testimony, to be kept as a sign for the rebels, that you may make an end of their grumblings against me, lest they die."

11 Thus did Moses; as the Lord commanded him, so he did.

12 And the people of Israel said to Moses, "Behold, we perish, we are undone, we are all undone.

13 Everyone who comes near, who comes near to the tabernacle of the Lord, shall die. Are we all to perish?"

Numbers 18

English Standard Version

Duties of Priests and Levites

1 So the Lord said to Aaron, "You and your sons and your father's house with you shall bear iniquity connected with the sanctuary, and you and your sons with you shall bear iniquity connected with your priesthood.

2 And with you bring your brothers also, the tribe of Levi, the tribe of your father, that they may join you and minister to you while you and your sons with you are before the tent of the testimony.

3 They shall keep guard over you and over the whole tent, but shall not come near to the vessels of the sanctuary or to the altar lest they, and you, die.

4 They shall join you and keep guard over the tent of meeting for all the service of the tent, and no outsider shall come near you.

5 And you shall keep guard over the sanctuary and over the altar, that there may never again be wrath on the people of Israel.

6 And behold, I have taken your brothers the Levites from among the people of Israel. They are a gift to you, given to the Lord, to do the service of the tent of meeting.

7 And you and your sons with you shall guard your priesthood for all that concerns the altar and that is within the veil; and you shall serve. I give your priesthood as a gift, and any outsider who comes near shall be put to death."

8 Then the Lord spoke to Aaron, "Behold, I have given you charge of the contributions made to me, all the consecrated things of the people of Israel. I have given them to you as a portion and to your sons as a perpetual due.

9 This shall be yours of the most holy things, reserved from the fire: every offering of theirs, every grain offering of theirs and every sin offering of theirs and every guilt offering of theirs, which they render to me, shall be most holy to you and to your sons.

10 In a most holy place shall you eat it. Every male may eat it; it is holy to you.

11 This also is yours: the contribution of their gift, all the wave offerings of the people of Israel. I have given them to you, and to your sons and daughters with you, as a perpetual due. Everyone who is clean in your house may eat it.

12 All the best of the oil and all the best of the wine and of the grain, the firstfruits of what they give to the Lord, I give to you.

13 The first ripe fruits of all that is in their land, which they bring to the Lord, shall be yours. Everyone who is clean in your house may eat it.

14 Every devoted thing in Israel shall be yours.

15 Everything that opens the womb of all flesh, whether man or beast, which they offer to the Lord, shall be yours. Nevertheless, the firstborn of man you shall redeem, and the firstborn of unclean animals you shall redeem.

16 And their redemption price (at a month old you shall redeem them) you shall fix at five shekels in silver, according to the shekel of the sanctuary, which is twenty gerahs.

17 But the firstborn of a cow, or the firstborn of a sheep, or the firstborn of a goat, you shall not redeem; they are holy. You shall sprinkle their blood on the altar and shall burn their fat as a food offering, with a pleasing aroma to the Lord.

18 But their flesh shall be yours, as the breast that is waved and as the right thigh are yours.

19 All the holy contributions that the people of Israel present to the Lord I give to you, and to your sons and daughters with you, as a perpetual due. It is a covenant of salt forever before the Lord for you and for your offspring with you."

20 And the Lord said to Aaron, "You shall have no inheritance in their land, neither shall you have any portion among them. I am your portion and your inheritance among the people of Israel.

21 "To the Levites I have given every tithe in Israel for an inheritance, in return for their service that they do, their service in the tent of meeting,

22 so that the people of Israel do not come near the tent of meeting, lest they bear sin and die.

23 But the Levites shall do the service of the tent of meeting, and they shall bear their iniquity. It shall be a perpetual statute throughout your generations, and among the people of Israel they shall have no inheritance.

24 For the tithe of the people of Israel, which they present as a contribution to the Lord, I have given to the Levites for an inheritance. Therefore I have said of them that they shall have no inheritance among the people of Israel."

25 And the Lord spoke to Moses, saying,

26 "Moreover, you shall speak and say to the Levites, 'When you take from the people of Israel the tithe that I have given you from them for your inheritance, then you shall present a contribution from it to the Lord, a tithe of the tithe.

27 And your contribution shall be counted to you as though it were the grain of the threshing floor, and as the fullness of the winepress.

28 So you shall also present a contribution to the Lord from all your tithes, which you receive from the people of Israel. And from it you shall give the Lord's contribution to Aaron the priest.

29 Out of all the gifts to you, you shall present every contribution due to the Lord; from each its best part is to be dedicated.'

30 Therefore you shall say to them, 'When you have offered from it the best of it, then the rest shall be counted to the Levites as produce of the threshing floor, and as produce of the winepress.

31 And you may eat it in any place, you and your households, for it is your reward in return for your service in the tent of meeting.

32 And you shall bear no sin by reason of it, when you have contributed the best of it. But you shall not profane the holy things of the people of Israel, lest you die.'"

Numbers 19

English Standard Version

Laws for Purification

1 Now the Lord spoke to Moses and to Aaron, saying,

2 "This is the statute of the law that the Lord has commanded: Tell the people of Israel to bring you a red heifer without defect, in which there is no blemish, and on which a yoke has never come.

3 And you shall give it to Eleazar the priest, and it shall be taken outside the camp and slaughtered before him.

4 And Eleazar the priest shall take some of its blood with his finger, and sprinkle some of its blood toward the front of the tent of meeting seven times.

5 And the heifer shall be burned in his sight. Its skin, its flesh, and its blood, with its dung, shall be burned.

6 And the priest shall take cedarwood and hyssop and scarlet yarn, and throw them into the fire burning the heifer.

7 Then the priest shall wash his clothes and bathe his body in water, and afterward he may come into the camp. But the priest shall be unclean until evening.

8 The one who burns the heifer shall wash his clothes in water and bathe his body in water and shall be unclean until evening.

9 And a man who is clean shall gather up the ashes of the heifer and deposit them outside the camp in a clean place. And they shall be kept for the water for impurity for the congregation of the people of Israel; it is a sin offering.

10 And the one who gathers the ashes of the heifer shall wash his clothes and be unclean until evening. And this shall be a perpetual statute for the people of Israel, and for the stranger who sojourns among them.

11 "Whoever touches the dead body of any person shall be unclean seven days.

12 He shall cleanse himself with the water on the third day and on the seventh day, and so be clean. But if he does not cleanse himself on the third day and on the seventh day, he will not become clean.

13 Whoever touches a dead person, the body of anyone who has died, and does not cleanse himself, defiles the tabernacle of the Lord, and that person shall be cut off from Israel; because the water for impurity was not thrown on him, he shall be unclean. His uncleanness is still on him.

14 "This is the law when someone dies in a tent: everyone who comes into the tent and everyone who is in the tent shall be unclean seven days.

15 And every open vessel that has no cover fastened on it is unclean.

16 Whoever in the open field touches someone who was killed with a sword or who died naturally, or touches a human bone or a grave, shall be unclean seven days.

17 For the unclean they shall take some ashes of the burnt sin offering, and fresh water shall be added in a vessel.

18 Then a clean person shall take hyssop and dip it in the water and sprinkle it on the tent and on all the furnishings and on the persons who

Numbers 19

were there and on whoever touched the bone, or the slain or the dead or the grave.

19 And the clean person shall sprinkle it on the unclean on the third day and on the seventh day. Thus on the seventh day he shall cleanse him, and he shall wash his clothes and bathe himself in water, and at evening he shall be clean.

20 "If the man who is unclean does not cleanse himself, that person shall be cut off from the midst of the assembly, since he has defiled the sanctuary of the Lord. Because the water for impurity has not been thrown on him, he is unclean.

21 And it shall be a statute forever for them. The one who sprinkles the water for impurity shall wash his clothes, and the one who touches the water for impurity shall be unclean until evening.

22 And whatever the unclean person touches shall be unclean, and anyone who touches it shall be unclean until evening."

Numbers 20

English Standard Version

The Death of Miriam

1 And the people of Israel, the whole congregation, came into the wilderness of Zin in the first month, and the people stayed in Kadesh. And Miriam died there and was buried there.

The Waters of Meribah

2 Now there was no water for the congregation. And they assembled themselves together against Moses and against Aaron.

3 And the people quarreled with Moses and said, "Would that we had perished when our brothers perished before the Lord!

4 Why have you brought the assembly of the Lord into this wilderness, that we should die here, both we and our cattle?

5 And why have you made us come up out of Egypt to bring us to this evil place? It is no place for grain or figs or vines or pomegranates, and there is no water to drink."

6 Then Moses and Aaron went from the presence of the assembly to the entrance of the tent of meeting and fell on their faces. And the glory of the Lord appeared to them,

7 and the Lord spoke to Moses, saying,

8 "Take the staff, and assemble the congregation, you and Aaron your brother, and tell the rock before their eyes to yield its water. So you shall bring water out of the rock for them and give drink to the congregation and their cattle."

9 And Moses took the staff from before the Lord, as he commanded him.

Moses Strikes the Rock

10 Then Moses and Aaron gathered the assembly together before the rock, and he said to them, "Hear now, you rebels: shall we bring water for you out of this rock?"

11 And Moses lifted up his hand and struck the rock with his staff twice, and water came out abundantly, and the congregation drank, and their livestock.

12 And the Lord said to Moses and Aaron, "Because you did not believe in me, to uphold me as holy in the eyes of the people of Israel, therefore you shall not bring this assembly into the land that I have given them."

13 These are the waters of Meribah, where the people of Israel quarreled with the Lord, and through them he showed himself holy.

Edom Refuses Passage

14 Moses sent messengers from Kadesh to the king of Edom: "Thus says your brother Israel: You know all the hardship that we have met:

15 how our fathers went down to Egypt, and we lived in Egypt a long time. And the Egyptians dealt harshly with us and our fathers.

16 And when we cried to the Lord, he heard our voice and sent an angel and brought us out of Egypt. And here we are in Kadesh, a city on the edge of your territory.

17 Please let us pass through your land. We will not pass through field or vineyard, or drink water from a well. We will go along the King's Highway. We will not turn aside to the right hand or to the left until we have passed through your territory." 1

8 But Edom said to him, "You shall not pass through, lest I come out with the sword against you."

19 And the people of Israel said to him, "We will go up by the highway, and if we drink of your water, I and my livestock, then I will pay for it. Let me only pass through on foot, nothing more."

20 But he said, "You shall not pass through." And Edom came out against them with a large army and with a strong force.

21 Thus Edom refused to give Israel passage through his territory, so Israel turned away from him.

The Death of Aaron

22 And they journeyed from Kadesh, and the people of Israel, the whole congregation, came to Mount Hor.

23 And the Lord said to Moses and Aaron at Mount Hor, on the border of the land of Edom,

24 "Let Aaron be gathered to his people, for he shall not enter the land that I have given to the people of Israel, because you rebelled against my command at the waters of Meribah.

25 Take Aaron and Eleazar his son and bring them up to Mount Hor.

26 And strip Aaron of his garments and put them on Eleazar his son. And Aaron shall be gathered to his people and shall die there."

27 Moses did as the Lord commanded. And they went up Mount Hor in the sight of all the congregation.

Numbers 20

28 And Moses stripped Aaron of his garments and put them on Eleazar his son. And Aaron died there on the top of the mountain. Then Moses and Eleazar came down from the mountain.

29 And when all the congregation saw that Aaron had perished, all the house of Israel wept for Aaron thirty days.

Numbers 21

English Standard Version

Arad Destroyed

1 When the Canaanite, the king of Arad, who lived in the Negeb, heard that Israel was coming by the way of Atharim, he fought against Israel, and took some of them captive.

2 And Israel vowed a vow to the Lord and said, "If you will indeed give this people into my hand, then I will devote their cities to destruction."

3 And the Lord heeded the voice of Israel and gave over the Canaanites, and they devoted them and their cities to destruction. So the name of the place was called Hormah.

The Bronze Serpent

4 From Mount Hor they set out by the way to the Red Sea, to go around the land of Edom. And the people became impatient on the way.

5 And the people spoke against God and against Moses, "Why have you brought us up out of Egypt to die in the wilderness? For there is no food and no water, and we loathe this worthless food."

6 Then the Lord sent fiery serpents among the people, and they bit the people, so that many people of Israel died.

7 And the people came to Moses and said, "We have sinned, for we have spoken against the Lord and against you. Pray to the Lord, that he take away the serpents from us." So Moses prayed for the people.

8 And the Lord said to Moses, "Make a fiery serpent and set it on a pole, and everyone who is bitten, when he sees it, shall live."

9 So Moses made a bronze serpent and set it on a pole. And if a serpent bit anyone, he would look at the bronze serpent and live.

The Song of the Well

10 And the people of Israel set out and camped in Oboth.

11 And they set out from Oboth and camped at Iye-abarim, in the wilderness that is opposite Moab, toward the sunrise.

12 From there they set out and camped in the Valley of Zered.

13 From there they set out and camped on the other side of the Arnon, which is in the wilderness that extends from the border of the Amorites, for the Arnon is the border of Moab, between Moab and the Amorites.

14 Therefore it is said in the Book of the Wars of the Lord, "Waheb in Suphah, and the valleys of the Arnon,

15 and the slope of the valleys that extends to the seat of Ar, and leans to the border of Moab."

16 And from there they continued to Beer; that is the well of which the Lord said to Moses, "Gather the people together, so that I may give them water."

17 Then Israel sang this song: "Spring up, O well!—Sing to it!—

18 the well that the princes made, that the nobles of the people dug, with the scepter and with their staffs."

And from the wilderness they went on to Mattanah,

19 and from Mattanah to Nahaliel, and from Nahaliel to Bamoth,

20 and from Bamoth to the valley lying in the region of Moab by the top of Pisgah that looks down on the desert.

King Sihon Defeated

21 Then Israel sent messengers to Sihon king of the Amorites, saying,

22 "Let me pass through your land. We will not turn aside into field or vineyard. We will not drink the water of a well. We will go by the King's Highway until we have passed through your territory."

23 But Sihon would not allow Israel to pass through his territory. He gathered all his people together and went out against Israel to the wilderness and came to Jahaz and fought against Israel.

24 And Israel defeated him with the edge of the sword and took possession of his land from the Arnon to the Jabbok, as far as to the Ammonites, for the border of the Ammonites was strong.

25 And Israel took all these cities, and Israel settled in all the cities of the Amorites, in Heshbon, and in all its villages.

26 For Heshbon was the city of Sihon the king of the Amorites, who had fought against the former king of Moab and taken all his land out of his hand, as far as the Arnon.

27 Therefore the ballad singers say, "Come to Heshbon, let it be built; let the city of Sihon be established.

28 For fire came out from Heshbon, flame from the city of Sihon.

It devoured Ar of Moab, and swallowed the heights of the Arnon.

29 Woe to you, O Moab! You are undone, O people of Chemosh! He has made his sons fugitives, and his daughters captives, to an Amorite king, Sihon.

30 So we overthrew them; Heshbon, as far as Dibon, perished; and we laid waste as far as Nophah; fire spread as far as Medeba."

King Og Defeated

31 Thus Israel lived in the land of the Amorites.

32 And Moses sent to spy out Jazer, and they captured its villages and dispossessed the Amorites who were there.

33 Then they turned and went up by the way to Bashan. And Og the king of Bashan came out against them, he and all his people, to battle at Edrei.

34 But the Lord said to Moses, "Do not fear him, for I have given him into your hand, and all his people, and his land. And you shall do to him as you did to Sihon king of the Amorites, who lived at Heshbon."

35 So they defeated him and his sons and all his people, until he had no survivor left. And they possessed his land.

Numbers 22

English Standard Version

Balak Summons Balaam

1 Then the people of Israel set out and camped in the plains of Moab beyond the Jordan at Jericho.

2 And Balak the son of Zippor saw all that Israel had done to the Amorites.

3 And Moab was in great dread of the people, because they were many. Moab was overcome with fear of the people of Israel.

4 And Moab said to the elders of Midian, "This horde will now lick up all that is around us, as the ox licks up the grass of the field." So Balak the son of Zippor, who was king of Moab at that time,

5 sent messengers to Balaam the son of Beor at Pethor, which is near the River in the land of the people of Amaw, to call him, saying, "Behold, a people has come out of Egypt. They cover the face of the earth, and they are dwelling opposite me.

6 Come now, curse this people for me, since they are too mighty for me. Perhaps I shall be able to defeat them and drive them from the land, for I know that he whom you bless is blessed, and he whom you curse is cursed."

Numbers 22

7 So the elders of Moab and the elders of Midian departed with the fees for divination in their hand. And they came to Balaam and gave him Balak's message.

8 And he said to them, "Lodge here tonight, and I will bring back word to you, as the Lord speaks to me." So the princes of Moab stayed with Balaam.

9 And God came to Balaam and said, "Who are these men with you?"

10 And Balaam said to God, "Balak the son of Zippor, king of Moab, has sent to me, saying,

11 'Behold, a people has come out of Egypt, and it covers the face of the earth. Now come, curse them for me. Perhaps I shall be able to fight against them and drive them out.'"

12 God said to Balaam, "You shall not go with them. You shall not curse the people, for they are blessed."

13 So Balaam rose in the morning and said to the princes of Balak, "Go to your own land, for the Lord has refused to let me go with you."

14 So the princes of Moab rose and went to Balak and said, "Balaam refuses to come with us."

15 Once again Balak sent princes, more in number and more honorable than these.

16 And they came to Balaam and said to him, "Thus says Balak the son of Zippor: 'Let nothing hinder you from coming to me,

17 for I will surely do you great honor, and whatever you say to me I will do. Come, curse this people for me.'"

18 But Balaam answered and said to the servants of Balak, "Though Balak were to give me his house full of silver and gold, I could not go beyond the command of the Lord my God to do less or more.

19 So you, too, please stay here tonight, that I may know what more the Lord will say to me."

20 And God came to Balaam at night and said to him, "If the men have come to call you, rise, go with them; but only do what I tell you."

21 So Balaam rose in the morning and saddled his donkey and went with the princes of Moab.

Balaam's Donkey and the Angel

22 But God's anger was kindled because he went, and the angel of the Lord took his stand in the way as his adversary. Now he was riding on the donkey, and his two servants were with him.

23 And the donkey saw the angel of the Lord standing in the road, with a drawn sword in his hand. And the donkey turned aside out of the road and went into the field. And Balaam struck the donkey, to turn her into the road.

24 Then the angel of the Lord stood in a narrow path between the vineyards, with a wall on either side.

25 And when the donkey saw the angel of the Lord, she pushed against the wall and pressed Balaam's foot against the wall. So he struck her again.

26 Then the angel of the Lord went ahead and stood in a narrow place, where there was no way to turn either to the right or to the left.

27 When the donkey saw the angel of the Lord, she lay down under Balaam. And Balaam's anger was kindled, and he struck the donkey with his staff.

28 Then the Lord opened the mouth of the donkey, and she said to Balaam, "What have I done to you, that you have struck me these three times?"

29 And Balaam said to the donkey, "Because you have made a fool of me. I wish I had a sword in my hand, for then I would kill you."

30 And the donkey said to Balaam, "Am I not your donkey, on which you have ridden all your life long to this day? Is it my habit to treat you this way?" And he said, "No."

31 Then the Lord opened the eyes of Balaam, and he saw the angel of the Lord standing in the way, with his drawn sword in his hand. And he bowed down and fell on his face.

32 And the angel of the Lord said to him, "Why have you struck your donkey these three times? Behold, I have come out to oppose you because your way is perverse before me.

33 The donkey saw me and turned aside before me these three times. If she had not turned aside from me, surely just now I would have killed you and let her live."

34 Then Balaam said to the angel of the Lord, "I have sinned, for I did not know that you stood in the road against me. Now therefore, if it is evil in your sight, I will turn back."

35 And the angel of the Lord said to Balaam, "Go with the men, but speak only the word that I tell you." So Balaam went on with the princes of Balak.

36 When Balak heard that Balaam had come, he went out to meet him at the city of Moab, on the border formed by the Arnon, at the extremity of the border.

37 And Balak said to Balaam, "Did I not send to you to call you? Why did you not come to me? Am I not able to honor you?"

38 Balaam said to Balak, "Behold, I have come to you! Have I now any power of my own to speak anything? The word that God puts in my mouth, that must I speak."

39 Then Balaam went with Balak, and they came to Kiriath-huzoth.

40 And Balak sacrificed oxen and sheep, and sent for Balaam and for the princes who were with him.

41 And in the morning Balak took Balaam and brought him up to Bamoth-baal, and from there he saw a fraction of the people.

Numbers 23

English Standard Version

Balaam's First Oracle

1 And Balaam said to Balak, "Build for me here seven altars, and prepare for me here seven bulls and seven rams."

2 Balak did as Balaam had said. And Balak and Balaam offered on each altar a bull and a ram.

3 And Balaam said to Balak, "Stand beside your burnt offering, and I will go. Perhaps the Lord will come to meet me, and whatever he shows me I will tell you." And he went to a bare height,

4 and God met Balaam. And Balaam said to him, "I have arranged the seven altars and I have offered on each altar a bull and a ram."

5 And the Lord put a word in Balaam's mouth and said, "Return to Balak, and thus you shall speak."

6 And he returned to him, and behold, he and all the princes of Moab were standing beside his burnt offering.

7 And Balaam took up his discourse and said, "From Aram Balak has brought me, the king of Moab from the eastern mountains: 'Come, curse Jacob for me, and come, denounce Israel!'

8 How can I curse whom God has not cursed? How can I denounce whom the Lord has not denounced?

9 For from the top of the crags I see him, from the hills I behold him; behold, a people dwelling alone, and not counting itself among the nations!

10 Who can count the dust of Jacob or number the fourth part of Israel? Let me die the death of the upright, and let my end be like his!"

11 And Balak said to Balaam, "What have you done to me? I took you to curse my enemies, and behold, you have done nothing but bless them."

12 And he answered and said, "Must I not take care to speak what the Lord puts in my mouth?"

Balaam's Second Oracle

13 And Balak said to him, "Please come with me to another place, from which you may see them. You shall see only a fraction of them and shall not see them all. Then curse them for me from there."

14 And he took him to the field of Zophim, to the top of Pisgah, and built seven altars and offered a bull and a ram on each altar.

15 Balaam said to Balak, "Stand here beside your burnt offering, while I meet the Lord over there."

16 And the Lord met Balaam and put a word in his mouth and said, "Return to Balak, and thus shall you speak."

17 And he came to him, and behold, he was standing beside his burnt offering, and the princes of Moab with him. And Balak said to him, "What has the Lord spoken?"

18 And Balaam took up his discourse and said, "Rise, Balak, and hear; give ear to me, O son of Zippor:

Numbers 23

19 God is not man, that he should lie, or a son of man, that he should change his mind. Has he said, and will he not do it? Or has he spoken, and will he not fulfill it?

20 Behold, I received a command to bless: he has blessed, and I cannot revoke it.

21 He has not beheld misfortune in Jacob, nor has he seen trouble in Israel. The Lord their God is with them, and the shout of a king is among them.

22 God brings them out of Egypt and is for them like the horns of the wild ox.

23 For there is no enchantment against Jacob, no divination against Israel; now it shall be said of Jacob and Israel, 'What has God wrought!'

24 Behold, a people! As a lioness it rises up and as a lion it lifts itself; it does not lie down until it has devoured the prey and drunk the blood of the slain."

25 And Balak said to Balaam, "Do not curse them at all, and do not bless them at all."

26 But Balaam answered Balak, "Did I not tell you, 'All that the Lord says, that I must do'?"

27 And Balak said to Balaam, "Come now, I will take you to another place. Perhaps it will please God that you may curse them for me from there."

28 So Balak took Balaam to the top of Peor, which overlooks the desert.

29 And Balaam said to Balak, "Build for me here seven altars and prepare for me here seven bulls and seven rams."

30 And Balak did as Balaam had said, and offered a bull and a ram on each altar.

Numbers 24

English Standard Version

Balaam's Third Oracle

1 When Balaam saw that it pleased the Lord to bless Israel, he did not go, as at other times, to look for omens, but set his face toward the wilderness.

2 And Balaam lifted up his eyes and saw Israel camping tribe by tribe. And the Spirit of God came upon him,

3 and he took up his discourse and said, "The oracle of Balaam the son of Beor, the oracle of the man whose eye is opened,

4 the oracle of him who hears the words of God, who sees the vision of the Almighty, falling down with his eyes uncovered:

5 How lovely are your tents, O Jacob, your encampments, O Israel!

6 Like palm groves that stretch afar, like gardens beside a river,

like aloes that the Lord has planted, like cedar trees beside the waters.

7 Water shall flow from his buckets, and his seed shall be in many waters; his king shall be higher than Agag, and his kingdom shall be exalted.

8 God brings him out of Egypt and is for him like the horns of the wild ox; he shall eat up the nations, his adversaries, and shall break their bones in pieces and pierce them through with his arrows.

9 He crouched, he lay down like a lion and like a lioness; who will rouse him up? Blessed are those who bless you, and cursed are those who curse you."

10 And Balak's anger was kindled against Balaam, and he struck his hands together. And Balak said to Balaam, "I called you to curse my enemies, and behold, you have blessed them these three times.

11 Therefore now flee to your own place. I said, 'I will certainly honor you,' but the Lord has held you back from honor."

12 And Balaam said to Balak, "Did I not tell your messengers whom you sent to me,

13 'If Balak should give me his house full of silver and gold, I would not be able to go beyond the word of the Lord, to do either good or bad of my own will. What the Lord speaks, that will I speak'?

14 And now, behold, I am going to my people. Come, I will let you know what this people will do to your people in the latter days."

Balaam's Final Oracle

15 And he took up his discourse and said, "The oracle of Balaam the son of Beor, the oracle of the man whose eye is opened,

16 the oracle of him who hears the words of God, and knows the knowledge of the Most High, who sees the vision of the Almighty, falling down with his eyes uncovered:

17 I see him, but not now; I behold him, but not near: a star shall come out of Jacob, and a scepter shall rise out of Israel; it shall crush the forehead of Moab and break down all the sons of Sheth.

18 Edom shall be dispossessed; Seir also, his enemies, shall be dispossessed. Israel is doing valiantly.

19 And one from Jacob shall exercise dominion and destroy the survivors of cities!"

20 Then he looked on Amalek and took up his discourse and said, "Amalek was the first among the nations, but its end is utter destruction."

21 And he looked on the Kenite, and took up his discourse and said, "Enduring is your dwelling place, and your nest is set in the rock.

22 Nevertheless, Kain shall be burned when Asshur takes you away captive."

23 And he took up his discourse and said, "Alas, who shall live when God does this?

24 But ships shall come from Kittim and shall afflict Asshur and Eber; and he too shall come to utter destruction."

25 Then Balaam rose and went back to his place. And Balak also went his way.

Numbers 25

English Standard Version

Baal Worship at Peor

1 While Israel lived in Shittim, the people began to whore with the daughters of Moab.

2 These invited the people to the sacrifices of their gods, and the people ate and bowed down to their gods.

3 So Israel yoked himself to Baal of Peor. And the anger of the Lord was kindled against Israel.

4 And the Lord said to Moses, "Take all the chiefs of the people and hang them in the sun before the Lord, that the fierce anger of the Lord may turn away from Israel."

5 And Moses said to the judges of Israel, "Each of you kill those of his men who have yoked themselves to Baal of Peor."

6 And behold, one of the people of Israel came and brought a Midianite woman to his family, in the sight of Moses and in the sight of the whole congregation of the people of Israel, while they were weeping in the entrance of the tent of meeting.

7 When Phinehas the son of Eleazar, son of Aaron the priest, saw it, he rose and left the congregation and took a spear in his hand

8 and went after the man of Israel into the chamber and pierced both of them, the man of Israel and the woman through her belly. Thus the plague on the people of Israel was stopped.

9 Nevertheless, those who died by the plague were twenty-four thousand.

The Zeal of Phinehas

10 And the Lord said to Moses,

11 "Phinehas the son of Eleazar, son of Aaron the priest, has turned back my wrath from the people of Israel, in that he was jealous with my jealousy among them, so that I did not consume the people of Israel in my jealousy.

12 Therefore say, 'Behold, I give to him my covenant of peace,

13 and it shall be to him and to his descendants after him the covenant of a perpetual priesthood, because he was jealous for his God and made atonement for the people of Israel.'"

14 The name of the slain man of Israel, who was killed with the Midianite woman, was Zimri the son of Salu, chief of a father's house belonging to the Simeonites.

15 And the name of the Midianite woman who was killed was Cozbi the daughter of Zur, who was the tribal head of a father's house in Midian.

16 And the Lord spoke to Moses, saying,

17 "Harass the Midianites and strike them down,

18 for they have harassed you with their wiles, with which they beguiled you in the matter of Peor, and in the matter of Cozbi, the daughter of the chief of Midian, their sister, who was killed on the day of the plague on account of Peor."

Numbers 26

English Standard Version

Census of the New Generation

1 After the plague, the Lord said to Moses and to Eleazar the son of Aaron, the priest,

2 "Take a census of all the congregation of the people of Israel, from twenty years old and upward, by their fathers' houses, all in Israel who are able to go to war."

3 And Moses and Eleazar the priest spoke with them in the plains of Moab by the Jordan at Jericho, saying,

4 "Take a census of the people,[a] from twenty years old and upward," as the Lord commanded Moses. The people of Israel who came out of the land of Egypt were:

5 Reuben, the firstborn of Israel; the sons of Reuben: of Hanoch, the clan of the Hanochites; of Pallu, the clan of the Palluites;

6 of Hezron, the clan of the Hezronites; of Carmi, the clan of the Carmites.

7 These are the clans of the Reubenites, and those listed were 43,730.

8 And the sons of Pallu: Eliab.

9 The sons of Eliab: Nemuel, Dathan, and Abiram. These are the Dathan and Abiram, chosen from the congregation, who contended against Moses and Aaron in the company of Korah, when they contended against the Lord

10 and the earth opened its mouth and swallowed them up together with Korah, when that company died, when the fire devoured 250 men, and they became a warning.

11 But the sons of Korah did not die.

12 The sons of Simeon according to their clans: of Nemuel, the clan of the Nemuelites; of Jamin, the clan of the Jaminites; of Jachin, the clan of the Jachinites;

13 of Zerah, the clan of the Zerahites; of Shaul, the clan of the Shaulites.

14 These are the clans of the Simeonites, 22,200.

15 The sons of Gad according to their clans: of Zephon, the clan of the Zephonites; of Haggi, the clan of the Haggites; of Shuni, the clan of the Shunites;

16 of Ozni, the clan of the Oznites; of Eri, the clan of the Erites;

17 of Arod, the clan of the Arodites; of Areli, the clan of the Arelites.

18 These are the clans of the sons of Gad as they were listed, 40,500.

19 The sons of Judah were Er and Onan; and Er and Onan died in the land of Canaan.

20 And the sons of Judah according to their clans were: of Shelah, the clan of the Shelanites; of Perez, the clan of the Perezites; of Zerah, the clan of the Zerahites.

21 And the sons of Perez were: of Hezron, the clan of the Hezronites; of Hamul, the clan of the Hamulites.

22 These are the clans of Judah as they were listed, 76,500.

23 The sons of Issachar according to their clans: of Tola, the clan of the Tolaites; of Puvah, the clan of the Punites;

24 of Jashub, the clan of the Jashubites; of Shimron, the clan of the Shimronites.

25 These are the clans of Issachar as they were listed, 64,300.

26 The sons of Zebulun, according to their clans: of Sered, the clan of the Seredites; of Elon, the clan of the Elonites; of Jahleel, the clan of the Jahleelites.

27 These are the clans of the Zebulunites as they were listed, 60,500.

28 The sons of Joseph according to their clans: Manasseh and Ephraim.

29 The sons of Manasseh: of Machir, the clan of the Machirites; and Machir was the father of Gilead; of Gilead, the clan of the Gileadites.

30 These are the sons of Gilead: of Iezer, the clan of the Iezerites; of Helek, the clan of the Helekites;

31 and of Asriel, the clan of the Asrielites; and of Shechem, the clan of the Shechemites;

32 and of Shemida, the clan of the Shemidaites; and of Hepher, the clan of the Hepherites.

33 Now Zelophehad the son of Hepher had no sons, but daughters. And the names of the daughters of Zelophehad were Mahlah, Noah, Hoglah, Milcah, and Tirzah.

34 These are the clans of Manasseh, and those listed were 52,700.

35 These are the sons of Ephraim according to their clans: of Shuthelah, the clan of the Shuthelahites; of Becher, the clan of the Becherites; of Tahan, the clan of the Tahanites.

36 And these are the sons of Shuthelah: of Eran, the clan of the Eranites.

37 These are the clans of the sons of Ephraim as they were listed, 32,500. These are the sons of Joseph according to their clans.

38 The sons of Benjamin according to their clans: of Bela, the clan of the Belaites; of Ashbel, the clan of the Ashbelites; of Ahiram, the clan of the Ahiramites;

39 of Shephupham, the clan of the Shuphamites; of Hupham, the clan of the Huphamites.

40 And the sons of Bela were Ard and Naaman: of Ard, the clan of the Ardites; of Naaman, the clan of the Naamites.

41 These are the sons of Benjamin according to their clans, and those listed were 45,600.

42 These are the sons of Dan according to their clans: of Shuham, the clan of the Shuhamites. These are the clans of Dan according to their clans.

43 All the clans of the Shuhamites, as they were listed, were 64,400.

44 The sons of Asher according to their clans: of Imnah, the clan of the Imnites; of Ishvi, the clan of the Ishvites; of Beriah, the clan of the Beriites.

45 Of the sons of Beriah: of Heber, the clan of the Heberites; of Malchiel, the clan of the Malchielites.

46 And the name of the daughter of Asher was Serah.

47 These are the clans of the sons of Asher as they were listed, 53,400.

48 The sons of Naphtali according to their clans: of Jahzeel, the clan of the Jahzeelites; of Guni, the clan of the Gunites;

49 of Jezer, the clan of the Jezerites; of Shillem, the clan of the Shillemites.

50 These are the clans of Naphtali according to their clans, and those listed were 45,400.

51 This was the list of the people of Israel, 601,730.

52 The Lord spoke to Moses, saying,

53 "Among these the land shall be divided for inheritance according to the number of names.

54 To a large tribe you shall give a large inheritance, and to a small tribe you shall give a small inheritance; every tribe shall be given its inheritance in proportion to its list.

55 But the land shall be divided by lot. According to the names of the tribes of their fathers they shall inherit.

56 Their inheritance shall be divided according to lot between the larger and the smaller."

57 This was the list of the Levites according to their clans: of Gershon, the clan of the Gershonites; of Kohath, the clan of the Kohathites; of Merari, the clan of the Merarites.

58 These are the clans of Levi: the clan of the Libnites, the clan of the Hebronites, the clan of the Mahlites, the clan of the Mushites, the clan of the Korahites. And Kohath was the father of Amram.

59 The name of Amram's wife was Jochebed the daughter of Levi, who was born to Levi in Egypt. And she bore to Amram Aaron and Moses and Miriam their sister.

60 And to Aaron were born Nadab, Abihu, Eleazar, and Ithamar.

61 But Nadab and Abihu died when they offered unauthorized fire before the Lord.

62 And those listed were 23,000, every male from a month old and upward. For they were not listed among the people of Israel, because there was no inheritance given to them among the people of Israel.

63 These were those listed by Moses and Eleazar the priest, who listed the people of Israel in the plains of Moab by the Jordan at Jericho.

64 But among these there was not one of those listed by Moses and Aaron the priest, who had listed the people of Israel in the wilderness of Sinai.

65 For the Lord had said of them, "They shall die in the wilderness." Not one of them was left, except Caleb the son of Jephunneh and Joshua the son of Nun.

Numbers 27

English Standard Version

The Daughters of Zelophehad

1 Then drew near the daughters of Zelophehad the son of Hepher, son of Gilead, son of Machir, son of Manasseh, from the clans of Manasseh the son of Joseph. The names of his daughters were: Mahlah, Noah, Hoglah, Milcah, and Tirzah.

2 And they stood before Moses and before Eleazar the priest and before the chiefs and all the congregation, at the entrance of the tent of meeting, saying,

3 "Our father died in the wilderness. He was not among the company of those who gathered themselves together against the Lord in the company of Korah, but died for his own sin. And he had no sons.

4 Why should the name of our father be taken away from his clan because he had no son? Give to us a possession among our father's brothers."

5 Moses brought their case before the Lord.

6 And the Lord said to Moses,

7 "The daughters of Zelophehad are right. You shall give them possession of an inheritance among their father's brothers and transfer the inheritance of

their father to them. 8 And you shall speak to the people of Israel, saying, 'If a man dies and has no son, then you shall transfer his inheritance to his daughter.

9 And if he has no daughter, then you shall give his inheritance to his brothers.

10 And if he has no brothers, then you shall give his inheritance to his father's brothers.

11 And if his father has no brothers, then you shall give his inheritance to the nearest kinsman of his clan, and he shall possess it. And it shall be for the people of Israel a statute and rule, as the Lord commanded Moses.'"

Joshua to Succeed Moses

12 The Lord said to Moses, "Go up into this mountain of Abarim and see the land that I have given to the people of Israel.

13 When you have seen it, you also shall be gathered to your people, as your brother Aaron was, 1

4 because you rebelled against my word in the wilderness of Zin when the congregation quarreled, failing to uphold me as holy at the waters before their eyes." (These are the waters of Meribah of Kadesh in the wilderness of Zin.)

15 Moses spoke to the Lord, saying,

16 "Let the Lord, the God of the spirits of all flesh, appoint a man over the congregation

17 who shall go out before them and come in before them, who shall lead them out and bring them in, that the congregation of the Lord may not be as sheep that have no shepherd."

18 So the Lord said to Moses, "Take Joshua the son of Nun, a man in whom is the Spirit, and lay your hand on him.

19 Make him stand before Eleazar the priest and all the congregation, and you shall commission him in their sight.

20 You shall invest him with some of your authority, that all the congregation of the people of Israel may obey.

21 And he shall stand before Eleazar the priest, who shall inquire for him by the judgment of the Urim before the Lord. At his word they shall go out, and at his word they shall come in, both he and all the people of Israel with him, the whole congregation."

22 And Moses did as the Lord commanded him. He took Joshua and made him stand before Eleazar the priest and the whole congregation,

23 and he laid his hands on him and commissioned him as the Lord directed through Moses.

Numbers 28

English Standard Version

Daily Offerings

1 The Lord spoke to Moses, saying,

2 "Command the people of Israel and say to them, 'My offering, my food for my food offerings, my pleasing aroma, you shall be careful to offer to me at its appointed time.'

3 And you shall say to them, This is the food offering that you shall offer to the Lord: two male lambs a year old without blemish, day by day, as a regular offering.

4 The one lamb you shall offer in the morning, and the other lamb you shall offer at twilight;

5 also a tenth of an ephah of fine flour for a grain offering, mixed with a quarter of a hin of beaten oil.

6 It is a regular burnt offering, which was ordained at Mount Sinai for a pleasing aroma, a food offering to the Lord.

7 Its drink offering shall be a quarter of a hin for each lamb. In the Holy Place you shall pour out a drink offering of strong drink to the Lord.

8 The other lamb you shall offer at twilight. Like the grain offering of the morning, and like its drink offering, you shall offer it as a food offering, with a pleasing aroma to the Lord.

Sabbath Offerings

9 "On the Sabbath day, two male lambs a year old without blemish, and two tenths of an ephah of fine flour for a grain offering, mixed with oil, and its drink offering:

10 this is the burnt offering of every Sabbath, besides the regular burnt offering and its drink offering.

Monthly Offerings

11 "At the beginnings of your months, you shall offer a burnt offering to the Lord: two bulls from the herd, one ram, seven male lambs a year old without blemish;

12 also three tenths of an ephah of fine flour for a grain offering, mixed with oil, for each bull, and two tenths of fine flour for a grain offering, mixed with oil, for the one ram;

13 and a tenth of fine flour mixed with oil as a grain offering for every lamb; for a burnt offering with a pleasing aroma, a food offering to the Lord.

14 Their drink offerings shall be half a hin of wine for a bull, a third of a hin for a ram, and a quarter of a hin for a lamb. This is the burnt offering of each month throughout the months of the year.

15 Also one male goat for a sin offering to the Lord; it shall be offered besides the regular burnt offering and its drink offering.

Passover Offerings

16 "On the fourteenth day of the first month is the Lord's Passover,

17 and on the fifteenth day of this month is a feast. Seven days shall unleavened bread be eaten.

18 On the first day there shall be a holy convocation. You shall not do any ordinary work,

19 but offer a food offering, a burnt offering to the Lord: two bulls from the herd, one ram, and seven male lambs a year old; see that they are without blemish;

20 also their grain offering of fine flour mixed with oil; three tenths of an ephah shall you offer for a bull, and two tenths for a ram;

21 a tenth shall you offer for each of the seven lambs;

22 also one male goat for a sin offering, to make atonement for you.

23 You shall offer these besides the burnt offering of the morning, which is for a regular burnt offering.

24 In the same way you shall offer daily, for seven days, the food of a food offering, with a pleasing aroma to the Lord. It shall be offered besides the regular burnt offering and its drink offering.

25 And on the seventh day you shall have a holy convocation. You shall not do any ordinary work.

Offerings for the Feast of Weeks

26 "On the day of the firstfruits, when you offer a grain offering of new grain to the Lord at your Feast of Weeks, you shall have a holy convocation. You shall not do any ordinary work,

27 but offer a burnt offering, with a pleasing aroma to the Lord: two bulls from the herd, one ram, seven male lambs a year old;

28 also their grain offering of fine flour mixed with oil, three tenths of an ephah for each bull, two tenths for one ram,

29 a tenth for each of the seven lambs;

30 with one male goat, to make atonement for you.

31 Besides the regular burnt offering and its grain offering, you shall offer them and their drink offering. See that they are without blemish.

Numbers 29

English Standard Version

Offerings for the Feast of Trumpets

1 "On the first day of the seventh month you shall have a holy convocation. You shall not do any ordinary work. It is a day for you to blow the trumpets,

2 and you shall offer a burnt offering, for a pleasing aroma to the Lord: one bull from the herd, one ram, seven male lambs a year old without blemish;

3 also their grain offering of fine flour mixed with oil, three tenths of an ephah for the bull, two tenths for the ram,

4 and one tenth for each of the seven lambs;

5 with one male goat for a sin offering, to make atonement for you;

6 besides the burnt offering of the new moon, and its grain offering, and the regular burnt offering and its grain offering, and their drink offering, according to the rule for them, for a pleasing aroma, a food offering to the Lord.

Offerings for the Day of Atonement

7 "On the tenth day of this seventh month you shall have a holy convocation and afflict yourselves. You shall do no work,

8 but you shall offer a burnt offering to the Lord, a pleasing aroma: one bull from the herd, one ram, seven male lambs a year old: see that they are without blemish.

9 And their grain offering shall be of fine flour mixed with oil, three tenths of an ephah for the bull, two tenths for the one ram,

10 a tenth for each of the seven lambs:

11 also one male goat for a sin offering, besides the sin offering of atonement, and the regular burnt offering and its grain offering, and their drink offerings.

Offerings for the Feast of Booths

12 "On the fifteenth day of the seventh month you shall have a holy convocation. You shall not do any ordinary work, and you shall keep a feast to the Lord seven days.

13 And you shall offer a burnt offering, a food offering, with a pleasing aroma to the Lord, thirteen bulls from the herd, two rams, fourteen male lambs a year old; they shall be without blemish;

14 and their grain offering of fine flour mixed with oil, three tenths of an ephah for each of the thirteen bulls, two tenths for each of the two rams,

15 and a tenth for each of the fourteen lambs;

16 also one male goat for a sin offering, besides the regular burnt offering, its grain offering and its drink offering.

17 "On the second day twelve bulls from the herd, two rams, fourteen male lambs a year old without blemish,

18 with the grain offering and the drink offerings for the bulls, for the rams, and for the lambs, in the prescribed quantities;

19 also one male goat for a sin offering, besides the regular burnt offering and its grain offering, and their drink offerings.

20 "On the third day eleven bulls, two rams, fourteen male lambs a year old without blemish,

21 with the grain offering and the drink offerings for the bulls, for the rams, and for the lambs, in the prescribed quantities;

22 also one male goat for a sin offering, besides the regular burnt offering and its grain offering and its drink offering.

23 "On the fourth day ten bulls, two rams, fourteen male lambs a year old without blemish,

24 with the grain offering and the drink offerings for the bulls, for the rams, and for the lambs, in the prescribed quantities;

25 also one male goat for a sin offering, besides the regular burnt offering, its grain offering and its drink offering.

26 "On the fifth day nine bulls, two rams, fourteen male lambs a year old without blemish,

27 with the grain offering and the drink offerings for the bulls, for the rams, and for the lambs, in the prescribed quantities;

28 also one male goat for a sin offering; besides the regular burnt offering and its grain offering and its drink offering.

29 "On the sixth day eight bulls, two rams, fourteen male lambs a year old without blemish,

30 with the grain offering and the drink offerings for the bulls, for the rams, and for the lambs, in the prescribed quantities;

31 also one male goat for a sin offering; besides the regular burnt offering, its grain offering, and its drink offerings.

32 "On the seventh day seven bulls, two rams, fourteen male lambs a year old without blemish,

33 with the grain offering and the drink offerings for the bulls, for the rams, and for the lambs, in the prescribed quantities;

34 also one male goat for a sin offering; besides the regular burnt offering, its grain offering, and its drink offering.

35 "On the eighth day you shall have a solemn assembly. You shall not do any ordinary work,

36 but you shall offer a burnt offering, a food offering, with a pleasing aroma to the Lord: one bull, one ram, seven male lambs a year old without blemish,

37 and the grain offering and the drink offerings for the bull, for the ram, and for the lambs, in the prescribed quantities;

38 also one male goat for a sin offering; besides the regular burnt offering and its grain offering and its drink offering.

39 "These you shall offer to the Lord at your appointed feasts, in addition to your vow offerings and your freewill offerings, for your burnt offerings, and for your grain offerings, and for your drink offerings, and for your peace offerings."

40 So Moses told the people of Israel everything just as the Lord had commanded Moses.

Numbers 30

English Standard Version

Men and Vows

1 Moses spoke to the heads of the tribes of the people of Israel, saying, "This is what the Lord has commanded.

2 If a man vows a vow to the Lord, or swears an oath to bind himself by a pledge, he shall not break his word. He shall do according to all that proceeds out of his mouth.

Women and Vows

3 "If a woman vows a vow to the Lord and binds herself by a pledge, while within her father's house in her youth,

4 and her father hears of her vow and of her pledge by which she has bound herself and says nothing to her, then all her vows shall stand, and every pledge by which she has bound herself shall stand.

5 But if her father opposes her on the day that he hears of it, no vow of hers, no pledge by which she has bound herself shall stand. And the Lord will forgive her, because her father opposed her.

6 "If she marries a husband, while under her vows or any thoughtless utterance of her lips by which she has bound herself,

7 and her husband hears of it and says nothing to her on the day that he hears, then her vows shall stand, and her pledges by which she has bound herself shall stand.

8 But if, on the day that her husband comes to hear of it, he opposes her, then he makes void her vow that was on her, and the thoughtless utterance of her lips by which she bound herself. And the Lord will forgive her.

9 (But any vow of a widow or of a divorced woman, anything by which she has bound herself, shall stand against her.)

10 And if she vowed in her husband's house or bound herself by a pledge with an oath,

11 and her husband heard of it and said nothing to her and did not oppose her, then all her vows shall stand, and every pledge by which she bound herself shall stand.

12 But if her husband makes them null and void on the day that he hears them, then whatever proceeds out of her lips concerning her vows or concerning her pledge of herself shall not stand. Her husband has made them void, and the Lord will forgive her.

13 Any vow and any binding oath to afflict herself, her husband may establish, or her husband may make void.

14 But if her husband says nothing to her from day to day, then he establishes all her vows or all her pledges that are upon her. He has established them, because he said nothing to her on the day that he heard of them.

15 But if he makes them null and void after he has heard of them, then he shall bear her iniquity."

16 These are the statutes that the Lord commanded Moses about a man and his wife and about a father and his daughter while she is in her youth within her father's house.

Numbers 31

English Standard Version

Vengeance on Midian

1 The Lord spoke to Moses, saying,

2 "Avenge the people of Israel on the Midianites. Afterward you shall be gathered to your people."

3 So Moses spoke to the people, saying, "Arm men from among you for the war, that they may go against Midian to execute the Lord's vengeance on Midian.

4 You shall send a thousand from each of the tribes of Israel to the war."

5 So there were provided, out of the thousands of Israel, a thousand from each tribe, twelve thousand armed for war.

6 And Moses sent them to the war, a thousand from each tribe, together with Phinehas the son of Eleazar the priest, with the vessels of the sanctuary and the trumpets for the alarm in his hand.

7 They warred against Midian, as the Lord commanded Moses, and killed every male.

8 They killed the kings of Midian with the rest of their slain, Evi, Rekem, Zur, Hur, and Reba, the five kings of Midian. And they also killed Balaam the son of Beor with the sword.

9 And the people of Israel took captive the women of Midian and their little ones, and they took as plunder all their cattle, their flocks, and all their goods.

10 All their cities in the places where they lived, and all their encampments, they burned with fire,

11 and took all the spoil and all the plunder, both of man and of beast.

12 Then they brought the captives and the plunder and the spoil to Moses, and to Eleazar the priest, and to the congregation of the people of Israel, at the camp on the plains of Moab by the Jordan at Jericho.

13 Moses and Eleazar the priest and all the chiefs of the congregation went to meet them outside the camp.

14 And Moses was angry with the officers of the army, the commanders of thousands and the commanders of hundreds, who had come from service in the war.

15 Moses said to them, "Have you let all the women live?

16 Behold, these, on Balaam's advice, caused the people of Israel to act treacherously against the Lord in the incident of Peor, and so the plague came among the congregation of the Lord.

17 Now therefore, kill every male among the little ones, and kill every woman who has known man by lying with him.

18 But all the young girls who have not known man by lying with him keep alive for yourselves.

19 Encamp outside the camp seven days. Whoever of you has killed any person and whoever has touched any slain, purify yourselves and your captives on the third day and on the seventh day.

20 You shall purify every garment, every article of skin, all work of goats' hair, and every article of wood."

21 Then Eleazar the priest said to the men in the army who had gone to battle: "This is the statute of the law that the Lord has commanded Moses:

22 only the gold, the silver, the bronze, the iron, the tin, and the lead,

23 everything that can stand the fire, you shall pass through the fire, and it shall be clean. Nevertheless, it shall also be purified with the water for impurity. And whatever cannot stand the fire, you shall pass through the water.

24 You must wash your clothes on the seventh day, and you shall be clean. And afterward you may come into the camp."

25 The Lord said to Moses,

26 "Take the count of the plunder that was taken, both of man and of beast, you and Eleazar the priest and the heads of the fathers' houses of the congregation,

27 and divide the plunder into two parts between the warriors who went out to battle and all the congregation.

28 And levy for the Lord a tribute from the men of war who went out to battle, one out of five hundred, of the people and of the oxen and of the donkeys and of the flocks.

29 Take it from their half and give it to Eleazar the priest as a contribution to the Lord.

30 And from the people of Israel's half you shall take one drawn out of every fifty, of the people, of the oxen, of the donkeys, and of the flocks,

of all the cattle, and give them to the Levites who keep guard over the tabernacle of the Lord."

31 And Moses and Eleazar the priest did as the Lord commanded Moses.

32 Now the plunder remaining of the spoil that the army took was 675,000 sheep,

33 72,000 cattle,

34 61,000 donkeys,

35 and 32,000 persons in all, women who had not known man by lying with him.

36 And the half, the portion of those who had gone out in the army, numbered 337,500 sheep,

37 and the Lord's tribute of sheep was 675.

38 The cattle were 36,000, of which the Lord's tribute was 72.

39 The donkeys were 30,500, of which the Lord's tribute was 61.

40 The persons were 16,000, of which the Lord's tribute was 32 persons.

41 And Moses gave the tribute, which was the contribution for the Lord, to Eleazar the priest, as the Lord commanded Moses.

42 From the people of Israel's half, which Moses separated from that of the men who had served in the army—

43 now the congregation's half was 337,500 sheep,

44 36,000 cattle,

45 and 30,500 donkeys,

46 and 16,000 persons—

47 from the people of Israel's half Moses took one of every 50, both of persons and of beasts, and gave them to the Levites who kept guard over the tabernacle of the Lord, as the Lord commanded Moses.

48 Then the officers who were over the thousands of the army, the commanders of thousands and the commanders of hundreds, came near to Moses

49 and said to Moses, "Your servants have counted the men of war who are under our command, and there is not a man missing from us.

50 And we have brought the Lord's offering, what each man found, articles of gold, armlets and bracelets, signet rings, earrings, and beads, to make atonement for ourselves before the Lord."

51 And Moses and Eleazar the priest received from them the gold, all crafted articles.

52 And all the gold of the contribution that they presented to the Lord, from the commanders of thousands and the commanders of hundreds, was 16,750 shekels.

53 (The men in the army had each taken plunder for himself.)

54 And Moses and Eleazar the priest received the gold from the commanders of thousands and of hundreds, and brought it into the tent of meeting, as a memorial for the people of Israel before the Lord.

Numbers 32

English Standard Version

Reuben and Gad Settle in Gilead

1 Now the people of Reuben and the people of Gad had a very great number of livestock. And they saw the land of Jazer and the land of Gilead, and behold, the place was a place for livestock.

2 So the people of Gad and the people of Reuben came and said to Moses and to Eleazar the priest and to the chiefs of the congregation,

3 "Ataroth, Dibon, Jazer, Nimrah, Heshbon, Elealeh, Sebam, Nebo, and Beon,

4 the land that the Lord struck down before the congregation of Israel, is a land for livestock, and your servants have livestock."

5 And they said, "If we have found favor in your sight, let this land be given to your servants for a possession. Do not take us across the Jordan."

6 But Moses said to the people of Gad and to the people of Reuben, "Shall your brothers go to the war while you sit here?

7 Why will you discourage the heart of the people of Israel from going over into the land that the Lord has given them?

8 Your fathers did this, when I sent them from Kadesh-barnea to see the land.

9 For when they went up to the Valley of Eshcol and saw the land, they discouraged the heart of the people of Israel from going into the land that the Lord had given them.

10 And the Lord's anger was kindled on that day, and he swore, saying,

11 'Surely none of the men who came up out of Egypt, from twenty years old and upward, shall see the land that I swore to give to Abraham, to Isaac, and to Jacob, because they have not wholly followed me,

12 none except Caleb the son of Jephunneh the Kenizzite and Joshua the son of Nun, for they have wholly followed the Lord.'

13 And the Lord's anger was kindled against Israel, and he made them wander in the wilderness forty years, until all the generation that had done evil in the sight of the Lord was gone.

14 And behold, you have risen in your fathers' place, a brood of sinful men, to increase still more the fierce anger of the Lord against Israel!

15 For if you turn away from following him, he will again abandon them in the wilderness, and you will destroy all this people."

16 Then they came near to him and said, "We will build sheepfolds here for our livestock, and cities for our little ones,

17 but we will take up arms, ready to go before the people of Israel, until we have brought them to their place. And our little ones shall live in the fortified cities because of the inhabitants of the land.

18 We will not return to our homes until each of the people of Israel has gained his inheritance.

19 For we will not inherit with them on the other side of the Jordan and beyond, because our inheritance has come to us on this side of the Jordan to the east."

20 So Moses said to them, "If you will do this, if you will take up arms to go before the Lord for the war,

21 and every armed man of you will pass over the Jordan before the Lord, until he has driven out his enemies from before him

22 and the land is subdued before the Lord; then after that you shall return and be free of obligation to the Lord and to Israel, and this land shall be your possession before the Lord.

23 But if you will not do so, behold, you have sinned against the Lord, and be sure your sin will find you out.

24 Build cities for your little ones and folds for your sheep, and do what you have promised."

25 And the people of Gad and the people of Reuben said to Moses, "Your servants will do as my lord commands.

26 Our little ones, our wives, our livestock, and all our cattle shall remain there in the cities of Gilead,

27 but your servants will pass over, every man who is armed for war, before the Lord to battle, as my lord orders."

28 So Moses gave command concerning them to Eleazar the priest and to Joshua the son of Nun and to the heads of the fathers' houses of the tribes of the people of Israel.

29 And Moses said to them, "If the people of Gad and the people of Reuben, every man who is armed to battle before the Lord, will pass with you over the Jordan and the land shall be subdued before you, then you shall give them the land of Gilead for a possession.

30 However, if they will not pass over with you armed, they shall have possessions among you in the land of Canaan."

31 And the people of Gad and the people of Reuben answered, "What the Lord has said to your servants, we will do.

32 We will pass over armed before the Lord into the land of Canaan, and the possession of our inheritance shall remain with us beyond the Jordan."

33 And Moses gave to them, to the people of Gad and to the people of Reuben and to the half-tribe of Manasseh the son of Joseph, the kingdom of Sihon king of the Amorites and the kingdom of Og king of Bashan, the land and its cities with their territories, the cities of the land throughout the country.

34 And the people of Gad built Dibon, Ataroth, Aroer,

35 Atroth-shophan, Jazer, Jogbehah,

36 Beth-nimrah and Beth-haran, fortified cities, and folds for sheep.

37 And the people of Reuben built Heshbon, Elealeh, Kiriathaim,

38 Nebo, and Baal-meon (their names were changed), and Sibmah. And they gave other names to the cities that they built.

39 And the sons of Machir the son of Manasseh went to Gilead and captured it, and dispossessed the Amorites who were in it.

40 And Moses gave Gilead to Machir the son of Manasseh, and he settled in it.

41 And Jair the son of Manasseh went and captured their villages, and called them Havvoth-jair.

42 And Nobah went and captured Kenath and its villages, and called it Nobah, after his own name.

Numbers 33

English Standard Version

Recounting Israel's Journey

1 These are the stages of the people of Israel, when they went out of the land of Egypt by their companies under the leadership of Moses and Aaron.

2 Moses wrote down their starting places, stage by stage, by command of the Lord, and these are their stages according to their starting places.

3 They set out from Rameses in the first month, on the fifteenth day of the first month. On the day after the Passover, the people of Israel went out triumphantly in the sight of all the Egyptians,

4 while the Egyptians were burying all their firstborn, whom the Lord had struck down among them. On their gods also the Lord executed judgments.

5 So the people of Israel set out from Rameses and camped at Succoth.

6 And they set out from Succoth and camped at Etham, which is on the edge of the wilderness.

7 And they set out from Etham and turned back to Pi-hahiroth, which is east of Baal-zephon, and they camped before Migdol.

8 And they set out from before Hahiroth and passed through the midst of the sea into the wilderness, and they went a three days' journey in the wilderness of Etham and camped at Marah.

9 And they set out from Marah and came to Elim; at Elim there were twelve springs of water and seventy palm trees, and they camped there.

10 And they set out from Elim and camped by the Red Sea.

11 And they set out from the Red Sea and camped in the wilderness of Sin.

12 And they set out from the wilderness of Sin and camped at Dophkah.

13 And they set out from Dophkah and camped at Alush.

14 And they set out from Alush and camped at Rephidim, where there was no water for the people to drink.

15 And they set out from Rephidim and camped in the wilderness of Sinai.

16 And they set out from the wilderness of Sinai and camped at Kibroth-hattaavah.

17 And they set out from Kibroth-hattaavah and camped at Hazeroth.

18 And they set out from Hazeroth and camped at Rithmah.

19 And they set out from Rithmah and camped at Rimmon-perez.

20 And they set out from Rimmon-perez and camped at Libnah.

21 And they set out from Libnah and camped at Rissah.

22 And they set out from Rissah and camped at Kehelathah.

23 And they set out from Kehelathah and camped at Mount Shepher.

24 And they set out from Mount Shepher and camped at Haradah.

25 And they set out from Haradah and camped at Makheloth.

26 And they set out from Makheloth and camped at Tahath.

27 And they set out from Tahath and camped at Terah.

28 And they set out from Terah and camped at Mithkah.

29 And they set out from Mithkah and camped at Hashmonah.

30 And they set out from Hashmonah and camped at Moseroth.

31 And they set out from Moseroth and camped at Bene-jaakan.

32 And they set out from Bene-jaakan and camped at Hor-haggidgad.

33 And they set out from Hor-haggidgad and camped at Jotbathah.

34 And they set out from Jotbathah and camped at Abronah.

35 And they set out from Abronah and camped at Ezion-geber.

36 And they set out from Ezion-geber and camped in the wilderness of Zin (that is, Kadesh).

37 And they set out from Kadesh and camped at Mount Hor, on the edge of the land of Edom.

38 And Aaron the priest went up Mount Hor at the command of the Lord and died there, in the fortieth year after the people of Israel had come out of the land of Egypt, on the first day of the fifth month.

39 And Aaron was 123 years old when he died on Mount Hor.

40 And the Canaanite, the king of Arad, who lived in the Negeb in the land of Canaan, heard of the coming of the people of Israel.

41 And they set out from Mount Hor and camped at Zalmonah.

42 And they set out from Zalmonah and camped at Punon.

43 And they set out from Punon and camped at Oboth.

44 And they set out from Oboth and camped at Iye-abarim, in the territory of Moab.

45 And they set out from Iyim and camped at Dibon-gad.

46 And they set out from Dibon-gad and camped at Almon-diblathaim.

47 And they set out from Almon-diblathaim and camped in the mountains of Abarim, before Nebo.

48 And they set out from the mountains of Abarim and camped in the plains of Moab by the Jordan at Jericho;

49 they camped by the Jordan from Beth-jeshimoth as far as Abel-shittim in the plains of Moab.

Drive Out the Inhabitants

50 And the Lord spoke to Moses in the plains of Moab by the Jordan at Jericho, saying,

51 "Speak to the people of Israel and say to them, When you pass over the Jordan into the land of Canaan,

52 then you shall drive out all the inhabitants of the land from before you and destroy all their figured stones and destroy all their metal images and demolish all their high places.

53 And you shall take possession of the land and settle in it, for I have given the land to you to possess it.

54 You shall inherit the land by lot according to your clans. To a large tribe you shall give a large inheritance, and to a small tribe you shall give a small inheritance. Wherever the lot falls for anyone, that shall be his. According to the tribes of your fathers you shall inherit.

55 But if you do not drive out the inhabitants of the land from before you, then those of them whom you let remain shall be as barbs in your eyes and thorns in your sides, and they shall trouble you in the land where you dwell.

56 And I will do to you as I thought to do to them."

Numbers 34

English Standard Version

Boundaries of the Land

1 The Lord spoke to Moses, saying,

2 "Command the people of Israel, and say to them, When you enter the land of Canaan (this is the land that shall fall to you for an inheritance, the land of Canaan as defined by its borders),

3 your south side shall be from the wilderness of Zin alongside Edom, and your southern border shall run from the end of the Salt Sea on the east.

4 And your border shall turn south of the ascent of Akrabbim, and cross to Zin, and its limit shall be south of Kadesh-barnea. Then it shall go on to Hazar-addar, and pass along to Azmon.

5 And the border shall turn from Azmon to the Brook of Egypt, and its limit shall be at the sea.

6 "For the western border, you shall have the Great Sea and its coast. This shall be your western border.

7 "This shall be your northern border: from the Great Sea you shall draw a line to Mount Hor.

8 From Mount Hor you shall draw a line to Lebo-hamath, and the limit of the border shall be at Zedad.

9 Then the border shall extend to Ziphron, and its limit shall be at Hazar-enan. This shall be your northern border.

10 "You shall draw a line for your eastern border from Hazar-enan to Shepham.

11 And the border shall go down from Shepham to Riblah on the east side of Ain. And the border shall go down and reach to the shoulder of the Sea of Chinnereth on the east.

12 And the border shall go down to the Jordan, and its limit shall be at the Salt Sea. This shall be your land as defined by its borders all around."

13 Moses commanded the people of Israel, saying, "This is the land that you shall inherit by lot, which the Lord has commanded to give to the nine tribes and to the half-tribe.

14 For the tribe of the people of Reuben by fathers' houses and the tribe of the people of Gad by their fathers' houses have received their inheritance, and also the half-tribe of Manasseh.

15 The two tribes and the half-tribe have received their inheritance beyond the Jordan east of Jericho, toward the sunrise."

List of Tribal Chiefs

16 The Lord spoke to Moses, saying,

17 "These are the names of the men who shall divide the land to you for inheritance: Eleazar the priest and Joshua the son of Nun.

18 You shall take one chief from every tribe to divide the land for inheritance.

19 These are the names of the men: Of the tribe of Judah, Caleb the son of Jephunneh.

20 Of the tribe of the people of Simeon, Shemuel the son of Ammihud.

21 Of the tribe of Benjamin, Elidad the son of Chislon.

22 Of the tribe of the people of Dan a chief, Bukki the son of Jogli.

23 Of the people of Joseph: of the tribe of the people of Manasseh a chief, Hanniel the son of Ephod.

24 And of the tribe of the people of Ephraim a chief, Kemuel the son of Shiphtan.

25 Of the tribe of the people of Zebulun a chief, Elizaphan the son of Parnach.

26 Of the tribe of the people of Issachar a chief, Paltiel the son of Azzan.

27 And of the tribe of the people of Asher a chief, Ahihud the son of Shelomi.

28 Of the tribe of the people of Naphtali a chief, Pedahel the son of Ammihud."

29 These are the men whom the Lord commanded to divide the inheritance for the people of Israel in the land of Canaan.

Numbers 35

English Standard Version

Cities for the Levites

1 The Lord spoke to Moses in the plains of Moab by the Jordan at Jericho, saying,

2 "Command the people of Israel to give to the Levites some of the inheritance of their possession as cities for them to dwell in. And you shall give to the Levites pasturelands around the cities.

3 The cities shall be theirs to dwell in, and their pasturelands shall be for their cattle and for their livestock and for all their beasts.

4 The pasturelands of the cities, which you shall give to the Levites, shall reach from the wall of the city outward a thousand cubits all around.

5 And you shall measure, outside the city, on the east side two thousand cubits, and on the south side two thousand cubits, and on the west side two thousand cubits, and on the north side two thousand cubits, the city being in the middle. This shall belong to them as pastureland for their cities.

6 "The cities that you give to the Levites shall be the six cities of refuge, where you shall permit the manslayer to flee, and in addition to them you shall give forty-two cities.

7 All the cities that you give to the Levites shall be forty-eight, with their pasturelands.

8 And as for the cities that you shall give from the possession of the people of Israel, from the larger tribes you shall take many, and from the smaller tribes you shall take few; each, in proportion to the inheritance that it inherits, shall give of its cities to the Levites."

Cities of Refuge

9 And the Lord spoke to Moses, saying,

10 "Speak to the people of Israel and say to them, When you cross the Jordan into the land of Canaan,

11 then you shall select cities to be cities of refuge for you, that the manslayer who kills any person without intent may flee there.

12 The cities shall be for you a refuge from the avenger, that the manslayer may not die until he stands before the congregation for judgment.

13 And the cities that you give shall be your six cities of refuge.

14 You shall give three cities beyond the Jordan, and three cities in the land of Canaan, to be cities of refuge.

15 These six cities shall be for refuge for the people of Israel, and for the stranger and for the sojourner among them, that anyone who kills any person without intent may flee there.

16 "But if he struck him down with an iron object, so that he died, he is a murderer. The murderer shall be put to death.

17 And if he struck him down with a stone tool that could cause death, and he died, he is a murderer. The murderer shall be put to death.

18 Or if he struck him down with a wooden tool that could cause death, and he died, he is a murderer. The murderer shall be put to death.

19 The avenger of blood shall himself put the murderer to death; when he meets him, he shall put him to death.

20 And if he pushed him out of hatred or hurled something at him, lying in wait, so that he died,

21 or in enmity struck him down with his hand, so that he died, then he who struck the blow shall be put to death. He is a murderer. The avenger of blood shall put the murderer to death when he meets him.

22 "But if he pushed him suddenly without enmity, or hurled anything on him without lying in wait

23 or used a stone that could cause death, and without seeing him dropped it on him, so that he died, though he was not his enemy and did not seek his harm,

24 then the congregation shall judge between the manslayer and the avenger of blood, in accordance with these rules.

25 And the congregation shall rescue the manslayer from the hand of the avenger of blood, and the congregation shall restore him to his city of refuge to which he had fled, and he shall live in it until the death of the high priest who was anointed with the holy oil.

26 But if the manslayer shall at any time go beyond the boundaries of his city of refuge to which he fled,

27 and the avenger of blood finds him outside the boundaries of his city of refuge, and the avenger of blood kills the manslayer, he shall not be guilty of blood.

28 For he must remain in his city of refuge until the death of the high priest, but after the death of the high priest the manslayer may return to the land of his possession.

29 And these things shall be for a statute and rule for you throughout your generations in all your dwelling places.

30 "If anyone kills a person, the murderer shall be put to death on the evidence of witnesses. But no person shall be put to death on the testimony of one witness.

31 Moreover, you shall accept no ransom for the life of a murderer, who is guilty of death, but he shall be put to death.

32 And you shall accept no ransom for him who has fled to his city of refuge, that he may return to dwell in the land before the death of the high priest.

33 You shall not pollute the land in which you live, for blood pollutes the land, and no atonement can be made for the land for the blood that is shed in it, except by the blood of the one who shed it.

34 You shall not defile the land in which you live, in the midst of which I dwell, for I the Lord dwell in the midst of the people of Israel."

Numbers 36

English Standard Version

Marriage of Female Heirs

1 The heads of the fathers' houses of the clan of the people of Gilead the son of Machir, son of Manasseh, from the clans of the people of Joseph, came near and spoke before Moses and before the chiefs, the heads of the fathers' houses of the people of Israel.

2 They said, "The Lord commanded my lord to give the land for inheritance by lot to the people of Israel, and my lord was commanded by the Lord to give the inheritance of Zelophehad our brother to his daughters.

3 But if they are married to any of the sons of the other tribes of the people of Israel, then their inheritance will be taken from the inheritance of our fathers and added to the inheritance of the tribe into which they marry. So it will be taken away from the lot of our inheritance.

4 And when the jubilee of the people of Israel comes, then their inheritance will be added to the inheritance of the tribe into which they marry, and their inheritance will be taken from the inheritance of the tribe of our fathers."

5 And Moses commanded the people of Israel according to the word of the Lord, saying, "The tribe of the people of Joseph is right.

6 This is what the Lord commands concerning the daughters of Zelophehad: 'Let them marry whom they think best, only they shall marry within the clan of the tribe of their father.

7 The inheritance of the people of Israel shall not be transferred from one tribe to another, for every one of the people of Israel shall hold on to the inheritance of the tribe of his fathers.

8 And every daughter who possesses an inheritance in any tribe of the people of Israel shall be wife to one of the clan of the tribe of her father, so that every one of the people of Israel may possess the inheritance of his fathers.

9 So no inheritance shall be transferred from one tribe to another, for each of the tribes of the people of Israel shall hold on to its own inheritance.'"

10 The daughters of Zelophehad did as the Lord commanded Moses,

11 for Mahlah, Tirzah, Hoglah, Milcah, and Noah, the daughters of Zelophehad, were married to sons of their father's brothers.

12 They were married into the clans of the people of Manasseh the son of Joseph, and their inheritance remained in the tribe of their father's clan.

13 These are the commandments and the rules that the Lord commanded through Moses to the people of Israel in the plains of Moab by the Jordan at Jericho.

Deuteronomy 1

English Standard Version

The Command to Leave Horeb

1 These are the words that Moses spoke to all Israel beyond the Jordan in the wilderness, in the Arabah opposite Suph, between Paran and Tophel, Laban, Hazeroth, and Dizahab.

2 It is eleven days' journey from Horeb by the way of Mount Seir to Kadesh-barnea.

3 In the fortieth year, on the first day of the eleventh month, Moses spoke to the people of Israel according to all that the Lord had given him in commandment to them,

4 after he had defeated Sihon the king of the Amorites, who lived in Heshbon, and Og the king of Bashan, who lived in Ashtaroth and in Edrei.

5 Beyond the Jordan, in the land of Moab, Moses undertook to explain this law, saying,

6 "The Lord our God said to us in Horeb, 'You have stayed long enough at this mountain.

7 Turn and take your journey, and go to the hill country of the Amorites and to all their neighbors in the Arabah, in the hill country and in the

lowland and in the Negeb and by the seacoast, the land of the Canaanites, and Lebanon, as far as the great river, the river Euphrates.

8 See, I have set the land before you. Go in and take possession of the land that the Lord swore to your fathers, to Abraham, to Isaac, and to Jacob, to give to them and to their offspring after them.'

Leaders Appointed

9 "At that time I said to you, 'I am not able to bear you by myself.

10 The Lord your God has multiplied you, and behold, you are today as numerous as the stars of heaven.

11 May the Lord, the God of your fathers, make you a thousand times as many as you are and bless you, as he has promised you!

12 How can I bear by myself the weight and burden of you and your strife?

13 Choose for your tribes wise, understanding, and experienced men, and I will appoint them as your heads.'

14 And you answered me, 'The thing that you have spoken is good for us to do.'

15 So I took the heads of your tribes, wise and experienced men, and set them as heads over you, commanders of thousands, commanders of hundreds, commanders of fifties, commanders of tens, and officers, throughout your tribes.

16 And I charged your judges at that time, 'Hear the cases between your brothers, and judge righteously between a man and his brother or the alien who is with him.

17 You shall not be partial in judgment. You shall hear the small and the great alike. You shall not be intimidated by anyone, for the judgment is God's. And the case that is too hard for you, you shall bring to me, and I will

hear it.' 18 And I commanded you at that time all the things that you should do.

Israel's Refusal to Enter the Land

19 "Then we set out from Horeb and went through all that great and terrifying wilderness that you saw, on the way to the hill country of the Amorites, as the Lord our God commanded us. And we came to Kadesh-barnea.

20 And I said to you, 'You have come to the hill country of the Amorites, which the Lord our God is giving us.

21 See, the Lord your God has set the land before you. Go up, take possession, as the Lord, the God of your fathers, has told you. Do not fear or be dismayed.'

22 Then all of you came near me and said, 'Let us send men before us, that they may explore the land for us and bring us word again of the way by which we must go up and the cities into which we shall come.'

23 The thing seemed good to me, and I took twelve men from you, one man from each tribe.

24 And they turned and went up into the hill country, and came to the Valley of Eshcol and spied it out.

25 And they took in their hands some of the fruit of the land and brought it down to us, and brought us word again and said, 'It is a good land that the Lord our God is giving us.'

26 "Yet you would not go up, but rebelled against the command of the Lord your God.

27 And you murmured in your tents and said, 'Because the Lord hated us he has brought us out of the land of Egypt, to give us into the hand of the Amorites, to destroy us.

28 Where are we going up? Our brothers have made our hearts melt, saying, "The people are greater and taller than we. The cities are great and fortified up to heaven. And besides, we have seen the sons of the Anakim there."'

29 Then I said to you, 'Do not be in dread or afraid of them.

30 The Lord your God who goes before you will himself fight for you, just as he did for you in Egypt before your eyes,

31 and in the wilderness, where you have seen how the Lord your God carried you, as a man carries his son, all the way that you went until you came to this place.'

32 Yet in spite of this word you did not believe the Lord your God,

33 who went before you in the way to seek you out a place to pitch your tents, in fire by night and in the cloud by day, to show you by what way you should go.

The Penalty for Israel's Rebellion

34 "And the Lord heard your words and was angered, and he swore,

35 'Not one of these men of this evil generation shall see the good land that I swore to give to your fathers,

36 except Caleb the son of Jephunneh. He shall see it, and to him and to his children I will give the land on which he has trodden, because he has wholly followed the Lord!'

37 Even with me the Lord was angry on your account and said, 'You also shall not go in there.

38 Joshua the son of Nun, who stands before you, he shall enter. Encourage him, for he shall cause Israel to inherit it.

39 And as for your little ones, who you said would become a prey, and your children, who today have no knowledge of good or evil, they shall go in there. And to them I will give it, and they shall possess it.

40 But as for you, turn, and journey into the wilderness in the direction of the Red Sea.'

41 "Then you answered me, 'We have sinned against the Lord. We ourselves will go up and fight, just as the Lord our God commanded us.' And every one of you fastened on his weapons of war and thought it easy to go up into the hill country.

42 And the Lord said to me, 'Say to them, Do not go up or fight, for I am not in your midst, lest you be defeated before your enemies.'

43 So I spoke to you, and you would not listen; but you rebelled against the command of the Lord and presumptuously went up into the hill country.

44 Then the Amorites who lived in that hill country came out against you and chased you as bees do and beat you down in Seir as far as Hormah.

45 And you returned and wept before the Lord, but the Lord did not listen to your voice or give ear to you.

46 So you remained at Kadesh many days, the days that you remained there.

Deuteronomy 2

English Standard Version

The Wilderness Years

1 "Then we turned and journeyed into the wilderness in the direction of the Red Sea, as the Lord told me. And for many days we traveled around Mount Seir.

2 Then the Lord said to me,

3 'You have been traveling around this mountain country long enough. Turn northward

4 and command the people, "You are about to pass through the territory of your brothers, the people of Esau, who live in Seir; and they will be afraid of you. So be very careful.

5 Do not contend with them, for I will not give you any of their land, no, not so much as for the sole of the foot to tread on, because I have given Mount Seir to Esau as a possession.

6 You shall purchase food from them with money, that you may eat, and you shall also buy water from them with money, that you may drink.

7 For the Lord your God has blessed you in all the work of your hands. He knows your going through this great wilderness. These forty years the Lord your God has been with you. You have lacked nothing."'

8 So we went on, away from our brothers, the people of Esau, who live in Seir, away from the Arabah road from Elath and Ezion-geber. "And we turned and went in the direction of the wilderness of Moab.

9 And the Lord said to me, 'Do not harass Moab or contend with them in battle, for I will not give you any of their land for a possession, because I have given Ar to the people of Lot for a possession.'

10 (The Emim formerly lived there, a people great and many, and tall as the Anakim.

11 Like the Anakim they are also counted as Rephaim, but the Moabites call them Emim.

12 The Horites also lived in Seir formerly, but the people of Esau dispossessed them and destroyed them from before them and settled in their place, as Israel did to the land of their possession, which the Lord gave to them.)

13 'Now rise up and go over the brook Zered.' So we went over the brook Zered.

14 And the time from our leaving Kadesh-barnea until we crossed the brook Zered was thirty-eight years, until the entire generation, that is, the men of war, had perished from the camp, as the Lord had sworn to them.

15 For indeed the hand of the Lord was against them, to destroy them from the camp, until they had perished.

16 "So as soon as all the men of war had perished and were dead from among the people,

17 the Lord said to me,

18 'Today you are to cross the border of Moab at Ar.

19 And when you approach the territory of the people of Ammon, do not harass them or contend with them, for I will not give you any of the land of the people of Ammon as a possession, because I have given it to the sons of Lot for a possession.'

20 (It is also counted as a land of Rephaim. Rephaim formerly lived there—but the Ammonites call them Zamzummim—

21 a people great and many, and tall as the Anakim; but the Lord destroyed them before the Ammonites, and they dispossessed them and settled in their place,

22 as he did for the people of Esau, who live in Seir, when he destroyed the Horites before them and they dispossessed them and settled in their place even to this day.

23 As for the Avvim, who lived in villages as far as Gaza, the Caphtorim, who came from Caphtor, destroyed them and settled in their place.)

24 'Rise up, set out on your journey and go over the Valley of the Arnon. Behold, I have given into your hand Sihon the Amorite, king of Heshbon, and his land. Begin to take possession, and contend with him in battle.

25 This day I will begin to put the dread and fear of you on the peoples who are under the whole heaven, who shall hear the report of you and shall tremble and be in anguish because of you.'

The Defeat of King Sihon

26 "So I sent messengers from the wilderness of Kedemoth to Sihon the king of Heshbon, with words of peace, saying,

27 'Let me pass through your land. I will go only by the road; I will turn aside neither to the right nor to the left.

28 You shall sell me food for money, that I may eat, and give me water for money, that I may drink. Only let me pass through on foot,

29 as the sons of Esau who live in Seir and the Moabites who live in Ar did for me, until I go over the Jordan into the land that the Lord our God is giving to us.'

30 But Sihon the king of Heshbon would not let us pass by him, for the Lord your God hardened his spirit and made his heart obstinate, that he might give him into your hand, as he is this day.

31 And the Lord said to me, 'Behold, I have begun to give Sihon and his land over to you. Begin to take possession, that you may occupy his land.'

32 Then Sihon came out against us, he and all his people, to battle at Jahaz.

33 And the Lord our God gave him over to us, and we defeated him and his sons and all his people.

34 And we captured all his cities at that time and devoted to destruction every city, men, women, and children. We left no survivors.

35 Only the livestock we took as spoil for ourselves, with the plunder of the cities that we captured.

36 From Aroer, which is on the edge of the Valley of the Arnon, and from the city that is in the valley, as far as Gilead, there was not a city too high for us. The Lord our God gave all into our hands.

37 Only to the land of the sons of Ammon you did not draw near, that is, to all the banks of the river Jabbok and the cities of the hill country, whatever the Lord our God had forbidden us.

Deuteronomy 3

English Standard Version

The Defeat of King Og

1 "Then we turned and went up the way to Bashan. And Og the king of Bashan came out against us, he and all his people, to battle at Edrei.

2 But the Lord said to me, 'Do not fear him, for I have given him and all his people and his land into your hand. And you shall do to him as you did to Sihon the king of the Amorites, who lived at Heshbon.'

3 So the Lord our God gave into our hand Og also, the king of Bashan, and all his people, and we struck him down until he had no survivor left.

4 And we took all his cities at that time—there was not a city that we did not take from them—sixty cities, the whole region of Argob, the kingdom of Og in Bashan.

5 All these were cities fortified with high walls, gates, and bars, besides very many unwalled villages.

6 And we devoted them to destruction, as we did to Sihon the king of Heshbon, devoting to destruction every city, men, women, and children.

7 But all the livestock and the spoil of the cities we took as our plunder.

8 So we took the land at that time out of the hand of the two kings of the Amorites who were beyond the Jordan, from the Valley of the Arnon to Mount Hermon

9 (the Sidonians call Hermon Sirion, while the Amorites call it Senir),

10 all the cities of the tableland and all Gilead and all Bashan, as far as Salecah and Edrei, cities of the kingdom of Og in Bashan.

11 (For only Og the king of Bashan was left of the remnant of the Rephaim. Behold, his bed was a bed of iron. Is it not in Rabbah of the Ammonites? Nine cubits was its length, and four cubits its breadth, according to the common cubit.)

12 "When we took possession of this land at that time, I gave to the Reubenites and the Gadites the territory beginning at Aroer, which is on the edge of the Valley of the Arnon, and half the hill country of Gilead with its cities.

13 The rest of Gilead, and all Bashan, the kingdom of Og, that is, all the region of Argob, I gave to the half-tribe of Manasseh. (All that portion of Bashan is called the land of Rephaim.

14 Jair the Manassite took all the region of Argob, that is, Bashan, as far as the border of the Geshurites and the Maacathites, and called the villages after his own name, Havvoth-jair, as it is to this day.)

15 To Machir I gave Gilead,

16 and to the Reubenites and the Gadites I gave the territory from Gilead as far as the Valley of the Arnon, with the middle of the valley as a border, as far over as the river Jabbok, the border of the Ammonites;

17 the Arabah also, with the Jordan as the border, from Chinnereth as far as the Sea of the Arabah, the Salt Sea, under the slopes of Pisgah on the east.

18 "And I commanded you at that time, saying, 'The Lord your God has given you this land to possess. All your men of valor shall cross over armed before your brothers, the people of Israel.

19 Only your wives, your little ones, and your livestock (I know that you have much livestock) shall remain in the cities that I have given you,

20 until the Lord gives rest to your brothers, as to you, and they also occupy the land that the Lord your God gives them beyond the Jordan. Then each of you may return to his possession which I have given you.'

21 And I commanded Joshua at that time, 'Your eyes have seen all that the Lord your God has done to these two kings. So will the Lord do to all the kingdoms into which you are crossing.

22 You shall not fear them, for it is the Lord your God who fights for you.'

Moses Forbidden to Enter the Land

23 "And I pleaded with the Lord at that time, saying,

24 'O Lord God, you have only begun to show your servant your greatness and your mighty hand. For what god is there in heaven or on earth who can do such works and mighty acts as yours?

25 Please let me go over and see the good land beyond the Jordan, that good hill country and Lebanon.'

26 But the Lord was angry with me because of you and would not listen to me. And the Lord said to me, 'Enough from you; do not speak to me of this matter again.

27 Go up to the top of Pisgah and lift up your eyes westward and northward and southward and eastward, and look at it with your eyes, for you shall not go over this Jordan.

28 But charge Joshua, and encourage and strengthen him, for he shall go over at the head of this people, and he shall put them in possession of the land that you shall see.'

29 So we remained in the valley opposite Beth-peor.

Deuteronomy 4

English Standard Version

Moses Commands Obedience

1 "And now, O Israel, listen to the statutes and the rules that I am teaching you, and do them, that you may live, and go in and take possession of the land that the Lord, the God of your fathers, is giving you.

2 You shall not add to the word that I command you, nor take from it, that you may keep the commandments of the Lord your God that I command you.

3 Your eyes have seen what the Lord did at Baal-peor, for the Lord your God destroyed from among you all the men who followed the Baal of Peor.

4 But you who held fast to the Lord your God are all alive today.

5 See, I have taught you statutes and rules, as the Lord my God commanded me, that you should do them in the land that you are entering to take possession of it.

6 Keep them and do them, for that will be your wisdom and your understanding in the sight of the peoples, who, when they hear all these statutes, will say, 'Surely this great nation is a wise and understanding people.'

7 For what great nation is there that has a god so near to it as the Lord our God is to us, whenever we call upon him?

8 And what great nation is there, that has statutes and rules so righteous as all this law that I set before you today?

9 "Only take care, and keep your soul diligently, lest you forget the things that your eyes have seen, and lest they depart from your heart all the days of your life. Make them known to your children and your children's children—

10 how on the day that you stood before the Lord your God at Horeb, the Lord said to me, 'Gather the people to me, that I may let them hear my words, so that they may learn to fear me all the days that they live on the earth, and that they may teach their children so.'

11 And you came near and stood at the foot of the mountain, while the mountain burned with fire to the heart of heaven, wrapped in darkness, cloud, and gloom.

12 Then the Lord spoke to you out of the midst of the fire. You heard the sound of words, but saw no form; there was only a voice.

13 And he declared to you his covenant, which he commanded you to perform, that is, the Ten Commandments, and he wrote them on two tablets of stone.

14 And the Lord commanded me at that time to teach you statutes and rules, that you might do them in the land that you are going over to possess.

Idolatry Forbidden

15 "Therefore watch yourselves very carefully. Since you saw no form on the day that the Lord spoke to you at Horeb out of the midst of the fire,

16 beware lest you act corruptly by making a carved image for yourselves, in the form of any figure, the likeness of male or female,

17 the likeness of any animal that is on the earth, the likeness of any winged bird that flies in the air,

18 the likeness of anything that creeps on the ground, the likeness of any fish that is in the water under the earth.

19 And beware lest you raise your eyes to heaven, and when you see the sun and the moon and the stars, all the host of heaven, you be drawn away and bow down to them and serve them, things that the Lord your God has allotted to all the peoples under the whole heaven.

20 But the Lord has taken you and brought you out of the iron furnace, out of Egypt, to be a people of his own inheritance, as you are this day.

21 Furthermore, the Lord was angry with me because of you, and he swore that I should not cross the Jordan, and that I should not enter the good land that the Lord your God is giving you for an inheritance.

22 For I must die in this land; I must not go over the Jordan. But you shall go over and take possession of that good land.

23 Take care, lest you forget the covenant of the Lord your God, which he made with you, and make a carved image, the form of anything that the Lord your God has forbidden you.

24 For the Lord your God is a consuming fire, a jealous God.

25 "When you father children and children's children, and have grown old in the land, if you act corruptly by making a carved image in the form of anything, and by doing what is evil in the sight of the Lord your God, so as to provoke him to anger,

26 I call heaven and earth to witness against you today, that you will soon utterly perish from the land that you are going over the Jordan to possess. You will not live long in it, but will be utterly destroyed.

27 And the Lord will scatter you among the peoples, and you will be left few in number among the nations where the Lord will drive you.

28 And there you will serve gods of wood and stone, the work of human hands, that neither see, nor hear, nor eat, nor smell.

29 But from there you will seek the Lord your God and you will find him, if you search after him with all your heart and with all your soul.

30 When you are in tribulation, and all these things come upon you in the latter days, you will return to the Lord your God and obey his voice.

31 For the Lord your God is a merciful God. He will not leave you or destroy you or forget the covenant with your fathers that he swore to them.

The Lord Alone Is God

32 "For ask now of the days that are past, which were before you, since the day that God created man on the earth, and ask from one end of heaven to the other, whether such a great thing as this has ever happened or was ever heard of.

33 Did any people ever hear the voice of a god speaking out of the midst of the fire, as you have heard, and still live?

34 Or has any god ever attempted to go and take a nation for himself from the midst of another nation, by trials, by signs, by wonders, and by war, by a mighty hand and an outstretched arm, and by great deeds of terror, all of which the Lord your God did for you in Egypt before your eyes?

35 To you it was shown, that you might know that the Lord is God; there is no other besides him.

36 Out of heaven he let you hear his voice, that he might discipline you. And on earth he let you see his great fire, and you heard his words out of the midst of the fire.

37 And because he loved your fathers and chose their offspring after them and brought you out of Egypt with his own presence, by his great power,

38 driving out before you nations greater and mightier than you, to bring you in, to give you their land for an inheritance, as it is this day,

39 know therefore today, and lay it to your heart, that the Lord is God in heaven above and on the earth beneath; there is no other.

40 Therefore you shall keep his statutes and his commandments, which I command you today, that it may go well with you and with your children after you, and that you may prolong your days in the land that the Lord your God is giving you for all time."

Cities of Refuge

41 Then Moses set apart three cities in the east beyond the Jordan,

42 that the manslayer might flee there, anyone who kills his neighbor unintentionally, without being at enmity with him in time past; he may flee to one of these cities and save his life:

43 Bezer in the wilderness on the tableland for the Reubenites, Ramoth in Gilead for the Gadites, and Golan in Bashan for the Manassites.

Introduction to the Law

44 This is the law that Moses set before the people of Israel.

45 These are the testimonies, the statutes, and the rules, which Moses spoke to the people of Israel when they came out of Egypt,

46 beyond the Jordan in the valley opposite Beth-peor, in the land of Sihon the king of the Amorites, who lived at Heshbon, whom Moses and the people of Israel defeated when they came out of Egypt.

47 And they took possession of his land and the land of Og, the king of Bashan, the two kings of the Amorites, who lived to the east beyond the Jordan;

48 from Aroer, which is on the edge of the Valley of the Arnon, as far as Mount Sirion (that is, Hermon),

49 together with all the Arabah on the east side of the Jordan as far as the Sea of the Arabah, under the slopes of Pisgah.

Deuteronomy 5

English Standard Version

The Ten Commandments

1 And Moses summoned all Israel and said to them, "Hear, O Israel, the statutes and the rules that I speak in your hearing today, and you shall learn them and be careful to do them.

2 The Lord our God made a covenant with us in Horeb.

3 Not with our fathers did the Lord make this covenant, but with us, who are all of us here alive today.

4 The Lord spoke with you face to face at the mountain, out of the midst of the fire,

5 while I stood between the Lord and you at that time, to declare to you the word of the Lord. For you were afraid because of the fire, and you did not go up into the mountain. He said:

6 "'I am the Lord your God, who brought you out of the land of Egypt, out of the house of slavery.

7 "'You shall have no other gods before me.

8 "'You shall not make for yourself a carved image, or any likeness of anything that is in heaven above, or that is on the earth beneath, or that is in the water under the earth.

9 You shall not bow down to them or serve them; for I the Lord your God am a jealous God, visiting the iniquity of the fathers on the children to the third and fourth generation of those who hate me,

10 but showing steadfast love to thousands of those who love me and keep my commandments.

11 "'You shall not take the name of the Lord your God in vain, for the Lord will not hold him guiltless who takes his name in vain.

12 "'Observe the Sabbath day, to keep it holy, as the Lord your God commanded you.

13 Six days you shall labor and do all your work,

14 but the seventh day is a Sabbath to the Lord your God. On it you shall not do any work, you or your son or your daughter or your male servant or your female servant, or your ox or your donkey or any of your livestock, or the sojourner who is within your gates, that your male servant and your female servant may rest as well as you.

15 You shall remember that you were a slave in the land of Egypt, and the Lord your God brought you out from there with a mighty hand and an outstretched arm. Therefore the Lord your God commanded you to keep the Sabbath day.

16 "'Honor your father and your mother, as the Lord your God commanded you, that your days may be long, and that it may go well with you in the land that the Lord your God is giving you.

17 "'You shall not murder.

18 "'And you shall not commit adultery.

19 "'And you shall not steal.

20 "'And you shall not bear false witness against your neighbor.

21 "'And you shall not covet your neighbor's wife. And you shall not desire your neighbor's house, his field, or his male servant, or his female servant, his ox, or his donkey, or anything that is your neighbor's.'

22 "These words the Lord spoke to all your assembly at the mountain out of the midst of the fire, the cloud, and the thick darkness, with a loud voice; and he added no more. And he wrote them on two tablets of stone and gave them to me.

23 And as soon as you heard the voice out of the midst of the darkness, while the mountain was burning with fire, you came near to me, all the heads of your tribes, and your elders.

24 And you said, 'Behold, the Lord our God has shown us his glory and greatness, and we have heard his voice out of the midst of the fire. This day we have seen God speak with man, and man still live.

25 Now therefore why should we die? For this great fire will consume us. If we hear the voice of the Lord our God any more, we shall die.

26 For who is there of all flesh, that has heard the voice of the living God speaking out of the midst of fire as we have, and has still lived?

27 Go near and hear all that the Lord our God will say, and speak to us all that the Lord our God will speak to you, and we will hear and do it.'

28 "And the Lord heard your words, when you spoke to me. And the Lord said to me, 'I have heard the words of this people, which they have spoken to you. They are right in all that they have spoken.

29 Oh that they had such a heart as this always, to fear me and to keep all my commandments, that it might go well with them and with their descendants forever!

30 Go and say to them, "Return to your tents."

31 But you, stand here by me, and I will tell you the whole commandment and the statutes and the rules that you shall teach them, that they may do them in the land that I am giving them to possess.'

32 You shall be careful therefore to do as the Lord your God has commanded you. You shall not turn aside to the right hand or to the left.

33 You shall walk in all the way that the Lord your God has commanded you, that you may live, and that it may go well with you, and that you may live long in the land that you shall possess.

Deuteronomy 6

English Standard Version

The Greatest Commandment

1 "Now this is the commandment—the statutes and the rules—that the Lord your God commanded me to teach you, that you may do them in the land to which you are going over, to possess it,

2 that you may fear the Lord your God, you and your son and your son's son, by keeping all his statutes and his commandments, which I command you, all the days of your life, and that your days may be long.

3 Hear therefore, O Israel, and be careful to do them, that it may go well with you, and that you may multiply greatly, as the Lord, the God of your fathers, has promised you, in a land flowing with milk and honey.

4 "Hear, O Israel: The Lord our God, the Lord is one.

5 You shall love the Lord your God with all your heart and with all your soul and with all your might.

6 And these words that I command you today shall be on your heart.

7 You shall teach them diligently to your children, and shall talk of them when you sit in your house, and when you walk by the way, and when you lie down, and when you rise.

8 You shall bind them as a sign on your hand, and they shall be as frontlets between your eyes.

9 You shall write them on the doorposts of your house and on your gates.

10 "And when the Lord your God brings you into the land that he swore to your fathers, to Abraham, to Isaac, and to Jacob, to give you—with great and good cities that you did not build,

11 and houses full of all good things that you did not fill, and cisterns that you did not dig, and vineyards and olive trees that you did not plant—and when you eat and are full,

12 then take care lest you forget the Lord, who brought you out of the land of Egypt, out of the house of slavery.

13 It is the Lord your God you shall fear. Him you shall serve and by his name you shall swear.

14 You shall not go after other gods, the gods of the peoples who are around you—

15 for the Lord your God in your midst is a jealous God—lest the anger of the Lord your God be kindled against you, and he destroy you from off the face of the earth.

16 "You shall not put the Lord your God to the test, as you tested him at Massah.

17 You shall diligently keep the commandments of the Lord your God, and his testimonies and his statutes, which he has commanded you.

18 And you shall do what is right and good in the sight of the Lord, that it may go well with you, and that you may go in and take possession of the good land that the Lord swore to give to your fathers

19 by thrusting out all your enemies from before you, as the Lord has promised.

20 "When your son asks you in time to come, 'What is the meaning of the testimonies and the statutes and the rules that the Lord our God has commanded you?'

21 then you shall say to your son, 'We were Pharaoh's slaves in Egypt. And the Lord brought us out of Egypt with a mighty hand.

22 And the Lord showed signs and wonders, great and grievous, against Egypt and against Pharaoh and all his household, before our eyes.

23 And he brought us out from there, that he might bring us in and give us the land that he swore to give to our fathers.

24 And the Lord commanded us to do all these statutes, to fear the Lord our God, for our good always, that he might preserve us alive, as we are this day.

25 And it will be righteousness for us, if we are careful to do all this commandment before the Lord our God, as he has commanded us.'

Deuteronomy 7

English Standard Version

A Chosen People

1 "When the Lord your God brings you into the land that you are entering to take possession of it, and clears away many nations before you, the Hittites, the Girgashites, the Amorites, the Canaanites, the Perizzites, the Hivites, and the Jebusites, seven nations more numerous and mightier than you,

2 and when the Lord your God gives them over to you, and you defeat them, then you must devote them to complete destruction. You shall make no covenant with them and show no mercy to them.

3 You shall not intermarry with them, giving your daughters to their sons or taking their daughters for your sons,

4 for they would turn away your sons from following me, to serve other gods. Then the anger of the Lord would be kindled against you, and he would destroy you quickly.

5 But thus shall you deal with them: you shall break down their altars and dash in pieces their pillars and chop down their Asherim and burn their carved images with fire.

6 "For you are a people holy to the Lord your God. The Lord your God has chosen you to be a people for his treasured possession, out of all the peoples who are on the face of the earth.

7 It was not because you were more in number than any other people that the Lord set his love on you and chose you, for you were the fewest of all peoples,

8 but it is because the Lord loves you and is keeping the oath that he swore to your fathers, that the Lord has brought you out with a mighty hand and redeemed you from the house of slavery, from the hand of Pharaoh king of Egypt.

9 Know therefore that the Lord your God is God, the faithful God who keeps covenant and steadfast love with those who love him and keep his commandments, to a thousand generations,

10 and repays to their face those who hate him, by destroying them. He will not be slack with one who hates him. He will repay him to his face.

11 You shall therefore be careful to do the commandment and the statutes and the rules that I command you today.

12 "And because you listen to these rules and keep and do them, the Lord your God will keep with you the covenant and the steadfast love that he swore to your fathers.

13 He will love you, bless you, and multiply you. He will also bless the fruit of your womb and the fruit of your ground, your grain and your wine and your oil, the increase of your herds and the young of your flock, in the land that he swore to your fathers to give you.

14 You shall be blessed above all peoples. There shall not be male or female barren among you or among your livestock.

15 And the Lord will take away from you all sickness, and none of the evil diseases of Egypt, which you knew, will he inflict on you, but he will lay them on all who hate you.

16 And you shall consume all the peoples that the Lord your God will give over to you. Your eye shall not pity them, neither shall you serve their gods, for that would be a snare to you.

17 "If you say in your heart, 'These nations are greater than I. How can I dispossess them?'

18 you shall not be afraid of them but you shall remember what the Lord your God did to Pharaoh and to all Egypt,

19 the great trials that your eyes saw, the signs, the wonders, the mighty hand, and the outstretched arm, by which the Lord your God brought you out. So will the Lord your God do to all the peoples of whom you are afraid.

20 Moreover, the Lord your God will send hornets among them, until those who are left and hide themselves from you are destroyed.

21 You shall not be in dread of them, for the Lord your God is in your midst, a great and awesome God.

22 The Lord your God will clear away these nations before you little by little. You may not make an end of them at once, lest the wild beasts grow too numerous for you.

23 But the Lord your God will give them over to you and throw them into great confusion, until they are destroyed.

24 And he will give their kings into your hand, and you shall make their name perish from under heaven. No one shall be able to stand against you until you have destroyed them.

25 The carved images of their gods you shall burn with fire. You shall not covet the silver or the gold that is on them or take it for yourselves, lest you be ensnared by it, for it is an abomination to the Lord your God.

26 And you shall not bring an abominable thing into your house and become devoted to destruction like it. You shall utterly detest and abhor it, for it is devoted to destruction.

Deuteronomy 8

English Standard Version

Remember the Lord Your God

1 "The whole commandment that I command you today you shall be careful to do, that you may live and multiply, and go in and possess the land that the Lord swore to give to your fathers.

2 And you shall remember the whole way that the Lord your God has led you these forty years in the wilderness, that he might humble you, testing you to know what was in your heart, whether you would keep his commandments or not.

3 And he humbled you and let you hunger and fed you with manna, which you did not know, nor did your fathers know, that he might make you know that man does not live by bread alone, but man lives by every word that comes from the mouth of the Lord.

4 Your clothing did not wear out on you and your foot did not swell these forty years.

5 Know then in your heart that, as a man disciplines his son, the Lord your God disciplines you.

6 So you shall keep the commandments of the Lord your God by walking in his ways and by fearing him.

7 For the Lord your God is bringing you into a good land, a land of brooks of water, of fountains and springs, flowing out in the valleys and hills,

8 a land of wheat and barley, of vines and fig trees and pomegranates, a land of olive trees and honey,

9 a land in which you will eat bread without scarcity, in which you will lack nothing, a land whose stones are iron, and out of whose hills you can dig copper.

10 And you shall eat and be full, and you shall bless the Lord your God for the good land he has given you.

11 "Take care lest you forget the Lord your God by not keeping his commandments and his rules and his statutes, which I command you today,

12 lest, when you have eaten and are full and have built good houses and live in them,

13 and when your herds and flocks multiply and your silver and gold is multiplied and all that you have is multiplied,

14 then your heart be lifted up, and you forget the Lord your God, who brought you out of the land of Egypt, out of the house of slavery,

15 who led you through the great and terrifying wilderness, with its fiery serpents and scorpions and thirsty ground where there was no water, who brought you water out of the flinty rock,

16 who fed you in the wilderness with manna that your fathers did not know, that he might humble you and test you, to do you good in the end.

17 Beware lest you say in your heart, 'My power and the might of my hand have gotten me this wealth.'

18 You shall remember the Lord your God, for it is he who gives you power to get wealth, that he may confirm his covenant that he swore to your fathers, as it is this day.

19 And if you forget the Lord your God and go after other gods and serve them and worship them, I solemnly warn you today that you shall surely perish.

20 Like the nations that the Lord makes to perish before you, so shall you perish, because you would not obey the voice of the Lord your God.

Deuteronomy 9

English Standard Version

Not Because of Righteousness

1 "Hear, O Israel: you are to cross over the Jordan today, to go in to dispossess nations greater and mightier than you, cities great and fortified up to heaven,

2 a people great and tall, the sons of the Anakim, whom you know, and of whom you have heard it said, 'Who can stand before the sons of Anak?'

3 Know therefore today that he who goes over before you as a consuming fire is the Lord your God. He will destroy them and subdue them before you. So you shall drive them out and make them perish quickly, as the Lord has promised you.

4 "Do not say in your heart, after the Lord your God has thrust them out before you, 'It is because of my righteousness that the Lord has brought me in to possess this land,' whereas it is because of the wickedness of these nations that the Lord is driving them out before you.

5 Not because of your righteousness or the uprightness of your heart are you going in to possess their land, but because of the wickedness of these nations the Lord your God is driving them out from before you, and that he

may confirm the word that the Lord swore to your fathers, to Abraham, to Isaac, and to Jacob.

6 "Know, therefore, that the Lord your God is not giving you this good land to possess because of your righteousness, for you are a stubborn people.

7 Remember and do not forget how you provoked the Lord your God to wrath in the wilderness. From the day you came out of the land of Egypt until you came to this place, you have been rebellious against the Lord.

8 Even at Horeb you provoked the Lord to wrath, and the Lord was so angry with you that he was ready to destroy you.

9 When I went up the mountain to receive the tablets of stone, the tablets of the covenant that the Lord made with you, I remained on the mountain forty days and forty nights. I neither ate bread nor drank water.

10 And the Lord gave me the two tablets of stone written with the finger of God, and on them were all the words that the Lord had spoken with you on the mountain out of the midst of the fire on the day of the assembly.

11 And at the end of forty days and forty nights the Lord gave me the two tablets of stone, the tablets of the covenant.

12 Then the Lord said to me, 'Arise, go down quickly from here, for your people whom you have brought from Egypt have acted corruptly. They have turned aside quickly out of the way that I commanded them; they have made themselves a metal image.'

The Golden Calf

13 "Furthermore, the Lord said to me, 'I have seen this people, and behold, it is a stubborn people.

14 Let me alone, that I may destroy them and blot out their name from under heaven. And I will make of you a nation mightier and greater than they.'

15 So I turned and came down from the mountain, and the mountain was burning with fire. And the two tablets of the covenant were in my two hands.

16 And I looked, and behold, you had sinned against the Lord your God. You had made yourselves a golden calf. You had turned aside quickly from the way that the Lord had commanded you.

17 So I took hold of the two tablets and threw them out of my two hands and broke them before your eyes.

18 Then I lay prostrate before the Lord as before, forty days and forty nights. I neither ate bread nor drank water, because of all the sin that you had committed, in doing what was evil in the sight of the Lord to provoke him to anger.

19 For I was afraid of the anger and hot displeasure that the Lord bore against you, so that he was ready to destroy you. But the Lord listened to me that time also.

20 And the Lord was so angry with Aaron that he was ready to destroy him. And I prayed for Aaron also at the same time.

21 Then I took the sinful thing, the calf that you had made, and burned it with fire and crushed it, grinding it very small, until it was as fine as dust. And I threw the dust of it into the brook that ran down from the mountain.

22 "At Taberah also, and at Massah and at Kibroth-hattaavah you provoked the Lord to wrath.

23 And when the Lord sent you from Kadesh-barnea, saying, 'Go up and take possession of the land that I have given you,' then you rebelled against the commandment of the Lord your God and did not believe him or obey his voice.

24 You have been rebellious against the Lord from the day that I knew you.

25 "So I lay prostrate before the Lord for these forty days and forty nights, because the Lord had said he would destroy you.

26 And I prayed to the Lord, 'O Lord God, do not destroy your people and your heritage, whom you have redeemed through your greatness, whom you have brought out of Egypt with a mighty hand.

27 Remember your servants, Abraham, Isaac, and Jacob. Do not regard the stubbornness of this people, or their wickedness or their sin,

28 lest the land from which you brought us say, "Because the Lord was not able to bring them into the land that he promised them, and because he hated them, he has brought them out to put them to death in the wilderness."

29 For they are your people and your heritage, whom you brought out by your great power and by your outstretched arm.'

Deuteronomy 10

English Standard Version

New Tablets of Stone

1 "At that time the Lord said to me, 'Cut for yourself two tablets of stone like the first, and come up to me on the mountain and make an ark of wood.

2 And I will write on the tablets the words that were on the first tablets that you broke, and you shall put them in the ark.'

3 So I made an ark of acacia wood, and cut two tablets of stone like the first, and went up the mountain with the two tablets in my hand.

4 And he wrote on the tablets, in the same writing as before, the Ten Commandments that the Lord had spoken to you on the mountain out of the midst of the fire on the day of the assembly. And the Lord gave them to me.

5 Then I turned and came down from the mountain and put the tablets in the ark that I had made. And there they are, as the Lord commanded me."

6 (The people of Israel journeyed from Beeroth Bene-jaakan to Moserah. There Aaron died, and there he was buried. And his son Eleazar ministered as priest in his place.

7 From there they journeyed to Gudgodah, and from Gudgodah to Jotbathah, a land with brooks of water.

8 At that time the Lord set apart the tribe of Levi to carry the ark of the covenant of the Lord to stand before the Lord to minister to him and to bless in his name, to this day.

9 Therefore Levi has no portion or inheritance with his brothers. The Lord is his inheritance, as the Lord your God said to him.)

10 "I myself stayed on the mountain, as at the first time, forty days and forty nights, and the Lord listened to me that time also. The Lord was unwilling to destroy you.

11 And the Lord said to me, 'Arise, go on your journey at the head of the people, so that they may go in and possess the land, which I swore to their fathers to give them.'

Circumcise Your Heart

12 "And now, Israel, what does the Lord your God require of you, but to fear the Lord your God, to walk in all his ways, to love him, to serve the Lord your God with all your heart and with all your soul,

13 and to keep the commandments and statutes of the Lord, which I am commanding you today for your good?

14 Behold, to the Lord your God belong heaven and the heaven of heavens, the earth with all that is in it.

15 Yet the Lord set his heart in love on your fathers and chose their offspring after them, you above all peoples, as you are this day.

16 Circumcise therefore the foreskin of your heart, and be no longer stubborn.

17 For the Lord your God is God of gods and Lord of lords, the great, the mighty, and the awesome God, who is not partial and takes no bribe.

18 He executes justice for the fatherless and the widow, and loves the sojourner, giving him food and clothing.

19 Love the sojourner, therefore, for you were sojourners in the land of Egypt.

20 You shall fear the Lord your God. You shall serve him and hold fast to him, and by his name you shall swear.

21 He is your praise. He is your God, who has done for you these great and terrifying things that your eyes have seen.

22 Your fathers went down to Egypt seventy persons, and now the Lord your God has made you as numerous as the stars of heaven.

Deuteronomy 11

English Standard Version

Love and Serve the Lord

1 "You shall therefore love the Lord your God and keep his charge, his statutes, his rules, and his commandments always.

2 And consider today (since I am not speaking to your children who have not known or seen it), consider the discipline of the Lord your God, his greatness, his mighty hand and his outstretched arm,

3 his signs and his deeds that he did in Egypt to Pharaoh the king of Egypt and to all his land,

4 and what he did to the army of Egypt, to their horses and to their chariots, how he made the water of the Red Sea flow over them as they pursued after you, and how the Lord has destroyed them to this day,

5 and what he did to you in the wilderness, until you came to this place,

6 and what he did to Dathan and Abiram the sons of Eliab, son of Reuben, how the earth opened its mouth and swallowed them up, with their households, their tents, and every living thing that followed them, in the midst of all Israel.

7 For your eyes have seen all the great work of the Lord that he did.

8 "You shall therefore keep the whole commandment that I command you today, that you may be strong, and go in and take possession of the land that you are going over to possess,

9 and that you may live long in the land that the Lord swore to your fathers to give to them and to their offspring, a land flowing with milk and honey.

10 For the land that you are entering to take possession of it is not like the land of Egypt, from which you have come, where you sowed your seed and irrigated it, like a garden of vegetables.

11 But the land that you are going over to possess is a land of hills and valleys, which drinks water by the rain from heaven,

12 a land that the Lord your God cares for. The eyes of the Lord your God are always upon it, from the beginning of the year to the end of the year.

13 "And if you will indeed obey my commandments that I command you today, to love the Lord your God, and to serve him with all your heart and with all your soul,

14 he will give the rain for your land in its season, the early rain and the later rain, that you may gather in your grain and your wine and your oil.

15 And he will give grass in your fields for your livestock, and you shall eat and be full.

16 Take care lest your heart be deceived, and you turn aside and serve other gods and worship them;

17 then the anger of the Lord will be kindled against you, and he will shut up the heavens, so that there will be no rain, and the land will yield no fruit, and you will perish quickly off the good land that the Lord is giving you.

18 "You shall therefore lay up these words of mine in your heart and in your soul, and you shall bind them as a sign on your hand, and they shall be as frontlets between your eyes.

19 You shall teach them to your children, talking of them when you are sitting in your house, and when you are walking by the way, and when you lie down, and when you rise.

20 You shall write them on the doorposts of your house and on your gates,

21 that your days and the days of your children may be multiplied in the land that the Lord swore to your fathers to give them, as long as the heavens are above the earth.

22 For if you will be careful to do all this commandment that I command you to do, loving the Lord your God, walking in all his ways, and holding fast to him,

23 then the Lord will drive out all these nations before you, and you will dispossess nations greater and mightier than you.

24 Every place on which the sole of your foot treads shall be yours. Your territory shall be from the wilderness to the Lebanon and from the River, the river Euphrates, to the western sea.

25 No one shall be able to stand against you. The Lord your God will lay the fear of you and the dread of you on all the land that you shall tread, as he promised you.

26 "See, I am setting before you today a blessing and a curse:

27 the blessing, if you obey the commandments of the Lord your God, which I command you today,

28 and the curse, if you do not obey the commandments of the Lord your God, but turn aside from the way that I am commanding you today, to go after other gods that you have not known.

29 And when the Lord your God brings you into the land that you are entering to take possession of it, you shall set the blessing on Mount Gerizim and the curse on Mount Ebal.

30 Are they not beyond the Jordan, west of the road, toward the going down of the sun, in the land of the Canaanites who live in the Arabah, opposite Gilgal, beside the oak of Moreh?

31 For you are to cross over the Jordan to go in to take possession of the land that the Lord your God is giving you. And when you possess it and live in it,

32 you shall be careful to do all the statutes and the rules that I am setting before you today

Deuteronomy 12

English Standard Version

The Lord's Chosen Place of Worship

1 "These are the statutes and rules that you shall be careful to do in the land that the Lord, the God of your fathers, has given you to possess, all the days that you live on the earth.

2 You shall surely destroy all the places where the nations whom you shall dispossess served their gods, on the high mountains and on the hills and under every green tree.

3 You shall tear down their altars and dash in pieces their pillars and burn their Asherim with fire. You shall chop down the carved images of their gods and destroy their name out of that place.

4 You shall not worship the Lord your God in that way.

5 But you shall seek the place that the Lord your God will choose out of all your tribes to put his name and make his habitation there. There you shall go,

6 and there you shall bring your burnt offerings and your sacrifices, your tithes and the contribution that you present, your vow offerings, your freewill offerings, and the firstborn of your herd and of your flock.

7 And there you shall eat before the Lord your God, and you shall rejoice, you and your households, in all that you undertake, in which the Lord your God has blessed you.

8 "You shall not do according to all that we are doing here today, everyone doing whatever is right in his own eyes,

9 for you have not as yet come to the rest and to the inheritance that the Lord your God is giving you.

10 But when you go over the Jordan and live in the land that the Lord your God is giving you to inherit, and when he gives you rest from all your enemies around, so that you live in safety,

11 then to the place that the Lord your God will choose, to make his name dwell there, there you shall bring all that I command you: your burnt offerings and your sacrifices, your tithes and the contribution that you present, and all your finest vow offerings that you vow to the Lord.

12 And you shall rejoice before the Lord your God, you and your sons and your daughters, your male servants and your female servants, and the Levite that is within your towns, since he has no portion or inheritance with you.

13 Take care that you do not offer your burnt offerings at any place that you see,

14 but at the place that the Lord will choose in one of your tribes, there you shall offer your burnt offerings, and there you shall do all that I am commanding you.

15 "However, you may slaughter and eat meat within any of your towns, as much as you desire, according to the blessing of the Lord your God that he has given you. The unclean and the clean may eat of it, as of the gazelle and as of the deer.

16 Only you shall not eat the blood; you shall pour it out on the earth like water.

17 You may not eat within your towns the tithe of your grain or of your wine or of your oil, or the firstborn of your herd or of your flock, or any of your vow offerings that you vow, or your freewill offerings or the contribution that you present,

18 but you shall eat them before the Lord your God in the place that the Lord your God will choose, you and your son and your daughter, your male servant and your female servant, and the Levite who is within your towns. And you shall rejoice before the Lord your God in all that you undertake.

19 Take care that you do not neglect the Levite as long as you live in your land.

20 "When the Lord your God enlarges your territory, as he has promised you, and you say, 'I will eat meat,' because you crave meat, you may eat meat whenever you desire.

21 If the place that the Lord your God will choose to put his name there is too far from you, then you may kill any of your herd or your flock, which the Lord has given you, as I have commanded you, and you may eat within your towns whenever you desire.

22 Just as the gazelle or the deer is eaten, so you may eat of it. The unclean and the clean alike may eat of it.

23 Only be sure that you do not eat the blood, for the blood is the life, and you shall not eat the life with the flesh.

24 You shall not eat it; you shall pour it out on the earth like water.

25 You shall not eat it, that all may go well with you and with your children after you, when you do what is right in the sight of the Lord.

26 But the holy things that are due from you, and your vow offerings, you shall take, and you shall go to the place that the Lord will choose,

27 and offer your burnt offerings, the flesh and the blood, on the altar of the Lord your God. The blood of your sacrifices shall be poured out on the altar of the Lord your God, but the flesh you may eat.

28 Be careful to obey all these words that I command you, that it may go well with you and with your children after you forever, when you do what is good and right in the sight of the Lord your God.

Warning Against Idolatry

29 "When the Lord your God cuts off before you the nations whom you go in to dispossess, and you dispossess them and dwell in their land,

30 take care that you be not ensnared to follow them, after they have been destroyed before you, and that you do not inquire about their gods, saying, 'How did these nations serve their gods?—that I also may do the same.'

31 You shall not worship the Lord your God in that way, for every abominable thing that the Lord hates they have done for their gods, for they even burn their sons and their daughters in the fire to their gods.

32 "Everything that I command you, you shall be careful to do. You shall not add to it or take from it.

Deuteronomy 13

English Standard Version

1 "If a prophet or a dreamer of dreams arises among you and gives you a sign or a wonder,

2 and the sign or wonder that he tells you comes to pass, and if he says, 'Let us go after other gods,' which you have not known, 'and let us serve them,'

3 you shall not listen to the words of that prophet or that dreamer of dreams. For the Lord your God is testing you, to know whether you love the Lord your God with all your heart and with all your soul.

4 You shall walk after the Lord your God and fear him and keep his commandments and obey his voice, and you shall serve him and hold fast to him.

5 But that prophet or that dreamer of dreams shall be put to death, because he has taught rebellion against the Lord your God, who brought you out of the land of Egypt and redeemed you out of the house of slavery, to make you leave the way in which the Lord your God commanded you to walk. So you shall purge the evil from your midst.

6 "If your brother, the son of your mother, or your son or your daughter or the wife you embrace or your friend who is as your own soul entices you

secretly, saying, 'Let us go and serve other gods,' which neither you nor your fathers have known,

7 some of the gods of the peoples who are around you, whether near you or far off from you, from the one end of the earth to the other,

8 you shall not yield to him or listen to him, nor shall your eye pity him, nor shall you spare him, nor shall you conceal him.

9 But you shall kill him. Your hand shall be first against him to put him to death, and afterward the hand of all the people.

10 You shall stone him to death with stones, because he sought to draw you away from the Lord your God, who brought you out of the land of Egypt, out of the house of slavery.

11 And all Israel shall hear and fear and never again do any such wickedness as this among you.

12 "If you hear in one of your cities, which the Lord your God is giving you to dwell there,

13 that certain worthless fellows have gone out among you and have drawn away the inhabitants of their city, saying, 'Let us go and serve other gods,' which you have not known,

14 then you shall inquire and make search and ask diligently. And behold, if it be true and certain that such an abomination has been done among you,

15 you shall surely put the inhabitants of that city to the sword, devoting it to destruction, all who are in it and its cattle, with the edge of the sword.

16 You shall gather all its spoil into the midst of its open square and burn the city and all its spoil with fire, as a whole burnt offering to the Lord your God. It shall be a heap forever. It shall not be built again.

17 None of the devoted things shall stick to your hand, that the Lord may turn from the fierceness of his anger and show you mercy and have compassion on you and multiply you, as he swore to your fathers,

18 if you obey the voice of the Lord your God, keeping all his commandments that I am commanding you today, and doing what is right in the sight of the Lord your God.

Deuteronomy 14

English Standard Version

Clean and Unclean Food

1 "You are the sons of the Lord your God. You shall not cut yourselves or make any baldness on your foreheads for the dead.

2 For you are a people holy to the Lord your God, and the Lord has chosen you to be a people for his treasured possession, out of all the peoples who are on the face of the earth.

3 "You shall not eat any abomination.

4 These are the animals you may eat: the ox, the sheep, the goat,

5 the deer, the gazelle, the roebuck, the wild goat, the ibex, the antelope, and the mountain sheep.

6 Every animal that parts the hoof and has the hoof cloven in two and chews the cud, among the animals, you may eat.

7 Yet of those that chew the cud or have the hoof cloven you shall not eat these: the camel, the hare, and the rock badger, because they chew the cud but do not part the hoof, are unclean for you.

8 And the pig, because it parts the hoof but does not chew the cud, is unclean for you. Their flesh you shall not eat, and their carcasses you shall not touch.

9 "Of all that are in the waters you may eat these: whatever has fins and scales you may eat.

10 And whatever does not have fins and scales you shall not eat; it is unclean for you.

11 "You may eat all clean birds.

12 But these are the ones that you shall not eat: the eagle, the bearded vulture, the black vulture,

13 the kite, the falcon of any kind;

14 every raven of any kind;

15 the ostrich, the nighthawk, the sea gull, the hawk of any kind;

16 the little owl and the short-eared owl, the barn owl

17 and the tawny owl, the carrion vulture and the cormorant,

18 the stork, the heron of any kind; the hoopoe and the bat.

19 And all winged insects are unclean for you; they shall not be eaten.

20 All clean winged things you may eat.

21 "You shall not eat anything that has died naturally. You may give it to the sojourner who is within your towns, that he may eat it, or you may sell it to a foreigner. For you are a people holy to the Lord your God. "You shall not boil a young goat in its mother's milk.

Tithes

22 "You shall tithe all the yield of your seed that comes from the field year by year.

23 And before the Lord your God, in the place that he will choose, to make his name dwell there, you shall eat the tithe of your grain, of your wine, and of your oil, and the firstborn of your herd and flock, that you may learn to fear the Lord your God always.

24 And if the way is too long for you, so that you are not able to carry the tithe, when the Lord your God blesses you, because the place is too far from you, which the Lord your God chooses, to set his name there,

25 then you shall turn it into money and bind up the money in your hand and go to the place that the Lord your God chooses

26 and spend the money for whatever you desire—oxen or sheep or wine or strong drink, whatever your appetite craves. And you shall eat there before the Lord your God and rejoice, you and your household.

27 And you shall not neglect the Levite who is within your towns, for he has no portion or inheritance with you.

28 "At the end of every three years you shall bring out all the tithe of your produce in the same year and lay it up within your towns.

29 And the Levite, because he has no portion or inheritance with you, and the sojourner, the fatherless, and the widow, who are within your towns, shall come and eat and be filled, that the Lord your God may bless you in all the work of your hands that you do.

Deuteronomy 15

English Standard Version

The Sabbatical Year

1 "At the end of every seven years you shall grant a release.

2 And this is the manner of the release: every creditor shall release what he has lent to his neighbor. He shall not exact it of his neighbor, his brother, because the Lord's release has been proclaimed.

3 Of a foreigner you may exact it, but whatever of yours is with your brother your hand shall release.

4 But there will be no poor among you; for the Lord will bless you in the land that the Lord your God is giving you for an inheritance to possess—

5 if only you will strictly obey the voice of the Lord your God, being careful to do all this commandment that I command you today.

6 For the Lord your God will bless you, as he promised you, and you shall lend to many nations, but you shall not borrow, and you shall rule over many nations, but they shall not rule over you.

7 "If among you, one of your brothers should become poor, in any of your towns within your land that the Lord your God is giving you, you shall not harden your heart or shut your hand against your poor brother,

8 but you shall open your hand to him and lend him sufficient for his need, whatever it may be.

9 Take care lest there be an unworthy thought in your heart and you say, 'The seventh year, the year of release is near,' and your eye look grudgingly on your poor brother, and you give him nothing, and he cry to the Lord against you, and you be guilty of sin.

10 You shall give to him freely, and your heart shall not be grudging when you give to him, because for this the Lord your God will bless you in all your work and in all that you undertake.

11 For there will never cease to be poor in the land. Therefore I command you, 'You shall open wide your hand to your brother, to the needy and to the poor, in your land.'

12 "If your brother, a Hebrew man or a Hebrew woman, is sold to you, he shall serve you six years, and in the seventh year you shall let him go free from you.

13 And when you let him go free from you, you shall not let him go empty-handed.

14 You shall furnish him liberally out of your flock, out of your threshing floor, and out of your winepress. As the Lord your God has blessed you, you shall give to him.

15 You shall remember that you were a slave in the land of Egypt, and the Lord your God redeemed you; therefore I command you this today.

16 But if he says to you, 'I will not go out from you,' because he loves you and your household, since he is well-off with you,

17 then you shall take an awl, and put it through his ear into the door, and he shall be your slave forever. And to your female slave you shall do the same.

18 It shall not seem hard to you when you let him go free from you, for at half the cost of a hired worker he has served you six years. So the Lord your God will bless you in all that you do.

19 "All the firstborn males that are born of your herd and flock you shall dedicate to the Lord your God. You shall do no work with the firstborn of your herd, nor shear the firstborn of your flock.

20 You shall eat it, you and your household, before the Lord your God year by year at the place that the Lord will choose.

21 But if it has any blemish, if it is lame or blind or has any serious blemish whatever, you shall not sacrifice it to the Lord your God.

22 You shall eat it within your towns. The unclean and the clean alike may eat it, as though it were a gazelle or a deer.

23 Only you shall not eat its blood; you shall pour it out on the ground like water.

Deuteronomy 16

English Standard Version

Passover

1 "Observe the month of Abib and keep the Passover to the Lord your God, for in the month of Abib the Lord your God brought you out of Egypt by night.

2 And you shall offer the Passover sacrifice to the Lord your God, from the flock or the herd, at the place that the Lord will choose, to make his name dwell there.

3 You shall eat no leavened bread with it. Seven days you shall eat it with unleavened bread, the bread of affliction—for you came out of the land of Egypt in haste—that all the days of your life you may remember the day when you came out of the land of Egypt.

4 No leaven shall be seen with you in all your territory for seven days, nor shall any of the flesh that you sacrifice on the evening of the first day remain all night until morning.

5 You may not offer the Passover sacrifice within any of your towns that the Lord your God is giving you,

6 but at the place that the Lord your God will choose, to make his name dwell in it, there you shall offer the Passover sacrifice, in the evening at sunset, at the time you came out of Egypt.

7 And you shall cook it and eat it at the place that the Lord your God will choose. And in the morning you shall turn and go to your tents.

8 For six days you shall eat unleavened bread, and on the seventh day there shall be a solemn assembly to the Lord your God. You shall do no work on it.

The Feast of Weeks

9 "You shall count seven weeks. Begin to count the seven weeks from the time the sickle is first put to the standing grain.

10 Then you shall keep the Feast of Weeks to the Lord your God with the tribute of a freewill offering from your hand, which you shall give as the Lord your God blesses you.

11 And you shall rejoice before the Lord your God, you and your son and your daughter, your male servant and your female servant, the Levite who is within your towns, the sojourner, the fatherless, and the widow who are among you, at the place that the Lord your God will choose, to make his name dwell there.

12 You shall remember that you were a slave in Egypt; and you shall be careful to observe these statutes.

The Feast of Booths

13 "You shall keep the Feast of Booths seven days, when you have gathered in the produce from your threshing floor and your winepress.

14 You shall rejoice in your feast, you and your son and your daughter, your male servant and your female servant, the Levite, the sojourner, the fatherless, and the widow who are within your towns.

15 For seven days you shall keep the feast to the Lord your God at the place that the Lord will choose, because the Lord your God will bless you in all your produce and in all the work of your hands, so that you will be altogether joyful.

16 "Three times a year all your males shall appear before the Lord your God at the place that he will choose: at the Feast of Unleavened Bread, at the Feast of Weeks, and at the Feast of Booths. They shall not appear before the Lord empty-handed.

17 Every man shall give as he is able, according to the blessing of the Lord your God that he has given you.

Justice

18 "You shall appoint judges and officers in all your towns that the Lord your God is giving you, according to your tribes, and they shall judge the people with righteous judgment.

19 You shall not pervert justice. You shall not show partiality, and you shall not accept a bribe, for a bribe blinds the eyes of the wise and subverts the cause of the righteous.

20 Justice, and only justice, you shall follow, that you may live and inherit the land that the Lord your God is giving you.

Forbidden Forms of Worship

21 "You shall not plant any tree as an Asherah beside the altar of the Lord your God that you shall make.

22 And you shall not set up a pillar, which the Lord your God hates.

Deuteronomy 17

English Standard Version

1 "You shall not sacrifice to the Lord your God an ox or a sheep in which is a blemish, any defect whatever, for that is an abomination to the Lord your God.

2 "If there is found among you, within any of your towns that the Lord your God is giving you, a man or woman who does what is evil in the sight of the Lord your God, in transgressing his covenant,

3 and has gone and served other gods and worshiped them, or the sun or the moon or any of the host of heaven, which I have forbidden,

4 and it is told you and you hear of it, then you shall inquire diligently, and if it is true and certain that such an abomination has been done in Israel,

5 then you shall bring out to your gates that man or woman who has done this evil thing, and you shall stone that man or woman to death with stones.

6 On the evidence of two witnesses or of three witnesses the one who is to die shall be put to death; a person shall not be put to death on the evidence of one witness.

7 The hand of the witnesses shall be first against him to put him to death, and afterward the hand of all the people. So you shall purge the evil from your midst.

Legal Decisions by Priests and Judges

8 "If any case arises requiring decision between one kind of homicide and another, one kind of legal right and another, or one kind of assault and another, any case within your towns that is too difficult for you, then you shall arise and go up to the place that the Lord your God will choose.

9 And you shall come to the Levitical priests and to the judge who is in office in those days, and you shall consult them, and they shall declare to you the decision.

10 Then you shall do according to what they declare to you from that place that the Lord will choose. And you shall be careful to do according to all that they direct you.

11 According to the instructions that they give you, and according to the decision which they pronounce to you, you shall do. You shall not turn aside from the verdict that they declare to you, either to the right hand or to the left.

12 The man who acts presumptuously by not obeying the priest who stands to minister there before the Lord your God, or the judge, that man shall die. So you shall purge the evil from Israel.

13 And all the people shall hear and fear and not act presumptuously again.

Laws Concerning Israel's Kings

14 "When you come to the land that the Lord your God is giving you, and you possess it and dwell in it and then say, 'I will set a king over me, like all the nations that are around me,'

15 you may indeed set a king over you whom the Lord your God will choose. One from among your brothers you shall set as king over you. You may not put a foreigner over you, who is not your brother.

16 Only he must not acquire many horses for himself or cause the people to return to Egypt in order to acquire many horses, since the Lord has said to you, 'You shall never return that way again.'

17 And he shall not acquire many wives for himself, lest his heart turn away, nor shall he acquire for himself excessive silver and gold.

18 "And when he sits on the throne of his kingdom, he shall write for himself in a book a copy of this law, approved by the Levitical priests.

19 And it shall be with him, and he shall read in it all the days of his life, that he may learn to fear the Lord his God by keeping all the words of this law and these statutes, and doing them,

20 that his heart may not be lifted up above his brothers, and that he may not turn aside from the commandment, either to the right hand or to the left, so that he may continue long in his kingdom, he and his children, in Israel.

Deuteronomy 18

English Standard Version

Provision for Priests and Levites

1 "The Levitical priests, all the tribe of Levi, shall have no portion or inheritance with Israel. They shall eat the Lord's food offerings as their inheritance.

2 They shall have no inheritance among their brothers; the Lord is their inheritance, as he promised them.

3 And this shall be the priests' due from the people, from those offering a sacrifice, whether an ox or a sheep: they shall give to the priest the shoulder and the two cheeks and the stomach.

4 The firstfruits of your grain, of your wine and of your oil, and the first fleece of your sheep, you shall give him.

5 For the Lord your God has chosen him out of all your tribes to stand and minister in the name of the Lord, him and his sons for all time.

6 "And if a Levite comes from any of your towns out of all Israel, where he lives—and he may come when he desires—to the place that the Lord will choose,

7 and ministers in the name of the Lord his God, like all his fellow Levites who stand to minister there before the Lord,

8 then he may have equal portions to eat, besides what he receives from the sale of his patrimony.

Abominable Practices

9 "When you come into the land that the Lord your God is giving you, you shall not learn to follow the abominable practices of those nations.

10 There shall not be found among you anyone who burns his son or his daughter as an offering, anyone who practices divination or tells fortunes or interprets omens, or a sorcerer

11 or a charmer or a medium or a necromancer or one who inquires of the dead,

12 for whoever does these things is an abomination to the Lord. And because of these abominations the Lord your God is driving them out before you.

13 You shall be blameless before the Lord your God,

14 for these nations, which you are about to dispossess, listen to fortune-tellers and to diviners. But as for you, the Lord your God has not allowed you to do this.

A New Prophet like Moses

15 "The Lord your God will raise up for you a prophet like me from among you, from your brothers—it is to him you shall listen—

16 just as you desired of the Lord your God at Horeb on the day of the assembly, when you said, 'Let me not hear again the voice of the Lord my God or see this great fire any more, lest I die.'

17 And the Lord said to me, 'They are right in what they have spoken.

18 I will raise up for them a prophet like you from among their brothers. And I will put my words in his mouth, and he shall speak to them all that I command him.

19 And whoever will not listen to my words that he shall speak in my name, I myself will require it of him.

20 But the prophet who presumes to speak a word in my name that I have not commanded him to speak, or who speaks in the name of other gods, that same prophet shall die.'

21 And if you say in your heart, 'How may we know the word that the Lord has not spoken?'—

22 when a prophet speaks in the name of the Lord, if the word does not come to pass or come true, that is a word that the Lord has not spoken; the prophet has spoken it presumptuously. You need not be afraid of him.

Deuteronomy 19

English Standard Version

Laws Concerning Cities of Refuge

19 "When the Lord your God cuts off the nations whose land the Lord your God is giving you, and you dispossess them and dwell in their cities and in their houses,

2 you shall set apart three cities for yourselves in the land that the Lord your God is giving you to possess. 3 You shall measure the distances and divide into three parts the area of the land that the Lord your God gives you as a possession, so that any manslayer can flee to them.

4 "This is the provision for the manslayer, who by fleeing there may save his life. If anyone kills his neighbor unintentionally without having hated him in the past—

5 as when someone goes into the forest with his neighbor to cut wood, and his hand swings the axe to cut down a tree, and the head slips from the handle and strikes his neighbor so that he dies—he may flee to one of these cities and live,

6 lest the avenger of blood in hot anger pursue the manslayer and overtake him, because the way is long, and strike him fatally, though the man did not deserve to die, since he had not hated his neighbor in the past.

7 Therefore I command you, You shall set apart three cities.

8 And if the Lord your God enlarges your territory, as he has sworn to your fathers, and gives you all the land that he promised to give to your fathers—

9 provided you are careful to keep all this commandment, which I command you today, by loving the Lord your God and by walking ever in his ways— then you shall add three other cities to these three,

10 lest innocent blood be shed in your land that the Lord your God is giving you for an inheritance, and so the guilt of bloodshed be upon you.

11 "But if anyone hates his neighbor and lies in wait for him and attacks him and strikes him fatally so that he dies, and he flees into one of these cities,

12 then the elders of his city shall send and take him from there, and hand him over to the avenger of blood, so that he may die.

13 Your eye shall not pity him, but you shall purge the guilt of innocent blood from Israel, so that it may be well with you.

Property Boundaries

14 "You shall not move your neighbor's landmark, which the men of old have set, in the inheritance that you will hold in the land that the Lord your God is giving you to possess.

Laws Concerning Witnesses

15 "A single witness shall not suffice against a person for any crime or for any wrong in connection with any offense that he has committed. Only on the evidence of two witnesses or of three witnesses shall a charge be established.

16 If a malicious witness arises to accuse a person of wrongdoing,

17 then both parties to the dispute shall appear before the Lord, before the priests and the judges who are in office in those days.

Deuteronomy 19

18 The judges shall inquire diligently, and if the witness is a false witness and has accused his brother falsely, 1

9 then you shall do to him as he had meant to do to his brother. So you shall purge the evil from your midst.

20 And the rest shall hear and fear, and shall never again commit any such evil among you.

21 Your eye shall not pity. It shall be life for life, eye for eye, tooth for tooth, hand for hand, foot for foot.

Deuteronomy 20

English Standard Version

Laws Concerning Warfare

1 "When you go out to war against your enemies, and see horses and chariots and an army larger than your own, you shall not be afraid of them, for the Lord your God is with you, who brought you up out of the land of Egypt.

2 And when you draw near to the battle, the priest shall come forward and speak to the people

3 and shall say to them, 'Hear, O Israel, today you are drawing near for battle against your enemies: let not your heart faint. Do not fear or panic or be in dread of them,

4 for the Lord your God is he who goes with you to fight for you against your enemies, to give you the victory.'

5 Then the officers shall speak to the people, saying, 'Is there any man who has built a new house and has not dedicated it? Let him go back to his house, lest he die in the battle and another man dedicate it.

6 And is there any man who has planted a vineyard and has not enjoyed its fruit? Let him go back to his house, lest he die in the battle and another man enjoy its fruit.

7 And is there any man who has betrothed a wife and has not taken her? Let him go back to his house, lest he die in the battle and another man take her.'

8 And the officers shall speak further to the people, and say, 'Is there any man who is fearful and fainthearted? Let him go back to his house, lest he make the heart of his fellows melt like his own.'

9 And when the officers have finished speaking to the people, then commanders shall be appointed at the head of the people.

10 "When you draw near to a city to fight against it, offer terms of peace to it.

11 And if it responds to you peaceably and it opens to you, then all the people who are found in it shall do forced labor for you and shall serve you.

12 But if it makes no peace with you, but makes war against you, then you shall besiege it.

13 And when the Lord your God gives it into your hand, you shall put all its males to the sword,

14 but the women and the little ones, the livestock, and everything else in the city, all its spoil, you shall take as plunder for yourselves. And you shall enjoy the spoil of your enemies, which the Lord your God has given you.

15 Thus you shall do to all the cities that are very far from you, which are not cities of the nations here.

16 But in the cities of these peoples that the Lord your God is giving you for an inheritance, you shall save alive nothing that breathes,

17 but you shall devote them to complete destruction, the Hittites and the Amorites, the Canaanites and the Perizzites, the Hivites and the Jebusites, as the Lord your God has commanded,

18 that they may not teach you to do according to all their abominable practices that they have done for their gods, and so you sin against the Lord your God.

19 "When you besiege a city for a long time, making war against it in order to take it, you shall not destroy its trees by wielding an axe against them. You may eat from them, but you shall not cut them down. Are the trees in the field human, that they should be besieged by you?

20 Only the trees that you know are not trees for food you may destroy and cut down, that you may build siegeworks against the city that makes war with you, until it falls.

Deuteronomy 21

English Standard Version

Atonement for Unsolved Murders

1 "If in the land that the Lord your God is giving you to possess someone is found slain, lying in the open country, and it is not known who killed him,

2 then your elders and your judges shall come out, and they shall measure the distance to the surrounding cities.

3 And the elders of the city that is nearest to the slain man shall take a heifer that has never been worked and that has not pulled in a yoke.

4 And the elders of that city shall bring the heifer down to a valley with running water, which is neither plowed nor sown, and shall break the heifer's neck there in the valley.

5 Then the priests, the sons of Levi, shall come forward, for the Lord your God has chosen them to minister to him and to bless in the name of the Lord, and by their word every dispute and every assault shall be settled.

6 And all the elders of that city nearest to the slain man shall wash their hands over the heifer whose neck was broken in the valley,

7 and they shall testify, 'Our hands did not shed this blood, nor did our eyes see it shed.

8 Accept atonement, O Lord, for your people Israel, whom you have redeemed, and do not set the guilt of innocent blood in the midst of your people Israel, so that their blood guilt be atoned for.'

9 So you shall purge the guilt of innocent blood from your midst, when you do what is right in the sight of the Lord.

Marrying Female Captives

10 "When you go out to war against your enemies, and the Lord your God gives them into your hand and you take them captive,

11 and you see among the captives a beautiful woman, and you desire to take her to be your wife,

12 and you bring her home to your house, she shall shave her head and pare her nails.

13 And she shall take off the clothes in which she was captured and shall remain in your house and lament her father and her mother a full month. After that you may go in to her and be her husband, and she shall be your wife.

14 But if you no longer delight in her, you shall let her go where she wants. But you shall not sell her for money, nor shall you treat her as a slave, since you have humiliated her.

Inheritance Rights of the Firstborn

15 "If a man has two wives, the one loved and the other unloved, and both the loved and the unloved have borne him children, and if the firstborn son belongs to the unloved,

16 then on the day when he assigns his possessions as an inheritance to his sons, he may not treat the son of the loved as the firstborn in preference to the son of the unloved, who is the firstborn,

17 but he shall acknowledge the firstborn, the son of the unloved, by giving him a double portion of all that he has, for he is the firstfruits of his strength. The right of the firstborn is his.

A Rebellious Son

18 "If a man has a stubborn and rebellious son who will not obey the voice of his father or the voice of his mother, and, though they discipline him, will not listen to them,

19 then his father and his mother shall take hold of him and bring him out to the elders of his city at the gate of the place where he lives,

20 and they shall say to the elders of his city, 'This our son is stubborn and rebellious; he will not obey our voice; he is a glutton and a drunkard.'

21 Then all the men of the city shall stone him to death with stones. So you shall purge the evil from your midst, and all Israel shall hear, and fear.

A Man Hanged on a Tree Is Cursed

22 "And if a man has committed a crime punishable by death and he is put to death, and you hang him on a tree,

23 his body shall not remain all night on the tree, but you shall bury him the same day, for a hanged man is cursed by God. You shall not defile your land that the Lord your God is giving you for an inheritance.

Deuteronomy 22

English Standard Version

Various Laws

1 "You shall not see your brother's ox or his sheep going astray and ignore them. You shall take them back to your brother.

2 And if he does not live near you and you do not know who he is, you shall bring it home to your house, and it shall stay with you until your brother seeks it. Then you shall restore it to him.

3 And you shall do the same with his donkey or with his garment, or with any lost thing of your brother's, which he loses and you find; you may not ignore it.

4 You shall not see your brother's donkey or his ox fallen down by the way and ignore them. You shall help him to lift them up again.

5 "A woman shall not wear a man's garment, nor shall a man put on a woman's cloak, for whoever does these things is an abomination to the Lord your God.

6 "If you come across a bird's nest in any tree or on the ground, with young ones or eggs and the mother sitting on the young or on the eggs, you shall not take the mother with the young.

7 You shall let the mother go, but the young you may take for yourself, that it may go well with you, and that you may live long.

8 "When you build a new house, you shall make a parapet for your roof, that you may not bring the guilt of blood upon your house, if anyone should fall from it.

9 "You shall not sow your vineyard with two kinds of seed, lest the whole yield be forfeited, the crop that you have sown and the yield of the vineyard.

10 You shall not plow with an ox and a donkey together.

11 You shall not wear cloth of wool and linen mixed together.

12 "You shall make yourself tassels on the four corners of the garment with which you cover yourself.

Laws Concerning Sexual Immorality

13 "If any man takes a wife and goes in to her and then hates her

14 and accuses her of misconduct and brings a bad name upon her, saying, 'I took this woman, and when I came near her, I did not find in her evidence of virginity,'

15 then the father of the young woman and her mother shall take and bring out the evidence of her virginity to the elders of the city in the gate.

16 And the father of the young woman shall say to the elders, 'I gave my daughter to this man to marry, and he hates her;

17 and behold, he has accused her of misconduct, saying, "I did not find in your daughter evidence of virginity." And yet this is the evidence of my daughter's virginity.' And they shall spread the cloak before the elders of the city.

18 Then the elders of that city shall take the man and whip him,

19 and they shall fine him a hundred shekels of silver and give them to the father of the young woman, because he has brought a bad name upon a virgin of Israel. And she shall be his wife. He may not divorce her all his days.

20 But if the thing is true, that evidence of virginity was not found in the young woman,

21 then they shall bring out the young woman to the door of her father's house, and the men of her city shall stone her to death with stones, because she has done an outrageous thing in Israel by whoring in her father's house. So you shall purge the evil from your midst.

22 "If a man is found lying with the wife of another man, both of them shall die, the man who lay with the woman, and the woman. So you shall purge the evil from Israel.

23 "If there is a betrothed virgin, and a man meets her in the city and lies with her,

24 then you shall bring them both out to the gate of that city, and you shall stone them to death with stones, the young woman because she did not cry for help though she was in the city, and the man because he violated his neighbor's wife. So you shall purge the evil from your midst.

25 "But if in the open country a man meets a young woman who is betrothed, and the man seizes her and lies with her, then only the man who lay with her shall die.

26 But you shall do nothing to the young woman; she has committed no offense punishable by death. For this case is like that of a man attacking and murdering his neighbor,

27 because he met her in the open country, and though the betrothed young woman cried for help there was no one to rescue her.

28 "If a man meets a virgin who is not betrothed, and seizes her and lies with her, and they are found,

29 then the man who lay with her shall give to the father of the young woman fifty shekels of silver, and she shall be his wife, because he has violated her. He may not divorce her all his days.

30 "A man shall not take his father's wife, so that he does not uncover his father's nakedness.

Deuteronomy 23

English Standard Version

Those Excluded from the Assembly

1 "No one whose testicles are crushed or whose male organ is cut off shall enter the assembly of the Lord.

2 "No one born of a forbidden union may enter the assembly of the Lord. Even to the tenth generation, none of his descendants may enter the assembly of the Lord.

3 "No Ammonite or Moabite may enter the assembly of the Lord. Even to the tenth generation, none of them may enter the assembly of the Lord forever,

4 because they did not meet you with bread and with water on the way, when you came out of Egypt, and because they hired against you Balaam the son of Beor from Pethor of Mesopotamia, to curse you.

5 But the Lord your God would not listen to Balaam; instead the Lord your God turned the curse into a blessing for you, because the Lord your God loved you.

6 You shall not seek their peace or their prosperity all your days forever.

7 "You shall not abhor an Edomite, for he is your brother. You shall not abhor an Egyptian, because you were a sojourner in his land.

8 Children born to them in the third generation may enter the assembly of the Lord.

Uncleanness in the Camp

9 "When you are encamped against your enemies, then you shall keep yourself from every evil thing.

10 "If any man among you becomes unclean because of a nocturnal emission, then he shall go outside the camp. He shall not come inside the camp,

11 but when evening comes, he shall bathe himself in water, and as the sun sets, he may come inside the camp.

12 "You shall have a place outside the camp, and you shall go out to it.

13 And you shall have a trowel with your tools, and when you sit down outside, you shall dig a hole with it and turn back and cover up your excrement.

14 Because the Lord your God walks in the midst of your camp, to deliver you and to give up your enemies before you, therefore your camp must be holy, so that he may not see anything indecent among you and turn away from you.

Miscellaneous Laws

15 "You shall not give up to his master a slave who has escaped from his master to you.

16 He shall dwell with you, in your midst, in the place that he shall choose within one of your towns, wherever it suits him. You shall not wrong him.

17 "None of the daughters of Israel shall be a cult prostitute, and none of the sons of Israel shall be a cult prostitute.

18 You shall not bring the fee of a prostitute or the wages of a dog into the house of the Lord your God in payment for any vow, for both of these are an abomination to the Lord your God.

19 "You shall not charge interest on loans to your brother, interest on money, interest on food, interest on anything that is lent for interest.

20 You may charge a foreigner interest, but you may not charge your brother interest, that the Lord your God may bless you in all that you undertake in the land that you are entering to take possession of it.

21 "If you make a vow to the Lord your God, you shall not delay fulfilling it, for the Lord your God will surely require it of you, and you will be guilty of sin.

22 But if you refrain from vowing, you will not be guilty of sin.

23 You shall be careful to do what has passed your lips, for you have voluntarily vowed to the Lord your God what you have promised with your mouth.

24 "If you go into your neighbor's vineyard, you may eat your fill of grapes, as many as you wish, but you shall not put any in your bag.

25 If you go into your neighbor's standing grain, you may pluck the ears with your hand, but you shall not put a sickle to your neighbor's standing grain.

Deuteronomy 24

English Standard Version

Laws Concerning Divorce

1 "When a man takes a wife and marries her, if then she finds no favor in his eyes because he has found some indecency in her, and he writes her a certificate of divorce and puts it in her hand and sends her out of his house, and she departs out of his house,

2 and if she goes and becomes another man's wife,

3 and the latter man hates her and writes her a certificate of divorce and puts it in her hand and sends her out of his house, or if the latter man dies, who took her to be his wife,

4 then her former husband, who sent her away, may not take her again to be his wife, after she has been defiled, for that is an abomination before the Lord. And you shall not bring sin upon the land that the Lord your God is giving you for an inheritance.

Miscellaneous Laws

5 "When a man is newly married, he shall not go out with the army or be liable for any other public duty. He shall be free at home one year to be happy with his wife whom he has taken.

6 "No one shall take a mill or an upper millstone in pledge, for that would be taking a life in pledge.

7 "If a man is found stealing one of his brothers of the people of Israel, and if he treats him as a slave or sells him, then that thief shall die. So you shall purge the evil from your midst.

8 "Take care, in a case of leprous disease, to be very careful to do according to all that the Levitical priests shall direct you. As I commanded them, so you shall be careful to do.

9 Remember what the Lord your God did to Miriam on the way as you came out of Egypt.

10 "When you make your neighbor a loan of any sort, you shall not go into his house to collect his pledge.

11 You shall stand outside, and the man to whom you make the loan shall bring the pledge out to you. 1

2 And if he is a poor man, you shall not sleep in his pledge.

13 You shall restore to him the pledge as the sun sets, that he may sleep in his cloak and bless you. And it shall be righteousness for you before the Lord your God.

14 "You shall not oppress a hired worker who is poor and needy, whether he is one of your brothers or one of the sojourners who are in your land within your towns.

15 You shall give him his wages on the same day, before the sun sets (for he is poor and counts on it), lest he cry against you to the Lord, and you be guilty of sin.

16 "Fathers shall not be put to death because of their children, nor shall children be put to death because of their fathers. Each one shall be put to death for his own sin.

17 "You shall not pervert the justice due to the sojourner or to the fatherless, or take a widow's garment in pledge,

18 but you shall remember that you were a slave in Egypt and the Lord your God redeemed you from there; therefore I command you to do this.

19 "When you reap your harvest in your field and forget a sheaf in the field, you shall not go back to get it. It shall be for the sojourner, the fatherless, and the widow, that the Lord your God may bless you in all the work of your hands.

20 When you beat your olive trees, you shall not go over them again. It shall be for the sojourner, the fatherless, and the widow.

21 When you gather the grapes of your vineyard, you shall not strip it afterward. It shall be for the sojourner, the fatherless, and the widow.

22 You shall remember that you were a slave in the land of Egypt; therefore I command you to do this.

Deuteronomy 25

English Standard Version

1 "If there is a dispute between men and they come into court and the judges decide between them, acquitting the innocent and condemning the guilty,

2 then if the guilty man deserves to be beaten, the judge shall cause him to lie down and be beaten in his presence with a number of stripes in proportion to his offense.

3 Forty stripes may be given him, but not more, lest, if one should go on to beat him with more stripes than these, your brother be degraded in your sight.

4 "You shall not muzzle an ox when it is treading out the grain.

Laws Concerning Levirate Marriage

5 "If brothers dwell together, and one of them dies and has no son, the wife of the dead man shall not be married outside the family to a stranger. Her husband's brother shall go in to her and take her as his wife and perform the duty of a husband's brother to her.

6 And the first son whom she bears shall succeed to the name of his dead brother, that his name may not be blotted out of Israel.

7 And if the man does not wish to take his brother's wife, then his brother's wife shall go up to the gate to the elders and say, 'My husband's brother refuses to perpetuate his brother's name in Israel; he will not perform the duty of a husband's brother to me.'

8 Then the elders of his city shall call him and speak to him, and if he persists, saying, 'I do not wish to take her,'

9 then his brother's wife shall go up to him in the presence of the elders and pull his sandal off his foot and spit in his face. And she shall answer and say, 'So shall it be done to the man who does not build up his brother's house.'

10 And the name of his house shall be called in Israel, 'The house of him who had his sandal pulled off.'

Miscellaneous Laws

11 "When men fight with one another and the wife of the one draws near to rescue her husband from the hand of him who is beating him and puts out her hand and seizes him by the private parts,

12 then you shall cut off her hand. Your eye shall have no pity.

13 "You shall not have in your bag two kinds of weights, a large and a small.

14 You shall not have in your house two kinds of measures, a large and a small.

15 A full and fair weight you shall have, a full and fair measure you shall have, that your days may be long in the land that the Lord your God is giving you.

16 For all who do such things, all who act dishonestly, are an abomination to the Lord your God.

17 "Remember what Amalek did to you on the way as you came out of Egypt,

18 how he attacked you on the way when you were faint and weary, and cut off your tail, those who were lagging behind you, and he did not fear God.

19 Therefore when the Lord your God has given you rest from all your enemies around you, in the land that the Lord your God is giving you for an inheritance to possess, you shall blot out the memory of Amalek from under heaven; you shall not forget

Deuteronomy 26

English Standard Version

Offerings of Firstfruits and Tithes

1 "When you come into the land that the Lord your God is giving you for an inheritance and have taken possession of it and live in it,

2 you shall take some of the first of all the fruit of the ground, which you harvest from your land that the Lord your God is giving you, and you shall put it in a basket, and you shall go to the place that the Lord your God will choose, to make his name to dwell there.

3 And you shall go to the priest who is in office at that time and say to him, 'I declare today to the Lord your God that I have come into the land that the Lord swore to our fathers to give us.'

4 Then the priest shall take the basket from your hand and set it down before the altar of the Lord your God.

5 "And you shall make response before the Lord your God, 'A wandering Aramean was my father. And he went down into Egypt and sojourned there, few in number, and there he became a nation, great, mighty, and populous.

6 And the Egyptians treated us harshly and humiliated us and laid on us hard labor.

7 Then we cried to the Lord, the God of our fathers, and the Lord heard our voice and saw our affliction, our toil, and our oppression.

8 And the Lord brought us out of Egypt with a mighty hand and an outstretched arm, with great deeds of terror, with signs and wonders.

9 And he brought us into this place and gave us this land, a land flowing with milk and honey.

10 And behold, now I bring the first of the fruit of the ground, which you, O Lord, have given me.' And you shall set it down before the Lord your God and worship before the Lord your God.

11 And you shall rejoice in all the good that the Lord your God has given to you and to your house, you, and the Levite, and the sojourner who is among you.

12 "When you have finished paying all the tithe of your produce in the third year, which is the year of tithing, giving it to the Levite, the sojourner, the fatherless, and the widow, so that they may eat within your towns and be filled,

13 then you shall say before the Lord your God, 'I have removed the sacred portion out of my house, and moreover, I have given it to the Levite, the sojourner, the fatherless, and the widow, according to all your commandment that you have commanded me. I have not transgressed any of your commandments, nor have I forgotten them.

14 I have not eaten of the tithe while I was mourning, or removed any of it while I was unclean, or offered any of it to the dead. I have obeyed the voice of the Lord my God. I have done according to all that you have commanded me.

15 Look down from your holy habitation, from heaven, and bless your people Israel and the ground that you have given us, as you swore to our fathers, a land flowing with milk and honey.'

16 "This day the Lord your God commands you to do these statutes and rules. You shall therefore be careful to do them with all your heart and with all your soul.

17 You have declared today that the Lord is your God, and that you will walk in his ways, and keep his statutes and his commandments and his rules, and will obey his voice.

18 And the Lord has declared today that you are a people for his treasured possession, as he has promised you, and that you are to keep all his commandments,

19 and that he will set you in praise and in fame and in honor high above all nations that he has made, and that you shall be a people holy to the Lord your God, as he promised.".

Deuteronomy 27

English Standard Version

The Altar on Mount Ebal

1 Now Moses and the elders of Israel commanded the people, saying, "Keep the whole commandment that I command you today.

2 And on the day you cross over the Jordan to the land that the Lord your God is giving you, you shall set up large stones and plaster them with plaster.

3 And you shall write on them all the words of this law, when you cross over to enter the land that the Lord your God is giving you, a land flowing with milk and honey, as the Lord, the God of your fathers, has promised you.

4 And when you have crossed over the Jordan, you shall set up these stones, concerning which I command you today, on Mount Ebal, and you shall plaster them with plaster.

5 And there you shall build an altar to the Lord your God, an altar of stones. You shall wield no iron tool on them;

6 you shall build an altar to the Lord your God of uncut stones. And you shall offer burnt offerings on it to the Lord your God,

7 and you shall sacrifice peace offerings and shall eat there, and you shall rejoice before the Lord your God.

8 And you shall write on the stones all the words of this law very plainly."

Curses from Mount Ebal

9 Then Moses and the Levitical priests said to all Israel, "Keep silence and hear, O Israel: this day you have become the people of the Lord your God.

10 You shall therefore obey the voice of the Lord your God, keeping his commandments and his statutes, which I command you today."

11 That day Moses charged the people, saying,

12 "When you have crossed over the Jordan, these shall stand on Mount Gerizim to bless the people: Simeon, Levi, Judah, Issachar, Joseph, and Benjamin.

13 And these shall stand on Mount Ebal for the curse: Reuben, Gad, Asher, Zebulun, Dan, and Naphtali.

14 And the Levites shall declare to all the men of Israel in a loud voice:

15 "'Cursed be the man who makes a carved or cast metal image, an abomination to the Lord, a thing made by the hands of a craftsman, and sets it up in secret.' And all the people shall answer and say, 'Amen.'

16 "'Cursed be anyone who dishonors his father or his mother.' And all the people shall say, 'Amen.'

17 "'Cursed be anyone who moves his neighbor's landmark.' And all the people shall say, 'Amen.'

18 "'Cursed be anyone who misleads a blind man on the road.' And all the people shall say, 'Amen.'

19 "'Cursed be anyone who perverts the justice due to the sojourner, the fatherless, and the widow.' And all the people shall say, 'Amen.'

20 "'Cursed be anyone who lies with his father's wife, because he has uncovered his father's nakedness.' And all the people shall say, 'Amen.'

21 "'Cursed be anyone who lies with any kind of animal.' And all the people shall say, 'Amen.'

22 "'Cursed be anyone who lies with his sister, whether the daughter of his father or the daughter of his mother.' And all the people shall say, 'Amen.'

23 "'Cursed be anyone who lies with his mother-in-law.' And all the people shall say, 'Amen.'

24 "'Cursed be anyone who strikes down his neighbor in secret.' And all the people shall say, 'Amen.'

25 "'Cursed be anyone who takes a bribe to shed innocent blood.' And all the people shall say, 'Amen.'

26 "'Cursed be anyone who does not confirm the words of this law by doing them.' And all the people shall say, 'Amen.'

Deuteronomy 28

English Standard Version

Blessings for Obedience

1 "And if you faithfully obey the voice of the Lord your God, being careful to do all his commandments that I command you today, the Lord your God will set you high above all the nations of the earth.

2 And all these blessings shall come upon you and overtake you, if you obey the voice of the Lord your God.

3 Blessed shall you be in the city, and blessed shall you be in the field.

4 Blessed shall be the fruit of your womb and the fruit of your ground and the fruit of your cattle, the increase of your herds and the young of your flock.

5 Blessed shall be your basket and your kneading bowl.

6 Blessed shall you be when you come in, and blessed shall you be when you go out.

7 "The Lord will cause your enemies who rise against you to be defeated before you. They shall come out against you one way and flee before you seven ways.

8 The Lord will command the blessing on you in your barns and in all that you undertake. And he will bless you in the land that the Lord your God is giving you.

9 The Lord will establish you as a people holy to himself, as he has sworn to you, if you keep the commandments of the Lord your God and walk in his ways.

10 And all the peoples of the earth shall see that you are called by the name of the Lord, and they shall be afraid of you.

11 And the Lord will make you abound in prosperity, in the fruit of your womb and in the fruit of your livestock and in the fruit of your ground, within the land that the Lord swore to your fathers to give you.

12 The Lord will open to you his good treasury, the heavens, to give the rain to your land in its season and to bless all the work of your hands. And you shall lend to many nations, but you shall not borrow.

13 And the Lord will make you the head and not the tail, and you shall only go up and not down, if you obey the commandments of the Lord your God, which I command you today, being careful to do them,

14 and if you do not turn aside from any of the words that I command you today, to the right hand or to the left, to go after other gods to serve them.

Curses for Disobedience

15 "But if you will not obey the voice of the Lord your God or be careful to do all his commandments and his statutes that I command you today, then all these curses shall come upon you and overtake you.

16 Cursed shall you be in the city, and cursed shall you be in the field.

17 Cursed shall be your basket and your kneading bowl.

18 Cursed shall be the fruit of your womb and the fruit of your ground, the increase of your herds and the young of your flock.

19 Cursed shall you be when you come in, and cursed shall you be when you go out.

20 "The Lord will send on you curses, confusion, and frustration in all that you undertake to do, until you are destroyed and perish quickly on account of the evil of your deeds, because you have forsaken me.

21 The Lord will make the pestilence stick to you until he has consumed you off the land that you are entering to take possession of it.

22 The Lord will strike you with wasting disease and with fever, inflammation and fiery heat, and with drought and with blight and with mildew. They shall pursue you until you perish.

23 And the heavens over your head shall be bronze, and the earth under you shall be iron.

24 The Lord will make the rain of your land powder. From heaven dust shall come down on you until you are destroyed.

25 "The Lord will cause you to be defeated before your enemies. You shall go out one way against them and flee seven ways before them. And you shall be a horror to all the kingdoms of the earth.

26 And your dead body shall be food for all birds of the air and for the beasts of the earth, and there shall be no one to frighten them away.

27 The Lord will strike you with the boils of Egypt, and with tumors and scabs and itch, of which you cannot be healed.

28 The Lord will strike you with madness and blindness and confusion of mind,

29 and you shall grope at noonday, as the blind grope in darkness, and you shall not prosper in your ways. And you shall be only oppressed and robbed continually, and there shall be no one to help you.

30 You shall betroth a wife, but another man shall ravish her. You shall build a house, but you shall not dwell in it. You shall plant a vineyard, but you shall not enjoy its fruit.

31 Your ox shall be slaughtered before your eyes, but you shall not eat any of it. Your donkey shall be seized before your face, but shall not be restored to you. Your sheep shall be given to your enemies, but there shall be no one to help you.

32 Your sons and your daughters shall be given to another people, while your eyes look on and fail with longing for them all day long, but you shall be helpless.

33 A nation that you have not known shall eat up the fruit of your ground and of all your labors, and you shall be only oppressed and crushed continually, 3

4 so that you are driven mad by the sights that your eyes see.

35 The Lord will strike you on the knees and on the legs with grievous boils of which you cannot be healed, from the sole of your foot to the crown of your head.

36 "The Lord will bring you and your king whom you set over you to a nation that neither you nor your fathers have known. And there you shall serve other gods of wood and stone.

37 And you shall become a horror, a proverb, and a byword among all the peoples where the Lord will lead you away.

38 You shall carry much seed into the field and shall gather in little, for the locust shall consume it.

39 You shall plant vineyards and dress them, but you shall neither drink of the wine nor gather the grapes, for the worm shall eat them.

40 You shall have olive trees throughout all your territory, but you shall not anoint yourself with the oil, for your olives shall drop off.

Deuteronomy 28

41 You shall father sons and daughters, but they shall not be yours, for they shall go into captivity. 4

2 The cricket shall possess all your trees and the fruit of your ground.

43 The sojourner who is among you shall rise higher and higher above you, and you shall come down lower and lower.

44 He shall lend to you, and you shall not lend to him. He shall be the head, and you shall be the tail.

45 "All these curses shall come upon you and pursue you and overtake you till you are destroyed, because you did not obey the voice of the Lord your God, to keep his commandments and his statutes that he commanded you.

46 They shall be a sign and a wonder against you and your offspring forever.

47 Because you did not serve the Lord your God with joyfulness and gladness of heart, because of the abundance of all things,

48 therefore you shall serve your enemies whom the Lord will send against you, in hunger and thirst, in nakedness, and lacking everything. And he will put a yoke of iron on your neck until he has destroyed you.

49 The Lord will bring a nation against you from far away, from the end of the earth, swooping down like the eagle, a nation whose language you do not understand,

50 a hard-faced nation who shall not respect the old or show mercy to the young.

51 It shall eat the offspring of your cattle and the fruit of your ground, until you are destroyed; it also shall not leave you grain, wine, or oil, the increase of your herds or the young of your flock, until they have caused you to perish.

52 "They shall besiege you in all your towns, until your high and fortified walls, in which you trusted, come down throughout all your land. And they

shall besiege you in all your towns throughout all your land, which the Lord your God has given you.

53 And you shall eat the fruit of your womb, the flesh of your sons and daughters, whom the Lord your God has given you, in the siege and in the distress with which your enemies shall distress you.

54 The man who is the most tender and refined among you will begrudge food to his brother, to the wife he embraces, and to the last of the children whom he has left,

55 so that he will not give to any of them any of the flesh of his children whom he is eating, because he has nothing else left, in the siege and in the distress with which your enemy shall distress you in all your towns.

56 The most tender and refined woman among you, who would not venture to set the sole of her foot on the ground because she is so delicate and tender, will begrudge to the husband she embraces, to her son and to her daughter,

57 her afterbirth that comes out from between her feet and her children whom she bears, because lacking everything she will eat them secretly, in the siege and in the distress with which your enemy shall distress you in your towns.

58 "If you are not careful to do all the words of this law that are written in this book, that you may fear this glorious and awesome name, the Lord your God,

59 then the Lord will bring on you and your offspring extraordinary afflictions, afflictions severe and lasting, and sicknesses grievous and lasting.

60 And he will bring upon you again all the diseases of Egypt, of which you were afraid, and they shall cling to you.

61 Every sickness also and every affliction that is not recorded in the book of this law, the Lord will bring upon you, until you are destroyed.

62 Whereas you were as numerous as the stars of heaven, you shall be left few in number, because you did not obey the voice of the Lord your God.

63 And as the Lord took delight in doing you good and multiplying you, so the Lord will take delight in bringing ruin upon you and destroying you. And you shall be plucked off the land that you are entering to take possession of it.

64 "And the Lord will scatter you among all peoples, from one end of the earth to the other, and there you shall serve other gods of wood and stone, which neither you nor your fathers have known.

65 And among these nations you shall find no respite, and there shall be no resting place for the sole of your foot, but the Lord will give you there a trembling heart and failing eyes and a languishing soul.

66 Your life shall hang in doubt before you. Night and day you shall be in dread and have no assurance of your life.

67 In the morning you shall say, 'If only it were evening!' and at evening you shall say, 'If only it were morning!' because of the dread that your heart shall feel, and the sights that your eyes shall see.

68 And the Lord will bring you back in ships to Egypt, a journey that I promised that you should never make again; and there you shall offer yourselves for sale to your enemies as male and female slaves, but there will be no buyer."

Deuteronomy 29

English Standard Version

The Covenant Renewed in Moab

1 These are the words of the covenant that the Lord commanded Moses to make with the people of Israel in the land of Moab, besides the covenant that he had made with them at Horeb.

2 And Moses summoned all Israel and said to them: "You have seen all that the Lord did before your eyes in the land of Egypt, to Pharaoh and to all his servants and to all his land,

3 the great trials that your eyes saw, the signs, and those great wonders.

4 But to this day the Lord has not given you a heart to understand or eyes to see or ears to hear.

5 I have led you forty years in the wilderness. Your clothes have not worn out on you, and your sandals have not worn off your feet.

6 You have not eaten bread, and you have not drunk wine or strong drink, that you may know that I am the Lord your God.

7 And when you came to this place, Sihon the king of Heshbon and Og the king of Bashan came out against us to battle, but we defeated them.

8 We took their land and gave it for an inheritance to the Reubenites, the Gadites, and the half-tribe of the Manassites.

9 Therefore keep the words of this covenant and do them, that you may prosper in all that you do.

10 "You are standing today, all of you, before the Lord your God: the heads of your tribes, your elders, and your officers, all the men of Israel,

11 your little ones, your wives, and the sojourner who is in your camp, from the one who chops your wood to the one who draws your water,

12 so that you may enter into the sworn covenant of the Lord your God, which the Lord your God is making with you today,

13 that he may establish you today as his people, and that he may be your God, as he promised you, and as he swore to your fathers, to Abraham, to Isaac, and to Jacob.

14 It is not with you alone that I am making this sworn covenant,

15 but with whoever is standing here with us today before the Lord our God, and with whoever is not here with us today.

16 "You know how we lived in the land of Egypt, and how we came through the midst of the nations through which you passed.

17 And you have seen their detestable things, their idols of wood and stone, of silver and gold, which were among them.

18 Beware lest there be among you a man or woman or clan or tribe whose heart is turning away today from the Lord our God to go and serve the gods of those nations. Beware lest there be among you a root bearing poisonous and bitter fruit,

19 one who, when he hears the words of this sworn covenant, blesses himself in his heart, saying, 'I shall be safe, though I walk in the

stubbornness of my heart.' This will lead to the sweeping away of moist and dry alike.

20 The Lord will not be willing to forgive him, but rather the anger of the Lord and his jealousy will smoke against that man, and the curses written in this book will settle upon him, and the Lord will blot out his name from under heaven.

21 And the Lord will single him out from all the tribes of Israel for calamity, in accordance with all the curses of the covenant written in this Book of the Law.

22 And the next generation, your children who rise up after you, and the foreigner who comes from a far land, will say, when they see the afflictions of that land and the sicknesses with which the Lord has made it sick—

23 the whole land burned out with brimstone and salt, nothing sown and nothing growing, where no plant can sprout, an overthrow like that of Sodom and Gomorrah, Admah, and Zeboiim, which the Lord overthrew in his anger and wrath—

24 all the nations will say, 'Why has the Lord done thus to this land? What caused the heat of this great anger?'

25 Then people will say, 'It is because they abandoned the covenant of the Lord, the God of their fathers, which he made with them when he brought them out of the land of Egypt,

26 and went and served other gods and worshiped them, gods whom they had not known and whom he had not allotted to them.

27 Therefore the anger of the Lord was kindled against this land, bringing upon it all the curses written in this book,

28 and the Lord uprooted them from their land in anger and fury and great wrath, and cast them into another land, as they are this day.'

29 "The secret things belong to the Lord our God, but the things that are revealed belong to us and to our children forever, that we may do all the words of this law.

Deuteronomy 30

English Standard Version

Repentance and Forgiveness

1 "And when all these things come upon you, the blessing and the curse, which I have set before you, and you call them to mind among all the nations where the Lord your God has driven you,

2 and return to the Lord your God, you and your children, and obey his voice in all that I command you today, with all your heart and with all your soul,

3 then the Lord your God will restore your fortunes and have mercy on you, and he will gather you again from all the peoples where the Lord your God has scattered you.

4 If your outcasts are in the uttermost parts of heaven, from there the Lord your God will gather you, and from there he will take you.

5 And the Lord your God will bring you into the land that your fathers possessed, that you may possess it. And he will make you more prosperous and numerous than your fathers.

6 And the Lord your God will circumcise your heart and the heart of your offspring, so that you will love the Lord your God with all your heart and with all your soul, that you may live.

7 And the Lord your God will put all these curses on your foes and enemies who persecuted you.

8 And you shall again obey the voice of the Lord and keep all his commandments that I command you today.

9 The Lord your God will make you abundantly prosperous in all the work of your hand, in the fruit of your womb and in the fruit of your cattle and in the fruit of your ground. For the Lord will again take delight in prospering you, as he took delight in your fathers,

10 when you obey the voice of the Lord your God, to keep his commandments and his statutes that are written in this Book of the Law, when you turn to the Lord your God with all your heart and with all your soul.

The Choice of Life and Death

11 "For this commandment that I command you today is not too hard for you, neither is it far off.

12 It is not in heaven, that you should say, 'Who will ascend to heaven for us and bring it to us, that we may hear it and do it?'

13 Neither is it beyond the sea, that you should say, 'Who will go over the sea for us and bring it to us, that we may hear it and do it?'

14 But the word is very near you. It is in your mouth and in your heart, so that you can do it.

15 "See, I have set before you today life and good, death and evil.

16 If you obey the commandments of the Lord your God that I command you today, by loving the Lord your God, by walking in his ways, and by

keeping his commandments and his statutes and his rules, then you shall live and multiply, and the Lord your God will bless you in the land that you are entering to take possession of it.

17 But if your heart turns away, and you will not hear, but are drawn away to worship other gods and serve them,

18 I declare to you today, that you shall surely perish. You shall not live long in the land that you are going over the Jordan to enter and possess.

19 I call heaven and earth to witness against you today, that I have set before you life and death, blessing and curse. Therefore choose life, that you and your offspring may live,

20 loving the Lord your God, obeying his voice and holding fast to him, for he is your life and length of days, that you may dwell in the land that the Lord swore to your fathers, to Abraham, to Isaac, and to Jacob, to give them."

Deuteronomy 31

English Standard Version

Joshua to Succeed Moses

1 So Moses continued to speak these words to all Israel.

2 And he said to them, "I am 120 years old today. I am no longer able to go out and come in. The Lord has said to me, 'You shall not go over this Jordan.'

3 The Lord your God himself will go over before you. He will destroy these nations before you, so that you shall dispossess them, and Joshua will go over at your head, as the Lord has spoken.

4 And the Lord will do to them as he did to Sihon and Og, the kings of the Amorites, and to their land, when he destroyed them.

5 And the Lord will give them over to you, and you shall do to them according to the whole commandment that I have commanded you.

6 Be strong and courageous. Do not fear or be in dread of them, for it is the Lord your God who goes with you. He will not leave you or forsake you."

7 Then Moses summoned Joshua and said to him in the sight of all Israel, "Be strong and courageous, for you shall go with this people into the land

that the Lord has sworn to their fathers to give them, and you shall put them in possession of it.

8 It is the Lord who goes before you. He will be with you; he will not leave you or forsake you. Do not fear or be dismayed."

The Reading of the Law

9 Then Moses wrote this law and gave it to the priests, the sons of Levi, who carried the ark of the covenant of the Lord, and to all the elders of Israel.

10 And Moses commanded them, "At the end of every seven years, at the set time in the year of release, at the Feast of Booths,

11 when all Israel comes to appear before the Lord your God at the place that he will choose, you shall read this law before all Israel in their hearing.

12 Assemble the people, men, women, and little ones, and the sojourner within your towns, that they may hear and learn to fear the Lord your God, and be careful to do all the words of this law,

13 and that their children, who have not known it, may hear and learn to fear the Lord your God, as long as you live in the land that you are going over the Jordan to possess."

Joshua Commissioned to Lead Israel

14 And the Lord said to Moses, "Behold, the days approach when you must die. Call Joshua and present yourselves in the tent of meeting, that I may commission him." And Moses and Joshua went and presented themselves in the tent of meeting.

15 And the Lord appeared in the tent in a pillar of cloud. And the pillar of cloud stood over the entrance of the tent.

16 And the Lord said to Moses, "Behold, you are about to lie down with your fathers. Then this people will rise and whore after the foreign gods

among them in the land that they are entering, and they will forsake me and break my covenant that I have made with them.

17 Then my anger will be kindled against them in that day, and I will forsake them and hide my face from them, and they will be devoured. And many evils and troubles will come upon them, so that they will say in that day, 'Have not these evils come upon us because our God is not among us?'

18 And I will surely hide my face in that day because of all the evil that they have done, because they have turned to other gods.

19 "Now therefore write this song and teach it to the people of Israel. Put it in their mouths, that this song may be a witness for me against the people of Israel.

20 For when I have brought them into the land flowing with milk and honey, which I swore to give to their fathers, and they have eaten and are full and grown fat, they will turn to other gods and serve them, and despise me and break my covenant.

21 And when many evils and troubles have come upon them, this song shall confront them as a witness (for it will live unforgotten in the mouths of their offspring). For I know what they are inclined to do even today, before I have brought them into the land that I swore to give."

22 So Moses wrote this song the same day and taught it to the people of Israel.

23 And the Lord commissioned Joshua the son of Nun and said, "Be strong and courageous, for you shall bring the people of Israel into the land that I swore to give them. I will be with you."

24 When Moses had finished writing the words of this law in a book to the very end,

25 Moses commanded the Levites who carried the ark of the covenant of the Lord,

26 "Take this Book of the Law and put it by the side of the ark of the covenant of the Lord your God, that it may be there for a witness against you.

27 For I know how rebellious and stubborn you are. Behold, even today while I am yet alive with you, you have been rebellious against the Lord. How much more after my death!

28 Assemble to me all the elders of your tribes and your officers, that I may speak these words in their ears and call heaven and earth to witness against them.

29 For I know that after my death you will surely act corruptly and turn aside from the way that I have commanded you. And in the days to come evil will befall you, because you will do what is evil in the sight of the Lord, provoking him to anger through the work of your hands."

The Song of Moses

30 Then Moses spoke the words of this song until they were finished, in the ears of all the assembly of Israel:

Deuteronomy 32

English Standard Version

1 "Give ear, O heavens, and I will speak, and let the earth hear the words of my mouth.

2 May my teaching drop as the rain, my speech distill as the dew, like gentle rain upon the tender grass, and like showers upon the herb.

3 For I will proclaim the name of the Lord; ascribe greatness to our God!

4 "The Rock, his work is perfect, for all his ways are justice. A God of faithfulness and without iniquity, just and upright is he.

5 They have dealt corruptly with him; they are no longer his children because they are blemished; they are a crooked and twisted generation.

6 Do you thus repay the Lord, you foolish and senseless people? Is not he your father, who created you, who made you and established you?

7 Remember the days of old; consider the years of many generations; ask your father, and he will show you, your elders, and they will tell you.

8 When the Most High gave to the nations their inheritance, when he divided mankind, he fixed the borders of the peoples according to the number of the sons of God.

Pearls of Wisdom

9 But the Lord's portion is his people, Jacob his allotted heritage.

10 "He found him in a desert land, and in the howling waste of the wilderness; he encircled him, he cared for him, he kept him as the apple of his eye.

11 Like an eagle that stirs up its nest, that flutters over its young, spreading out its wings, catching them, bearing them on its pinions,

12 the Lord alone guided him, no foreign god was with him.

13 He made him ride on the high places of the land, and he ate the produce of the field, and he suckled him with honey out of the rock, and oil out of the flinty rock.

14 Curds from the herd, and milk from the flock, with fat of lambs, rams of Bashan and goats, with the very finest of the wheat— and you drank foaming wine made from the blood of the grape.

15 "But Jeshurun grew fat, and kicked; you grew fat, stout, and sleek; then he forsook God who made him and scoffed at the Rock of his salvation.

16 They stirred him to jealousy with strange gods; with abominations they provoked him to anger.

17 They sacrificed to demons that were no gods, to gods they had never known, to new gods that had come recently, whom your fathers had never dreaded.

18 You were unmindful of the Rock that bore you, and you forgot the God who gave you birth.

19 "The Lord saw it and spurned them, because of the provocation of his sons and his daughters.

20 And he said, 'I will hide my face from them; I will see what their end will be, for they are a perverse generation, children in whom is no faithfulness.

21 They have made me jealous with what is no god; they have provoked me to anger with their idols. So I will make them jealous with those who are no people; I will provoke them to anger with a foolish nation.

22 For a fire is kindled by my anger, and it burns to the depths of Sheol,

devours the earth and its increase and sets on fire the foundations of the mountains.

23 "'And I will heap disasters upon them; I will spend my arrows on them;

24 they shall be wasted with hunger, and devoured by plague and poisonous pestilence; I will send the teeth of beasts against them, with the venom of things that crawl in the dust.

25 Outdoors the sword shall bereave, and indoors terror, for young man and woman alike, the nursing child with the man of gray hairs.

26 I would have said, "I will cut them to pieces; I will wipe them from human memory,"

27 had I not feared provocation by the enemy, lest their adversaries should misunderstand, lest they should say, "Our hand is triumphant,

28 "For they are a nation void of counsel, and there is no understanding in them.

29 If they were wise, they would understand this; they would discern their latter end!

30 How could one have chased a thousand, and two have put ten thousand to flight, unless their Rock had sold them, and the Lord had given them up?

31 For their rock is not as our Rock; our enemies are by themselves.

32 For their vine comes from the vine of Sodom and from the fields of Gomorrah; their grapes are grapes of poison; their clusters are bitter;

33 their wine is the poison of serpents and the cruel venom of asps.

34 "'Is not this laid up in store with me, sealed up in my treasuries?

35 Vengeance is mine, and recompense, for the time when their foot shall slip; for the day of their calamity is at hand, and their doom comes swiftly.'

36 For the Lord will vindicate[g] his people and have compassion on his servants, when he sees that their power is gone and there is none remaining, bond or free.

37 Then he will say, 'Where are their gods, the rock in which they took refuge,

38 who ate the fat of their sacrifices and drank the wine of their drink offering? Let them rise up and help you; let them be your protection!

39 "'See now that I, even I, am he, and there is no god beside me; I kill and I make alive; I wound and I heal; and there is none that can deliver out of my hand.

40 For I lift up my hand to heaven and swear, As I live forever,

41 if I sharpen my flashing sword and my hand takes hold on judgment, I will take vengeance on my adversaries and will repay those who hate me.

42 I will make my arrows drunk with blood, and my sword shall devour flesh—with the blood of the slain and the captives, from the long-haired heads of the enemy.'

43 "Rejoice with him, O heavens; bow down to him, all gods, for he avenges the blood of his children and takes vengeance on his adversaries. He repays those who hate him and cleanses his people's land."

44 Moses came and recited all the words of this song in the hearing of the people, he and Joshua the son of Nun.

45 And when Moses had finished speaking all these words to all Israel,

46 he said to them, "Take to heart all the words by which I am warning you today, that you may command them to your children, that they may be careful to do all the words of this law.

47 For it is no empty word for you, but your very life, and by this word you shall live long in the land that you are going over the Jordan to possess."

Moses' Death Foretold

48 That very day the Lord spoke to Moses,

49 "Go up this mountain of the Abarim, Mount Nebo, which is in the land of Moab, opposite Jericho, and view the land of Canaan, which I am giving to the people of Israel for a possession.

50 And die on the mountain which you go up, and be gathered to your people, as Aaron your brother died in Mount Hor and was gathered to his people,

51 because you broke faith with me in the midst of the people of Israel at the waters of Meribah-kadesh, in the wilderness of Zin, and because you did not treat me as holy in the midst of the people of Israel.

52 For you shall see the land before you, but you shall not go there, into the land that I am giving to the people of Israel."

Deuteronomy 33

English Standard Version

Moses' Final Blessing on Israel

1 This is the blessing with which Moses the man of God blessed the people of Israel before his death.

2 He said, "The Lord came from Sinai and dawned from Seir upon us; he shone forth from Mount Paran; he came from the ten thousands of holy ones, with flaming fire at his right hand.

3 Yes, he loved his people, all his holy ones were in his hand; so they followed in your steps, receiving direction from you,

4 when Moses commanded us a law, as a possession for the assembly of Jacob.

5 Thus the Lord became king in Jeshurun, when the heads of the people were gathered, all the tribes of Israel together.

6 "Let Reuben live, and not die, but let his men be few."

7 And this he said of Judah: "Hear, O Lord, the voice of Judah, and bring him in to his people. With your hands contend for him, and be a help against his adversaries."

8 And of Levi he said, "Give to Levi your Thummim, and your Urim to your godly one, whom you tested at Massah, with whom you quarreled at the waters of Meribah;

9 who said of his father and mother, 'I regard them not'; he disowned his brothers and ignored his children. For they observed your word and kept your covenant.

10 They shall teach Jacob your rules and Israel your law; they shall put incense before you and whole burnt offerings on your altar.

11 Bless, O Lord, his substance, and accept the work of his hands; crush the loins of his adversaries, of those who hate him, that they rise not again."

12 Of Benjamin he said, "The beloved of the Lord dwells in safety. The High God surrounds him all day long, and dwells between his shoulders."

13 And of Joseph he said, "Blessed by the Lord be his land, with the choicest gifts of heaven above, and of the deep that crouches beneath,

14 with the choicest fruits of the sun and the rich yield of the months,

15 with the finest produce of the ancient mountains and the abundance of the everlasting hills,

16 with the best gifts of the earth and its fullness and the favor of him who dwells in the bush. May these rest on the head of Joseph, on the pate of him who is prince among his brothers.

17 A firstborn bull—he has majesty, and his horns are the horns of a wild ox; with them he shall gore the peoples, all of them, to the ends of the earth; they are the ten thousands of Ephraim, and they are the thousands of Manasseh."

18 And of Zebulun he said, "Rejoice, Zebulun, in your going out, and Issachar, in your tents.

19 They shall call peoples to their mountain; there they offer right sacrifices; for they draw from the abundance of the seas and the hidden treasures of the sand."

20 And of Gad he said, "Blessed be he who enlarges Gad! Gad crouches like a lion; he tears off arm and scalp.

21 He chose the best of the land for himself, for there a commander's portion was reserved; and he came with the heads of the people, with Israel he executed the justice of the Lord, and his judgments for Israel."

22 And of Dan he said, "Dan is a lion's cub that leaps from Bashan."

23 And of Naphtali he said, "O Naphtali, sated with favor, and full of the blessing of the Lord, possess the lake and the south."

24 And of Asher he said, "Most blessed of sons be Asher; let him be the favorite of his brothers, and let him dip his foot in oil.

25 Your bars shall be iron and bronze, and as your days, so shall your strength be.

26 "There is none like God, O Jeshurun,mwho rides through the heavens to your help, through the skies in his majesty.

27 The eternal God is your dwelling place, and underneath are the everlasting arms. And he thrust out the enemy before you and said, 'Destroy.'

28 So Israel lived in safety, Jacob lived alone, in a land of grain and wine,mwhose heavens drop down dew.

29 Happy are you, O Israel! Who is like you, a people saved by the Lord, the shield of your help, and the sword of your triumph! Your enemies shall come fawning to you, and you shall tread upon their backs."

Deuteronomy 34

English Standard Version

The Death of Moses

1 Then Moses went up from the plains of Moab to Mount Nebo, to the top of Pisgah, which is opposite Jericho. And the Lord showed him all the land, Gilead as far as Dan,

2 all Naphtali, the land of Ephraim and Manasseh, all the land of Judah as far as the western sea,

3 the Negeb, and the Plain, that is, the Valley of Jericho the city of palm trees, as far as Zoar.

4 And the Lord said to him, "This is the land of which I swore to Abraham, to Isaac, and to Jacob, 'I will give it to your offspring.' I have let you see it with your eyes, but you shall not go over there."

5 So Moses the servant of the Lord died there in the land of Moab, according to the word of the Lord,

6 and he buried him in the valley in the land of Moab opposite Beth-peor; but no one knows the place of his burial to this day.

7 Moses was 120 years old when he died. His eye was undimmed, and his vigor unabated.

8 And the people of Israel wept for Moses in the plains of Moab thirty days. Then the days of weeping and mourning for Moses were ended.

9 And Joshua the son of Nun was full of the spirit of wisdom, for Moses had laid his hands on him. So the people of Israel obeyed him and did as the Lord had commanded Moses.

10 And there has not arisen a prophet since in Israel like Moses, whom the Lord knew face to face,

11 none like him for all the signs and the wonders that the Lord sent him to do in the land of Egypt, to Pharaoh and to all his servants and to all his land,

12 and for all the mighty power and all the great deeds of terror that Moses did in the sight of all Israel.

www.ingramcontent.com/pod-product-compliance
Lightning Source LLC
Chambersburg PA
CBHW060407010526
44107CB00005B/609